COMMERCIAL AND MARITIME LAW IN CHINA AND EUROPE

MARITIME AND TRANSPORT LAW LIBRARY

MARITIME AND TRANSPORT LAW LIBRARY

COMMERCIAL AND MARITIME LAW IN CHINA AND EUROPE

EDITED BY SHENGNAN JIA AND LIJUN LIZ ZHAO

informa law
from Routledge

First published 2023
By Informa Law from Routledge
4 Park Square, Milton Park, Abingdon, Oxon OX14 4RN

and by Informa Law from Routledge
605 Third Avenue, New York, NY 10158

Informa Law from Routledge is an imprint of the Taylor & Francis Group, an informa business

British Library Cataloguing-in-Publication Data
A catalogue record for this book is available from the British Library

ISBN: 978-0-367-74927-9 (hbk)
ISBN: 978-0-367-74928-6 (pbk)
ISBN: 978-1-003-16029-8 (ebk)

DOI: 10.4324/9781003160298

Typeset in Times New Roman
by Deanta Global Publishing Services, Chennai, India

CONTENTS

PART II LAW IN ACTION: LITIGATION AND ALTERNATIVE DISPUTE
RESOLUTION

PART III LIABILITY REGIMES

TABLE OF CONVENTIONS, LEGISLATION AND RULES

Chinese Legislation: Regulations and Statutory Instruments

Chinese Legislation: Statutes

Dutch Legislation

EU Legislation

German Legislation

International Conventions

Japanese Legislation

Singaporean Legislation

UK Legislation

US Legislation

TABLE OF CASES

Cases Decided by the Supreme People's Court of PR China

English Cases

LIST OF TABLES

AUTHORS' BIOGRAPHIES

Editors

Dr Shengnan Jia was awarded the degree of PhD in Commercial Maritime Law by City, University of London and obtained her first LL.M. in China and second LL.M. in Sweden. She is an Associate Professor at Navigation College, Jimei University, Xiamen, China; an Adjunct Lecturer, the School of Juris Master, China University of Political Science of Law; and Partner, Tahota Law Firm, China.

In her practical career, Shengnan mainly disposes of litigation and arbitration disputes over international trade, commercial, financial and maritime domains involving banking, finance, shipping, logistic and energy industries. During her practice, she has been involved in some important and complex cases (*inter alia*, disputes over Bank's Acceptance Bill; Guarantee Agreements; Loan Contract; Asset Transfer and Equity Interests Management Contract; a Contract on Assignment of Claims/Factoring) in the Supreme Court of P.R. of China and different high courts around China. She has been appointed as arbitrator in a range of international commercial disputes, such as Hainan International Association Court, Zhuhai Court of International Arbitration, China; LMAA, UK; an Arbitrator of Caspian Arbitration Society, Geneva and Energy Disputes Arbitration Centre, Ankara. As an expert witness, she has been invited by international law firms to submit the expert witness opinion on Chinese commercial maritime law in the London Court of International Arbitration. In addition, she has been appointed to an Expert of Advisory Panel for China Council for Promotion of International Trade as UNCITRAL Observer on Judicial Sale of Ships since 2021.

Beyond her practical career, Shengnan is Co-Founding Director, China–Europe Commercial Collaboration Association (CECCA) (London) and Chair of the Board, Stichting CECCA (Netherlands). She is the author of *Comparative Analysis of Interim Measures—Interim Remedies (England & Wales) v Preservation Measures (China)* (publisher: Routledge) and has contributed chapters to many legal profession books, such as *Maritime Law in Motion* (Springer), *New Trends in Maritime Law: Maritime Liens, Arrest of Ships, Mortgages and Forced Sale* (Thomson Reuters). She has also organised a few international commercial law and maritime law conferences in London and online seminars. She has founded two journals: Journal of Transnational and Chinese Maritime Law (ISSN 2634-4777) and Journal of Transnational and Chinese Commercial Law (ISSN 2634-8209).

Dr Lijun (Liz) Zhao is Senior Lecturer (Associate Professor equivalent) in law and Director of Academic Visitor Programme, at City, University of London. Her expertise lies in commercial and corporate law, maritime law, international trade and policy. Lijun has published extensively on these areas in international peer-reviewed journals. Also, she has attended and presented her research at several high-profile international conferences, including the WTO Ministerial Conference M11 Academic Forum, and Harvard Global Law and Policy conferences. Besides this, Lijun has been awarded Senior Fellowship by the UK Higher Education Academy.

Beyond academia, Lijun is Co-Founding Director of the China–Europe Commercial Collaboration Association (CECCA), London, Member of Advisory Board of Stichting CECCA, Netherlands, and a member of several professional bodies, such as the London Maritime Arbitrators Association (LMAA) and the China Bar Council. Since September 2018, Lijun has joined a Working Group at the International Maritime Committee (CMI) as a Member and Law Expert, and currently is working on the Restatement of General Maritime Law (*Lex Maritima*).

Contributors

Professor Simon Baughen was appointed as Professor of Shipping Law in September 2013 (previously Reader at the University of Bristol Law School). Simon Baughen studied law at Oxford and practised in maritime law for several years before joining academia.

His research interests lie mainly in the field of shipping law, but also include the law of trusts and the environmental law implications of the activities of multinational corporations in the developing world. Simon is a member of the Institute of International Shipping and Trade Law (IISTL) at Swansea University.

Professor Jason Chuah FRSA is Professor of Commercial and Maritime Law and, formerly, Head of Department. He has held scholarships from Barclays Bank and the UK Overseas Development Authority at St Johns College, Cambridge University. He was the holder of the Cambridge Commonwealth Trust Award and the Cambridge Commonwealth Fellowship and also has a Certificate in Export with Distinction from the Institute of Export, winning the Clive Schmitthoff Commercial Law prize and the Sweet & Maxwell book prize.

Jason is Executive Director of the London Universities Maritime Law and Policy Group and has been nominated three times for the Oxford University Press Award for Best Law Teacher of the Year. He teaches Commercial, Maritime, Energy and Project Finance Law.

He is a peer review of the Arts and Humanities Research Council and has been involved in various consultations with the Ministry of Justice, the OECD, the ICC, the Association of British Insurers, the UNCITRAL, etc. He also serves as a member of the Consultative Group on Sustainable Shipping for the UN Global Compact and has contributed to the highly influential ICC-ECCO International Good Practice Guide for Offsets.

He is especially interested in the regulatory role of Private Law, especially mercantile law, in the common law tradition. He has written thus about how contract law might respond to the sustainability imperative. As a commercial maritime lawyer, he also examines how shipping law has been shaping general contract and property law thinking. His works have been cited by the CJEU, EU Institutions, courts and tribunals in the US, UK and Asia. He is also a Fellow of the Royal Society of Arts.

Simon Croall QC has a global practice with a depth of experience working with Chinese and South East Asian clients. This was recognised by his ranking as a leader in International Arbitration by Chambers Asia Pacific 2018 and Legal 500 Asia Pacific Guides. He is an established commercial leader frequently appearing in international arbitrations. He is particularly well known for his work with South East Asian (especially Chinese clients). He is recognised by both Chambers Asia Pacific and Legal 500 Asia Pacific editions for his internal arbitration work in the region. He has been described as "*a trusted name in international arbitration*" (Who's Who Legal UK Bar). Simon also sits as an arbitrator. He is a supporting member of the LMAA and is a panel arbitrator for the Asian International Arbitration Centre.

Recently, he has acted in a series of international disputes relating to the construction of commercial vessels such as VLCCs, capesize bulk carriers and other bulk carriers; has acted for Chinese clients in disputes over long carriage and import contracts for iron ore both in London and Hong Kong; has appeared in a series of International Arbitrations (LCIA, ICC, LMAA) in relation to matters as diverse as copper trading, Liner Conferences, international franchise agreements and petrochemical refining and trading; has acted for a major Middle East airline in an international arbitration against a software provider for online booking about unpaid commissions. He appeared in *ASM v Harris and others* [2008] 1 Lloyd's Rep. 61 (Comm Court) following on from related cases on bias in the same dispute, namely *ASM Shipping v TTMI* [2007] 1 Lloyd's Rep. 155 (CA) and *ASM Shipping v TTMI* [2007] 1 Lloyd's Rep. 131.

Fa Chen, (MPhil., LL.M., and LL.B.) Chinese lawyer, and formerly, served as a judge in a Beijing court in China for several years.

Dr Tobias Eckardt studied law in Hanover and completed his doctorate on the electronic "Bolero Bill of Lading under German and English Law". Since his admission to the bar in 2005, he has been working the law firm Ahlers & Vogel and became a partner in 2012. He advises on all aspects of national and international road, rail, inland waterway and sea transport and on international sales. He is co-publisher and editor of the journals for International Trade Law ("Zeitschrift für Internationales Handelsrecht – IHR") and transport law ("Transportrecht"), editor of the "European Journal of Commercial Contract Law" (EJCCL) and member of the advisory board to the Journal of Transnational and Chinese Commercial Law.

Dr. Eckardt contributes to German and English commentaries on national and international land and maritime transport regulations. Dr. Eckardt is the lecturer for both international trade law and transport law at the University of Applied Science Emden/Leer. He is Member of Advisory Board of Stichting CECCA, Netherlands.

Professor Dr. Michael G. Faure LL.M. became academic director of the Maastricht European institute for transnational legal research (METRO) and professor of Comparative and International Environmental Law at the law faculty of Maastricht University in September 1991. He still holds both positions today. In addition, he is, since its foundation in 1995, academic director of the Ius Commune Research School, a collaboration between the Universities of Amsterdam, Leuven, Utrecht and Maastricht, containing more than 500 members.

Since the first of February 2008, he is half time professor of comparative private law and economics at the Rotterdam Institute of Law & Economics (RILE) of the Erasmus University in Rotterdam and academic director of the European Doctorate in Law and Economics (EDLE) programme.

Since 1982 he is equally attorney at the Antwerp Bar. He is board member of the European Centre of Tort and Insurance Law (ECTIL) in Vienna and was elected member of the Netherlands Royal Academy of Arts and Sciences. He has numerous publications in internationally refereed journals such as Law & Policy, Oxford Journal of Legal Studies, International Review of Law and Economics, European Journal of Law and Economics, Review of Law and Economics, Environmental Policy and Governance and the Geneva Papers on Risk and Insurance. He also published many articles in American law reviews such as the Stanford Journal of International Law, the Virginia International Law Journal and the New York University Journal of Law and Finance. He published books with renowned international publishers, such as MIT Press, Edward Elgar, Hart Publishing and Cambridge University Press. He has often provided policy advice to various ministerial departments in Belgium and the Netherlands and to the European Commission.

Ian Gaunt is an English Barrister (non-practising). Since 2008 he has practised as a full-time arbitrator in international commercial cases and particularly maritime cases. He was President of the London Maritime Arbitrators Association from 2016 to 2019. He is a Member of the Baltic & Mercantile Exchange and a Director of Maritime London. He is the co-author of *The Law of Shipbuilding Contracts* (5th edition, 2020) published by Informa.

Catherine Green is a barrister, arbitrator, adjudicator and mediator, practising in the area of commercial and construction disputes. Before commencing her private dispute resolution practice, Catherine practised as a litigator both onshore and offshore in New Zealand, London, and the Cayman Islands, acting for clients on a wide variety of commercial disputes across the globe covering the Asia-Pacific, Europe, the Middle East, the Americas, the Caribbean, and Africa. Catherine is also currently the Executive Director of the New Zealand International Arbitration Centre (NZIAC).

Professor Dr James Zhengliang Hu B.Sc. (nautical science), LL.M. and Ph.D. (maritime and shipping law)

James is Professor of Law, Director of Institute of Maritime Law, Shanghai Maritime University.

He also serves as Legal advisor of the Ministry of Transport and the Maritime Safety Administration (MSA) of P.R. China. Besides this, he is one of the draftsmen of Chinese Maritime Code, Chinese Port Law, Chinese Shipping Law under drafting, the revision of Chinese Maritime Traffic Safety Law and various shipping regulations; Member of the Chinese delegation to UNCITRAL Working Group in formulating the Rotterdam Rules.

In addition, James is a practicing lawyer & partner, Shanghai Wintell & Co Law Firm, Member of Standing Committee, China Maritime Experts Commission; Member of Board of Standing Directors, China Maritime Law Association; Arbitrator, China Maritime Arbitration Commission & Shanghai Arbitration Court of International Shipping.

He also holds several Visiting professorships, including visiting professor of Swansea University of UK, Guest research fellow of Waseda University of Japan, visiting scholar of University of Antwerp, Belgium (1994–1995), and senior visiting scholar, Catholic University of Leuven, Belgium (2001).

Professor Proshanto K. Mukherjee was previously Vice President (Research), Director, Doctoral Programmes and ITF Professor of Maritime Safety and Environmental Protection at World Maritime University; Director of LL.M. and Ph.D. Programmes in Maritime Law at Lund University, Sweden; IMO Legal Adviser for the Caribbean Region; Senior Adviser, Maritime Policy and International Affairs, Canadian Hydrographic Service, Fisheries and Oceans, Canada; Senior Deputy Director and Professor of Maritime Law, International Maritime Law Institute (IMLI), Malta and Member of Advisory Board of Stichting CECCA, Netherlands.

He practiced as a barrister and solicitor in Ontario, Canada, was Legal Consultant and Adviser in maritime and marine environmental matters to the International Maritime Organization of the United Nations, numerous governments, shipping companies, and law firms in Malta, Cayman Islands, Dhaka, London, Amsterdam and Oslo. He presently acts as Maritime Law Consultant to the Governments of Mauritius and Bangladesh. He was previously visiting faculty at the Hague Academy of the International Court of Justice. He is Honorary Research Fellow, Swansea University; Honorary Professor of Law, National Law University Odisha, Cuttack, India; Visiting or Adjunct Professor at University of Antwerp, Shanghai Maritime University; Jimei University; Graduate School of Human Resource Development, Chung-Ang University, Seoul; BSMR Maritime University, Dhaka and Yangon University, Myanmar. He is associated with West Bengal University of Juridical Sciences, Kolkata, Gujarat National Law University, Gujarat Maritime University and Kerala Law Academy Law College in India; He spent 16 years in a seafaring career culminating as Master before entering legal studies and the legal profession. He is a member of the Canadian Maritime Law Association and the CMI Working Group on Fair Treatment of Seafarers. He is the author of *Mukherjee on Maritime Legislation*, lead author of Farthing on International Shipping, Fourth Edition and Lead Editor of *Maritime Law in Motion* and Editor of *Maritime Law Perspectives Old and New*, Volume I among numerous publications on virtually every aspect maritime affairs and maritime law.

Professor Avv. Francesco Munari is professor of EU Law, University of Genoa Law School. Adjunct Professor of EU Law and International and European Environmental Law at LUISS – Università Guido Carli, Rome; partner at Munari Giudici Maniglio Panfili & Associati, Genoa-Milan.

Dr Desai Shan is Assistant Professor at Faculty of Medicine, Memorial University of Newfoundland. She received her PhD from Cardiff University in 2017. As a dedicated researcher in the fields of international maritime law and occupational health and safety (OHS), she has published 15 research articles and book chapters on Canadian and international seafarers' rights to occupational health and safety. She sat on the expert panel of the Ministry of Foreign affairs of the Republic of Indonesia to develop guidelines on international seafarer abandonment cases.

Desai is now conducting research projects on Maritime Occupational Health and Safety in Canada, including Arctic maritime occupational health and safety issues, occupational noise exposure on merchant and fishing vessels. Her research projects have been funded by the Ocean Frontier Institute, Memorial University of Newfoundland, Social Sciences and Humanities Research Council through the On the Move Partnership.

Professor D Rhidian Thomas, Emeritus Professor of Maritime Law, Founding Director of the Institute of International Shipping and Trade Law, Swansea University, UK.

James M. Turner QC specialises in cross-border commercial and shipping disputes, notably shipbuilding and offshore construction, wet and dry shipping and related banking disputes. In 2021, Lloyd's List named James as one of its Top Ten Maritime Lawyers. Arbitration is the chosen forum in most matters on which James acts or advises. Many of those disputes come before LMAA panels, but James also has considerable experience of other arbitral settings, including the ICC, LCIA and HKIAC. He has frequently been instructed and appeared in cases for arbitration in other jurisdictions, such as Rotterdam, Singapore and Hong Kong.

He has extensive experience of working with and representing Far Eastern (especially Chinese) clients in London arbitration, and has a particular eye for appreciating and addressing commercial, legal and cultural barriers in international arbitration, born of his *"rich experience of representing clients in Asia-Pacific and [his] thorough understanding of the cultural, commercial and legal aspects of dispute resolutions in the region"* (Chambers UK).

James accepts appointments as arbitrator in a range of international commercial disputes. His experience as arbitrator over more than 20 years includes ICC, LCIA, NAI (Netherlands Arbitration Institute), LMAA and ad hoc references. He is a supporting member of the LMAA and is on the arbitration and mediation panels of the Shanghai and the Asian International Arbitration Centres, as well as being the only English lawyer on the arbitration panel of UNUM, the leading Dutch maritime disputes resolution centre.

Jing Wang, Director of the Maritime Law Committee of All China Lawyers Association and former Director, founding partner of Wang Jing & Co. Law Firm, is now Chairman of Board of Directors and Managing Partner of Wang Jing & GH Law Firm. Mr. Wang is a listed arbitrator at Shenzhen Court of International Arbitration, and Hainan International Arbitration Court. Mr. Wang has practiced law for more than 30 years, and founded and managed Wang Jing & Co. for more than 25 years. He has handled and instructed nearly a thousand foreign-related cases, many of which have been recognised as classic maritime and admiralty cases in China. Mr. Wang is a prestigious legal practitioner in the international shipping circle. He maintains close cooperation and contact with many well-known overseas shipping lawyers, law firms, English barristers, insurers, etc. Mr. Wang is the legal counsel in China for various international P&I clubs, banks, large SOEs and multi-national corporations. He is often invited as China law expert to provide advice to courts or arbitration courts in London, Singapore and Hong Kong.

Mr. Wang has been consistently recognised as one of the top lawyers in shipping and commercial matters in China by Chambers & Partners, The Legal 500, Asia Law & Practice, Asia Law Profiles and other international rating institutions. He is also in the National List of 1,000 Foreign-related Lawyers (practice areas: Cross-Border Investment and M&A, Maritime & Admiralty) by the PRC Ministry of Justice.

Weisheng (Wilson) Wang graduated from Dalian Maritime University (LL.B.) and Tulane Law School (LL.M.) and is now a degree candidate at London School of Economics and Political Science. He was a partner at the Admiralty Department of Wang Jing & Co., and is now a partner at Wang Jing & GH Law Firm. Mr. Wilson Wang is qualified to practice laws in both China and England & Wales. He is a fellow member of the Chartered Institute of Arbitrators, a listed arbitrator at Shenzhen Court of International Arbitration, and Hainan International Arbitration Court. He handles matters concerning admiralty, maritime and off-shore engineering, insurance, banking and finance, international trade and L/C, cross-border investment and general commercial dispute resolution (litigation and arbitration). His clients include insurance companies, shipping companies, P&I clubs, international banks and financial institutions, large SOEs and other multinational corporations. Mr. Wilson Wang has handled many maritime and commercial arbitration cases conducted at LCIA, HKIAC, SIAC, or by members of the LMAA.

Wilson was awarded as the "Practice Head" by The Legal 500 Asia Pacific shipping ranking in 2022. He is recognised as one of the Thousand Talented Lawyers in foreign related practice (practice areas: cross-border investment and M&A, maritime & admiralty) in China; "the Leading Lawyer in Foreign-Related Legal Service" by All China Lawyers Association; and "the Leading Lawyer in Foreign-Related Legal Service" by Guangdong Lawyers Association.

Dr Hui Wang received her Ph.D from Erasmus University Rotterdam, the Netherlands.

Dr Rui Zheng received his Ph.D. from Swansea University, UK. He is currently an Associate Professor and Director of Maritime Law Division at the School of Law, Shanghai Maritime University of China. His principal teaching and research interests lie on the contract law, maritime law, insurance law, sales law and arbitration law in both China and UK. He is a member of China Insurance Law Association, China Maritime Law Association, the Deputy Secretary General of the Insurance and Legal Committee of China Shipowners Association and Senior Member of CECCA, London. He is also a member of the working group entrusted by the Ministry of Transportation of China on the revision of China Maritime Code.

Dr Pengfei Zhang has been working in the maritime industry for over 20 years, previously working as a master mariner, maritime lawyer dually qualified in England and Wales and China, senior executive in a large shipping group. He is Member of Advisory Board of Stichting CECCA, Netherlands. He has gained hands-on experience covering almost the full spectrum of maritime business, from shipbuilding to ship operations and to ship recycling. He has practised as a maritime lawyer at Shanghai AllBrights Law offices since 2008, specialising in shipbuilding and financing, ship collision and SNP disputes.

With a Ph.D. in international maritime studies, Pengfei has a distinguished track record in publications and conference speeches. He has authored/co-authored several books on maritime management and over 80 articles carried by prestigious journals, including (inter alia) Economic and Labour Relations Review, Industrial Relations Journal, Marine Policy, Journal of Navigation, International Economic Law. Pengfei has extensive teaching experience in the UK (Solent University), China (Dalian Maritime University and Shanghai Maritime University), and HK (VTC program).

FOREWORD

Both China and Europe have a long tradition of commercial and maritime law, and this new book examining various topics from their particular perspectives is both timely and important.

The editors have performed a remarkable task in bringing together highly respected academics and practitioners from Europe and China each with considerable knowledge and expertise covering a wide field, including commercial law, insurance law, salvage, EU maritime law and Brexit, carriage of goods by sea, arbitration, mediation, litigation, the recently formed China International Commercial Court and different liability regimes, as well as a brief look forward into new initiatives and artificial intelligence in the digital age.

In these challenging times, we all have much to learn from each other in seeking to find answers to what are often difficult problems. This book provides a welcome opportunity for anyone interested in commercial and maritime law to engage in that learning exercise and, looking ahead, thereby to help solve such problems as may arise in the future – in a practical and fair manner.

The Hon. Sir Bernard Eder
London.
March 2022

CHAPTER 1

Introduction

An Overview of Commercial and Maritime Law in China and Europe

Shengnan Jia and Lijun Liz Zhao

No man is an island, entire of itself; every man is a piece of the continent, a part of the main.
John Donne

Introduction: Making Connections between China and Europe

In human history, countries and civilisations do not exist in isolation. Back to the ages of early agrarian civilisations, societies started to connect into large exchange networks through trade. One of the most important exchange systems in the past is known today as "the Silk Road" that connected China with Europe. As thousands of years have passed, the cross-border trade between Europe and China has escalated significantly and revived. Today we live in this vast, connected, globalised world.

Nowadays, the EU, China and the USA are the world's three most significant trading partners.[1] According to the World Bank statistics, China is one of the largest trading partners of the European countries.[2] Over the past decades, "made in China" products have been shipped to end users in Europe.

In addition, trade has stimulated the development of "new" international trade centres beyond the Western developed countries. Apart from the long-established trade centres in the West, like London and Rotterdam, China is playing an increasingly prominent role in global trade. This is demonstrated by some trade hubs that are located in China, such as Shanghai, Hong Kong and several globally leading container ports in China, to name a few.

The Scope, Aims and Structure of This Book

In the context of globalised trade and the rise of China, this very timely book explores commercial and maritime law from the Europe–China perspective. To avoid confusion and repetitions for readers, it goes without repeating that expressions such as "Europe" and "the West" in this book refer to European countries, including the UK, albeit the latter has voted in favour of Brexit.

---

1 Europe Commission, EU–China Trade, https://ec.europa.eu/trade/policy/countries-and-regions/countries/china/index_en.htm#:~:text=The%20European%20Union%2C%20China%20and,World%20Trade%20Organization%20(WTO).

2 World Bank, Trade Stats, https://wits.worldbank.org/countrysnapshot/en/EUN.

DOI: 10.4324/9781003160298-1

This book draws on a collection of essays that are revised, updated and enhanced versions of papers that were presented in the inaugural ceremony of the China–Europe Commercial Collaboration Association and the follow-up global forum, organised by this Association in London in 2017, and the recurring annual forums. The collective sentiment has been that there has been relatively limited academic discourse on issues relating to the current development of commercial and maritime law and, particularly, the interplay between China and Europe. As such, this book has been an excellent opportunity to bring together learned scholars and practitioners from the UK, EU countries and China to debate and test ideas of making connections and exchange viewpoints between China and Europe, from the lenses of legislators, policymakers, legal professionals and merchants.

Much research has been conducted in the areas of trade statistics, business and economics in terms of Europe–China relations.[3] However, in the area of law, more is yet to be done. Since the 1900s, it has been a long tradition that the Chinese learn English law and laws of European countries and respective legal transplantation from the West to China. Now, the influence between Europe and China tends to be more mutual and two-way. Moreover, with the establishment of "new" international trade hubs in China, Chinese law is not only of interest but has become more critical.

The scope of the subject is indeed so wide that merely one book would not be able to do it perfectly. The aims shared among all chapters in this book are to employ a Europe–China perspective and evaluate the mutual influence and interplay between the two leading trading partners – China and Europe.

The overall aim of this book is to explore the interplay between China and Europe, through the lens of commercial and maritime law. This is because maritime transport is the backbone of international trade and the global economy. According to the UN agency, International Maritime Organization (IMO),

> Around today, around 90% of world trade is carried by the international shipping industry. Without shipping the import and export of goods on the scale necessary to sustain the modern world would not be possible. [S]eaborne trade continues to expand, bringing benefits for consumers across the world through competitive freight costs[4] ... Without shipping the import and export of goods on the scale necessary to sustain the modern world would not be possible. Yet the fact remains that most of the world's population is not aware of the vital role shipping plays in their everyday lives.[5]

Based on the aims mentioned above, this book tackles this highly intricate subject matter in four interlinked parts:

Part I Law in the Books: When East Meets West

Part I is concerned with exploring how and to what extent commercial and maritime law should be reformed and developed in the existing legal frameworks. In particular, it is worth sketching out how China has been seeking new approaches in lawmaking over recent years, whether Chinese law should continue to "incorporate" international and European rules when several pieces of Chinese legislation on commercial and maritime law, which

---

3 For example the EU statics mentioned above.
4 IMO, Shipping: indispensable to the world, 2015 www.imo.org/en/MediaCentre/PressBriefings/Pages/47 -WMD-theme-2016-.aspx
5 Ibid.

are very internationalised fields of law, are being revised. We have witnessed a more two-way influence between China and Europe. In addition, how the unexpected political issues and considerations arising from Brexit impact the application of both the European Union law and English law has attracted attention of the scholars and practitioners.

Part II Law in Action: Litigation and Alternative Dispute Resolution

Part II mainly focuses on the international commercial and maritime law dispute resolution arena. This part examines new developments, innovations and challenges in the fields of dispute resolution mechanisms, including litigation, arbitration and mediation, with the purpose to draw up lessons for legislators, policymakers, merchants and legal professionals, in Europe, China and other jurisdictions globally.

Part III Liability Regimes

Part III concentrates on the liability regimes in the commercial and maritime law domain from the perspective of substantive law. It is safe to say that the fundamental purpose of the research on the liability regimes is to address the question of how and to what extent stakeholders in law can be protected and indemnified effectively. Accordingly, this Part explores liability issues over charterparties, carriage of goods by sea, vessel-related marine pollution and work-related incidents involving vulnerable seafarers.

Part IV Looking Forward: New Initiatives in the Digital Age

This part is forward-looking and examines the emerging legal regimes in the West and China in the digital age. Many jurisdictions, such as the EU, UK and China, have published various position papers and policy statements on regulating AI in response to this impact. It is self-evident that the continuing impact of AI on global maritime trade is inevitable. This part explores the emerging influence of artificial intelligence in shipping and international commerce.

Concluding Remarks

Last but not least, we would like to express our sincere gratitude to our distinguished contributors who devoted their precious time and efforts to our conferences, events and this book. Additionally, we greatly appreciate the patience of each contributor. Without their support and input before and during the COVID pandemic, we would not be able to conclude this book project.

In addition, we would like to thank our editors, Guy Loft, and Amelia Bashford. This book would not have been possible without the support of our publisher and editors.

Special thanks go to our funders the UK Higher Education Innovation Fund for supporting two of the annual forums, and the support from the China–Europe Commercial Collaboration Association.

The law and legal instruments in this book are as stated as of 19 April 2022.

PART I

LAW IN THE BOOKS

When East Meets West

CHAPTER 2

The Curious Concept of Employment Salvage in Chinese Law

The Case of *Archangelos Gabriel*

Proshanto K. Mukherjee[1]

I. Preface

I am writing this piece in the first person because of a number of factors which feature in the text. I normally do not write in the first person as I do not consider it sound legal writing etiquette, but in the present instance I am making an exception mainly because I have expressed several subjective views and conclusions; also, because I have referred to an interview with a local television channel in Beijing, and to my specific answers given to a questionnaire which I was requested by the Supreme People's Court to address. My responses in English were translated into Chinese and published in *China Trial*, a magazine of the Supreme People's Court.

A fundamental question that arises in the context of the phrase "Chinese law" in the title is – what exactly is "law" in the first place? I have addressed this question in my writings and lectures in a holistic and jurisprudential context, encapsulating both the common and civil law traditions. I consider these two systems as two dimensions of the same commonality and believe that the common denominator of both systems is the foundation on which the superstructures of the law is built, even though, at least in terms of European continental civil law, the roots of which can be traced to the Justinian *corpus iuris civilis*, codes are the primary source of law.[2] In my latest book *Mukherjee on Maritime Legislation*, as in its first editions, I have stated unabashedly that "law defies description" and

> is indeed a proposition that is thought-provoking to say the least. To some, law is an amorphous concept, to others it is a necessary evil; to yet others, a straight-jacket designed by the elite for the rest of humanity. Whatever may be one's perception, its existence is indisputable.[3]

Throughout human history, law has evolved from customs and practices which were institutionalised even in primitive societies. In juxtaposition, legal systems provide the

---

1 LL.B. (Dalhousie), Ph.D. (Wales), LL.D. juris dr. honoris causa (Lund) Professor of Law & Foreign Expert, Dalian Maritime University; Emeritus Professor of Maritime Law and Policy, Ex-Vice President (Research) World Maritime University; Chancellor, CINEC Campus, Colombo; Barrister-at-Law (Osgoode Hall, Law Society of Ontario), Solicitor of the Supreme Court of Ontario, Notary Public (Ontario), Master Mariner (Canada), A.F.R.I.N., F.N.I. (UK)

2 William Tetley, "Mixed Jurisdictions: Common Law v. Civil Law (Codified and Uncodified)", 60 *La L.Rev.* pp. 677, 683 (2000).

3 Proshanto K. Mukherjee, *Mukherjee on Maritime Legislation*, Malmo: WMU Publications, 2021, p. 7.

DOI: 10.4324/9781003160298-3

jurisprudential infrastructure for the effectuation of law.[4] What I mean by this will crystalize as the discussion unfolds.

I will now proceed with the main theme of this chapter which is salvage law particularised in the form of the expression "employment salvage". I call it a "curious concept" as the appellation is without precedent in any other jurisdiction but the essence of the notion is not unknown.

II. Introduction

A. Background

The well-known author Christopher Hill has rightly stated – "it is misleading to refer to 'salvage contracts'. It implies that we are exclusively in the 'world of the law of contract. We are not. We are into the law of salvage".[5] Salvage law is *sui generis* but is associated with property law as it applies only to maritime property as subjects of salvage. The essential ingredients of traditional salvage law are danger, voluntariness and success, without which salvage remuneration is not payable. If any or all of these ingredients are absent, a rescue or saving of a ship or cargo would fall under the ordinary law of contract. This is sometimes referred to as "contract salvage", an expression that can potentially cause confusion with the term "salvage contract". The latter is a well-established phrase and concept but it essentially refers to an agreement as distinguished from a contract. In a typical salvage agreement such as the Lloyd's Open Form of Salvage Agreement, the element of consideration, which is one of the three necessary elements defining a contract, is not provided for in the written representation of the transaction but is left to be decided by arbitration or by a court. That is the significance of the word "Open" in the description of that Agreement. Thus, the "Agreement" falls short of a full-fledged contract.[6]

Traditional salvage law was first codified in the Salvage Convention of 1910[7] which was subsequently superseded by the International Salvage Convention of 1989[8] adopted under the auspices of the International Maritime Organization (IMO). The 1989 Convention largely represents the current international regime of salvage. Almost all maritime states subscribe to it.

B. Fundamental Principles and Ingredients of Salvage Law

The fundamental principles of salvage law have their roots in both Roman law as well as the English law of equity. The principles of equity emanated from the decisions of Roman Praetors who were akin to English judges in the courts of chancery.[9] In *The Calypso*, Sir Christopher Robinson, in the context of salvage, made reference to "a general principle

---

4 Ibid.

5 Christopher Hill, *Maritime Law*, 6th Edition, London, Hong Kong: LLP, 2003, p. 335.

6 See Proshanto K. Mukherjee, "Salvage Agreement and Contract Salvage: Risk Dynamics in Salvage Law", *Revisiting Trade, Transport, and Marine Law: Risk and Technology in Perspective, Liber Amicorum Lars-Goran Malmberg*, Brill, UK, 2021.

7 Convention for the Unification of Certain Rules of Law relating to Assistance and Salvage at Sea, Brussels, 1910, 1953 *UNTS* 165

8 International Convention on Salvage, 1989, 327 *UNTS* 3; 41 *ILM* 40.

9 Sir Henry Maine, *Ancient Law*, Oxford University Press, London: Humphrey Milford, 1931, "The World's Classics", pp. 23, 53–54.

of natural equity" and stated that it gave rise to "a cause of action in the Roman law".[10] Underlying this principle are the doctrines of restitution for unjust enrichment and *quantum meruit*. It is noted that in circumstances where one receives a benefit at the expense of another, the former is *prima facie* unjustly enriched and must make restitution for it to the latter.[11] It is a vital principle of Roman law, a legal system which has profoundly influenced the admiralty jurisprudence of England.[12] It is said that the description "quasi contract" or "implied contract" given to salvage, indeed any association of salvage with contract, is manifestly misleading and has been rejected.[13]

As regards the doctrine of *quantum meruit*, the payment of a reward for meritorious salvage services can be higher than an assessment made simply on the basis of *quantum meruit* as that notion obtains in English law. Indeed, if *quantum meruit* were to be strictly interpreted, payment for salvage services would simply be a reasonable amount corresponding to the detriment suffered by the salvor, in conferring a benefit. Thus, a salvage reward is often in excess of re-imbursement on a *quantum meruit* basis, especially where the value of the saved *res* is relatively high.

Under the customary or traditional law of salvage, there are three main ingredients to a salvage claim, namely, danger, voluntariness and success. They are often referred to as the triumvirate of customary salvage law.[14] If any of these ingredients are absent, a salvage claim cannot subsist; neither can a maritime lien arise in respect of such a claim. All of these three ingredients are alluded to in the two international Salvage Conventions referred to above. As mentioned, the Conventions represent a codification of international custom and practice, which in essence has been, and still reflects the law as it is known. These ingredients indubitably have their roots in the historical evolution of salvage law.

C. Salvage Agreements

Salvage operations are usually conducted pursuant to "agreements", as mentioned previously which are based on the ingredients of traditional salvage law as outlined above. The best-known of these is the Lloyd's Open Form of Salvage Agreement (LOF) which is uniquely characterised by the appellation "no cure, no pay" appearing at the top of the Form signifying the requirement for success ostensibly extending to the notion of "ultimate preservation of the *res*".[15] Incidentally, the LOF has been on the decline for some time now. In 1980, there were some 255 cases involving the LOF, but in 2007 this figure has decreased to only 107 cases.[16]

---

10 (1828), 2 Hagg. 209, pp. 217–218.

11 Francis D. Rose, *Kennedy and Rose: Law of Salvage*, Ninth Edition, London: Thompson Reuters/Sweet & Maxwell, paragraph 1-034, p. 16.

12 Ibid., paragraph 1-003, p. 2.

13 Ibid., paragraph 1-035, pp. 16–17.

14 Edgar Gold, Aldo Chircop, Hugh Kindred, *Essentials of Canadian Law, Maritime Law*, Toronto: Irwin Law, 2003, pp. 605–608; Proshanto K. Mukherjee, "Refuge and Salvage" in Aldo Chircop and Olof Linden (Eds), Places of Refuge for Ships, Leiden/Boston: Martinus Nijhoff Publishers, 2006, p. 274.

15 Mukherjee, ibid., pp. 274–276.

16 See Martin Davies, "Whatever Happened to the Salvage Convention 1989?", *Journal of Maritime Law and Commerce*, 39(4) February 2009.

III. The *Archangelos Gabriel* Case

The full name of the case under discussion in this chapter is *Nanhai Rescue Bureau of the Ministry of Transport of PRC (Appellants) v. Archangelos Investments E.N.E. (Respondents)* (*The Archangelos Gabriel*).[17] The Final Appeal in this case was made to the Supreme People's Court of the People's Republic of China before five justices presided over by the Vice-President of the Court, Madame Justice He Rong. The decision was rendered on 7 July 2016.

A. Facts of the Case[18]

On 12 August 2011, the 40,682 DWT Greek tanker *Archangelos Gabriel*, owned by Archangelos Investments E.N.E. of Athens, Greece and carrying 54,580 tonnes of Cabinda crude from Qinzhou to Hong Kong grounded in the Qiongzhou Strait outside the port of Guangzhou in southern China. The cause of the grounding was reported to be navigational error of the master. There was no pollution damage.

The owners contracted with Nanhai Rescue Bureau of the Ministry of Transport of PRC to refloat the vessel on the basis of what is known in China as an "employment contract for salvage" in respect of which the contract provided for joint liability of the shipowner and its Shanghai agents. It was not a typical salvage contract or agreement such as the Lloyd's Open Form (LOF) which is predicated on the principle of "no cure, no pay".

Under the employment contract for salvage, Archangelos Investments agreed to pay the Nanhai Rescue Bureau the amount of RMB 6.59 million, the equivalent of USD 985,000. But after the task of refloating the vessel was completed and the cargo was transhipped, Archangelos Investments refused to pay the contracted amount on two grounds. One was the allegation that, whereas the contract called for the use of three tugs, based on which the contract amount was agreed, only one tug was used in the operation. The other ground was that in any case the shipowners would only be liable to pay for the proportion of the amount attributable to salvage of the ship. The salvors would have to recover from the cargo owners by separate legal action, the amount attributable to saving of cargo.

The Nanhai Rescue Bureau as plaintiffs brought an action against the shipowners in the Guangzhou Maritime Court for payment of the contracted amount and received judgment for their claim.

B. Decision of the First Instance Court

The court of first instance ruled that the operation was fully successful and under the "no cure, no pay" principle entrenched in the Maritime Code of the People's Republic of China (CMC) giving effect to the International Salvage Convention, 1989 to which China was a party, the full contract amount of RMB 6.59 million was payable by the shipowners to the plaintiffs without any apportionment of liability between the shipowners and cargo owners as there was no privity of contract between plaintiffs and the cargo owners.

---

17 [2017] 7 CMCLR 1; [2016] SPC civil Retrial No. 61.

18 Extracted from Proshanto K. Mukherjee, "Salvage and Related Services" (2016) 22 *JIML* pp. 262–263, Issue 4, Digest of Contemporary Developments.

C. Decision of the Intermediary Court on Appeal from the First Instance Court

The shipowners appealed against that decision to the Guangdong High People's Court which decided that the appellants were liable, but only for 38.85% of the claim. The Court was of the opinion that the contract amount should be allocated separately as between shipowners and cargo owners. It also held that the "no cure, no pay" principle in Article 179 of the CMC was not applicable to the case.

D. Appeal to Supreme People's Court

The original plaintiffs then appealed to the Supreme People's Court, and contended, *inter alia*, that the fact that the shipowners had obtained an "average guaranty", namely, a guaranty of indemnification by the insurer for general average contribution paid by the shipowner, constituted new evidence. Under the Civil Procedure Law of PRC, new evidence coming to light is grounds for a "retrial" which in essence is an appeal to the Supreme People's Court. The appeal was heard on 7 July 2016.

E. Decision of the Supreme People's Court and Reasons for the Decision

The Supreme People's Court reversed the decision of the Guangdong High People's Court and held that the respondent shipowners were liable to pay the whole contract amount of RMB 6.59 million. The Court recognised that China was a party to the 1989 Salvage Convention which has been given effect through the CMC but held that this case did not fall within the purview of the Convention which in essence incorporates the customary law principle of "no cure, no pay".[19] Rather, this was an employment contract for salvage under which the shipowners were liable to pay the whole contract price regardless of whether or not the salvors were successful in salving the vessel. The Supreme People's Court applied the Contract Law of PRC under which, whatever was indicated as the price for the task in the contract had to be paid by the shipowner. In this regard, notably, the parties had agreed in the court of first instance that Chinese law was the applicable law in this case.

On the question of "new evidence" relating to the average guaranty, the Supreme People's Court rejected the submission made by the Rescue Bureau.

Overall, the judgment rendered was largely in favour of the appellants Nanhai Rescue Bureau.

IV. Critical Analysis of the Case

First of all, in my observation, the so-called "employment contract for salvage" is akin to what is sometimes referred to as "contract salvage" mentioned earlier, which in essence is a contract in the ordinary sense and does not bear the hallmarks of salvage which is considered to be *sui generis*. Thus, danger, voluntariness and success, which are the necessary ingredients for a saving act to qualify as salvage under the customary or traditional law of salvage, need not be present. In point of fact, in the present case these were absent.

---

19 This principle reflects the requirement for success and ultimate preservation of the *res* as a condition for payment of salvage remuneration.

Incidentally, the notion of "contract salvage" is exemplified in the Donjon-Smit standard form contract, one version of which carries the heading "Donjon-Smit, LLC Oil Pollution Act of 1990, Salvage, Firefighting and Lightering Contract and Funding Agreement". A perusal of this standard form indicates that it is in the nature of a contractual instrument not based on the "no cure, no pay" principle. As mentioned earlier, parties involved in salvage operations are increasingly moving away from "no cure, no pay" into fixed remuneration arrangements.

In terms of Chinese case law jurisprudence, this decision represents a landmark by virtue of the fact that salvage-related cases are relatively uncommon in China. That, in the opinion of the Supreme People's Court, this case did not fall under salvage law pursuant to the 1989 Salvage Convention, is laudable and significant in my view. The Convention, which has been given effect through the Maritime Code of China, admittedly represents a codification of the customary law of salvage. On the facts of the case, the apex Court held, however, that the case did not fall within the ambit of the relevant provisions of the Maritime Code. Rather, it fell within the purview of the Contract Law of China which governs contracts in general. Thus, this case was not considered a salvage matter coming under salvage law but was simply a matter of contract.

In my opinion which I communicated to the Supreme People's Court through my answer in the questionnaire and the interview to which I have referred earlier, this was a sound judgment based on the factual situation of the case and the extant state of the Chinese law. I hold the view that the decision was also consistent with the law and practice in other jurisdictions pertaining to similar factual situations involving the notion of contract salvage referred to as "employment salvage" in this decision.

On the issue of applicable law, grounding being a maritime tort, under the conflict of laws principle of *lex loci deliciti commissi*, Chinese law would be the proper law. China is a Code-based civil law jurisdiction and there is no express provision in the Maritime Code squarely governing this kind of factual situation involving salvage. In those circumstances, the decision reflects a functional judicial attitude conducive to significant advancement in maritime jurisprudence in this jurisdiction and reflecting a degree of judicial activism.

V. *Connotation of "Law" in the Context of the Supreme People's Court Decision*

In the previous section(s), I have used such phraseology as "Chinese law", "Chinese case law jurisprudence", "Maritime Code of China", "sound judgment" (referring to the Supreme People's Court decision in the *Archangelos Gabriel* case) and the likes. In the Preface to this discussion, I have already dealt with the issue of what is "law" and have cited my own writings on the subject. On the question of what is "law" in the context of China's legal regime, I hold the firm and steadfast view that, when expressed entirely in the lower case, the word "law" should be construed holistically, unlike the case where the word is expressed as "Law" with "L" capitalised. Based on a holistic approach, "law" encompasses all sources of law. I concede nevertheless that in terms of the legal regime prevailing in China, legislation, in the form of a Code or otherwise, is invariably the principal or primary source of law, but there are other sources of law that may be characterised as secondary. Thus, I believe that in the Chinese context, "law" and "Law" are distinguishable as they are in a number of other jurisdictions, in particular, one where I served as a legal adviser and legislative draftsman for several years and which happens to be a common law jurisdiction.

I have been fortunate to have had vast experience in the drafting of maritime, commercial, port, marine environmental and maritime labour legislation of all varieties, including principal and subordinate, in both common and civil law jurisdictions totalling approximately 30 in number. I completed my doctoral research on this subject and am the author of the only book (first and second editions) of its kind dedicated exclusively to maritime legislation. I therefore feel I am qualified to speak to this issue with some authority. In my considered opinion, any proposition stated categorically that in a Code-based civil law jurisdiction such as China, law can only mean codes or other varieties of statutes; and as an extension of it, that there is no place in law for the pronouncements of judges, even those of the Supreme Court, whether oral or written, is simply fallacious. Yet, that was precisely what I once heard stated in a public forum. It was an utterance with which I respectfully but manifestly beg to disagree for reasons which will unfold as I proceed to bring this discourse to its finality.

My contention is borne out by two relatively recent developments in the Chinese legal milieu. One is "Interpretations" of statutory provisions given by the Supreme People's Court; the other is the notion of "Guiding Cases" issued by the apex Court. No one will argue that in any legal system, a basic task of the judiciary is to interpret not only legislation but also any other variety of legal instrument relevant to that jurisdiction including contracts and treaties. Be that as it may, in common law jurisdictions, interpretation of legislation, which is the kind of legal instrument with which we are concerned in this discourse, is the province of the judiciary at any level of court, but only where the court is confronted with an issue of construction in the context of a case before it.

Needless to say, it is the Supreme Court in the jurisdiction which has the final say in matters of statutory construction or interpretation of a legal instrument including a treaty and a contract. In contrast, "Interpretations" handed down by the Supreme People's Court of China are not constrained by the instance of an actual case before it. The apex Court is free to provide an Interpretation to any statutory provision that has come to its attention from any source, whether incidental to a real case, or otherwise. Often it is in the form of a request from a lower level court which is virtually unheard of in the common law system.[20] An Interpretation once so issued, seemingly becomes a part of the law of the land, and arguably, is binding on all lower courts even though in terms of legal significance it is weaker in effectuation than legislative interpretation given by the Standing Committee of the National People's Congress and administrative interpretation given by the State Council through Administrative Rules.[21] Nevertheless, it is said that as a source of law, judicial interpretation is becoming increasingly indispensable.[22]

The advent of Interpretations issued by the Supreme People's Court has at once altered the legal landscape of China from the hitherto almost unshakable belief that the law is

---

20 Notably, in the legal systems of the International Court of Justice (ICJ) and the International Tribunal for the Law of the Sea (ITLOS) the judicial mechanism of "Advisory Opinions" in available. In the legal system of the European Court of Justice (ECJ), it is possible to "refer" to the ECJ for a preliminary ruling as was done by the High Court of England and Wales in the infamous "Intertanko" case involving ship-source pollution.

21 See Li Wei, "Judicial Interpretation in China", *Willamette J. of Intl L. and Dispute Resolution*, p. 87 and footnote 1 at that page.

22 Ibid. See also Jinrong Wang, "On the Judicial Interpretation of China's Supreme People's Court", 3 *China L.* 9 (1995).

invariably circumscribed by the four corners of a Code or Regulations or other form of statute, to a more dynamic portrayal and conception of the law in holistic terms.

The notion of Guiding Cases is the other significant development to which I have made reference in the foregoing discussion. Literature on this topic is ample emanating from both Chinese as well as foreign scholars.[23] Jiang Xiayi and Shao Ling have stated in their article "The Guiding Case System in China", that the Supreme People's Court has significantly altered the Chinese legal system for the better by creating the system of Guiding Cases. It serves to improve the quality of judgments and consistency of trials in the judicial system and as a law reform mechanism has far-reaching potential. Some scholars have expressed the view that the concept is akin to precedents in the common law system.[24] One author has described the phenomenon as imbued with "*stare decisis*-like authority".[25] The use of this terminology is consonant with some of the rhetoric describing Guiding Cases, seemingly bringing Chinese law into closer alignment with the common law tradition.[26]

But in my view such statements are less than accurate. While the Guiding Cases system calls for courts at all levels to refer to Guidance Cases when faced with a case posing similar factual situations and legal implications, they do not serve as binding precedents as in the common law milieu. Rather, the system serves the aim of encapsulating judicial experience in a timely fashion, giving guidance to courts at all levels, providing for uniformity of judicial standards and regulating judicial discretion. On the other hand, it is said that the Guiding Cases system does not empower judges to alter the law or to develop it. Unlike their common law counterparts, in China, judges do not make law. But these are also categorical statements that are somewhat imprecise. In my view, Guiding Cases do not make the "Law" but they do make "law" in the generic and holistic sense, and they are ostensibly a source of law, albeit secondary in status and at a lower threshold.

Some scholars argue that by using Guiding Cases, judges interpret the application of the law, in other words, how the "Law" should be applied. Even though there is close connectivity between the two, Guiding Cases and Judicial Interpretations are distinctively different when it comes to their respective characters. Judicial Interpretations provide general guidance; in contradistinction to that, Guiding Cases provide guidance in specific circumstances and are not binding in the same sense as Interpretations of the Supreme People's Court. But they can be said to be binding *de facto* which implies that they can be binding on future adjudications by the courts. At any rate, no proposition has thus far been cast in concrete; there are varying views. Thus, it is fair to say that both these concepts are still evolving but, in my view and observation, they are contributing immensely to a more holistic vision of what "law" is in the Chinese context.

---

23 See for example, Fengping Gao, "China's Guiding Cases System as the Instrument to Improve the System" *Intl J. of Legal Information*, Vol. 45, Issue 3, pp. 230–243, Cambridge University Press, (2017); Jeremy Daum, "The Curious Case of the Chinese Guiding Cases System" www.chinalawtranslate.com/author/jeremy-daum/?lang=en; Björn Ahl, "Retaining Judicial Professionalism: The New Guiding Cases Mechanism of the Supreme People's Court", 217 *China Q.* pp. 121, 123, (2014); Jinting Deng, "Functional Analysis of China's Guiding Cases", *China Intl J.* (CIJ), Vol. 2, (May 2016), pp. 44–70; Mo Zhang, "Pushing the Envelope: Application of Guiding Cases in Chinese Courts and Development of Case Law in China", *Washington Intl L.J.* Vol. 26, No. 2, (2017).

24 See "Chinese Common Law? Guiding Cases and Judicial Reform" *Note* in *Harvard L. Rev.* 2213, Vol. 129, No. 8, 10 June 2016.

25 Taisu Zhang, "The Pragmatic Court: Reinterpreting the Supreme People's Court of China", *Colum J. of Asian L.*, Vol. 25, No 1 (2012) 8.

26 *Supra*, note 21 above.

VI. Conclusion

In closing, and as a matter of interest in the context of the main theme of this discussion, recent statistics indicate that as of July 2022, 185 Guiding Cases have been published of which 7 are maritime cases. Most importantly, No. 110 on the list is the *Archangelos Gabriel* decision. The subject is identified as "Dispute Over Contract of Salvage at Sea".[27] Undoubtedly, therefore, the decision of the Supreme People's Court in this case has made a significant contribution to the maritime jurisprudence of China.

I humbly rest my case.

---

27 Others include Nos. 16 and 112 – "Application for Constitution of Limitation Fund for Maritime Claims"; No. 31 – "Dispute Over Damage Caused by Ship's Collision at Sea"; No. 52 – "Dispute Over Contract of Marine Cargo Insurance"; No. 108 – "Dispute Over Contract of Carriage of Goods by Sea"; and No. 111 – Dispute Over Issuing a Letter of Credit".

CHAPTER 3

What Is EU Maritime Law – and Will the UK Miss It after Brexit?

*Simon Baughen**

I. Introduction

On 23 June 2016 the people of the United Kingdom voted in a referendum to leave the EU. The immediate reaction of many in the maritime sector was "How will this affect shipping law?" which leads to the further question of "What is EU maritime law?" This chapter will endeavour to answer both those questions. The initial reaction on social media of some in China's maritime circles was that the UK would be finished as a maritime law centre. As this chapter will demonstrate, nothing could be further from the truth. This chapter will examine the nature of EU maritime law, identifying its increasing regulatory reach in the last two decades and the potential conflicts that has had with international law. It will then consider the Brexit process and show what, if anything, changed on the UK's leaving the EU on 31 January 2020 and what changed and is likely to change following the end of the transition period on 31 December 2020.

II. The Nature of EU Maritime Law

EU Maritime law has had very little substantive impact on private law in the shipping arena. English dry shipping is based on common law, and a few key statutes, such as the Carriage of Goods by Sea Act 1992 (COGSA 1992), and the implementation of international carriage conventions through domestic legislation – such as the Carriage of Goods by Sea Act 1971 (COGSA 1971) with the Hague-Visby Rules. With "wet" shipping, the 1992 CLC and the Fund, and the Supplementary Fund, are part of our national law through domestic law implementing international conventions. Similarly, the 2007 Nairobi Wreck Removal Convention, the 1989 Salvage Convention, and the 1976 Limitation Convention. There has been very little EU legislation that impacts directly on civil liability in the maritime sphere. There is the 2009 Passenger Liability Regulation, and the EU's accession to the 2002 Athens Convention which means the Convention applies throughout the EU on all Member States, whether or not they have individually ratified the Convention (which the UK has). There is the 2004 Environmental Liability Directive which institutes a public law clean up regime for "environmental damage" throughout the EU which was extended from coastal waters of Member States to their exclusive economic zone by the

---

* Professor of Shipping Law, Institute of International Shipping and Trade Law, Swansea University.

 DOI: 10.4324/9781003160298-4

2013 Offshore Safety Directive (2013.30/EU). This would have an impact on pollution from oil and gas operations in the UK's continental shelf,[1] and from pollution from shipping but not on pollution arising from an incident covered by one of the IMO civil liability conventions which is specifically excluded from the scope of the Environmental Liability Directive. The public law intervention powers granted by the Directives largely existed already under domestic UK law.[2] Civil liability is also indirectly affected by the mandatory liability insurance provisions in Directive 2009/20/EC on the insurance of shipowners for maritime claims[3] and by the financial security requirements for offshore oil and gas licensee under the Offshore Safety Directive 2013 OSD.[4]

The government issued a series of technical notices advising on the position in the event of a no-deal Brexit. There were no plans to repeal any of the EU legislation, which will take effect as domestic UK law on "exit day", concerning maritime regulation, other than in respect of the Brussels Recast Judgment Regulation and the Recast European Insolvency Regulation. However, some existing EU legislation was to be modified to make it work as domestic legislation.

Procedurally, UK shipping law is very much affected by European legislation to be found in three Regulations on jurisdiction and choice of law. These are: the Brussels Recast Judgment Regulation 1215/2012; the Rome I Regulation 593/208 on choice of law for contracts; the Rome II Regulation 864/207 on choice of law in non-contractual matters. Arbitration falls outside the Judgments Regulation so will be unaffected by Brexit. The enforcement of arbitration awards in foreign states will continue to fall under the 1958 New York Convention.

EU maritime law has had a substantial input in the regulation of shipping. EU competition law generally bans agreements between companies that restrict competition, and the

---

1 Article 7 requires Member States to ensure that the licensee is financially liable for the prevention and remediation of "environmental damage" – ie damage falling within the ELD – caused by offshore oil and gas operations carried out by, or on behalf of, the licensee or the operator.

2 The SOSREP has extensive intervention powers in relation to ships which are contained in the Marine Safety Act 2003, Schedule 1 Section 1 which appends a new schedule 3A to the Merchant Shipping Act 1995 – Safety Directions. There is specific provision for recovery of costs from the shipowner when action is taken by a public authority. The SOSREP has also been given wide powers of intervention in respect of offshore installations under the Offshore Installations Regulations 2002 and in respect of ships under Schedule 3A to the Merchant Shipping Act 1995 – Safety Directions, introduced in the Marine Safety Act 2003. Contrary to the position with ships, the Offshore Installation Regulations gives no right to claim costs incurred by the SOSREP and those acting under him. However, a contractual right would be given under the model clauses for offshore licences contained in the schedule to the Petroleum Licensing (Production) (Seaward Areas) Regulations 2008 (SI 2008/225).

3 Directive 2009/20/EC of the European Parliament and of the Council of 23 April 2009 on the insurance of shipowners for maritime claims applies to ships of 300 gross tonnage or more and imposes an obligation on Member States to require that shipowners of ships flying its flag have insurance covering such ships and to require shipowners of ships flying a flag other than its own to have insurance in place when such ships enter a port under the Member State's jurisdiction. The insurance is to cover maritime claims subject to limitation under the 1996 Convention. The amount of the insurance for each and every ship per incident shall be equal to the relevant maximum amount for the limitation of liability as laid down in the 1996 Convention.

4 Article 4 requires Member States "to require the licensee to maintain sufficient capacity to meet their financial obligations resulting from liabilities for offshore oil and gas operations" and, when granting or transferring licenses, to take due account of, *inter alia*, "the applicant's financial capabilities, including any financial security, to cover liabilities potentially deriving from the offshore oil and gas operations in question including liability for potential economic damages where such liability is provided for by national law". The liabilities in question are not limited to those imposed under the ELD for "environmental damage", as is the case with Article 7, but encompass "liabilities potentially deriving from the offshore oil and gas operations".

maritime sphere is no exception, subject only to the Consortia Block Exemption Regulation 906/2009 under which shipping lines with a combined market share of below 30% are allowed to enter into cooperation agreements to provide joint cargo transport services and are exempted from the prohibition of anticompetitive agreements in Article 101(1) of the Treaty on the Functioning of the European Union (TFEU).[5] P&I Clubs have been the subject of anti-trust investigation by the Commission in connection with the International Group Agreement and the pooling agreement between the Clubs. A Commission Decision of 12 April 1999 (IP/99/230) exempted the agreements concluded within the International Group of P&I Clubs from the competition rules of the European Union, until 20 February 2009. A further investigation was opened in August 2010 (IP/10/1072), but was not sufficiently conclusive to confirm the Commission's initial concerns and was closed in August 2012. A further competition measure is Regulation (EU) 2017/352 on Port Services (the Port Services Regulation) which came into effect five days before the original exit day of 29 March 2019.

Environmental Pollution has been high on the agenda post the "Erika" and "Prestige" spills. A raft of measures was introduced following the "Erika" oil spill in 1999. The "Erika I" package saw measures to ensure the accelerated phasing in of double hull design requirements for of single hulled tankers,[6] and measures on Port State Control[7] and on Classification Societies,[8] the establishment of the Committee on Safe Seas. The "Erika II" package saw the introduction of a Community monitoring, control and information system for maritime traffic,[9] and the establishment of the European Maritime Safety Agency (EMSA).[10] EMSA's remit is:

(i) monitoring the implementation of EU legislation in the maritime sphere.
(ii) to operate, maintain, and develop maritime information capabilities at EU l evel.[11]
(iii) marine pollution preparedness, detection and response capability. European wide stand-by oil spill response vessels and satellite oil spill monitoring and vessel detection service (CleanSeaNet).
(iv) Provision of technical and scientific advice to Commission in the field of maritime safety and prevention of pollution by ships.

---

5 The Regulation is currently in force until 25 April 2024.
6 Regulation 417/2002.
7 Directive 2001/106/EC amending Directive 95/21 Directive 2001/106/EC amending Directive 95/21.
8 Directive 2001/105/EC amending Directive 94/57.
9 Directive 2002/59/EC and
10 Regulation (EC) No 1406/2002 of the European Parliament and of the Council of 27 June 2002 establishing a European Maritime Safety Agency, as amended by:

Regulation (EC) No 1644/2003 of the European Parliament and of the Council of 22 July 2003;
Regulation (EC) No 724/2004 of the European Parliament and of the Council of 31 March 2004;
Regulation (EU) No 100/2013 of the European Parliament and of the Council of 15 January 2013;
Regulation (EU) No 911/2014 of the European Parliament and of the Council of 23 July 2014;
Regulation (EU) No 2016/1625 of the European Parliament and of the Council of 14 September 2016.

11 SafeSeaNet enables EU wide tracking of vessels and cargoes.

The "Erika III" package of 2009 saw the following maritime regulatory legislation: Directive 2009/21/EC on compliance with flag state requirements; Directive 2009/15/EC and Regulation (EC) No. 391/2009 on common rules and standards for ship inspections and survey organisations; Directive 2009/16/EC on port State control; Directive 2009/17/EC establishing a Community vessel traffic monitoring and information system; Directive 2009/18/EC establishing the fundamental principles governing the investigation of accidents in the maritime transport sector; Regulation (EC) No. 392/2009 on the liability of carriers of passengers by sea in the event of accidents; Directive 2009/20/EC on the insurance of shipowners for maritime claims.

III. The Expanding Competence of the EU over International Treaties and Conventions

The EU is not a State and is therefore unable to ratify or accede to most international conventions. There are some limited exceptions which provide for ratification or accession by Regional Economic Integration Organisations ("REIOs"), notably the 1982 UN Convention on the Law of the Sea and the IMO's 2002 Protocol to the Athens Convention, and also the 2005 Hague Convention on Choice of Court Agreements. The Court of Justice has decided that the EU's participation in UNCLOS precludes Member States from taking proceedings against each other before the International Tribunal for the Law of the Sea in respect of alleged violations of its provisions in matters of marine pollution.[12]

Furthermore, the freedom of Member States to sign up to international agreements will be constrained by the 1970 *ERTA* decision of the CJEU[13] whereby, when the EU obtains internal regulatory competence, a corresponding external power to negotiate and conclude international agreements is implied. With Council Regulation (EC) No 44/2001 of 22 December 2000 on jurisdiction and the recognition and enforcement of judgments in civil and commercial matters, the EU then obtained exclusive external power over international agreements covering the subject matter of the Regulation. This has been followed by the 2012 Recast Regulation and the two Regulations on choice of law, as well as EU ratification of the 2005 Hague Convention on Choice of Court Agreements 2005 (Hague Convention), which came into force as between the Member States and Mexico on 1 October 2015 (for intra-EU matters the Recast Regulation prevails). The Convention deals with exclusive jurisdiction clauses in favour of a Contracting State and provides for recognising and enforcing judgments within Contracting States in respect of contracts with such clauses. The Convention does not apply to contracts for the carriage of goods or passengers, although it would apply to contracts by way of time charter or demise charter. The EU has exclusive competence over anything jurisdictional, and agreements with third party states must be made by the EU acting on behalf of the Member States – hence it was the EU that ratified the 2005 Hague Convention and not the Member States.

---

12 The agreement is a mixed agreement with different competences between the EU and the Member States. Where the EU has competence, in matters of prevention of marine pollution, that will preclude one Member State from proceeding against another Member State before ITLOS in respect of alleged breaches of UNCLOS relating to environmental protection. *Commission v Ireland (c-459/03)* 2 C.M.L.R. The provisions of UNCLOS relied on by Ireland had become part of the Community legal order and the ECJ had exclusive jurisdiction to deal with disputes relating to their interpretation or application and to determine whether a Member State had complied with them.

13 Case 22/70 *Commission v Council (ERTA)* (1971) ECR 263.

Most maritime conventions will contain provisions on jurisdiction and enforcement of judgments.[14] After Brussels I, such conventions have become mixed agreements whereby Member States have competence to enter into such agreements as regards the liability and compensation regime, but it is the EU which has the competence over jurisdiction and enforcement of judgments. Member States cannot now sign up to these conventions without authorisation from the EU. The EU has been keen for Member States to do this and there have been a series of Council Decisions setting out three steps to this end. First the Member States are authorised to sign, ratify or accede to the convention. Second, the Member States are required to express their consent to be bound to the convention within a reasonable time and if possible by a specified date. Third, in doing so the Member States must make a declaration preserving the effect, as between Member States that are party to the convention, of the provisions of Brussels I relating to the recognition and enforcement of judgments.[15]

The conventions in question are: the International Convention on Liability and Compensation for Damage in Connection with the Carriage of Hazardous and Noxious Substances by Sea, 1996 (the HNS Convention);[16] the International Convention on Civil Liability for Bunker Oil Pollution Damage, 2001 (the Bunkers Convention);[17] the Protocol of 2010 to the International Convention on Liability and Compensation for Damage in Connection with the Carriage of Hazardous and Noxious Substances by Sea.[18]

Two other international conventions have been affected by the expansion of EU competence following Brussels I. The first is the 2002 Protocol to the Athens Convention. This was the first, and so far only, IMO Convention that allowed an REIO to become a party. The negotiations for the Protocol by the Commission on behalf of the Community resulted in the removal of a fifth ground of jurisdiction from Article 10, that of the State of the claimant's own domicile or permanent residence on the basis of the defendant's providing services to or from that State and being subject to jurisdiction in that State. As regards recognition and enforcement of judgments, Article 11(3) of the Protocol provides that Contracting Parties may apply, as between themselves, other rules for the recognition and enforcement of judgments, provided that their effect is that judgments are recognised and enforced "at least to the same extent" as under the rules of the Protocol.

The problems of co-ordinating ratification by the Community and the Member States in their respective areas of competence led to the adoption of Regulation 392/2009 which brought the provisions of the Convention into EU law, but with a wider ambit of application. Under the ERTA doctrine the EU now had exclusive competence to ratify or accede to the entirety of the Athens Convention which was done on 23 April 2014. Under Article 216(2) international agreements acceded to by the EU bind the internal legal order of all Member States, even those that are not themselves party to the agreement. Such international agreements take priority over EU secondary legislation, such as Regulation 392/2009. Therefore, passenger claims involving international carriage fall under the

---

14 The 2008 Rotterdam Rules have optional chapters on jurisdiction and arbitration. Member States would be completely free to ratify the Rotterdam Rules provided they did not opt for the jurisdiction chapter.

15 "Judgments on matters covered by the Convention shall, when given by a court of ((1) ...), be recognised and enforced in ((2) ...) according to the relevant internal Community rules on the subject (*)".

16 Council Decision (2002/971/EC).

17 Council Decision (2002/762/EC)

18 Council Decisions (EU) 2017/769 and 2017/770.

Athens Convention 2002 which has direct effect in all Member States. However, certain matters that fall outside the scope of the Convention, such as non-international sea carriage within Member States, and Articles 4, 6 and 7 of the Regulation, still fall within the Regulation.

Second, there is the Protocol of 2003 to the International Convention on the Establishment of an International Fund for Compensation for Oil Pollution Damage, 1992, (the Supplementary Fund Protocol).[19] The Council Decision did not require any declaration as to enforceability of judgments but the Commission's negotiations on behalf of the Community did result in the insertion of a new paragraph into Article 8 of the Supplementary Fund Protocol, which is the same as that in Article 11(3) of the Athens Protocol. The Council Decision also addressed the fact that two members of the Community, Austria and Luxembourg, were not parties to the two legal instruments underlying the Supplementary Fund, the 1992 Protocol to the CLC and the 1992 Fund Convention. Austria and Luxembourg were authorised to accede to all three of these instruments and it was stated that they should accede to them as far as possible by 31 December 2005.

The UK has implemented the Bunkers Convention through a statutory instrument pursuant to the powers given to the Secretary of State under s2(2) of the European Communities Act 1972. Accordingly, on the UK ceasing to be a member of the EU with the repeal of the Act, the legislation would cease to have effect. This is also the case with the Merchant Shipping (Carriage of Passengers by Sea) Regulations 2012 which implemented the Protocol and also applied it to domestic voyages within the UK on board Class A ships on or after 30 December 2016 and Class B ships on or after 30 December 2018.[20] When the Protocol entered into force internationally on 23 April 2014, the UK ratified the Protocol by means of the Merchant Shipping (Convention relating to the Carriage of Passengers and their Luggage by Sea) (Amendment) (Order) 2014 no 361 and made consequential amendments to Parts I and II of Schedule 6 to the Merchant Shipping Act 1995. This was done in exercise of the powers conferred by Sections 183(4) and (6) and 184(1) and (3) of the Merchant Shipping Act 1995, and therefore the Protocol itself will remain part of the law of the UK after Brexit. The same is the case with the Supplementary Fund protocol which was implemented through the Merchant Shipping (Pollution) Act 2006.

IV. Gold Plating

One of the EU's legislative functions has been ensuring consistent implementation within EU of IMO Treaties such as MARPOL 73/78, SOLAS, ISM. However, there have been an increasing number of instances of "gold plating" where EU legislation goes beyond the implementation of Regulations in the IMO conventions.

A. Ship Recycling

The Hong Kong International Convention for the Safe and Environmentally Sound Recycling of Ships. Council Decision (2014/241/EU) of 24 April 2014 authorises Member

---

19 Council Decisions (EU) 2011/22 and 2011/23.

20 Class B ships being passenger ships engaged on domestic voyages where they are at no point more than 20 miles from the coast and Class A ships being those engaged on domestic voyages operating at a greater distance from the coast.

States to ratify or accede to, for the parts falling under the exclusive competence of the Union, the Hong Kong International Convention for the Safe and Environmentally Sound Recycling of Ships, 2009. The EU obtained exclusive competence with The Ship Recycling Regulation 1257/2013.[21] The Regulation entered into force on 1 January 2019 and all vessels sailing under an EU flag will be required to use an approved ship recycling facility at the end of their operating lives. The Regulation sets high standards for ship recycling facilities that effectively exclude the sub-standard beaching method – something which is not excluded under the Convention. The Commission has produced a list of approved recycling facilities within the EU and is now due to produce a list of approved recycling facilities outside the EU. The approved list contains a few yards from outside the EU, in Norway, Turkey, and the US, even though there are yards in India and Bangladesh which are compliant with the requirements of the Hong Kong Convention, but which use beaching, and which have not made it onto the approved list.[22] New vessels carrying the flag of an EU Member State must have on board a certified IHM (Inventory Hazardous Material), a list of hazardous materials that are present on a ship, starting 31 December 2018. In addition, for vessels in operation and flying the flag of an EU Member State, the certified IHM has been required from 31 December 2020 and this will also be required of ships flying a third-country flag (non-EU flag, such as that of the UK) calling at a port or anchorage of an EU Member State.

The Regulation provides that ships which come under the scope of that Regulation do not come under the provisions of Regulation 1013/2006 on the shipment of waste. It has been argued that this establishes a unilateral exemption from the Basel Convention of 22 March 1989 on the Control of the Transboundary Movements of Hazardous Wastes and their Disposal, to which the EU is a party, which is not allowed under the provisions of that Convention.[23]

B. The Sulphur Directive

Both the IMO and the EU have adopted measures regulating the maximum sulphur content in fuel oil used on board ships. Until 1 January 2020 the IMO Regulations provided for a global fuel sulphur limit of 3.5% and 0.10% After that date a global limit of 0.50% has applied. As from 1 January 2020 under the EU's Sulphur Directive[24] the same global limit applies for vessels within EU waters.[25] Until 2016 the IMO's global cap of 0.50% was planned to be introduced between 2020 and 2025 which would have left a period of up

---

21 Regulation (EU) No 1257/2013 of the European Parliament and of the Council of 20 November 2013 on ship recycling and amending Regulation (EC) No 1013/2006 and Directive 2009/16/EC.

22 The European List was first established on 19 December 2016 and last updated on 22 January 2020. It now contains 41 yards, including 34 facilities located in 12 EU Member States and in Norway, 6 facilities in Turkey and 1 facility in the United States of America.

23 Within the EU, Regulation (EC) No 1013/2006 on the shipment of waste implements that Convention, as well as an amendment to the Convention adopted in 1995, which has not yet entered into force at international level, but which establishes a ban on exports on hazardous waste to countries which are not members of the Organisation for Economic cooperation and Development (OECD). Since ships contain hazardous material, they are generally classified as hazardous waste, and are therefore prohibited from being exported for recycling in facilities in countries which are not members of the OECD.

24 Directive 1999/32/EC and subsequent amendments. most recently Directive 2012/33/EU.

25 Defined as the Economic Exclusive Zone (EEZ) which stretches 200 nautical miles from shore of its Member States, except where that encroaches on the EEZ of non-EU countries.

to five years when different caps would have applied for EU waters and non-EU waters. However, the IMO position was harmonised with that under the Sulphur Directive with its decision in October 2016 at the 70th meeting of the Marine Environment Protection Committee (MEPC70) to introduce a global cap of 0.50% on 1 January 2020.[26] Both IMO and EU measures stipulate a lower figure of 0.10% for ships operating within emission control areas (ECAs), but the EU Sulphur Directive also applies it for ships at berth in any EU port.

C. The Monitoring, Reporting and Verification (MRV) Regulation

Both the EU and the IMO[27] have produced similar requirements for reporting of CO_2 emissions from shipping. The four main differences are. First, the EU Monitoring, Reporting and Verification Regulation 2015/757[28] requires reporting of three items: actual cargo carried onboard; fuel consumed and; CO_2 emitted. The IMO requires reporting only of fuel consumed. Second, the Regulation requires MRV calculations to be verified by an accredited verifier and sent to a central European Commission (EC) database, likely to be managed by the European Maritime Safety Agency (EMSA), whereas the IMO requires verification by the flag ship administration, under national procedures. Third, the Regulation provides for this information to be publicly available, as opposed to the IMO where raw data is restricted to the IMO and flag states and aggregated anonymised data is then made public. Fourth, the EU monitoring scheme started on 1 January 2018, with the IMO scheme starting on 1 January 2019.

In the UK the EU Regulation has been modified post-Brexit so that it applies to ships visiting ports within the United Kingdom in respect of voyages between ports in the United Kingdom and to and from ports outside the United Kingdom.[29] Ships visiting ports in the United Kingdom are required to carry a Document of Compliance which will be issued under the United Kingdom regulatory framework. However, the legislation does not require ships to monitor and report on voyages which do not start or end at a port in the United Kingdom. Vessels visiting both EU ports and UK ports will then be required to comply with both schemes. EU voyages and emissions would continue to be reported to the European Commission while UK voyages and emissions would have to be reported to the UK Secretary of State separately. All other provisions of the EU MRV regulation will

---

26 A further ban on carriage of fuel with a sulphur content in excess of 0.5% by 1 March 2020 was introduced in October 2018.

27 The IMO scheme is through amendments to the Ship Energy Efficiency Management Plan (SEEMP) guidelines for fuel-consumption data collection. It was adopted by the IMO's Marine Environment Protection Committee (MEPC70) on 28th October 2016 as amendments to chapter 4 of annex VI of MARPOL, adding a new Regulation 22A on Collection and reporting of ship fuel oil consumption data and new appendices covering Information to be submitted to the IMO Ship Fuel Oil Consumption Database.

28 Regulation (EU) 2015/757 of the European Parliament and of the Council of 29 April 2015 on the monitoring, reporting and verification of carbon dioxide emissions from maritime transport, and amending Directive 2009/16/EC

29 The Merchant Shipping (Monitoring, Reporting and Verification of Carbon Dioxide Emissions) (Amendment) (EU Exit) Regulations 2018 SI 2018/1358 amends Regulation (EU) No. 2015/757 Commission Implementing Regulation (EU) 2016/1927 of 4 November 2016 on templates for monitoring plans, emissions reports and documents of compliance pursuant to Regulation (EU) 2015/757 ("the Implementing regulation"). The instrument also amends the Merchant Shipping (Monitoring, Reporting and Verification of Carbon Dioxide Emissions) and Port State Control (Amendment) Regulations 2017 ("the 2017 Regulations") which provide an enforcement mechanism for the EU Regulation in the United Kingdom.

continue to apply. Any proposed amendments to the EU MRV that take effect after the end of the transition period will not affect the UK.

D. The IMO's 2018 Strategy on Reduction of Greenhouse Gas Emissions from Ships

The EU Parliament's proposal on 10 November 2017 to add shipping to the revised E.U. Emissions Trading System (ETS) from 2023 if IMO progress in a CO2 strategy was considered insufficient, is widely believed to have encouraged the IMO to adopt a plan in April 2018 to reduce greenhouse gas emissions from shipping by 50% over 2008 levels by 2050. The issue of the ETS has become live again with the Commission proposing an amendment to the MRV Regulation to harmonise its reporting requirements with those in the IMO regime, most notably in removing the need to report cargo carried. The proposed amendment has led to counter-amendments which would see international shipping from and to ports in the EU come into the ETS regime, and which were approved by the European Parliament on 16 September 2020.

The EU Commission's response came on 14 July 2021 with a proposed amendment to Directive 2003/87/EC, which established the ETS. Maritime transport services would fall within the Directive which would apply in respect of: CO2 emissions from intra-EU voyages; half of the CO2 emissions from extra-EU voyages and; CO2 emissions occurring at berth in an EU port. There would be phased entry into the ETS for Shipping companies which are to be liable to surrender allowances according to the following schedule: (a) 20% of verified emissions reported for 2023; (b) 45% of verified emissions reported for 2024; (c) 70% of verified emissions reported for 2025; (d) 100% of verified emissions reported for 2026 and each year thereafter.

Post-Brexit, a UK Emissions Trading Scheme (UK ETS)[30] replaced the UK's participation in the EU ETS on 1 January 2021. The scheme does not include shipping. Under the Carbon Budget Order 2021 (SI 2021 No. 750) international shipping is included in the sixth carbon budget under the Climate Change Act 2008 with the projections for international shipping emissions representing the estimated emissions from fuel sold in the UK for use in international shipping.

V. Conflicts with International Law

It is possible that EU legislation in the maritime field may conflict with the provisions of UNCLOS or with the provisions of the IMO Conventions such as MARPOL 73/78 and SOLAS. This notably occurred with the *Intertanko* case.[31] A joint action was brought before the High Court in England aimed at challenging the proposed implementation of Directive 2005/35, which introduces criminal penalties for ship-source discharges of polluting substances if committed "with intent, recklessly or by serious negligence".

The case raised four issues. First, was it lawful to legislate independently of MARPOL for third country vessels on the high seas or in the EEZ? Article 211 of UNCLOS indicates

---

30 The Greenhouse Gas Emissions Trading Scheme Order 2020 SI/2020/1265.

31 *The Queen on the application of: International Association of Independent Tanker Owners (Intertanko) and Others v. Secretary of State for Transport* (Case C-308/06) (Decision of the Grand Chamber of 3 June 2008).

that a state only has jurisdiction in relation to discharges on the high seas in relation to ships which are flying its flag, or where its legislation implements international rules. With regard to the EEZ Article 211(5) authorises state to legislate only to give effect to general international standards. Therefore, insofar as the Directive went beyond MARPOL by imposing criminal liability from third country ships in cases of serious negligence by persons other than the owner, master or crew, it would seem that the EU had exceeded its legislative competence under UNCLOS.

Second, was it lawful for the EU to legislate for the territorial sea otherwise than in accordance with MARPOL? Article 211(4) of UNCLOS provides that coastal states retain sovereignty over and may legislate for their territorial sea, subject to rights of innocent passage and there is nothing in MARPOL that provides that its provisions should be the sole source of applicable standards within the territorial sea or that coastal states may not adopt more stringent requirements. However, it was argued that UNCLOS and MARPOL, read together, can properly be understood as decisions by coastal states to limit their sovereign rights over their territorial seas. MARPOL is an example of states agreeing to exercise sovereign powers in an agreed uniform manner. Once they have entered into laws and Regulations for the prevention, reduction and control of marine pollution as provided for in UNCLOS Article 211(4) and in MARPOL, they have limited their rights over the territorial seas.

The third issue was whether the standard of liability of serious negligence in the Directive breached the right of innocent passage provided for under Article 17 of UNCLOS whereby ships of all states enjoy the right of innocent passage through the territorial sea. Article 19 provides that passage is innocent so long as it is not prejudicial to the peace, good order or security of the coastal state, which will be the case with "any act of wilful and serious pollution contrary to this Convention".[32] In a paper given in 2005, Dr Thomas A Mensah, the now retired, but former Presiding Judge of the Law of the Sea Tribunal in Hamburg, argued that "in the absence of a wilful and serious act of pollution, passage by a foreign vessel in the territorial sea of a coastal state must be considered to be 'innocent passage'".[33] The EC Directive lowers the requirement for the application of sanctions to a discharge from a foreign vessel involving "serious negligence" which is not provided for in either MARPOL or UNCLOS and therefore the "serious negligence" standard hampers innocent passage of a foreign vessel through the territorial sea. In his view:

> In particular a member state of the EU which enacts legislation to implement the Directive would be in breach of its obligations to another state party to MARPOL if it seeks to apply sanctions to the vessel of that other state for a discharge that results solely from "serious negligence".

Fourthly, did the phrase "serious negligence" in Article 4 of the Directive infringe the principle of legal certainty, and, if so, was Article 4 invalid to that extent?

The Court of Justice dodged the issues relating to UNCLOS and MARPOL. First, the Directive could not be reviewed in the light of MARPOL, as the European Community was not a party to MARPOL, although all the Member States were. However, the Court stated that this fact "[t]hat all its Member States are contracting parties to it is liable to

---

32 Article 19(2)(h).
33 Paper for the Eighth Cadwallader Memorial Lecture LSLC, www.shippinglbc.com/wp-content/uploads/2019/03/8_cad.pdf, last access on 4 April 2022.

have consequences for the interpretation of European Union law, in particular the provisions of secondary law which fall within the field of application of such an agreement. Therefore, it is incumbent upon the court to interpret those provisions taking account of the latter".[34] Having said so, it then failed to show how those consequences manifested in the interpretation of the provisions of the Directive which did fall within the field of application of MARPOL. Second, although the Community was a party to UNCLOS, that Convention did not establish rules intended to apply directly and immediately to individuals and to confer upon them rights or freedoms capable of being relied upon against states, irrespective of the attitude of the ship's flag state. Therefore, the nature and the broad logic of that Convention prevented the Court from being able to assess the validity of a Community measure in the light of UNCLOS. The Court of Justice concluded that there had been no infringement of the general principle of legal certainty. Although not defined in Art 4 of the Directive, the reference to "serious negligence" meant an unintentional act or omission by which the person responsible commits a patent breach of the duty of care which he should have and could have complied with in view of his attributes, knowledge, abilities and individual situation.

The second case *Mattia Manzi and Compagnia Naviera Orchestra v Capitaneria di Porto di Genova*[35] concerned the interpretation of Article 4 a(4) of Directive 1999/32/EC, relating to a reduction in the sulphur content of certain liquid fuels, as amended by Directive 2005/33/EC. The 1997 Protocol to MARPOL 73/78 included a new Annex VI, Rule 14(1) of which provided that the sulphur content in marine fuels must not exceed 4.5% by mass, which entered into force on 19 May 2005. The Directive provided that as from 11 August 2006 the sulphur content used by passenger ships operating on regular services to or from any Community port if the sulphur content should not exceed 1.5% by mass. Member States were to be responsible for the enforcement of this requirement at least in respect of vessels flying their flag and vessels of all flags while in their ports. An Italian court issued a penalty on the Captain of a Panamanian flagged cruise ship which had called at Genoa and had used fuel with a sulphur content exceeding the 1.5% limit.

The Italian court remitted three questions to the Court of Justice for a preliminary ruling. The first was whether cruise ships ran "regular services" within the meaning of Articles 4a(4) and 2(3g) of Directive 1999/32. The Court found that they did, and a series of crossings for the purpose of tourism was to be regarded as traffic within the meaning of Article 2(3g). The second was whether the 1.5% sulphur limit in Article 4a(4) of Directive 1999/32 was invalid on the basis that it was contrary to the general principle of international law *pacta sunt servanda* and to the principle of cooperation in good faith as between the EU and its Member States, in that it required Member States which had agreed to and ratified Annex VI to MARPOL 73/78 to act in breach of the obligations entered into towards the other states which were party to MARPOL 73/78. The third was whether, in light of the general principle of international law requiring international agreements to be implemented and interpreted in good faith, Article 4a(4) of Directive 1999/32 was to be interpreted as meaning that the sulphur limit of 1.5% in marine fuels did not apply to ships flying the flag of a non-EU state which was party to MARPOL 73/78, where such ships were in the port of a EU state which was itself a party to MARPOL 73/78.

---

34 [52].
35 (Case C-537/11) (23 January 2014) Judgment of the Court (Fourth Chamber).

The Fourth Chamber held that the validity of this provision of the Directive could not be challenged on the ground that it might lead to an infringement of Annex VI of MARPOL 73/78 The validity of Article 4a(4) of Directive 1999/32 cannot be determined in the light of Annex VI since the European Union is not a contracting party to the MARPOL 73/78 Convention, including Annex VI, and is not bound by it. If all the Member States had been a party to Annex VI that might affect the interpretation of the Directive, as stated in paragraph 52 of the *Intertanko* judgment, but that was not the case here as not all the Member States were parties to the 1997 Protocol.[36] Further

> Even assuming that the Court could interpret Article 4a(4) of Directive 1999/32 in the light of the sulphur content laid down in Annex VI, it suffices to state that, in the light of the objective pursued by that annex and set out in the title thereof, namely to protect the atmosphere by a reduction in harmful emissions produced by marine transport, that provision, in so far as it fixes a maximum limit on the sulphur content of marine fuel lower than that provided for by that annex, does not appear to be incompatible with such an objective.[37]

The end result of these decisions is that the EU will not allow its legislative competence to be challenged in the light of UNCLOS, or with regard to the effect of IMO Conventions to which Member States are party. In addition, disputes under UNCLOS between Member States in relation to pollution must be kept in-house within the EU, and not brought before the International Tribunal for the Law of the Sea.

EU legislation on waste has also entailed some conflict with the obligations of Member States under the IMO's civil liability conventions. Following the "Erika spill", the Commune de Mesquer attempted to recover its clean-up costs from the vessel's charterer, and the seller of the oil, Total SA, under the provisions of Law No 75-633 on the disposal of waste and the recovery of materials. The case proceeded up to the Cour de Cassation who considered that the case raised a serious problem of interpretation of Directive 75/442, and referred various questions to the European Court of Justice ("ECJ") for a preliminary ruling.[38] Article 15 of Directive 75/442 provides:

> "In accordance with the "polluter pays" principle, the cost of disposing of waste must be borne by:
>
> - the holder who has waste handled by a waste collector or by an undertaking as referred to in Article 9, and/or
> - the previous holders or the producer of the product from which the waste came".

The ECJ held that the oil became waste once it entered the sea following the shipwreck at which stage it became a product that could be reused without prior processing.[39] Although the shipwreck occurred in the exclusive economic zone of France, it was sufficient that the accidentally spilled hydrocarbons were eventually washed up on France's land territory. The obligation to dispose of the waste fell on the shipowner as the holder of the waste and under the "polluter pays" principle the charterer as the previous holder of the waste

---

36 The Czech Republic, Hungary and the Republic of Austria.

37 *Mattia Manzi and Compagnia Naviera Orchestra* v *Capitaneria di Porto di Genova* [53].

38 C-188/07 *Commune de Mesquer v Total France SA* [2008] ECR I-04501.

39 Applying its decision in *Paul Van de Walle and Others v Texaco Belgium SA* Case C-1/03 ECR 2004 I-07613.

or even the producer of the product from which the waste came, would also be liable for the costs of disposal in full, if they had contributed to the creation of the waste and to the consequent risk of pollution caused by the shipwreck. The national court could find that the charterer had contributed to this risk by failing to take measures to prevent such an incident, such as measures concerning the choice of the ship.[40] The CJEU found that the EU was not bound by the CLC, which it had not ratified,[41] and that if the waste fell within such a regime, correct transposition of Article 15 would require national law "[t]o make provision for that cost to be borne by the producer of the product from which the waste thus spread came".[42]

The logic of the decision also affects the right of a shipowner or charterer to limit under the LLMC for other marine pollution claims. Recovery of clean–up costs by a public authority would be recoverable in full, even though the constitution of a limitation fund would give only a pro-rata recovery. However, the Directive does not have direct effect, and for it to override the CLC and Fund regime, and the LLMC, national laws implementing the conventions would need to be amended, which has not been the case in the United Kingdom.

On 20 October 2020 the European Parliament proposed a new regulation on civil liability of operators of artificial intelligence for loss or damage in the territory of the Union, which has the capacity to cut across the existing IMO liability Conventions, in the same way as seen in *Commun de Mesquer*, as regards liabilities arising out of the operation of unmanned vessels when they come into operation.

VI. Brexit – and Beyond

Notice to leave the EU under Art 50 of the Treaty was given on 29 March 2017. Under the European Union (Withdrawal) Act 2018, which came into effect on "exit day" at 11pm on 31 January 2020,[43] the European Communities Act 1972 was repealed but EU legislation was retained as part of UK law.[44] Directly applicable EU law, such as EU Regulations was converted and incorporated into UK law immediately before exit from the EU. Domestic UK law which has implemented EU Directives through primary and secondary legislation pursuant to s 2(2) of the European Communities Act 1972 was preserved as it exists immediately before exit from the EU. From the EU perspective, Article 50(3) provides that

> the Treaties shall cease to apply to the state in question from the date of entry into force of the withdrawal agreement, or failing that, two years after the notification [of withdrawal] … unless the European Council, in agreement with the Member State concerned, unanimously decides to extend this period.

---

40 *Commune de Mesquer* [78].

41 [85].

42 [89].

43 This was originally scheduled for 29 March 2019 at 11.00 pm, but was extended till 31 January 2020.

44 Under the terms of Part 4 of the Withdrawal Agreement, it will be necessary to ensure that the EU Treaties and other EU law continues to apply in the UK during the implementation period. This will be achieved by way of transitional provision, inserting a new s1A into the EU (Withdrawal) Act 2018 so that the effect of the ECA is saved for the time-limited implementation period. The Bill also modifies the saved ECA provisions to reflect the fact that the UK has left the EU, and that the UK's relationship with EU law during this period is determined by the UK's obligations under the Withdrawal Agreement, rather than as a Member State.

The Treaties are the Treaty on European Union (TEU) and the Treaty on the Functioning of the European Union (TFEU).

After much absorbing politics throughout 2019 the UK and the EU managed to negotiate a revised withdrawal agreement to cover the period after "exit day" on 31 January 2020 at 11pm UK time, during which the future relationship between the parties would be negotiated. This was the so-called implementation, or transition, period,[45] which lasted until 31 December 2020 11pm UK time. During this period the UK remained subject to EU law, including new legislation coming into effect in the implementation period, but would not participate in the EU institutions. The UK would continue to benefit from the free trade agreements negotiated by the EU with third party states but would be free to start negotiating its own such agreements, although these could not come into effect until the end of the implementation period.[46]

A. Jurisdiction and Applicable Law

During the implementation period to 31 December 2020 the Brussels Recast Judgment Regulation 1215/2012, the Rome I Regulation on choice of law for contracts, and the Rome II Regulation on choice of law in non-contractual matters continued to apply as UK law by virtue of the EU Withdrawal Act 2018.[47] Article 66 of the UK–EU withdrawal agreement provided for Rome I to apply in respect of contracts concluded before the end of the implementation period and for Rome II to apply in respect of events giving rise to damage, where such events occurred before the end of the implementation period. Article 67 provided for the Brussels Regulation to apply to the recognition and enforcement of judgments given in legal proceedings instituted before the end of the implementation period, and to authentic instruments formally drawn up or registered and court settlements approved or concluded before the end of the implementation period;[48] and for the Insolvency Regulation to apply to insolvency proceedings, and actions referred to in Article 6(1) of that Regulation, provided that the main proceedings were opened before the end of the implementation period.

At the end of the implementation period, the UK became a third state and EU Regulations ceased to apply to it. From the UK's perspective the Regulations would continue to apply as UK domestic law. With the two choice of law Regulations there is no

---

45 The withdrawal agreement covers: the position of EU citizens in the UK on exit day and the position of UK citizens in EU Member States on exit day; the "divorce" settlement to be paid by the UK; the avoidance of a hard border on the island of Ireland; the role of the CJEU in supervising the withdrawal treaty.

46 In August 2019, following Jeremy Hunt's visit to China, China's commerce ministry said that the two countries agreed to "actively explore the possibility of discussing a "top-notch free trade agreement between the two sides after Brexit".

47 Sections 6 and 7. Section 8 gives ministers of the Crown a power to make secondary legislation to deal with deficiencies that would arise on exit in retained EU law. These powers can only be used for up to two years after exit day, as it expires at that point. It is also subject to various restrictions – it cannot be used to impose or increase taxation, make retrospective provision, create a relevant criminal offence, establish a public authority or amend, repeal or revoke the Human Rights Act 1998 or the legislation made under it, amend the devolution Acts (except in certain specific and limited ways) or for the purposes of implementing the withdrawal agreement. Section 9 gives ministers of the Crown a power to make secondary legislation to implement the withdrawal agreement agreed between the UK and the EU under Article 50(2) of the TEU. The power expires on exit day. It is also subject to various restrictions – it cannot be used to impose or increase taxation, make retrospective provision, create a relevant criminal offence, establish a public authority or amend, repeal or revoke the Human Rights Act 1998, or the legislation made under it.

48 Similarly, Article 69(2) regarding Denmark.

problem with reciprocity as their provisions are of universal application, and these remain part of domestic UK law,[49] with consequential amendments to reflect the fact that the UK is no longer a member of the EU. [50]

The problem is with the applicability of the Judgments Regulation. No UK litigant will lose their right to sue in another Member State, for the jurisdictional rules of the Regulation, with few exceptions apply just as much to non-Member State nationals as to everybody else.[51] However, the provisions of Article 25 the Recast Regulation regarding jurisdiction clauses in favour of the courts of a Member State would cease to apply as regards English jurisdiction clauses. The UK would be a third country and proceedings in the UK would fall under Articles 33 and 34 of the Regulation. The virtually automatic recognition of a UK judgment in a Member State of the EU ceased, although that does not mean that such judgments have ceased to be enforceable. That will depend on the mechanism for enforcing foreign judgments established under the national law of the Member State in question. Generally, for a foreign judgment to be enforced it must be established that the foreign court had jurisdiction, the defendant was properly served, the proceedings were not vitiated by fraud and the judgment is not contrary to the public policy of the foreign court.

On 13 September 2018 the UK government stated that in the event of a no-deal Brexit, it would repeal most of the existing civil judicial cooperation rules and instead use the domestic rules which each UK legal system currently applies in relation to non-EU countries. This was then put into a statutory instrument, the Civil Jurisdiction and Judgments (Amendment) (EU Exit) Regulations 2019 No. 479,[52] under which the following pieces of EU legislation were repealed with effect from the end of the implementation period: The 2012 Brussels Regulation (Recast); The Enforcement Order, Order for Payment and Small Claims Regulations;[53] the EU/Denmark Agreement.[54]

The Regulations also repealed The Lugano Convention 2007 which is the basis of the UK's civil judicial relationship with Norway, Iceland and Switzerland. The UK has made provision in domestic legislation for the Lugano Convention to apply to proceedings seised before the end of the transition period.[55]

The UK government indicated it would like to sign up to the Lugano Convention 2007 and applied to do so on 8 April 2020. The main differences between the Lugano Convention and the Brussels Regulation are that the former replicates the effect of the initial 2001 Brussels Regulation and not the 2012 Recast Regulation. For the UK to

---

49 Under Article 2 the Rome I Regulation is of universal application, whether or not the relevant law is that of a Member State, and the same is true of the Rome II Regulation under Article 3.

50 The Law Applicable to Contractual Obligations and Non-Contractual Obligations (Amendment, etc.) (EU Exit) Regulations 2019 (SI 2019/384).

51 C-412/98 *Universal General Insurance Co v Groupe Josi Reinsurance Co SA* [2000] ECR I-5925

52 The statutory instrument is supplemented by the Civil Procedure Rules 1998 (Amendment) (EU Exit) Regulations 2019 (SI 2019/521) which specify the effects on the Civil Procedure Rules.

53 This establishes EU procedures for dealing with, respectively, uncontested debts and claims worth less than EUR 5,000

54 This provides rules to decide where a case would be heard when it raises cross-border issues between Denmark and EU countries, and the recognition and enforcement of civil and commercial judgments between the EU and Denmark.

55 The Civil Jurisdiction and Judgments (Amendment) (EU Exit) Regulations 2019 (SI 2019/92). Norway has agreed to reciprocate application of the Lugano Convention in such cases under Article 2(1) of the UK–Norway Agreement of 13 October 2020. The EU–UK Withdrawal Agreement does not provide for the continued application of the Lugano Convention to proceedings instituted before the end of the transition period.

join the Lugano Convention an invitation is needed from all the existing state parties. Iceland, Norway,[56] Switzerland have indicated they would be happy for the UK to join the Convention. But what about the EU? On 4 May 2021, the Commission, in a communication to the European parliament and the council, rejected the entry of the UK to the Lugano Convention.

The UK was also, by virtue of its membership of the EU, a party to the Hague Convention. During the implementation period the UK continued to participate in the Convention through the EU's membership. On 29 September 2020 the UK government made a declaration agreeing to be bound by the Hague Convention on Choice of Law 2005 in its own right from the end of the transition period at 11pm, UK time, on 31 December 2020.[57] It has also made a reservation under Art 21 of the Convention that it will not apply the Convention to insurance contracts except as stated below:

1.   ...
    (a) where the contract is a reinsurance contract;
    (b) where the choice of court agreement is entered into after the dispute has arisen;
    (c) where, without prejudice to Article 1 (2) of the Convention, the choice of court agreement is concluded between a policyholder and an insurer, both of whom are, at the time of the conclusion of the contract of insurance, domiciled or habitually resident in the same Contracting State, and that agreement has the effect of conferring jurisdiction on the courts of that State, even if the harmful event were to occur abroad, provided that such an agreement is not contrary to the law of that State;
    (d) where the choice of court agreement relates to a contract of insurance which covers one or more of the following risks considered to be large risks:
        (i) any loss or damage arising from perils which relate to their use for commercial purposes, of, or to:
            (a) seagoing ships, installations situated offshore or on the high seas or river, canal and lake vessels;
            (b) aircraft;
            (c) railway rolling stock;
        (ii) any loss of or damage to goods in transit or baggage other than passengers' baggage, irrespective of the form of transport;
        (iii) any liability, other than for bodily injury to passengers or loss of or damage to their baggage, arising out of the use or operation of:
            (a) ships, installations or vessels as referred to in point (i)(a);
            (b) aircraft, in so far as the law of the Contracting State in which such aircraft are registered does not prohibit choice of court agreements regarding the insurance of such risks;
            (c) railway rolling stock;

---

56 In November 2020 the UK and Norway agreed to continued mutual recognition and enforcement of civil court judgments from each jurisdiction by extending and updating their 1961 Convention for the Reciprocal Recognition and Enforcement of Judgments in Civil Matters. The revived Convention will apply to the extent that, and during any period that, the 2007 Lugano Convention between EU Member States and Iceland, Norway and Switzerland does not apply to the UK.

57 The Hague Convention has been implemented into domestic law through the Private International Law (Implementation of Agreements) Act 2020.

(iv) any liability, other than for bodily injury to passengers or loss of or damage to their baggage, for loss or damage caused by goods in transit or baggage as referred to in point (ii);

(v) any financial loss connected with the use or operation of ships, installations, vessels, aircraft or railway rolling stock as referred to in point (i), in particular loss of freight or charter-hire;

(vi) any risk or interest connected with any of the risks referred to in points (i) to (v);

(vii) any credit risk or suretyship risk where the policy holder is engaged professionally in an industrial or commercial activity or in one of the liberal professions and the risk relates to such activity;

(viii) any other risks where the policy holder carries on a business of a size which exceeds the limits of at least two of the following criteria:

    (a)   a balance-sheet total of EUR 6,2 million;

    (b)   a net turnover of EUR 12,8 million;

    (c)   an average number of 250 employees during the financial year.

2. (where is "1") The United Kingdom of Great Britain and Northern Ireland declares that it may, at a later stage in the light of the experience acquired in the application of the Convention, reassess the need to maintain its declaration under Article 21 of the Convention".

Temporally the Convention only applies to exclusive choice of court agreements concluded after its entry into force in the state of the chosen court and only to proceedings instituted after its entry into force. For the EU and Mexico that date is 1 October 2015, for Singapore 1 October 2016, for Montenegro 1 August 2018 and for Denmark 1 September 2018. With the UK ratifying in its own right it would apply to exclusive jurisdiction agreements entered into from that date, and to proceedings instituted after that date, but there would be uncertainty as to the position with regard to exclusive jurisdiction agreements entered into after 1 October 2015 when the UK participated in the Convention through the EU. The UK's position as set out in its Declaration of 29 September 2020 is that:

> Whilst acknowledging that the Instrument of Accession takes effect at 00:00 CET on 1 January 2021, the United Kingdom considers that the 2005 Hague Convention entered into force for the United Kingdom on 1 October 2015 and that the United Kingdom is a Contracting State without interruption from that date.

The EU's position is that is that the date is 1 January 2021, after the end of the Brexit transition period, when the Convention entered into force in the UK by virtue of the UK being a party to it in its own right.[58]

Accordingly, as of 11pm UK time 31 December 2020, there has been a return to the common law rules determining when the English courts will have jurisdiction, and the enforcement of foreign judgments, except where the Hague Convention applies. This means that the anti-suit injunction may be used to restrain proceedings in EU and EFTA

---

58 Brussels, 9.7.2020 COM (2020) 324 final communication from the Commission to the European Parliament, the Council, the European Economic and Social Committee and the Committee of the Regions Getting ready for changes Communication on readiness at the end of the transition period between the European Union and the United Kingdom.

state parties brought in breach of an exclusive jurisdiction clause or arbitration clause.[59] This is not precluded by the Hague Convention which does not apply to interim measures.[60] The doctrine of *forum non conveniens*, which was precluded by the decision of the Court of Justice in *Owusu v Jackson*[61] now re-emerges to enable proceedings against English defendant in the English courts to be stayed on this ground. However, this is not the case where jurisdiction is covered by the Hague Convention.[62]

B. Insolvency

The UK is currently party to two cross-border insolvency Regulations. There are the Cross-Border Insolvency Regulations (CBIR) which implement the UNCITRAL Model Law on Insolvency and there is the EU Insolvency Regulation. Where the insolvency proceedings take place in a Member State of the EU, except Denmark,[63] the Regulation on Insolvency Proceedings (recast)[64] will apply. Unlike the CBIR, which has only procedural effect, the Regulation has a substantive effect. Article 3(1) provides that the courts of the Member State within the territory of which the centre of a debtor's main interests (the "COMI")[65] is situated are to have jurisdiction to open insolvency proceedings.[66] Article 20 provides that the effect of opening these proceedings shall "[p]roduce the same effects in any other Member State as under this law of the State of the opening of proceedings"[67] Article 7(1) provides that the law applicable to insolvency proceedings and their effects shall be that of the Member State within the territory of which such proceedings are

---

59 Prior to the end of the implementation period this would have been precluded by the decisions of the Court of Justice in *Turner v Grovit* (Case C-159/02) EU:C:2004:228), and *West Tankers v Allianz* (Case C-185/07) EU:C:2009:69). where an action in the other EU Member State court would be in breach of an arbitration agreement. The decisions no longer have effect as they are not "retained EU case law", as defined in Section 6(7) of the European Union (Withdrawal) Act 2018, being interpretative of the Brussels jurisdictional instruments which have not been retained in UK law.

60 Article 7 Interim measures of protection.

Interim measures of protection are not governed by this Convention. This Convention neither requires nor precludes the grant, refusal or termination of interim measures of protection by a court of a Contracting State and does not affect whether or not a party may request or a court should grant, refuse or terminate such measures.

61 (Case C-281/02) [2005] ECR I-1383.

62 Article 5 Jurisdiction of the chosen court (1)The court or courts of a Contracting State designated in an exclusive choice of court agreement shall have jurisdiction to decide a dispute to which the agreement applies, unless the agreement is null and void under the law of that State.

(2) A court that has jurisdiction under paragraph 1 shall not decline to exercise jurisdiction on the ground that the dispute should be decided in a court of another State.

(3)The preceding paragraphs shall not affect rules – a) on jurisdiction related to subject matter or to the value of the claim; b) on the internal allocation of jurisdiction among the courts of a Contracting State. However, where the chosen court has discretion as to whether to transfer a case, due consideration should be given to the choice of the parties.

63 Denmark does not participate in the judicial cooperation between the EU Member States.

64 The recast Regulation applies to insolvency proceedings commenced on or after 26 June 2017. Proceedings commenced before that date fall under Council Regulation (EC) No 1346/2000 of 29 May 2000 on Insolvency Proceedings.

65 In the case of a company or legal person, the place of the registered office shall be presumed to be the centre of its main interests in the absence of proof to the contrary.

66 Where the debtor has an establishment in another Member State, the courts of that Member State may open secondary insolvency proceedings

67 Formerly Article 17.

opened.[68] Article 4(2) provides a list of particular matters which the law of that Member State is to determine, such as

> (b) the assets which form part of the estate and the treatment of assets acquired by or devolving on the debtor after the opening of the insolvency proceedings ... (f) the effects of the insolvency proceedings on proceedings brought by individual creditors, with the exception of lawsuits pending ... (m) the rules relating to the voidness, voidability or unenforceability of legal acts detrimental to all the creditors.[69]

Article 8[70] provides an exception to the general rule in relation to pre-existing *in rem* rights over assets within the territory of another Member State.

The Insolvency (Amendment) (EU Exit) Regulations 2019, no146 provides for the repeal of most of the European Insolvency Regulation on "exit day" although the EU rules that provide for the UK courts to have jurisdiction where a company or individual is based in the UK will be retained. These provisions will continue in force as part of domestic UK law during the implementation period but have ceased as from the end of the implementation period as of 11pm 31 December 2020.

C. The European Maritime Safety Agency (EMSA)

After exit day the UK ceased to be a member of EMSA. Article 17 provides for the participation of third countries as follows:[71]

1. The Agency shall be open to the participation of third countries, which have entered into agreements with the European Community, whereby they have adopted and are applying the Community law in the field of maritime safety, maritime security, prevention of pollution and response to pollution caused by ships.
2. Under the relevant provisions of these agreements, arrangements will be developed which shall, inter alia, specify the nature and the extent of the detailed rules for the participation by these countries in the work of the Agency, including provisions on financial contributions and staff.

UK participation in EMSA after "exit day" looks unlikely given the requirement for a third country to have entered an agreement to adopt and apply "the Community law in the field of maritime safety, maritime security, prevention of pollution and response to pollution caused by ships" which would involve acceptance of the role of the CJEU over that law. However, the political declaration of Mrs May's agreement with the EU and the political framework agreement negotiated by Mr Johnson both provide:

> The future relationship should facilitate cooperation on maritime safety and security, including exchange of information between the European Maritime Safety Agency (EMSA) and the United Kingdom Maritime and Coastguard Agency (MCA), consistent with the United Kingdom's status as a third country.[72]

---

68 Formerly Article 4(1).
69 Formerly Article 4(2).
70 Formerly Article 5.
71 Norway and Iceland participate in EMSA as do candidate states for EU membership, Albania, Turkey, Serbia, Montenegro and Bosnia-Herzegovina.
72 [65] and [63] respectively.

D. Seafarers and Shipping Services

The International Convention on Standards of Training, Certification and Watchkeeping for Seafarers (STCW), 1978 requires crew members to have a Certificate of Competence which must be renewed every five years. The UK allows crew members who have trained outside the UK to work on a UK vessel if they have a certificate of equivalent competency issued by the Maritime and Coastguard Agency. Under EU law there are two procedures for recognising seafarers' qualifications. Under EC Directive 2005/45/EC there is mutual recognition by EU Member States of certificates issued to seafarers by other Member States which must be accompanied by an endorsement by the recognising State. Certificates from non-EU countries may be endorsed under EC Directive 2008/106/EC. After exit day existing UK endorsed certificates would enable UK seafarers to work on vessels flagged with EU Member States but on expiry renewal would be under the procedure set up under Directive 2008/106. EU Member States are required to write to the Commission if they wish to continue accepting new UK certificates of competence.

Article 6 of EC Regulation 725/2004 requires shipping companies (including ferries carrying passengers and lorries) prior to entering an EU port to submit security information, such as: particulars of the ship; last 10 port facilities of call; crew and passenger list. Article 7 allows a Member State to exempt companies which operate scheduled services between ports in their territory and that of another Member State. After "exit day" no exemptions are available for vessels operating scheduled services from the UK.

E. The IMO

The International Maritime Organization ("IMO") is a UN body of which most countries, and all EU Member States, are members. The EU is not a member but the Commission has observer status. However, the Commission ensures that Member States follow a predetermined EU line in meetings of the IMO as outlined in this extract from the European Parliament's 2016 briefing.

> To ensure that the EU speaks with one voice in IMO meetings, it applies an informal process for coordinating the positions of the EU Member States, Norway and Iceland. For most IMO meetings, the European Commission prepares a coordination paper, suggesting the positions for the Member States to follow. Moreover, several weeks before key IMO sessions, a coordination meeting is held in Brussels for Member States' representatives to agree on joint positions. In practice though, while during IMO meetings the EU Council presidency advances the coordinated position, individual EU Member States can take the floor and express their own position, sometimes departing slightly from the joint one.

The key word in the last sentence is "slightly". EU Member States have to toe the line in IMO meetings both in how they vote and what they say. After "exit day" the UK will be free to go its own way in the IMO.

F. Marine Insurance and P&I Cover

With Brexit the EU "passporting" regime for financial services came to an immediate end for the UK at the end of the implementation period agreed in the withdrawal agreement, as financial services did not form part of the agreement reached between the UK and the EU. Passporting previously operated so that firms, financial market infrastructures, and funds authorised in any European Economic Area (EEA) country[73] can carry out many activities in any other EEA country as a direct result of their EU authorisation, or via similar arrangements. If, for example, an insurer is authorised in the UK they can currently provide services to customers in other Member States, without requiring authorisation or supervision from the local regulator. After Brexit EEA clients will no longer be able to use the services of UK-based insurers. Furthermore, rules in Member States may prevent payments being made to an insured in that state by a UK insurer on a contract made before Brexit when the passporting regime was still in effect. The UK government proposed to use the powers under the European Withdrawal Act 2018 to establish temporary permissions regimes to enable these providers of financial services in the EEA to continue to provide those services to UK customers for up to three years after exit, so allowing those providers time to apply for authorisation to continue operating in the UK. The government has also committed to legislate, if necessary, to ensure that contractual obligations between EEA firms and UK-based customers that are not covered by the temporary permissions regime can continue to be met.

The insurance market has reacted to the increasing unlikelihood of any agreement on financial services by exit day by establishing subsidiaries based within EU Member States that will be able to underwrite EU risks directly. P&I Clubs have set up subsidiaries in Eire, Cyprus and The Netherlands. However, that still leaves the problem of contractual continuity for pre-Brexit contracts between UK insurers and an insured in an EEA state. The only possibility is for UK insurers to transfer their EU liabilities to new EU subsidiaries, a long, costly and complex process involving a Part VII transfer in the courts. The EU has so far given no commitments as to the recognition of pre-Brexit contracts. However, if national regulators in Member States were to prevent payment out on a UK policy to persons domiciled in their territory, that would almost certainly amount to an expropriation of possessions and amount to a violation of the rights granted under Article 1 of Protocol 1 of the European Convention on Human Rights, as well as a violation of similar rights guaranteed by the EU Fundamental Charter of Human Rights.

Contractual rights are capable of amounting to a possession if they give rise to an asset. Case law of the European Court of Human Rights (ECHR) indicates that this will be the case when the contract in question "gave rise to financial rights and interests and thus had an economic value". The UK case law on this issue as regards the ECHR is that the relevant criteria for determining whether a contract amounts to a "possession" are tangibility, transmissibility or assignability, realisability and economic value.[74] Although the right to property is qualified, in that the state may interfere with the right on certain permitted grounds in the public interest, the state must show (a) that its interference with the right to property is necessary to achieve legitimate aims and (b) that any action taken was proportionate to the legitimate aim pursued. This would be difficult to establish where the contract between the UK insurer and the EEA customer will carry on being regulated in the UK for the foreseeable future under the same standards as in the EEA and by a regulator that was, until Brexit, an EU regulator.

---

73 EU Member States and Norway, Iceland and Liechtenstein.

74 *Murungaru v Secretary of State for the Home Department and Others*, [2008] EWCA Civ 1015, para 58; *Breyer Group Plc v Department of Energy and Climate Change* [2014] EWHC 2257 (QB) para 51.

G. The Port Services Regulation 2017/352

The services covered by the EU Port Services Regulation are bunkering (provision of fuel), cargo-handling, mooring, passenger services, the collection of ship-generated waste and cargo residues, pilotage, and towage. Dredging is only covered to the extent that the EU Port Services Regulation requires ports to keep separate accounts of public funding received for dredging. Chapter II of the EU Port Services Regulation provides that access to the market for the provision of port services in maritime ports may be subject to: minimum requirements for the provision of port services; limitations on the number of providers; public service obligations and restrictions related to internal operators. It provides safeguards for employees' rights and an exemption from the requirements for cargo-handling, passenger services and pilotage. Chapter III sets out how port infrastructure charges are to be levied and requirements for port users and their representatives or associations to be made informed of the nature and level of these charges. Chapter IV sets out general requirements for the training of staff; consultation with port users and other stakeholders; and the handling of complaints, appeals and penalties

The Regulation has not been popular in the UK. In October 2017 the then shipping minister John Hayes told members of the UK Major Ports Group that the Regulation would be "consigned to the dustbin in the UK due to Brexit". But the Port Services Regulation was not immediately repealed. It was supplemented in domestic legislation by practical and procedural provisions in the Port Services Regulations 2019 (SI 2019/575). The Pilotage and Port Services (Amendment) (EU Exit) Regulations 2020 (SI 2020/671) covers the situation as from 1.1.21.[75] The Regulation also covers the Pilotage Act 1987 and contains amendments which remove or amend:

- provisions which have no value;
- confer functions on or refer to EU entities;
- deal with reciprocal arrangements which are no longer appropriate and, in the case of the Pilotage Act 1987, reflect the fact that the UK is no longer part of the EEA.

---

75 The amendments: restrict the scope of the retained version of the EU Port Services Regulation to ports in the UK rather than all of the EU;

- Remove provisions which allowed Member States to extend the scope of the Regulation to other ports or to pilotage;
- Remove provisions for certain reports to the European Commission designed to enable the Commission to monitor the application of the EU Port Services Regulation across Member States;
- Replace a reference to Directive 2000/59/EC (which will not be retained by the Withdrawal Act) with a reference to the Merchant Shipping and Fishing Vessels (Port Waste Reception Facilities) Regulations 2003 (S.I. 2003/1809);
- Substitute any references to "Member State" with "relevant authority" and define relevant authority as the Secretary of State and Scottish and Welsh Ministers so that in the future any obligations of Member State may be carried out by appropriate Minister.
- Omit Articles 6(7), 11(8) and amend 13(1) on the basis that these provisions have already been transposed by the UK into domestic legislation by way of the Port Services Regulations 2019 (S.I. 2019/575).
- Change references to EU procurement and employment law, which would no longer be appropriate when the UK is not a member of the EU, to the relevant UK regulations (including, where appropriate, the applicable legislation in the Devolved Administrations).

The government has recently signalled its intention to revoke the Port Service Regulation. On 16 September 2021, Lord Frost told the House of Lords: "We also intend to repeal the EU's Port Services Regulation – which is a very good example of a regulation that was geared heavily towards EU interests and never worked properly for the UK". The government has opened a consultation period from 22 March–22 April 2022.

VII. Conclusion

Following the substantial majority obtained by the conservative party in the general election on 12 December 2019 the UK–EU Withdrawal Agreement passed into law[76] and the UK left the EU at 11pm on 31 January 2020 and entered the implementation period during which the future relationship with the EU was to be negotiated. During the implementation period which ended on 31 December 2020 the UK remained subject to EU law, although was no longer a Member State and was not able to participate in EU institutions. In December 2020 a limited EU–UK Trade and Cooperation Agreement was concluded which set out preferential arrangements in areas such as trade in goods and in services, digital trade, intellectual property, public procurement, aviation and road transport, energy, fisheries, social security coordination, law enforcement and judicial cooperation in criminal matters, thematic cooperation and participation in Union programmes. It is underpinned by provisions ensuring a level playing field and respect for fundamental rights. Most EU legislation prior to the end of the implementation period continues as domestic legislation, but the Brussels Judgments Regulation, the Lugano Convention and the Insolvency Regulation all ceased to have effect as from that date.

However, as far as UK shipping law is concerned, there has been be very little change. There is nothing to change the position of the UK as the venue of choice, either through arbitration or reference to the jurisdiction of the High Court, for disputes under commercial contracts. Arbitration is unaffected by EU law and international enforcement of awards is subject to the New York Convention 1957. The parties' choice of English Law will be unaffected, and Rome I and Rome II will continue to apply throughout the EU and, as domestic law, within the UK. The UK acceded to the Hague Convention in its own right at 11pm UK time on 31 December 2020.

The end of the implementation period has brought one significant change, with the repeal of the Brussels Recast Regulation 2012, as there has been no agreement on civil jurisdiction and the EU declined to consent to the UK joining the Lugano Convention 2007. At the end of the transition period jurisdiction and enforcement of judgments in civil proceedings as between the UK and the EU and EFTA States is as follows.

The Hague Convention 2005 will apply in international cases to exclusive choice of court agreements, subject to a list of exclusions, those applicable to maritime matters being:

e) insolvency, composition and analogous matters; f) the carriage of passengers and goods; g) marine pollution, limitation of liability for maritime claims, general average, and emergency towage and salvage. Exclusive choice of court of agreements in time charters and bareboat charters therefore fall under the Convention but not those in contracts for the carriage of goods, such as voyage charters, bills of lading, sea waybills. Anti-suit

---

76 European Union (Withdrawal Agreement) Act 2020.

injunctions are not precluded under the Hague Convention but the English Courts would not be able to dismiss a Hague Convention claim on grounds of *forum non conveniens*.

Jurisdiction and enforcement of non-Hague Convention claims will be dealt with by national law in the UK and in the Member States. Anti-suit injunctions will return to restrain proceedings before courts in EU Member States which are brought in breach of arbitration clauses in a contract. *Forum non conveniens* will once more be able to justify staying proceedings against UK domiciled individuals and companies.

Enforcement of foreign judgments will be dealt with under the Hague Convention where it applies.[77] Otherwise enforcement will be dealt with under the common law grounds, under which a foreign judgment would not be recognised on various grounds, such as: where there was a previous final and conclusive judgment in relation to the dispute by a court having jurisdiction in the matter; it was a judgment obtained by fraud; it was a judgment contrary to domestic public policy; the defendant was not duly served and did not receive sufficient notice of the proceedings (for the statutory regimes) or the rules of procedure in the court of origin breached the rules of natural justice (for the common law regime).

The Recast European Insolvency Regulation 2015 has gone the same way as the Brussels Regulation and the Lugano Convention, and as of 1 January 2021 the framework for cross-border insolvency in the UK is exclusively governed by the Cross-Border Insolvency Regulation 2006, and common law principles in relation to EU Member States that are not parties to the UNCITRAL Model Law on Cross-Border Insolvency. There have also been impacts on the qualifications of seafarers working on ships flagged in an EU Member State and on security information required by shipping companies entering an EU port.

So, apart from the Judgments Regulation and the Insolvency Regulation and, prospectively, the Port Services Regulation, existing EU created maritime law in the UK after 1 January 2021 has continued as domestic UK law: *"plus ça change, plus c'est la même chose"*.[78]

---

77 Article 8 (1) provides:

"A judgment given by a court of a Contracting State designated in an exclusive choice of court agreement shall be recognised and enforced in other Contracting States in accordance with this Chapter. Recognition or enforcement may be refused only on the grounds specified in this Convention".

78 The epigram provided by Jean-Baptiste Alphonse Karr in the January 1849 issue of his journal *Les Guêpes* (*"The Wasps"*). It means that the more things change, the more they stay the same.

CHAPTER 4

The Modernisation of the Chinese Maritime Code

The Revision of the Hybrid Regime Governing Carriage of Goods by Sea

James Zhengliang Hu[1] and Lijun Liz Zhao[2]

I. Introduction

After modernising the Chinese law governing *domestic* carriage of goods *by waterways*,[3] China has shifted its focus to the law on *international* carriage of goods *by sea*. While the law on the domestic carriage is now governed by the Chinese Civil Code 2020,[4] the international carriage of goods by sea remains be governed by the Maritime Code of the PRC[5] (hereinafter "the Chinese Maritime Code", "Maritime Code", "the Code", or CMC) of 1992.[6]

---

1 Ph.D., Professor of Law, Director of Institute of Maritime Law, Shanghai Maritime University; Lawyer & Partner, Shanghai Wintell & Co Law Firm.

2 Dr Lijun Liz Zhao, Senior Lecturer in Corporate and Commercial Law, City, University of London.

3 Chapter 17 of Chinese Contract Law, which governed domestic carriage of goods by waterways has been consolidated into the Chinese Civil Code (Book Three (Contract Law Part), Chapter XIX) of 2020.

4 Chapter XIX "Contracts of Carriage" of Book Three within the Chinese Civil Code 2020, which was recently adopted on 28 March 2020 and came into force as of 1 January 2021.

5 In this Chapter, "the People's Republic of China" or "China" refers to the Mainland China unless otherwise expressly indicated. The carriage between or among the Mainland China, Taiwan and Macau is in the nature of domestic carriage, but is currently treated generally as international carriage in the sense of maritime law as they are of different jurisdictions in law

6 Chapter IV of the Maritime Code is not applicable to the contracts of domestic carriage of goods by sea, as Para 2 of Art. 2 of the Code provides: "The provisions concerning contracts of carriage of goods by sea as contained in Chapter IV of this Code shall not be applicable to the maritime transport of goods between the ports of the People's Republic of China". The provision of such inapplicability was mainly due to the differences between the legal regime applicable to the international carriage goods by sea and that to the domestic carriage of goods by waterways including the coastal carriage by sea and the carriage in inland navigation in 1992 when the Code was adopted. The differences were: (a) the State transport plans should be followed in the domestic carriage and formed part of the contract, whereas there was no such plan in the international carriage; (b) the carrier's liability was based upon the fault of the carrier, the master and the crew, his other servants or agents in the domestic carriage, whereas the carrier's liability based upon the Hague or Hague-Visby Rules was followed in the practice of international carriage by means of incorporating the Hague or Hague-Visby Rules into bills of lading; (c) the carrier could not avail of any limitation of liability for loss of or damage to goods in the domestic carriage, whereas the limit of carrier's liability was based upon the Hague or Hague-Visby Rules in the international carriage, in particular, the COSCO Bill of Lading stipulated the Chinese currency RMB700 Yuan per package or unit; (d) the transport documents used in the domestic carriage were waterway cargo transport waybills, whereas bills of lading were used in the international carriage. It was recognised that the regime of the domestic carriage of goods by waterways needed to be maintained and consequently above significant differences were unable to be eliminated.

DOI: 10.4324/9781003160298-5

The Maritime Code was enacted nearly 30 years ago and has demonstrated some gaps. In this context, both the Chinese public and private stakeholders have widely recognised that it is now time to revise the Code and modernise the law governing the international carriage of goods by sea under this Code.[7] In order to accomplish this mission, a law revision committee has been established. However, little research in English language has explored this significant ongoing law revision in this important trade country. With the aim to bridge the gap, this chapter evaluates the Chinese Maritime Code, particularly the regime governing the international carriage of goods by sea, and probes into the relevant ongoing law revision to modernise the Code.

The law on international carriage of goods by sea is a fundamental part of maritime law. Unlike some common law and civil law countries, each of which has a standing-alone statute to govern the international carriage of goods by sea,[8] China does not have such a statute. Instead, Chinese law governing contracts of international carriage of goods by sea is mainly consolidated in Chapter IV "Contract of Carriage of Goods By Sea" of the Maritime Code. So, this chapter pinpoints Chapter IV of the Code.

Remarkably, Chapter IV of the Code has adopted a hybrid regime. The regime is different from any of the three existing international conventions, which came into force before the Code, on the international carriage of goods by sea. Instead, only some provisions of the conventions were partially incorporated into the Code. These conventions consist of the Hague Rules (HR), the Hague-Visby Rules (HVR), and the Hamburg Rules (HBR).

II. Reasons that China adopted the Hybrid Regime: A Historical Review

At the late stage of drafting the Maritime Code, i.e. in 1991–1992, it was widely recognised that the international carriage of goods by sea called for international uniformity of law and that China – as a shipping and maritime trading country – should promote the legal uniformity. Individual maritime trade countries should either ratify or accede to a relevant international convention, or convert provisions of the convention into its domestic law, or do both. While doing so, China had difficulty in choosing any of the three existing international conventions:

> On the one hand, the Ministry of Communications, which represented the shipping companies such as China Ocean Shipping Company (COSCO),[9] preferred the Hague Rules, i.e.

---

7 Revision of the Maritime Code is necessitated by the facts including that the maritime shipping and trading situation in China and in the world, the contents of the principles followed in the making of the Maritime Code and the relevant domestic general laws have undergone a significant development, that the Maritime Code does not apply to domestic carriage of goods by sea and lacks legal regime governing compensation for marine pollution damage from ships and that the admiralty judicial practice has demonstrated the existence of ambiguities, uncertainties and gaps in some aspects in the Maritime Code. See James Zhengliang Hu, *The Chinese Maritime Code needs to be modernized (in Chinese)*, China Ocean Shipping, Vol. 107, March 2015, p. 67.

8 E.g. the UK Carriage of Goods by Sea Act (COGSA) 1971, the US Carriage of Goods by Sea Act (COGSA) 1936, the Australian Carriage of Goods by Sea Regulations 1998, the Japanese Law Concerning International Carriage of Goods by Sea 2018.

9 At the time of 1991–1992, COSCO was state-owned and subordinated to the Ministry of Communications. COSCO developed into COSCO Group at a later stage. In 2016, COSCO Group and China Shipping Group, another large state-owned shipping company, were merged into China COSCO Shipping Group and became the largest shipping group in the world. In 2008, the Ministry of Communications was reorganised as the Ministry of Transport responsible for shipping, road transport, rail transport and air transport.

"the International Convention for the Unification of Certain Rules of Law Relating to Bills of Lading, 1924". At the same time, the Ministry of Communications and COSCO favoured the Hague-Visby Rules, i.e. "the Hague Rules as amended by the Visby Rules (the Protocol of 1968 to amend the Hague Rules, and by the 1979 SDR Protocol)". The stance of the Ministry of Communications and COSCO was based upon the facts that: first, most shipping countries in the world had ratified or acceded to the Hague or Hague-Visby Rules; second, China, as one of the largest shipping countries, should act in line with the cluster of majority countries through adopting the Hague or Hague-Visby Rules in the forthcoming Maritime Code.

On the other hand, the Ministry of Foreign Economic and Trade Cooperation, representing the large international trading companies,[10] strongly insisted that the Maritime Code should adopt the Hamburg Rules, i.e. "the United Nations Convention in the Carriage of Goods By Sea, 1978". Their stance was based on the facts as follows: first, China was also one of the largest maritime trade countries, and this necessitated sufficient protection of cargo interests in the Maritime Code; second, the Chinese government strongly supported the adoption of the Hamburg Rules, when the Rules were negotiated before the United Nations Commission on International Trade Law (UNCITRAL).

It should be noted that the former group expressed firm opposition against the latter. The Ministry of Communications and COSCO claimed that incorporating the Hamburg Rules into the Maritime Code would make Chinese law concerning contracts of international carriage of goods by sea, under the Code, inconsistent with standard international practice. Furthermore, they pointed out that adopting the Hamburg Rules would likely have adverse effects on the competitiveness of the Chinese merchant fleets in the international shipping market due to the significantly increased carriers' liabilities.

Eventually, following lengthy discussions, the drafters of the Maritime Code, the State Council, and the National People's Congress jointly reached some conclusions as follows:

First, provisions governing contracts of international carriage of goods by sea in the Code should be consistent with the primary international trade practice that prevails around the globe. This is because of the need for international legal uniformity in this subject matter and the dual role of China – as a large shipping country on the one hand, and a maritime trading country on the other.

Second, *some* provisions of the Hague-Visby Rules should be incorporated into the Code. This is because of the wide acceptance of the Rules by large shipping and maritime trading countries.

Third, some mature and reasonable provisions of the Hamburg Rules also should be incorporated into the Code. This would help to overcome deficiencies of the Hague-Visby Rules, which were too simple as a whole, with some provisions being outdated.

Fourth, some provisions of the Code should reflect China's particularity.

Consequently, under Chapter IV of the Code, the hybrid regime governing the international carriage of goods by sea has been employed. As shown, the regime was in fact a pack of compromises between the shipping interests and the cargo interests in China.

---

10 Similarly, the largest international trading companies were state-owned and were subordinated to the Ministry of Foreign Economic and Trade Cooperation which was reorganised as the Ministry of Commerce in 2003.

The hybrid regime – Chapter IV of the Code – is different from any of the three pre-exisiting international conventions, i.e. the Hague Rules, the Hague-Visby Rules, and the Hamburg Rules. After the promulgation of the regime, there arose some negative comments from the international community that claiming the regime might be the fourth set of rules and added extra complexity to the fragementation of the legal uniformity on the international carriage of goods by sea. Nevertheless, it should be noted that four Scandinavian countries – Sweden, Denmark, Norway and Finland – adopted similar hybrid regimes in their respective maritime codes in 1994, roughtly at the same time with China.[11] Russia also adopted a similar hybrid regime in Chapter VIII "Contract of Carriage of Goods by Sea", of the Merchant Shipping Code of the Russian Federation as amended in 1999.[12]

III. An Overview of the Hybrid Regime: Major Contents

As discussed above, under Chapter IV of the Maritime Code, the hybrid regime consists of three categories of provisions, i.e. those based upon the Hague-Visby Rules as amended by its 1979 SDR Protocol, those based upon the Hamburg Rule, and those of China's particularity. In details:

A. Incorporated Provisions from the Hague-Visby Rules

In Chapter IV of the Code, the provisions concerning the carrier's liability regime, including the carrier's obligations, liability, exemptions, and the limits of liability, are largely identical with those under the Hague-Visby Rules as amended by the 1979 SDR Protocol.[13] These relevant provisions in the Code are identified as follows:

1) The obligation of the carrier to exercise *due diligence* to make the ship *seaworthy* (Art. 47) and care for the goods (Art. 48);
2) The exemptions of the carrier's liability (Art. 51);
3) The (upper) limit of the carrier's liability for loss of or damage to goods (Art. 56), and loss of the right to limit (Art. 59).

B Incorporated Provisions from the Hamburg Rules

The following provisions in Chapter IV of the Code are made by absorbing or by referring to the corresponding provisions of the Hamburg Rules:

1) The definitions of the carrier, shipper, actual carrier, consignee, and goods (Art. 42);
2) The provisions concerning obligations and liabilities of the "actual carrier" (Arts. 60–65);

---

11 Han Lixin, Wang Xiufeng et.al., *A Collection of Maritime Laws of Various Countries (Regions)*, Vol. 2, Dalian Maritime University Press, 2003, pp. 1485–1508.

12 Ibid.

13 An unofficial English version of the Maritime Code can be found on the website of https://china.findlaw.cn/jingjifa/shewaifalv/swflfg/20110414/91707.html or Westlaw database. All internet sources were last accessed 1 February 2022.

3) The provisions concerning obligations and liability of the shipper (Arts. 66, 68, and 70);

4) The provisions concerning carriage of live animal (Art. 52)[14] and deck cargo (Art. 53);

5) The provisions of non-contractual claims (Art. 58);

6) The provisions of bills of lading and other transport documents (Arts. 71–77 and 80).[15]

C Provisions of the Code Reflecting China's Particularity

Some particular provisions, different from both the Hague-Visby and Hamburg Rules, have been adopted in Chapter IV of the Code. Such particular provisions are identfied as follows:

Art. 46 of the Code provides the period of the carrier's responsibility for containerised and non-containerised goods, respectively. First, regarding the containerised goods, the period of the carrier's responsibility is from the time of receiving goods at the loading port to the time of delivery at the port of discharge, *which is the same as the Hamburg Rules Art. 4(1)*.[16] Second, as to the non-containerised goods, the period of the carrier's responsibility is from the time when the goods are loaded onboard the ship to the point of time when goods are discharged, *which is similar to the definition of carriage of goods contained in the Hague-Visby Rules Arts I(e) and VII*.[17]

Art. 50(1) of the Code states that delay in delivering goods occurs when the goods have not been delivered at the designated discharge port within the time *expressly agreed* upon. Thus, this article adopted the criterion of "agreed time" *only*, deviating from Art. 5(2) of the Hamburg Rules that adopted *both* the criteria of the "agreed time" and that of "reasonable time" in the absence of agreed time. This deviation from the Hamburg Rules was because, first, it is usually challenging in reality to prove the reasonable time needed for the performance of a particular voyage, and thus the "reasonable time" under the Hamburg Rules may easily cause disputes in practice. Second, Art. 50(1) was also a compromise between the carriers' interests and the cargo interests mentioned above.

Art. 55 of the Code governs indemnity measures concerning loss of or damage to goods subject to actual value of the goods in question. This "actual value" is that at the time of shipment, plus the cost of insurance and freight, i.e. the CIF price. So, a claimant cannot claim under the Code for loss of market value or other economic loss, arising from loss of or damage to goods.[18] In contrast, Subparagraph 2 of Art. 4(5)(b) of the Hague-Visby Rules

---

14 Under Art. 5(5) of the Hamburg Rules, carrier's proof of compliance with any special instructions given by the shipper respecting the animals constitutes partly a presumption that the loss, damage or delay in delivery of live animals was caused by the special risks inherent in the carriage of live animals. However, under Art. 52 of the Maritime Code, such a proof is a condition for the carrier to avail of the exemption of the special risks inherent in the carriage of live animals.

15 Art. 71 of the Maritime Code is identical to the definition of bill of lading contained in Art. 1(7) of the Hamburg Rules. However, Art. 71 provides that the carrier also undertakes to deliver the goods against surrender of bill of lading in the case of straight bill of lading, whereas such an undertaking is applicable only to an order or bearer bill of lading under Art. 1(7) of the Hamburg Rules.

16 Emphasis added.

17 Emphasis added.

18 Paras 1 and 2 of Art. 55 of the Maritime Code provides that "The amount of indemnity for the loss of the goods shall be calculated on the basis of the actual value of the goods so lost, while that for the damage to

prescribes that the "actual value" of goods shall be the "commodity exchange price", or, if no such price, be the "current market price", or, if there be no commodity exchange price or current market price, by reference to the "normal value" of goods of *the same kind and quality*. This deviation from the Hague-Visby Rules is because of, first, the lack of commodity exchange price, and second, the difficulty in proving the commodity market price, in the era of the State's planned economy in China when the Code was adopted in 1992.

Art. 57 of the Code governs that the liability of the carrier for the economic loss resulting from delay in delivering the goods shall be limited to an amount equivalent to the "freight payable" for the goods so delayed, while Art. 6(1)(b) of the Hamburg Rules provides the limit equivalent *to two and a half times*[19] of the freight payable for the goods delayed, but not exceeding the total freight payable under the contract of carriage of goods by sea. This deviation from the Hamburg Rules was also a compromise between the carriers' interests and the cargo interests mentioned above.

Art. 67 of the Code addresses the shipper's obligation to perform cargo formalities and its liability in the case of defective performance.[20] This is an important provision for China's cross-border trade practice, because the Chinese regulations on imports and exports require shippers to fulfil various cargo formalities.

Art. 78 of the Code provides the relationship between carriers on the one hand, and the consignee or the holder of bills of lading, whose rights and obligations are based on clauses of bills of lading, on the other. This article further states that neither the consignee nor the holder of the bill of lading shall be liable for demurrage, dead freight, and all other expenses in respect of loading goods that occurred at the loading port unless the bill of lading clearly states that such liability shall be borne by the consignee or the holder of the bill of lading.

Art. 79 of the Code provides the "negotiability" of bills of lading. First, a *straight* bill of lading is not negotiable; second, an *order* bill of lading may be negotiated through an endorsement to order or endorsement in blank; and third, a *bearer* bill of lading is negotiable without endorsement.[21]

Art. 81 of the Code provides the time required for submitting a notice claiming damages. When the loss of or damage to goods is not apparent, the notice shall be given by the consignee, within *7 days* concerning *non-containerised* goods, or within *15 days* regarding *containerised* goods, from the next day of the delivery thereof.[22] So, Article 81 here is different from Art. 19(2) of the Hamburg Rules, which provides 15 days for *both* non-containerised and containerised goods.

---

the goods shall be calculated on the basis of the difference between the values of the goods before and after the damage, or on the basis of the expenses for the repair. The actual value shall be the value of the goods at the time of shipment plus insurance and freight".

19 Emphasis added.

20 Art. 67 of the Maritime Code provides that "The shipper shall perform all necessary procedures at the port, customs, quarantine, inspection or other competent authorities with respect to the shipment of the goods and shall furnish to the carrier all relevant documents concerning the procedures the shipper has gone through. The shipper shall be liable for any damage to the interest of the carrier resulting from the inadequacy or inaccuracy or delay in delivery of such documents".

21 Emphasis added by the authors.

22 Emphasis added by the authors.

Art. 86 of the Code governs the disposal of undelivered goods. If the goods are not collected at the discharge port, the ship master may discharge the goods at warehouses or other appropriate places, and the consignee shall bear any expenses or risks.

Art. 87 of the Code states the carrier may exercise of lien on goods. If the freight, general average contributions, demurrage or other charges owed to the carrier have not been paid in full, nor has appropriate security been given, the carrier may exercise the lien over the goods to a reasonable extent.[23] Art. 88 further provides how the carrier may enforce the lien.[24]

IV. Modernising the Hybrid Regime: Reasons and Opportunities

A. Reasons for Modernising the Hybrid Regime

1. Gaps, Ambiguities and Uncertainties of Existing Rules

Due to the significant development in global maritime trade and the accumulated judicial experience in implementing the Code over the past three decades,[25] gaps in the current hybrid regime have emerged and revealed that the Code has fallen behind merchants' and industry practice.

2. A Summary of Major Gaps under the Current Hybrid Regime

Major gaps in the hybrid regime can be summarised as follows:

First, with the arrival of the digital age, the Code has no rules governing the use of electronic transport documents. To bridge this gap is increasingly important, because of the developments of electronic commerce, the internet and emerging blockchain and AI technologies.

Second, the Code lacks express rules governing the legal position of port operators. Such parties perform cargo loading, stowage, handling and discharge in port, in cross-border trade practice. However, the rights, obligations and liabilities of such parties are legally ambiguous under the Code. In addition, it is urgent to bridge the gap in the case of China because of the delima between the dramatic demand from the trade pratice – the

---

23 Noticeably, the goods subject to lien should be owned by the person who is obliged to pay the freight or other charges to the carrier under Art. 87 of the Maritime Code. In the domestic carriage of goods by sea or in inland navigation, however, there is not such a requirement, provided the freight or other charges occurred in the carriage of the goods concerned under Art. 836 of the Chinese Civil Code.

24 Art. 88 of the Maritime Code provides that: "If the goods under lien in accordance with the provisions of Article 87 of this Code have not been taken delivery of within 60 days from the next day of the ship's arrival at the port of discharge, the carrier may apply to the court for an order on selling the goods by auction; where the goods are perishable or the expenses for keeping such goods would exceed their value, the carrier may apply for an earlier sale by auction. The proceeds from the auction sale shall be used to pay off the expenses for the storage and auction sale of the goods, the freight and other related charges to be paid to the carrier. If the proceeds fall short of such expenses, the carrier is entitled to claim the difference from the shipper, whereas any amount in surplus shall be refunded to the shipper. If there is no way to make the refund and such surplus amount has not been claimed at the end of one full year after the auction sale, it shall go to the State Treasury".

25 There are 11 maritime courts in China for the trial of maritime cases in the first instance among which 9 are located in the coastal cities, i.e. Dalian, Tianjin, Qingdao, Shanghai, Ningbo, Xiamen, Guangzhou, Haikou and Beihai and two located along the Yangtze River, i.e. Wuhan and Nanjing. The courts of appeals are the high people's courts of a municipality directly under the State Council, province or autonomous region where a maritime court is located. A case will be retried by the Supreme People's Court where an application for retrial is approved by it after the second instance.

total turnover of the Chinese ports has been ranking the largest in the world for years – and the absence clear statutory provisions governing the port cargo operation activities.[26]

Third, the Code has no express rules governing "the identification of the carrier" under a bill of lading, the respective burden of proof in cargo claims, and the right of control.[27] Although Art. 829 of the Chinese Civil Code 2020 might potentially fill in this gap, this article is not appropriate for the international carriage, because this article does not provide any restrictions on the consignor' exercise of its rights, nor a guarantee to be provided by the consignor for compensation for the losses on demand of the carrier.

Other gaps in the hybrid regime comprise the ambiguities concerning a FOB seller's legal position and such a seller's rights and obligations, as opposed to the carrier, the identification of the "actual carrier", and the legal position of a "freight forwarder", to name a few. All these legal loopholes in the Code have brought about many disputes in practice.

B. The Adoption of the Rotterdam Rules

The Rotterdam Rules, i.e. "the United Nations Convention on Contracts for the International Carriage of Goods Wholly or Partly by Sea", were adopted in 2008. Among the stated principles of the drafters regarding the Maritime Code, one is to consider the tendency of international maritime legislation.[28] Although having not come into force yet, the Rotterdam Rules may indicate the latest international tendency of the law governing carriage of goods by sea. As mentioned above, the Rules are well supported in China since they contain some reasonable and mature provisions that need to be incorporated to improve the hybrid regime, while the Maritime Code is being revised.

C. The Consistency with General Civil Laws

In China, maritime law is deemed as an an area of special law, as opposed to general civil laws. This classification matters in terms of the hierarchy of the applications of legal rules:

---

26 The Rules on Port Cargo Operations of 2000 promulgated by the former Ministry of Communications were abolished in 2016. In the case of claim for cargo damage occurred during discharge against Guangzhou Container Terminal Co., Ltd., the High People's Court of Guangdong Province in the second instance reversed the judgement of the Guangzhou Maritime Court in the first instance and held that the discharge of containerised goods by the terminal as entrusted by the carrier did not come within carriage under Art. 58 which provides that the carrier shall properly and carefully load, handle, stow, carry, keep, care for and discharge the goods carried and therefore the terminal was not an actual carrier, and consequently was not entitled to avail of the limitation of liability available to the carrier under Art. 56 of the Maritime Code. See the Civil Judgement (2005) yue gao fa min si zhong No. 122.

27 Art. 829 of the Chinese Civil Code provides: "Before a carrier delivers the goods to the consignee, the consignor may ask the carrier to stop carriage, return the goods, change the place of destination, or deliver the goods to another consignee, provided that the consignor shall compensate for the losses thus caused to the carrier".

28 For example, Chapter IX "Salvage at Sea" is basically a copy of the 1989 Salvage Convention as the draftsmen of the Maritime Code realised that this Convention represented the tendency of international legislation on salvage at sea, although this Convention had not come into force yet in 1992. This Convention is now widely accepted in the world. The other principles are (a) starting from the actual situations of maritime transport, economy and trade; (b) taking the widely-adopted maritime conventions as the legislative basis; (c) absorbing the non-governmental rules in the nature of international shipping customs and usages; (d) using the widely-used contract forms for reference. See: James Zhengliang Hu: *On the necessity, principles to be followed and focuses in revising the Chinese Maritime Code (in Chinese)*, www.law-walker.net/news.asp?ctlgid =75&id=32919.

first, the maritime law as the special law shall enjoy *priority* over the general civil laws, where there are contradictions between the two; second, the relevant general civil law shall apply where the special law does *not* prescribe relevant provisions.

Also, it should be ntoed that, maritime law, as the special law, shall be consistent with the general civil laws as much as possible. That is to say, the scope of application of maritime law shall be confined within some areas as follows:

1) Those which are necessary to be regulated concerning legal relationships that are associated with maritime transport or ships which are distinctive from the general civil laws;
2) Specific provisions which are subordinate to and implement guiding principles stated within the general civil laws, which might be abstract and general;
3) Provisions that are identical to that of the general civil laws, but such provisions are essential for the integrity of the maritime law and affecting its application.

In order to make the Maritime Code consistent with the Chinese general civil laws, the precondition is to enact the general civil law before the Maritime Code. However, this was not the case in China's law-making trajectory. Except for the General Principles of Civil Law of 1986, China had not passed the general civil laws before the Maritime Code 1992.

The Chinese general civil laws, as opposed to the Maritime Code, include the Insurance Law of 1995, the Contract Law of 1999, the Tort Law of 2010, the Property Law of 2007, the Labour Contract Law of 2007, and the Law on Application of Law in the Foreign-related Civil Relations of 2010.

However, all these general civil laws had not been adopted before the passage of the Maritime Code 1992. This mismatch in China's law-making trajectory has led to many unnecessary contradictions between the Maritime Code and the Chinese general civil laws. For example, contractual parties to a marine insurance contract are "the insurer" and "the assured" under Art. 216 of the Maritime Code 1992, whereas those to an insurance contract are "the insurer" and "the applicant" under Art. 10 of the Insurance Law 1995.

In addition, the Chinese Civil Code was enacted on 28 May 2020 and came into force as of 1 January 2021. The Civil Code has consolidated some of the preexisting general civil laws, i.e. the General Principles of Civil Law of 1986, the Contract Law of 1999, the Tort Law of 2010, and the Property Law of 2007.

Therefore, to summarise, in order to eliminate the unnecessary contradictions with the Chinese general civil laws, the Maritime Code needs to be amended accordingly to be consistent with the Insurance Law of 1995, the Labour Contract Law of 2007, and the Law on Application of Law in the Foreign-related Civil Relations of 2010, and more importantly the consolidated legislation – the Civil Code 2020.

D. The Opportunity of Modernising the Hybrid Regime

The primary aim of revising the Maritime Code is to modernise the Code. Specificlly speaking, the revision of the Code need:

First, to accomodate the developments of the international shipping practice, the maritime economy and commercial pratice in China and the world, the international maritime legislation and the post-1992 standard maritime contract forms,

Second, to be consistent with the aforesaid general civil laws, and

Third, to consolidate the post-1992 statutory provisions that have been developed from the judicial interpretations, adopted by the Supreme People's Court of China.[29]

So far, a law revision committee has been established to revise the Code. In the Chinese legal system, the enactment or revision of a statute shall first be listed in the National Legislation Plan, made by the National People's Congress, every five years. Concerning maritime law, the revision of the Code has been listed in the current National Legislation Plan, by the Thirteenth National People's Congress, for the period from 2018 to 2023.

In this Plan, the Code is one of the 47 pieces of draft legislation in the second tier of the hierarchy to be submitted before the National Congress.[30] Nevertheless, apart from the 47 pieces of the second tier drafts legislation, the first tier comprises another 69 pieces of draft legislation which shall be submitted for the Congress to review definitely within the period of the Plan. In addition, the revision of existing legislation involves complicated legislative formalities and usually takes a long time. Therefore, it will not be easy to initiate the reading process of the draft Code before the National Congress before 2023 – less than one year from now on.

However, the need to revise the Code, especially Chapter IV thereof, is well recognised by the academic and judicial circles and the relevant industries in China. So far, research for the purpose to revise the Code has been conducted several times, as commissioned by the Ministry of Transport. Besides this, the Ministry of Transport submitted a piece of preliminary draft legislation to the Ministry of Justice in 2020. Therefore, the official readings and revision process of the Code before the National Congress will be initiated in the near future.

V. Proposed Amendments to the Hybrid Regime

A. Adopting the Reasonable and Mature Provisions of the Rotterdam Rules

To improve the hybrid regime under Chapter IV of the Code, it is of use to refer to some provisions of the Rotterdam Rules, which is the latest international convention concerning the carriage of goods by sea. For this reason, this chapter probes into China's attitude toward how to incorporate the Rules into the Code.

1. China's Attitude towards the Rotterdam Rules

There were many discussions and arguments regarding China's attitude toward the Rotterdam Rules before and after the adoption of the Rules in 2008.

---

29 As provided for in Art. 32 of the Law on the Organization of the People's Courts of 1979 as amended, the Supreme People's Court has the power to make judicial interpretations on legal issues concerning specific application of laws and decrees in the judicial trials of cases. So far, the Supreme People's Court has promulgated maritime judicial interpretations of general application in the following aspects: ship's collision in 1995 and 2008, marine insurance in 2006, delivery of goods without production of bills of lading in 2009, limitation fund for maritime claims in 2010, compensation for oil pollution damage from ships in 2011, freight forwarders in 2012, and shipmasters and crew in 2020.

30 See the website of the National People's Congress of the People's Republic of China: www.npc.gov.cn/npc/c30834/201809/f9bff485a57f498e8d5e22e0b56740f6.shtml.

There are four primary schools of viewpoints, summarised as follows. First, while the Rules are not perfect and have some deficiencies, China shall sign and ratify the Rules, because the Rules are a relatively advanced international convention concerning carriage of goods by sea.[31] Second, China shall not sign and ratify the Rules at the present stage and wait to see whether other countries adopt the Rules, because the contents of the Rules are too complicated, the innovative rules therein need to be tested in practice, and therefore China shall maintain a proactive but prudent attitude when considering adopting them or not.[32] Third, while China shall not sign and ratify the Rules at this stage, those reasonable, mature and advanced rules contained in the Rules shall be adopted by the current revision of the Maritime Code.[33]

The fourth school of viewpoint stems from the industry players. The attitudes of the shipping and the maritime trading industries are important in the eyes of the Chinese government in order to decide whether and when China shall ratify the Rotterdam Rules, though the industry is always interest-oriented.

Regarding the shipping industry in China, they claimed that the provisions of the Rotterdam Rules concerning the transport documents and electronic transport records and those for solving the practical issues commonly existing in shipping practice, such as provisions on delivery of goods in Chapter 9 of the Rules, will or may be beneficial to the shipping industry. However, the shipping industry, as a whole, does not support the Rules, because the industry, especially the small- or even some medium-sized shipping companies, are not satisfied with the Rules in the field of the carrier's liability. First, the Rules increase the carrier's liability by deleting the exemption of nautical fault and fault in fire,[34] which are available under Chapter IV of the Maritime Code and the Hague-Visby Rules. Second, the Rules also increase the upper limit of the carrier's liability.[35] Third, the industry is not satisfied with the special rules concerning "volume contracts" in Article 80 of the Rotterdam Rules, which may put the small- and even medium-sized shipping companies in an unequal and less favourable position when facing large shippers/cargo owners.

---

31 Yuzuo Si, *Evaluation and prospects of the Rotterdam Rules*, Annual of China Maritime Law (in Chinese), 2009, Vols. 1–2, p. 3. Yuechuan Jiang, Shihui Yu, *Question of the questioned: how to evaluate the Rotterdam Rules*, Tsinghua Forum of Law (in Chinese), 2014, Vol. 2, pp. 62–63.

32 Yongjian Zhang, *How to evaluate the Rotterdam Rules*, Annual of China Maritime Law (in Chinese), 2010, Vol. 1, p. 25. Yingying Zou, *Understanding of the assessment of the Rotterdam Rules under the perspective of the Chinese law*, Law Science (in Chinese), 2010, Vol. 11, p. 108.

33 James Zhengliang Hu, *The Chinese Maritime Code needs to be modernized*, China's Ocean Shipping (in Chinese), 2015, Vol. 3, p. 67. Faqiang Yuan, *Prudent step forward: the attitude to be maintained by China towards the Rotterdam Rules*, Contemporary Law Review, 2013, Vol. 4, p. 139.

34 Nautical fault means an act, neglect or default of the master, mariner, pilot or the servants of the carrier in the navigation or in the management of the ship as provided for in Art. 4(a) of the Hague-Visby Rules. Art. 51(1) of the Maritime Code contains similar provisions, i.e. "fault of the Master, crew members, pilot or servant of the carrier in the navigation or management of the ship". The deletion of the fault in the management of the ship in Art. 17 of the Rotterdam Rules is identical to the provision of the carrier's continuous obligation to exercise due diligence to make and maintain the ship seaworthy during the voyage in Art. 14 and consequently the shipping industry does not accept it. Art. 4(b) of the Hague-Visby Rules provides "fire, unless caused by the actual fault or privity of the carrier" as an exemption of liability. Art. 51(2) of the Maritime Code contains similar provisions, i.e. "fire, unless caused by the actual fault of the carrier". These provisions mean that the carrier is not liable for loss of or damage to goods caused by the fault in causing or extinguishing fire onboard committed by the master, mariner, pilot or the servants or agents of the carrier.

35 Para 1 of Art. 59 of the Rotterdam Rules stipulates that the carrier's liability for breaches of its obligations under this Convention is limited to 875 SDR per package or other shipping unit, or 3 SDR per kilogram of the gross weight of the goods, whichever is the higher.

From the perspective of China-based maritime trade industry, they supported provisions under the Rotterdam Rules concerning the carrier's liability regime, transport documents and electronic transport records. Especially, they welcomed the deletion of the carrier's exemption of nautical fault and fault in fire, and the increase of upper limits of carrier's liability. This is because these provisions are in favour of their interests. However, they claimed that the Rules are too complicated. Moreover, the small- and some medium-sized trading companies expressed concerns over the following provisions of the Rules:

1) The provisions regarding "documentary shipper" may jeopardise the interests of FOB sellers;
2) The special rules for "volume contracts" in Article 80 of the Rules may put the small- and even medium-sized trading companies in an unequal and less favourable position when they are facing large liner companies;
3) The provisions delivery of goods without surrender of transport documents or electronic transport records – under Arts. 46 or 47 of the Rules – may harm the FOB sellers' right to be paid for the sale of goods; and
4) The provisions in Chapter 14 "Jurisdiction" and Chapter 15 "Arbitration" of the Rules. Under these two chapters, a choice of court agreement or an arbitration agreement contained in a volume contract may be binding upon a person who is not a contractual party of the carriage thereto without his consent. Thus, these provisions may compel a consignee to be bound by the jurisdiction of a foreign court or arbitral tribunal.

After debates, a consensus has been reached among the various interest groups that China should not ratify the Rules at the present stage. Considering the *status quo* of the shipping and trading industries in China as mentioned above, especially the fact that most Chinese shipping companies or maritime trading companies are small- or medium-sized, they do not have sufficient competitive advantages in the global maritime trade markets. Therefore, China's ratification of the Rules at this stage would not benefit the overall economic interests of China. Moreover, the Rotterdam Rules would adversely impact China if China were to ratify the Rules shortly. To strike a balance, China should take a "wait-and-see" attitude toward the Rules, at least before most significant trading countries ratify the Rules.

Besides the above consensus, it is also widely agreed that, when the Maritime Code is being revised, some provisions of the Rules may be adopted and incorporated into Chinese law shortly to modernise the Code and the Chinese hybrid regime of carriage of goods by sea contained in Chapter IV of the Code.[36] Also, due to the complexity of the Rotterdam Rules as pointed out above, it is not advisable to incorporate some favourable but complicated provisions of the Rules without modification into the Maritime Code.

2. Identification of Suitable Provisions of the Rotterdam Rules to Adopted in the Maritime Code to Be Revised

Based on the discussions above, the hybrid regime under Chapter IV of the Code, when it is being revised, may incorporate some provisions of the Rotterdam Rules as follows:

---

36 James Zhengliang Hu, Siqi Sun, *China's attitude towards the Rotterdam Rules in the authors' view*, Papers Collection of the 8th International Conference on Maritime Law, Dalian, China, October 2015.

The first group of suitable provisions under the Rotterdam Rules comprise:

1) The transport documents and electronic transport records (Chapter 3 "Electronic Transport Records, Chapter 8 "Transport Documents and Electronic Transport Records"),
2) The "identity of the carrier" (Art. 37),[37] except the provision of Art. 35 concerning the "documentary shipper".[38]

The second group of suitable provisions under the Rotterdam Rules relates to carriers and their liability. These include:

1) The carrier's liability (Chapter 5 "Liability of the carrier for loss, damage or delay"),
2) The period of the carrier's responsibility of (Art. 12),
3) The specific obligations (Art. 13),
4) the basis of the carrier's liability (Art. 17), *provided that the exemptions of nautical fault and fault in fire shall be maintained,*[39]
5) The liability of "maritime performing parties", *provided that the concepts of "performing carrier" and "maritime performing carrier" are not to be incorporated,* but the concept of "actual carrier" shall be maintained (Art. 19),[40]
6) The notice in case of loss, damage or delay (Art. 23).

The third group of suitable provisions relate to deck cargo. Namely, deck cargo on ships (Art. 25), especially the provision of Paragraph 1(b) to the effect that the goods may be carried on deck if they are carried in or on containers or vehicles that are fit for deck carriage, and the decks are specially fitted to carry such containers or vehicles.

The fourth group of suitable provisions under the Rotterdam Rules relates to shippers and their obligations. These include the provisions within Chapter 7 "Obligations of the Shipper to the Carrier"), except the ambiguous Art. 32 "Special rules on dangerous goods". It is noted that the current Chinese law, CMC Art. 68, which is similar to Art. 13, has been proved appropriate in practice, thus, this article needs no modification).

The fifth group of suitable provisions of the Rotterdam Rules includes Chapter 10 "Rights of the Controlling Party", and Chapter 11 "Transfer of Rights".

---

37 Art. 37 provides: "1. If a carrier is identified by name in the contract particulars, any other information in the transport document or electronic transport record relating to the identity of the carrier shall have no effect to the extent that it is inconsistent with that identification. 2. If no person is identified in the contract particulars as the carrier as required pursuant to article 36, subparagraph 2 (b), but the contract particulars indicate that the goods have been loaded on board a named ship, the registered owner of that ship is presumed to be the carrier, unless it proves that the ship was under a bareboat charter at the time of the carriage and it identifies this bareboat charterer and indicates its address, in which case this bareboat charterer is presumed to be the carrier. Alternatively, the registered owner may rebut the presumption of being the carrier by identifying the carrier and indicating its address. The bareboat charterer may rebut any presumption of being the carrier in the same manner. 3. Nothing in this article prevents the claimant from proving that any person other than a person identified in the contract particulars or pursuant to paragraph 2 of this article is the carrier".

38 The documentary shipper, under RR Art. 35, is entitled to obtain a transport document and an electronic transport record, subject to the shipper's consent.

39 Emphasis added by the authors. This is the modification to the Rotterdam Rules due to China's particularity.

40 Ibid.

The sixth group of suitable provisions of the Rotterdam Rules is those on the dispute resolution mechanism, including "the period of time for suit" (Art. 62) and "the actions against the person identified as the carrier" (Art. 65).

Regarding electronic transport records, it should be noted that while the relevant provisions of the Rotterdam Rules adapt to the rapid developments in electronic commerce, these have not been tested sufficiently by practice. Thus, the enforceability of such provisions seems uncertain, unlike most traditional provisions that reflect the commercial practice and have been tested for a very long time.

3. Unsuitable Provisions of the Rotterdam Rules to Be
   Adopted in the Maritime Code to Be Revised

Moreover, some provisions of the Rotterdam Rules are also identified as those not suitable for the Maritime Code to be revised. Such provisions are summarised below:

(1) DOCUMENTARY SHIPPER

The first group of unsuitable provisions relate to "documentary shipper". A FOB seller shall be a documentary shipper if named as "shipper" in a transport document or electronic transport record as it has agreed, and shall assume the shipper's rights and obligations, according to Art. 33 "Assumption of shipper's rights and obligations by the documentary shipper". However, under provisions of Art. 35 "Issuance of the transport document or the electronic transport record", a documentary shipper's entitlement to obtaining a transport document or an electronic transport record from the carrier is *subject to the shipper's consent*.[41] That is to say, *if the shipper does not consent*, a FOB seller (even if it is a documentary shipper) cannot obtain a transport document or an electronic transport record from the carrier. Consequently, it seems clear that FOB sellers, according to the Rotterdam Rules, have no right against the carrier or maritime performing party based upon a transport document or an electronic transport record.

However, the definition of 'shipper' contained in current CMC Art. 42 (3) states that a person who has delivered the goods to the carrier is a "statutory shipper", and he assumes the shipper's rights and obligations "without the need of the contractual shipper's consent". Moreover, in the international trade practice in China, a considerable part of the commodities is exported on FOB terms by small- or medium-sized companies, so protecting FOB sellers' interests is of particular importance through expressly stipulating the FOB seller's legal position, rights (such as the right to obtain a bill of lading) and obligations. Nevertheless, the provisions of the Rotterdam Rules regarding the documentary shipper cannot serve China's particularity, although these provisions comply with the principle of privity of contract.

(2) VOLUME CONTRACTS

The second group of unsuitable provisions concerns "volume contracts". Art. 80 "Special rules for volume contracts" of the Rotterdam Rules allows a volume contract to conditionally derogate from the mandatory provisions of the Rules stated in Art. 79 thereof. As a result, a volume contract between the carrier and the shipper may provide for greater or lesser rights, obligations, and liabilities than those mandatory provisions imposed by the

---

41 Emphasis added by the authors.

Rules. Art. 80(2) provides the conditions for such a derogation.[42] Moreover, Art. 80(4) states the rights and obligations of contractual parties which cannot be derogated; such rights and obligations are provided in Art. 14(a)–(b),[43] Art. 29 "Shipper's obligation to provide information, instructions and documents", and Art. 32 "Special rules on dangerous goods" or the liability arising from the breach thereof, and the liability arising from an act or omission referred to in Art. 61 "Loss of the benefit of limitation of liability". In addition, Art. 80(5) further provides that a volume contract that derogates from the mandatory provisions can be conditionally binding upon any person other than the shipper, subject to its express agreement.[44]

In addition, the provisions of the Rotterdam Rules concerning dispute resolution of volume contracts are also unsuitable, as will be explained shortly in sections on Jurisdiction and Arbitration.

Furthermore, while volume contracts are widely used in the form of "service contracts" in the modern liner transport sector, Art. 80 of the Rotterdam Rules is not appropriate to be incorporated into the Maritime Code to be revised, because derogation of a volume contract from the mandatory provisions may potentially harm the interests of a large number of small- and medium-sized shipping companies and cargo traders, as well as the overall national economic interests, for several reasons as follows:

First, the presumptions of the volume contract regime under the Rotterdam Rules may not be fulfilled in practice. Although the derogation of a volume contract from the mandatory provisions adheres to the traditional principle of freedom of contract, the regime is based upon some presumptions that the contract parties to a volume contract have equal or similar bargaining power and that such a contract is concluded through sufficient negotiations. In reality, however, this is not always the case. A volume contract is likely concluded between a large container liner company and a small or medium-sized cargo trader, or *vice versa*. In these circumstances, the parties to a volume contract do not have equal or similar bargaining power *ex facto*. In addition, such a volume contract is possibly concluded without sufficient negotiations in reality, especially where the parties to a volume contract do not have equal or similar bargaining power. In China, most cargo traders and shipping companies are small or medium-sized and do not have equal or similar

---

42 Art. 80(2) provides: "A derogation pursuant to paragraph 1 of this article is binding only when: (a) The volume contract contains a prominent statement that it derogates from this Convention; (b) The volume contract is (i) individually negotiated or (ii) prominently specifies the sections of the volume contract containing the derogations; (c) The shipper is given an opportunity and notice of the opportunity to conclude a contract of carriage on terms and conditions that comply with this Convention without any derogation under this article; and (d) The derogation is neither (i) incorporated by reference from another document nor (ii) included in a contract of adhesion that is not subject to negotiation". Art. 80(3) further provides: "A carrier's public schedule of prices and services, transport document, electronic transport record or similar document is not a volume contract pursuant to paragraph 1 of this article, but a volume contract may incorporate such documents by reference as terms of the contract".

43 Art. 14 provides: "The carrier is bound before, at the beginning of, and during the voyage by sea to exercise due diligence to: (a) Make and keep the ship seaworthy; ... (c) Make and keep the holds and all other parts of the ship in which the goods are carried, and any containers supplied by the carrier in or upon which the goods are carried, fit and safe for their reception, carriage and preservation".

44 Art. 80(5) provides: "The terms of the volume contract that derogate from this Convention, if the volume contract satisfies the requirements of paragraph 2 of this article, apply between the carrier and any person other than the shipper provided that: (a) Such person received information that prominently states that the volume contract derogates from this Convention and gave its express consent to be bound by such derogations; and (b) Such consent is not solely set forth in a carrier's public schedule of prices and services, transport document or electronic transport record".

bargaining power when facing large shipping companies or cargo traders. Hence, both presumptions may not be fulfilled in terms of China, when considering the trade realities and China's particularity.

Second, a volume contract that derogates from the mandatory provisions can be conditionally binding upon any person other than the shipper, subject to express terms. In practice, such an express term may possibly be imposed upon, not wholly in conformity with the free will of, a small or medium-sized consignee. In practice, such a party may be compelled to give its consent, due to its weak bargaining power.

Third, the small- or medium-sized cargo traders or shipping companies, say in China, who are parties to volume contracts, may be bound by a foreign jurisdiction or arbitration agreement contained in a volume contract, even if they have not agreed so. As a result, they may be compelled to be involved in foreign litigation or arbitration, which will be inconvenient for them and harm their interests. In addition, the effect of a jurisdiction or arbitration agreement to be binding upon a person that is not a party to the volume contract even without its agreement is contrary to the current Chinese law.

(3) DELIVERY OF GOODS WITHOUT PRODUCTION OF TRANSPORT DOCUMENTS

Delivery of goods without the production of bills of lading is common in practice, especially in the carriage of liquid/containerised goods or in the short sea trades. However, if such delivery is made, sellers' interest may be prejudiced, because possibly such sellers have not been paid for the sale of goods and have to pursue a claim against the carrier and/or the buyer. In practice, however, pursuing such a claim may be difficult, as the carrier and/or the buyer may be financially insolvent, or such a claim has to be pursued in a foreign jurisdiction.

Accordingly, delivery of goods without production of bills of lading shall be prohibited, or at least strictly restricted, to protect the interests of unpaid sellers. It is of particular importance for the Maritime Code in order to protect so many small or medium-sized traders in China. That is why CMC Art. 71 requires the carrier to deliver the goods against surrendering an original bill of lading (including a straight bill of lading). On the one hand, it is anticipated that, unless the electronic transport documents are widely used in reality, the delivery of goods without the production of bills of lading will still exist in practice, and even becomes more common.[45] On the other hand, the necessity of protecting the interests of the small- or medium-sized traders in China will remain unchanged by requiring the delivery of goods with the production of bills of lading.

However, Arts. 46 or 47 of the Rotterdam Rules allow delivery of goods without tendering transport documents or electronic transport records to some extent.[46] It is a question

---

45 This is because ships sail faster due to the development of technology in shipbuilding and maritime transport.

46 By virtue of Art. 46, when a non-negotiable transport document has been issued that indicates that it shall be surrendered in order to obtain delivery of the goods, the carrier may delivers the goods upon instruction of the shipper or the documentary shipper pursuant to subparagraph (b) of this Article and such delivery shall discharge the carrier from its obligation to deliver the goods under the contract of carriage; if a non-negotiable transport document does not indicates that it shall be surrendered in order to obtain delivery of the goods, the carrier may deliver the goods upon the proof of the consignee's proper identity. By virtue of Art. 47, when a negotiable transport document or a negotiable electronic transport record has been issued that expressly states that the goods may be delivered without surrender of the transport document or the electronic transport record, the carrier may deliver the goods without surrender of the negotiable transport document or without demonstration of a negotiable electronic transport record, but upon instruction of the shipper or the

of whether China should adopt them into the Maritime Code to be revised. It is recommended that China not adopt Arts. 46 and 47 into Chapter IV of the Maritime Code to be revised, when considering China's particularity, such as the commodity export trade practice in China, and striking a balance between sellers' (especially FOB sellers) and the carriers' interests. This recommendation is an appropriate choice after striking a balance between the safety and efficacy of maritime trade prevailing in China. In detail, justifications for this recommendation are illustrated below:

It is acknowledged that allowing delivery of goods without the surrender of the transport document or the electronic transport record may facilitate the timely delivery of goods at the destination port. However, such delivery may cause harm to sellers, especially the FOB sellers' right to be paid for the sale of goods. In particular, if a FOB seller is not a "documentary shipper", it cannot control the goods in transit and has no right to claim against the carrier, in the case of delivery of goods without the surrender of the transport document or the electronic transport record.

In addition, where the goods cannot be timely delivered after they arrive at the destination port, the carrier is entitled to maintain an action in respect of the goods, at the risk and expense of the person entitled to claim the goods according to Art. 48 "Goods remaining undelivered". This article reduces the necessity of delivering goods without surrendering the transport document or electronic transport record. Furthermore, the increasingly widespread use of electronic transport records can help solve the problem of delays in the transfer of bills of lading and consequently significantly reduce the situations of delivery of goods without surrendering bills of lading.

(4) LIMITS OF CARRRIERS' LIABILITY FOR LOSS OF OR DAMAGE TO GOODS

Art. 59(a) of the Rotterdam Rules provides the package/unit/kilogram limit of carrier's liability, i.e. the carrier's liability for breaching its obligations under this convention is limited to 875 SDR per package or other shipping unit, or 3 SDR per kilogram of the gross weight of the goods that are the subject of the claim or dispute, whichever is the *higher*. The limit of 875 SDR is 31% higher than the limit of 666.67 SDR under the Hague-Visby Rules, and 5% higher than the limit of 835 SDR under the Hamburg Rules. The limit of 3 SDR is 50% higher than the limit of 2 SDR under the Hague-Visby Rules, and 20% higher than the limit of 2.5 SDR under the Hamburg Rules.[47]

The above upper limits of carriers' liability under the Rotterdam Rules exceed the current need of China's trading companies with a surplus, according to the statistics published by the National Bureau of Statistics of China regarding the average value per kilogram of main imported commodities in China.[48] Furthermore, the statistical data show that the average value per kilogram of such goods is lower than the limit of 2 SDR per kilogram of the goods as provided in Art. 56 of the Maritime Code or Art. 4(5) of the Hague-Visby Rules. Thus, the limit of 3 SDR per kilogram provided in the Rotterdam Rules is

---

documentary shipper in accordance with subparagraph 2 (a) of that article and such delivery shall discharge the carrier from its obligation to deliver the goods under the contract of carriage to the holder.

47 Noticeably, the percent of increase of the package or unit limit in the Rotterdam Rules is much lower than that of the kilo limit. This is because the Rotterdam Rules are mainly applicable to container liner transport and the use of containers makes the packages or units of goods smaller in practice.

48 See the National Bureau of Statistics of China, *Statistical Communiqué of the People's Republic of China on National Economic and Social Development in 2020 (in Chinese)*, www.stats.gov.cn/tjsj/zxfb/202102/t20210227_1814154.html.

excessively high, and the limit of 2 SDR per kilogram in the Hague-Visby Rules or the Maritime Code remains appropriate for the containerised goods, let alone the Rotterdam Rules are also applicable between carriers (including maritime performing parties) and consignees under contracts of carriage evidenced by or contained in a transport document or electronic transport record issued under a charterparty or other contracts for the use of a ship or of any space thereon. In addition, during the negotiations of the Rotterdam Rules, most delegations recognised that the limits of carriers' liability provided in the Rotterdam Rules are too high and beyond the commercial need, but such limits were still adopted due to the so-called "political considerations".[49]

(5) JURISDICTION AND ARBITRATION

Arts. 67(2) and 75(4) of the Rotterdam Rules are unsuitable provisions to incorporate into the Chinese legal system and the Maritime Code. Besides the considerations mentioned above, both jurisdiction and arbitration are procedural issues, and these matters are prescribed in other Chinese statutes on maritime procedural law rather than the Maritime Code, which consolidates maritime substantive law in China.[50]

By virtue of Art. 67(2) of Chapter 14 "Jurisdiction", an exclusive choice of court agreement contained in a volume contract may conditionally be binding upon a person that is not a party to the volume contract even without its agreement.[51] Similarly, by virtue of Art. 75(4) of Chapter 15 "Arbitration", an arbitration agreement contained in a volume contract may conditionally be binding upon a person who is not a party to the volume contract, even without its consent.[52] Thus, if such provisions were incorporated into the Code, a consignee might be compelled to join litigation or arbitration held in a foreign country. Consequently, the interests of small- or medium-sized shipping companies or cargo traders, and even the overall national economic interests, may be harmed.

B. Filling the Gaps in Chapter IV of the Code through Revising the Hybrid Regime

As mentioned above, the nearly 30 years of judicial practice have revealed the ambiguities and uncertainties of Chapter IV in the Maritime Code and the lack of provisions to govern some practical issues that emerged after 1992. Thus, Chapter IV is to be revised to bridge

---

49 Some delegations firmly insist that the new limits should be higher than the counterpart limits in the Hamburg Rules

50 The jurisdiction, arbitration and other procedural issues arising from or in connection with carriage of goods by sea are subject to the Special Maritime Procedure Law of 1999, the Civil Procedure Code of 1991 as amended or the Arbitration Law of 1994.

51 Art. 67(2) provides: "A person that is not a party to the volume contract is bound by an exclusive choice of court agreement concluded in accordance with paragraph 1 of this article only if: (a) The court is in one of the places designated in article 66, paragraph (a); (b) That agreement is contained in the transport document or electronic transport record; (c) That person is given timely and adequate notice of the court where the action shall be brought and that the jurisdiction of that court is exclusive; and (d) The law of the court seized recognises that that person may be bound by the exclusive choice of court agreement".

52 Art. 75(4) provides: "When an arbitration agreement has been concluded in accordance with paragraph 3 of this article, a person that is not a party to the volume contract is bound by the designation of the place of arbitration in that agreement only if: (a) The place of arbitration designated in the agreement is situated in one of the places referred to in subparagraph 2 (b) of this article; (b) The agreement is contained in the transport document or electronic transport record; (c) The person to be bound is given timely and adequate notice of the place of arbitration; and (d) Applicable law permits that person to be bound by the arbitration agreement".

these gaps to solve the matters that often give rise to disputes in practice and enhance its enforceability. The main issues are analysed as follows:

1. FOB seller's legal position and its rights and obligations

Like the Rotterdam Rules, it is advisable to revise the Code to distinguish an "actual shipper", who has not concluded a contract of carriage with the carrier but delivers the goods to the carrier (or actual carrier), from 'the shipper'. Here, the Maritime Code needs to define the "actual shipper" as "a consignor" and stipulate its rights and obligations based upon its delivery of goods for carriage. So the analysis below refers to the "actual shipper" as "consignor".

The consignor shall be responsible for providing goods suitable for carriage, accurate information of the goods and instructions required by the carrier, and for completing all necessary procedures at the port, customs (e.g. quarantine and commodity inspection) or other necessary procedures at the port competent authorities when the goods are shipped. If failing in performing its obligations, first, the consignor shall be liable for damage to the ship, carrier, or actual carrier, and second, the consignor shall bear joint or several liabilities with the shipper.

The consignor is entitled to obtain a bill of lading, other transport document or electronic transport record, without the shipper's consent, after he delivers goods to the carrier or actual carrier. In addition, if both the consignor and the shipper demand the carrier to issue a transport document or electronic transport record, it shall be issued to the consignor.

2. Port operator's rights and obligations

For the reasons explained in Sections II-IV, it is advisable to fill in the gap and stipulate the main rights and obligations of a port operator, which performs loading, stowage, handling and/or discharge of goods upon the entrustment of either the carrier and actual carrier, or the shipper, the consignor or the consignee. Furthermore, it seems unnecessary to differentiate whether the entrusting party is from either the ship interests or the cargo interests in each case, because the port operator performs the same operation services regarding goods, before or after the carriage, based on the same rate of operation charges.

There are three areas of provisions that need to be introduced to Chapter IV of the Maritime Code to be revised:

> First, the port operator shall carefully and adequately perform the entrusted cargo operations. When it is liable for the loss of or damage to the goods or delays in cargo operation, the port operator shall be entitled to all statutory exemptions, other defence, or limits of liability available to the carrier.
> Second, the port operator shall enjoy a lien on the goods, if the operation charges are unpaid, irrespective of the ownership of the goods, provided that the charge occurred during the operation of the goods on which the port operator exercises lien.
> Third, the operator shall deliver the goods to the person named in the delivery order (D/o) or other delivery instructions issued by the carrier or its agent.

3. Freight forwarder's legal position and its rights and obligations

For similar reasons, the Maritime Code also needs to introduce provisions to cover freight forwarders. They are active and essential intermediaries in the maritime transport of goods and act as a carrier (e.g., a non-vessel operator),[53] shipper, consignee, or an agent of the shipper or consignee, depending on the circumstances of a specific case. In container liner trade, notably, a freight forwarder usually concludes one contract of carriage with a seller/buyer of goods on the one hand and another contract of carriage, in its own name, with a container lines company. Thus, under the former contract of carriage with a seller/buyer, the freight forwarder is "the carrier", while the seller/buyer is "the shipper"; under the latter contract of carriage with the container liner company, the freight forwarder is "the shipper", and the container liner company is "the carrier".

In the judicial practice in China, around 40% of the maritime commercial disputes that the maritime courts handle every year arise between freight forwarders and sellers/buyers of goods, or between freight forwarders and shipping companies (e.g. container lines). These legal issues result from the lack of explicit statutory provisions regarding the legal position of freight forwarders, and legal ambiguity in their rights and obligations.

Thus, the Supreme People's Court of China promulgated "the Provisions on Certain Issues regarding the Trial of Cases of Disputes over Maritime Freight Forwarding of 2012". This judicial interpretation stipulates that the courts shall determine the freight forwarder's legal position and its consequential rights and obligations according to the legal nature of its particular conducts. Therefore, the legal position of a freight forwarder might be the carrier, shipper, consignee, and others, as explained above, or their agents under some specific circumstances. Thus, it seems appropriate to incorporate the main rules under the 2012 judicial interpretation into the Maritime Code to be revised.

C. Improving the Measures of Indemnity for Loss of or Damage to Goods

As discussed above, as one of the remarkable provisions of the Chinese particularity, Art. 55 of the Maritime Code provides the measures of indemnity for loss of or damage to goods to the effect that the actual value of the goods shall be the value of the goods at the time of shipment plus insurance and freight, i.e. the CIF price, and consequently the claimant is unable to claim for loss of market or other economic loss arising from loss of or damage to goods. However, the cargo interests have severely criticised this article, because it is unreasonable to deprive the cargo claimant of its claim for such losses and thus excessively protects the ship interests. Consequently, Art. 55 of the Code needs to be improved in the Maritime Code to be revised.

Noticeably, Subparagraph 2 of Art. 4(5)(b) under the Hague-Visby Rules and Art. 22 "Calculation of compensation" under the Rotterdam Rules provide that the actual value of goods shall be fixed according to the commodity exchange price, or, if there be no such price according to the current market price, or, if there be no commodity exchange price or current market price, by reference to the normal value of goods of the same kind and quality. In practice, however, only a small number of goods after carriage by sea have exchange prices, which are normally the CIF price. In addition, the normal value of goods of the same kind and quality as the goods in question is difficult to prove, or the proof thereof may easily cause disputes between the claimant and the carrier/actual carrier.

---

53 The concept of Non-Vessel Operator which is similar to Non-Vessel Operating Common Carrier (NVOCC) contained in the US Ocean Shipping Reform Act of 1998 is adopted in the Regulations on International Maritime Transport of 2001.

Therefore, it seems inappropriate to incorporate such controversial provisions into the Maritime Code.

In summary, by striking a balance between the fairness and practicability, it seems advisable to revise the Code to provide that the calculation of compensation for damages should be based upon

1) the "proven market value" of the goods in question at the time when they are delivered or when they should have been delivered at the destination, or
2) "the CIF price" of the goods in question, where there is no proven market value.

VI. Conclusion

First, this chapter discusses that it is necessary to improve the hybrid regime governing the carriage of goods by sea contained in Chapter IV of the Chinese Maritime Code. Considering the significant developments in the global maritime trade since the adoption of the Maritime Code in 1992, the adoption of the Rotterdam Rules, and the enactment of post-1992 domestic general civil laws, it is time to revise the hybrid regime in order to resolve the legal gaps, ambiguities and uncertainties under Chapter IV of the Code.

While it is challenging to be revised and complete the reading process before the National Congress up to 2023 as planned, the Chinese Maritime Code will be revised and modernised in the near future. So, the hybrid regime will be updated and modernised within the foreseeable future by the National Congress.

Second, while China still takes, and would probably maitain, a "wait and see approach" toward the Rules, the hybrid regime will be improved by incorporating some suitable provisions of the Rotterdam Rules into the Code to be revised. Detailed analysis can be found in Section V. The suitable Rotterdam Rules provisions comprise provisions concerning electronic transport records, the identification of the carrier, the burden of proof in cargo claims, and the right of control. Incorporating such provisions will help remove the exsiting legal gaps and ambiguities under the hybrid regime.

Third, several aforementioned controversial issues of the hybrid regime, such as the legal positions of FOB sellers, port operators, freight forwarders, and their rights and obligations, need to be clarified by revising the Maritime Code. The provision of indemnity measures for loss of or damage to goods also needs to be updated.

CHAPTER 5

Duty to Make Fair Presentation of the Risk under the UK Insurance Act 2015

D Rhidian Thomas[1]

I. An Outline of the Pre-2015 Act Law

The designation in English law of a contract of insurance as a contract of good faith was confirmed in the latter decades of the 18th century, and the derivative law developed by the common law was subsequently codified by the UK Marine Insurance Act 1906 (hereafter 1906 Act).[2] Although the Act is expressly identified with marine insurance, its main principles apply to insurance contracts generally.[3]

A significant part of the 1906 Act, under the sectional title 'Disclosure and Representations', is devoted to the principle of good faith. Section 17 sets out the fundamental principle in the following terms:

> A contract of marine insurance is a contract based upon the utmost good faith, and, if the utmost good faith be not observed by either party, the contract may be avoided by either party.

What is meant by 'utmost good faith' is not defined, but other matters are unambiguous. The duty is owed by both parties to the contract, assured and insurer, and in the event of breach the contract of insurance may be avoided by the other party. In other words, the contract may be retrospectively erased. No alternative remedy is made available.[4]

The 1906 Act did not develop the duties of the parties any further, except for the pre-contract duty of an assured. In sections 18 and 20, the pre-contract duties of an assured to make disclosure and accurate representations of material facts were set out in some detail. This area of the law became the major focus of disputes and litigation, and a substantial body of case-law was generated over the decades.

There can be no doubting that these duties weighed heavily on assureds and imposed significant obligations when placing the risk. The demands were potentially very wide, a point constantly reinforced by the growing body of case-law, with it uncertain where the line was to be drawn. There was no obligation to establish fraud or negligence on

---

1 Emeritus Professor of Maritime Law, Founding Director of the Institute of International Shipping and Trade Law, Swansea University, UK.

2 For a detailed analysis of the 1906 Act, see J. Gilman QC et al., Arnould, *Law of Marine Insurance and Average*, 20th edn (London, Sweet & Maxwell Ltd, 2021); R Merkin et al., *Marine Insurance Legislation*, 5th edn (Informa Law from Routledge, 2014).

3 *Pan Atlantic Insurance Ltd v Pine Top Ltd* [1995] 1 AC 501; *Manifest Shipping Co Ltd v Uni-Polaris Insurance Co Ltd (The Star Sea)* [2003] 1 AC 469.

4 *Banque Financiere de la Cite SA v Westgate Insurance Company* [1991] 2 A.C. 249.

---

the part of an assured, the duty might be breached innocently and in all cases avoidance was the sole remedy.[5] So dominant was this aspect of the good faith principle that there existed the understandable tendency to reflect upon and expound the law solely from the perspective of the pre-contract duties of assureds. This can be observed even in the earliest judicial *dicta*. Lord Mansfield observed:

> Insurance is a contract upon speculation. The special facts, upon which the contingent chance is to be computed, lie most commonly in the knowledge of the insured only: the underwriter trusts to his representation, and proceeds upon the confidence that he does not keep back any circumstances to his knowledge, to mislead the underwriter into a belief that the circumstance does not exist, and to induce him to estimate the risqué as if it did not exist.[6]

The developing law added greatly to the defensive armoury of insurers. The fact an insurer had accepted a proposal of insurance did not preclude it from subsequently raising a defence based on breach of the pre-contract duty of the assured. The only direct cost of avoiding liability was the obligation to return the premium in the absence of fraud, which might be thought a small price to pay. The strength of the insurer's position was all the greater for the cost of any litigation the assured might contemplate, which also served to increase the attractiveness of even a mean settlement proposal.

Sections 18 and 20 defined exclusively the pre-contract duties of an assured. It was not possible to contend for the enlargement of these duties by reference to the general principle in section 17. By contrast, all other duties of good faith could only develop by derivation from section 17. This was the case with regard to the pre-contract duties of insurers and the post-contract duties of assureds and insurers. The recognition of such wider duties has been slow to develop and this is probably understandable. It is also a peculiarity of the law that fraudulent claims were never characterised as breach of the duty of good faith. This particular issue has been closed by the emergence of a statutory provision prescribing the consequences of a fraudulent claim.[7]

Under the 1906 Act the duties of an agent to insure, the placing broker, is dealt with by section 19. Under the section the placing broker is under an obligation to disclose (a) material circumstances made known to him as agent by the assured, and (b) also material circumstances known to himself. The duties are separate and independent; the broker, in additional to his role as agent, owing an independent duty of disclosure to insurers. This could entail the agent being obliged to disclose information which was not known to the assured.

It was against this background that the Law Commissions for England and Wales, and Scotland, commenced a major enquiry into insurance law and the necessity of reform. Many topics were identified as meriting enquiry, with the pre-contract duties of assureds and intermediaries to the forefront, and a valuable series of Issues Papers, Consultation Papers and a Final Report published.[8] The latter was accompanied by a draft Insurance Bill and Explanatory Notes, from which the Insurance Act 2015 emerged and which applies to

---

5 For a review of the law, see P.E. Eggers et al., *Good Faith and Insurance Contracts*, 3rd edn (Lloyd's List 2010).

6 *Carter v Boehm* (1766) 3 Burr 1905, 1909.

7 Insurance Act 2015 ('IA' hereinafter), ss 12 & 13.

8 Law Commissions' Final Report: Insurance Contract Law: Business Disclosure; Warranties; Insurers' Remedies for Fraudulent Claimant; and Late Payment (July 2014).

all parts of the UK.[9] The remainder of this chapter examines the impact made by the new legislation. It represents the first significant legislation to appear since the codification by the Marine Insurance Act 1906. It expressly applies to all insurance contracts (including reinsurance and contractual variations)[10] which are not consumer insurance contracts.[11]

II. The UK Insurance Act 2015

The impact of the 2015 Act is examined only with regard to the principle of good faith and the particular duty of an assured to make fair presentation of the risk. The Act also introduced reforms to the law relating to warranties and other terms, fraudulent claims and delay in settling claims, which are outside the scope of the current subject.[12]

A. Principle of Good Faith

The first impact of the 2015 Act is to amend the definition of the principle of good faith in section 17 of the MIA 1906 by omitting any reference to the remedy for breach. The section as amended reads:

> A contract of marine insurance is a contract based upon the utmost good faith.

The express reference to the principle of good faith applying to both parties is also omitted for being superfluous. The omission of the consequence of breach is of far greater significance. It opens the way to the legislation expressly providing for the remedies that may result from breach of the pre-contract duty of assureds.[13]

It has also removed an obstacle to the development of the principle of good faith pre-contract in relation to insurers and post-contract in relation to both assureds and insurers. The availability of the sole remedy of avoidance for breach of good faith in all circumstances had long been considered harsh and probably resulted in the judicial reluctance to apply the principle too readily. In removing the mandatory remedy and not replacing it with a new provision, the legislature has left it to the common law to determine the consequences of breach.

B. Assured's Duty to Make Fair Presentation of the Risk

The assured's duty to make fair presentation of the risk is set out in Part 2 of the 2015 Act, sections 2–8. The duty is defined in the following terms:[14]

> Before a contract of insurance is entered into, the insured must make to the insurer a fair presentation of the risk.

---

9 See Clarke & Soyer (eds), *The Insurance Act 2015: A New Regime for Commercial and Marine Insurance Law* (Informa Law from Routledge, 2016).

10 E.g. *AXA Versicherung AG v Arab Insurance Group (BSC)* [207]EWCA Civ 96, [2017] Lloyd's Rep IR 216 (reinsurance case).

11 IA, s. 2(1). Consumer insurance is governed by the Consumer Insurance (Disclosure and Representations) Act 2012 which provides a definition of 'consumer insurance contract' in section 1.

12 See Hertzell, The Insurance Act 2015: Background and Philosophy, chapter 1 in Clarke and Soyer, supra n. 7.

13 Considered later in the text.

14 IA, s. 3(1).

The duty applies to both the original contract of insurance and any subsequent agreement to vary the contract,[15] and also to contracts of reinsurance.[16] As with the preceding law the duty is constituted of two parts, a duty to disclose material circumstances and a duty not to misrepresent material circumstances, both pre-contract duties.[17] The duty exists up until the offer of insurance is accepted by the insurer and a contract is concluded. They are unambiguously legal and not contractual duties[18] but they may be amended, modified and excluded, by contract.[19]

In all instances it is a question of fact whether an assured has discharged the duty to make fair presentation of the risk. To amount to a fair presentation it need not be made in a single document or oral communication.[20] The position is to be judged by an examination of the entire placement process.

It is now proposed to analyse the two duties – duty to disclose material circumstances, and duty not to misrepresent material circumstances – separately.

1. Duty of Disclosure of Material Circumstances
The duty has both substantive and formal elements. The assured has the duty:[21]

(a) to disclose every material circumstance which the insured knows or ought to now, or
(b) in the alternative, make disclosure which gives the insurer sufficient information to put a prudent insurer on notice that it needs to make further enquires for the purpose of revealing those material circumstances.

In each case the disclosure must be reasonably clear and accessible to a prudent insurer.[22] This makes it clear that simply engaging in the mechanical act of disclosing is not sufficient, as when information is hidden in the body of a pile of documents with the insurer left to its own devices, possible in the tacit hope that the disclosure will not be discovered.[23] The disclosure must be made in a way such that it can be discovered and its relevance understood by a reasonable insurer. This suggests, for example, that a material document should be physically separated when contained in a pile of documents or otherwise identified: or that the pile should be prefaced by an index and summary of the documentary contents.[24] But beyond identifying a material document, the information it contains must also be clear, as opposed to cryptic or oblique.[25]

---

15 IA, s. 2(2).
16 The Act applies technically to non-consumer insurance contracts. S. 2(1).
17 See infra.
18 In the course of the history of this branch of the law the duty has been associated with contract but this is no longer a credible analysis. Cf. *Manifest Shipping Co Ltd v Uni-Polaris Shipping Co Ltd and Others (The Star Sea)* [2001] UKHL1; [2001] Lloyd's Rep I R 247(HL), per Lord Hobhouse.
19 *HIH Casualty and General Insurance Ltd v Chase Manhattan Bank [2003] 2 Lloyd's Rep 61; Mutual Energy Ltd v Starr Underwriting Agents Ltd and another* [2016] Lloyd's Rep IR 550.
20 IA, s. 7(1).
21 IA, ss. 3(3)(a) and 3(4).
22 IA, s. 3(3)(b).
23 This practice is customarily labelled "data dumps".
24 Law Commissions Final Report, para. 7.44, supra n. 7.
25 Ibid. para 7.46.

When it is alleged that the assured is in breach of duty, the burden of proof is borne by the insurer.[26]

The duty in (a), which may be described as the primary duty, reproduces the preceding law.

The duty in (b), which may be described as the secondary duty, is a new statutory addition. Whether it represents new law is uncertain, because similar judicial *dicta* are to be found in the common law.[27] There is also an obvious association with the concept of waiver.[28]

The secondary duty applies when the primary duty has not been properly discharged. It follows that the duty to make fair presentation is discharged if sufficient disclosure has been made to place the insurer on notice that enquires on his part may reveal further material circumstances that have not been declared.[29]

The evidentiary effect of the secondary duty is to move the burden of responsibility from the assured to a position where it is shared by assured and insurer. The insurer is no longer entitled to sit back passively and place the entire burden on the insured to disclose all material circumstances. Where the circumstances are as indicated in (b) the insurer is obliged to assume responsibility for the acquisition of material information and make the necessary enquires of the assured. If the insurer does not take the opportunity, the assured cannot be accused of failing to perform its duty of disclosure, and the insurer cannot complain about not being informed of the circumstances and information that would have been revealed had enquires been made. To this extent, the rule can be described as being based on the concept of a waiver.

The expectation is that the insurer will be moved to respond to the partial disclosure and make further enquires, but this need not necessarily be the case. The Act makes no provision for this possibility or for any wider consequences for relations between the parties over the course of the contract.[30]

The key concepts in both the primary and secondary duties of disclosure are 'material circumstances' and what an assured 'knows or ought to know'. It is now proposed to analyse these concepts:

'MATERIAL CIRCUMSTANCES'

What is a 'material circumstance' is to be judged by the objective standard of a prudent insurer. In the language of the Act, a circumstance is material 'if it would influence the judgement of a prudent insurer in determining whether to take the risk and, if so, on what terms'. The word 'judgement' has exerted a significant influence on the application of the test, with a clear distinction drawn between the 'decision' and 'judgement' of a prudent insurer. The test relates to what the prudent insurer would wish to know in exercising a judgement. It is not confined to circumstances which are decisive, that relate directly to

---

26 IA, s. 8(1).

27 Iron Trade Mutual Insurance Co Ltd v Compania de Seguros Imperio (1992) 1 Re L R 214 per Hobhouse J; WISE (Underwriting Agency) Ltd v Grupa Nacional Provincial SA [200] 2 Lloyd's Rep 283, per Rix LJ (dissenting judgment); Garnat Trading & Shipping (Singapore) Pte Ltd v Baominh Insurance Corporation [2011] Lloyd's Rep IR 366.

28 See infra.

29 Cf. *Iron Trades Mutual Insurance Co Ltd v Compania de Seguros Imperio* (1992) 1 Re L R 213; *Garnat Trading & Shipping (Singapore) Pte Ltd v Baominh Ins. Corpn* [2011] Lloyd's Rep I R 366.

30 See infra n. 88 for waiver of material circumstances by insurers.

the decision of the insurer whether or not to accept the risk, or the terms and/or premium rating.[31] This interpretation of the test plainly broadens the ambit of the assured's duty of disclosure.

In this context, 'circumstance' is to be understood in the broadest sense as relating to anything pertinent to the risk. The Act does not attempt a definition of the word save to indicate that it includes any communication made to, or information receive by, the assured.[32] At the same time, a circumstance is only relevant, if it is material to the risk and relates to 'every' material circumstance.

Whether a circumstance is material is a question of fact. It turns on a careful scrutiny of the facts and circumstances of individual situations. The Act does, however, provide broad indications as to when a circumstance might be considered material. They are:

(a) special or unusual facts relating to the risk,
(b) any particular concerns which led the assured to seek insurance cover for the risk and
(c) anything which those concerned with the class of insurance and field of activity would generally understand as being something that should be dealt with in a fair presentation of the risks of the type in question.[33]

Of these categories, (c) is likely to be most elusive to assureds, because it requires an awareness of what an underwriter in the area of insurance in question would customarily expect to be disclosed. Unlike (a) and (b), this may be outside the experience of the assured and even his agent.

KNOWLEDGE OF THE ASSURED

The duty of disclosure is logically tied to the knowledge of the assured but the Act on grounds of policy does not restrict what is known to the actual knowledge of the assured. This would limit the scope of the duty to disclose unduly and give too great a credit to actual or contrived ignorance. The Act therefore extends knowledge to include constructive knowledge, indicating knowledge which in a general sense the assured ought to know.[34] The legislation, addresses not only with what the assured actually knows but also what the assured is deemed, presumed or ought to know.[35]

The question of knowledge is further complicated by the fact that an assured may act through an agent and consequently the knowledge of the agent must be integrated into the question of the knowledge of the assured. It is also the case that the assured in commercial and maritime insurance will invariably be a legal person in the eyes of the law, an incorporated or unincorporated entity. To meet this position rules must be devised to determine how the knowledge of the assured entity is to be established. This gives rise to questions of attribution: whose knowledge represents the knowledge of the assured entity. The Act provides specific answers to this question.

---

31 *Pan Atlantic Insurance Co Ltd v Pine Top Insurance Co Ltd* [1995] 1 A C 501(HL)
32 IA, s. 7(2).
33 IA, s. 7(4).
34 IA, ss 4 & 6. The same was the case in the preceding law, see *Australia and New Zealand Bank v Colonial and Eagle Wharves Ltd* [1960] 2 Lloyd's Rep 241.
35 IA, s. 4(1).

The Act in stating what an assured knows is providing an exclusive statement, thereby excluding the possibility of wider contentions. Apart from the specific provisions in the Act knowledge cannot be attributed to an assured.[36] The Act is also resetting this branch of the law and endeavouring to be comprehensive. Aspects of the preceding law are amended and new provisions introduced. Unsurprisingly this on occasions creates uncertainty about the meaning and application of the provisions.

Knowledge of the Assured as an Individual   Where the assured is an individual (a natural person) the assured knows *only* the following:[37]

(a) What is known to him as an individual.

This alludes to the assured's actual knowledge when placing the risk. In each case this is to be determined as a question of fact.[38]

(b) What is known to one or more of the individuals who are responsible for the assured's insurance.[39]

This alludes to individuals who participate on behalf of the assured in the process of procuring the assured's insurance, whether as the assured's employee or agent, or as employee of the agent (which includes any person working for the agent in whatever capacity)[40] or in any other capacity.[41] This is a very broad provision and may encompass a large range of individuals.

The process of procuring insurance may include a range of functions, such as collecting data and records of previous claims, referring to external advisers, negotiating policy terms and the placement of the risk with an insurer.

This provision most clearly applies to agents, brokers and any other category of intermediary; and also to any person within the assured's business activity with authority to procure insurance. The knowledge of such a person is imputed to the assured and is defined under the Act as including that person's actual knowledge, knowledge which ought to be known, and 'blind-eye' knowledge.[42] Where the intermediary, for example, a broker, is an incorporated or unincorporated entity, it is the knowledge of the employee or other person acting for the broker, who directly assumes responsibility for the insurance, which is relevant. The broking entity itself is not within the provision.

The relation between placing brokers and the pre-contract duties of assureds has been changed significantly by the 2015 Act. Under section 19 of the MIA 1906, brokers, beyond being a conduit to disclosures by their principal, the assured, were under an independent obligation to disclose to the insurer material circumstances known to them.[43] This statutory provision is repealed by the 2015 Act, which provides that the knowledge of the

---

36 This is made clear by the introduction of the word 'only' to the drafting of s. 4.

37 This makes it clear that the definition of what is known is exclusive. Beyond the statutory definition knowledge cannot be attributed to the assured.

38 IA, ss. 4(2)(a) & 6(1).

39 IA, s. 4(2)(b).

40 IA, s. 4(8)(a).

41 IA, s. 4(8)(b).

42 IA, ss. 4(6) & 6(1). The concepts of what ought to be known and "blind-eye" knowledge are considered infra.

43 See supra, An outline of the Pre-2015 Law; *Blackburn Low & Co v Vigors* (1887) 12 App Cas 531; *The Litsion Pride* [1985] 1 Lloyd's Rep 437.

broker is attributed to the assured. This is a position more consistent with the common law of agency.

The changed law does not affect in any way the contractual relationship between assured and placing broker. In the event that the broker fails or omits to bring to the attention of the assured any material circumstance or information known to the broker, and as a consequence of which the assured is in breach of the duty to make fair presentation of the risk. The assured retains a right of redress against the broker for breach of the agency contract.[44]

(c) What ought to be known by the assured.[45]

This category lacks precision and may be challenging to assureds and those who act on their behalf in procuring insurance. The failure to obtain and disclose this category of information also hints at negligence. Its relationship to the preceding law is uncertain, and it is possible that it increases the duty of insureds to seek out by reasonable research material information. This, it may be assumed, is viewed as representing good insurance placement practice.

This category of knowledge identifies information that would reasonably have been revealed by a reasonable search of information available to the assured, whether the search is conducted by making enquires or by any other means.[46] This is a broad provision with the potential to raise abundant questions of fact. The test in all matters would seem to be objective with two tests of reasonableness at play, one relating to the research and the other to the revelation.[47] This is rich terrain for disputes but many of the potential difficulties may be avoided by the parties agreeing the precise obligation of the assured in this regard. Such an agreement, for example, may specify the precise research the insured is obliged to undertake.

The information must be 'available'. Whether information was 'available' will again be a question of fact. It may be anticipated that information that is available includes that held within the assured's organisation or by any other person such as the assured's agent or a person for whom cover is provided by the contract of insurance.[48] It will presumably include paper files, information in electronic data bases, and online and electronic media.

(d) 'Blind-eye' or 'Nelsonian' knowledge.

The assured as an individual knows of matters which were suspected, and would have had knowledge of, but for deliberately refraining from confirming or enquiring about them.[49]

This is a familiar concept and one of the identifying tags is associated with the conduct of Admiral Nelson at the Battle of Copenhagen. In the course of the conflict, he placed his telescope to his blind-eye so as not to see what he knew would be a signal to disengage. He remained engaged and was ultimately victorious.

---

44 Cf HIH Casualty and General Insurance Co v Chase Manhattan Bank [2003] Lloyd's Rep IR 230.

45 IA, s. 4(6).

46 Ibid.

47 Cf. Australia & Colonial Bank v Colonialand Eagle Wharves [1960] 2 Lloyd's Rep 241; Simner v New India Assurance Co [1995] L.R.L.R. 240.

48 IA, s. 4(7).

49 IA, s. 6(1).

Lord Scott has explained the principle very precisely in the following terms 'an imputation of blind-eye knowledge requires an amalgam of suspicion that certain facts may exist and a decision to refrain from taking any step to confirm their existence'.[50]

Knowledge of Assured when Not an Individual[51]   When the assured is not an individual, but an incorporated or unincorporated body or organisation, the assured knows *only* what is known to one or more of the individuals who are drawn from one of the following two groups:

(a) The assured's senior management.[52]

'Senior management' in this context means those individuals who play a significant role in making decisions about how the insured's activities are to be managed or organised.[53]

This is not a precisely drafted provision, and consequently there is much surrounding ambiguity. Clearly a director or equivalent is within the provision, but the intention appears to be that it may extend to individuals below board level who assume the necessary responsibilities. Where the line is to be drawn is uncertain. It will in each case be a question of fact. It would be possible for parties to agree who is to qualify as 'senior management'.

The key indicator is that the individual, whatever the person's precise status, is involved in the decision as '*to how* the assured's activities are to be managed or organised'. Activities in this context would appear to include the commercial and business activities generally of the assured. It may include, but is not restricted to, insurance matters. This implies a person who occupies a policy role, with the authority to make decisions and provide guidance; but it probably does not include individuals with administrative responsibilities solely.

What is known to an individual who is a member of the senior management includes that individual's actual knowledge,[54] what ought to be known by him by conducting reasonable research[55] and blind-eye knowledge.[56]

(b) Responsible for the assured's insurance.

The concept of an individual 'responsible for the assured's insurance' has already been examined, and that analysis applies equally to individuals in the present position.[57]

The knowledge of each individual within this provision includes, beyond actual knowledge, blind-eye knowledge[58] and information that would have been reasonably revealed by reasonable research of available information.[59]

---

50 Manifest Shipping Co v Uni-Polaris Insurance Co (The Star Sea) [2001] UKHL 1, [2003] 1 AC 469[112].

51 IA, s. 4(3).

52 Ibid.

53 IA, s. 4(8)(c).

54 IA, s. 6(1).

55 IA, s.5(6).

56 IA, s. 6(1).

57 Supra n. 38.

58 IA, s. 6(1). Considered supra n. 48.

59 IA, s. 4(6). Considered supra n. 44. It would seem that this must be the position notwithstanding that section 4(6) expressly applies to an insured, whether an individual or not. It begs the question whether an individual acting for an incorporated or unincorporated insured Is under the same obligation. Logic would suggest that this must be the case.

Where the assured is a corporate or unincorporated entity the person with responsibility for the insurance may be located within or outside the insured entity. A director or a member of senior management may be responsible to decide on the market, insurer, policy terms and on the development of a placement and/or claims strategy. The assured entity may have an in-house insurance and/or legal department. But a person involved in handling claims on a daily basis or placing insurance as per instruction would not be within the category of persons 'responsible' for the assured's insurance.

As for persons outside an incorporated or unincorporated entity who may fall into this category, the previous discussion in the text continues to be relevant.[60] The emphasis given to the word 'responsibility' does mean that the external person must be charged with strategic responsibilities and do much more than merely complying with instructions emanating from the assured entity.

WHAT IS NOT KNOWN BY AN ASSURED

The Act recognises two kinds of knowledge that are not attributable to assureds:

The first is confidential information known by the assured's agent or an employee of that agent, and which was acquired by the agent or his employee through a business relationship with a person who was not connected with the contract of insurance.[61] For the purpose of this provision, persons connected with the contract of insurance are the assured and any other person provided with cover under the contract. And with regard to a contract of reinsurance, the connected persons are the assured and any other persons provided with cover under the primary insurance.[62]

The second instance relates to situations where an individual has knowledge of fraud which is not known by and not attributable to the assured. More specifically, where an individual who is responsible for an individual's insurance, or in the case of an incorporated or unincorporated assured, is part of the senior management or responsible for the insurance, commits a fraud on the insured, knowledge of that fraud is not attributable to the assured.[63]

2. Circumstances Which Need Not Be Disclosed

The Act in keeping with the preceding law identifies circumstances which need not be disclosed to the insurer.[64] These again represent the exclusive position as is made clear by the use of word 'only', in section 4(2)–(3). It follows that a broader approach cannot be adopted by reference to considerations outside the statutory provisions.

These exceptions apply to the duty of disclosure only, and not to the duty not to misrepresent.[65] They also apply only in circumstances when a relevant express enquiry has not been made by the insurer.[66] If an enquiry is directed to the assured, the assured is required to respond; and if the answer is false or incorrect, it amounts to a misrepresentation.[67]

---

60 See supra n. 41
61 IA, s. 4(4).
62 IA, s. 4(5).
63 IA, s. 6(2)(a). Cf. *Arab Bank v Zurich Insurance Co* [1999] 1 Lloyd's Rep 262; *Moore Stephens v Stone & Rolls Ltd* [2009] UKHL 39.
64 IA, s. 3(5).
65 Ibid.
66 Ibid.
67 See infra, Duty not to misrepresent material circumstances.

In the absence of an enquiry, the assured is not required to disclose any circumstance if:

(a) 'it diminishes the risk'.[68]

If the assured fails to disclose a circumstance which diminishes the risk, the assured is acting contrary to its own best interests. The risk has been overrated, and the insurer is receiving an inflated premium. The omission is not prejudicial to the insurer, which has been led to believe that the risk is greater than it actually is and rated the risk on that basis. Consequently, there is no breach of duty on the part of the insured.[69]

Whether the information which is not disclosed would have indicated a reduction in the risk raises a question of fact. The answer may be straightforward or call for expert determination.[70] A straightforward example is provided when insurance on goods in storage is obtained by an assured which runs a commercial warehouse. The assured failed to disclose that the warehouse was fitted with security alarms and related equipment when placing the risk. In the event of a claim for loss by burglary, the non-disclosure was discovered. There had been a clear failure to disclose material information, but the non-disclosure was not prejudicial to the interests of the insurer. The actual risk underwritten was of a lower order than that the insurer presumed it to be when assessing, accepting and rating the cover. In the circumstances the assured has failed to act in its best interests, and the insurer had not been prejudiced. There had been no breach of duty.

This principle serves to emphasise that the duty of disclosure relates *only* to information which results in the insurer under-rating the risk. In this circumstance the non-disclosure is prejudicial. The actual risk is greater than that which the insurer has been led to believe.[71]

(b) it is known to the insurer.[72]

If the insurer has knowledge of any material circumstance, it is obviously unnecessary for the assured to inform the insurer anew by making disclosure. This again raises the question as to what is known by the insurer to which the Act provides a comprehensive answer.[73] In this context it must be remembered that the insurer is always a corporate entity.

The Act sets out the following rules relating to the knowledge of the insurer:

(i) The actual knowledge of the insurer.[74]

If the insurer 'knows it', in other words has actual knowledge of something, there is no obligation for the assured to disclose that same information.[75]

A corporate insurer knows something if it is known to one or more of the individuals who participate on behalf of the insurer in the decision whether to take the risk, and if

---

68 IA, s. 3(5)(a).
69 This exception has been recognised since the judgment of Lord Mansfield in *Carte v Boehm* (1766) 3 Burr 1905.
70 *Inversiones Manria SA v Sphere Drake Insurance Co (The Dora)* [1989] 1 Lloyd's Rep 69, [89]–[90].
71 *Carter v Boehm* (1766) 3 Burr 1905; *Pawson v Watson* (1778) 2 Cowp 785.
72 IA, ss. 3(5)(b)–(d) & 5.
73 IA, s. 5.
74 IA, s. 3(5)(b).
75 Ibid.

so, on what terms. This is the case whether such an individual does so as the insurer's employee or agent or as an employee of the insurer's agent or in any other capacity.[76]

This provision relates to the particular insurer in question and is addressing the actual knowledge of the insurer. The knowledge of the individuals acting on behalf of the insurer is attributed to the insurer. What any such individual knows extends beyond the individual's actual knowledge, to include blind-eye knowledge.[77]

The attribution of knowledge relates to an individual who participates on behalf of the insurer 'in *the decision* whether to take the risk and if so on what terms'.[78] These words indicate a person of seniority who assumes the ultimate responsibility for the decision whether to accept the risk and, if so, on what terms. The words do not embrace individuals otherwise involved in the underwriting.

A further qualification, if any individual identified above commits a fraud on the insurer, knowledge of that fraud is not attributable to the insurer.[79]

(ii) 'the insurer ought to know it'.[80]

The insurer ought to know of something, if:

(a) an employee or agent knows it and ought reasonably to have passed on the relevant information to an individual mentioned in para (i) above, or
(b) the relevant information is held by the insurer and is readily available to an individual mentioned in para (i) above.[81]

Paragraph (a) above is a reflection of the pre-Act concept of 'agent to know', alluding to agents whose knowledge was imputed to insurers who engaged them.[82] The statutory provision applies to employees and agents (not within (i) above) who are not engaged in underwriting, for example surveyors or experts engaged to assess a risk, but who ought nonetheless to pass on the information they acquire to underwriters. It could also apply to individuals employed in the claims departments of insurance companies. Whether information 'ought' to be passed on could represent a difficult question and ultimately will turn on the circumstances of individual cases.

Paragraph (b) above refers inclusively to information held by departments within insurance companies and to reports produced for assessing risk, such as medical and survey reports, which are readily available to underwriters. It may be assumed that this kind of information will be increasingly stored in centralised electronic records. It must be noted that the information must 'be held' by the insurer which excludes information available on the internet. The question of ready availability may be the source of difficulties but ultimately it will in each case be a question of fact.

(iii) 'The insurer is presumed to know'.[83]

---

76 IA, s. 5(1).
77 IA, s. 6(1).
78 Emphasis added for emphasis.
79 IA, s. 6(2)(b).
80 IA, s. 3(5)(c).
81 IA, s. 5(2).
82 *London General Insurance Co Ltd v General Marine Underwriters Association Ltd* (1920) 2 Ll. L Rep 199.
83 IA, s. 3(5)(d).

The insurer is presumed to know (a) matters of common knowledge and (b) which an insurer offering insurance of the class in question and in the field of activity in question would reasonably be expected to know in the ordinary course of business.[84]

Whether a matter may be considered one of common knowledge raises a question of fact to be determined objectively by the court. In a world of the internet, social media and a vast array of news outlets, what is to be considered common knowledge to any particular underwriter may be increasingly difficult to resolve. It is nonetheless possible to think of straightforward examples, such as the prevalence of piracy on the seas off Nigeria and Somalia, but how much wider the concept may be stretched is a troublesome question. The mere fact that something is or has been the subject of social comment would not of itself justify it being viewed as a matter of common knowledge. It may be that it must further be something that should have been in the mind of the insurer when accepting the risk.[85]

The case of *Carter v Boehm*[86] provides an early example of information which at the time was considered a matter of common knowledge. The Governor of Fort Marlborough, a trading station in Sumatra, insured against possible capture by a foreign enemy. Within a year, the fort was captured by the French. On an action under the policy, the insurer claimed that the policy was void 'because the circumstances had not been sufficiently disclosed'. The defence failed, because in the international political climate that prevailed at the time, the risk to the fort was a matter of common knowledge and deemed to be known by the insurer.

The second head of presumed knowledge follows a familiar commercial theme. An insurer providing insurance of a particular class ought to be aware of the practices and circumstances relating to that class of insurance and also the sphere of commercial activity in which the insurance is to apply. The Act couples the class of insurance with the field of activity to which the cover relates. Thus, to provide an example, the insurer of risks associated with oil trading would be expected to be familiar with circumstances relating to the insurance of oil in transit and also to the particular line of trade in which the insurance is to apply.[87]

(iv) the insurer has waived the information.[88]

It is always open to the insurer to waive the assured's obligation to disclose what otherwise is a material circumstance. The possibility of a waiver is probably the most significant element in the present discussion of what need not be disclosed to the insurer. In ordinary language, a waiver arises when the insurer indicates to the assured expressly or impliedly that specific information or circumstances need not be disclosed.

A waiver, as a matter of law, is an unequivocal unilateral representation by the insurer that specified circumstances or information need not be disclosed, and on which the assured places reliance. It is at least in part a waiver by estoppel,[89] as compared to a waiver

---

84 IA, s. 5(3).

85 *Bates v Hewitt* (1867) LR 2 QB 595.

86 (1766) 3 Burr 1905.

87 *Glencore International AG v Alpina Insurance Co* Ltd [2004] 1 Lloyd's Rep 111.

88 IA, s. 3(5)(e). There appears to be no reason to doubt that the concept of waiver in the 2015 Act follows the understanding in the preceding law. Cf. *Young v Royal Sun Alliance Insurance Plc* [2019] CSOH 32 [2019] Lloyd's Rep IR 482; [2020] CSIH 25; [2020] Lloyd's Rep IR 388.

89 Which means it is founded on an unequivocal promise which binds the promisor independently of contract, see the leading case *Hughes v Metropolitan Railway* (1877) 2 App Cas 439.

by election.[90] Whether there has been an effective waiver is in each case a question of fact, with the burden of proof borne by the assured.[91]

A waiver may be *express* or *implied* and relate to all or only a part of the body of information or circumstances that otherwise might be characterised as material:[92]

> An express waiver may be contractual or otherwise communicated to the insurer. For example, the insurer may indicate when enquiring about the assured's claims record that small claims for less than £1,000 need not be disclosed.
>
> A waiver may arise by implication in various circumstances including the following. When an insurer indicates to an assured in relation to a particular commercial circumstance that only specific information is required to be disclosed, this may amount to an implied waiver of all other information relating to the same commercial circumstance.[93] Also, an assured may communicate information to the insurer which alerts it to the possibility that there may exist further material facts that could be unearthed by making enquires, but which the insurer does not pursue. This omission may be construed as an implied waived of the information that would have been acquired had further enquires been made.[94] However, as a broad rule, a waiver does not arise by implication from the simple failure by an insurer to ask a question.[95]

Precisely how the concept of waiver operates in the context of the 2015 Act has been made more complex, because of what has been described in this chapter above as the secondary rule of disclosure.[96] This is in the nature of a waiver. An obvious question concerns the relation between this rule and the present discussion of waiver. There is no clear answer to this question. It would, however, be a little odd if a non-disclosure which did not preclude the duty of fair presentation being properly discharged was not also capable of amounting to a waiver in the context of what an insurer knows.

3. Duty Not to Misrepresent Material Circumstances

To make the point colloquially, beyond the duty to speak, when the assured does speak the communication must be accurate, considered and honest. This is a duty which attaches to every material representation made by the assured, whether spoken, in writing or evidenced by writing, and in traditional or digital format. It matters not if the representation is volunteered or made in response to oral or written questions: nor if the misrepresentation is innocent, negligent or fraudulent. In common with the duty to disclose, an assured may misrepresent without the presence of bad faith. But with regard to a negligent or fraudulent misrepresentation additional liabilities may arise in tort;[97] and in the case of non-fraudulent misrepresentation damages may be award in lieu of avoidance of the

---

90 *The Kanchenjunga* [1990] 1 Lloyd's Rep 391.

91 *Noblebright Ltd v Sirius International Corpn* [2007] Lloyd's Rep IR 584.

92 Emphasis added by the author. *HIH Casualty and General Insurance Co v Chase Manhattan Bank* [2003] Lloyd's Rep IR 230.

93 *Economides v Commercial Union Assurance Co plc* [1998] Lloyd's Rep IR9; *R & R Developments Ltd v AXA Insurance UK plc* [2010] Lloyd's Rep IR 521; Ristorante Ltd (T/A Bar Massimo) v Zurich Insurance Plc EWHC 2538(Ch); [2022] Lloyd's Rep IR 109.

94 *Pan Atlantic Insurance Co Ltd v Pine Top Insurance Co Ltd [1995] 1 A.C. 501; Wise (Underwriting Agency) Ltd v Grupo Nacional Provincial SA* [2004] 2 Lloyd's Rep 483; Dobeny v New India Assurance Co Ltd [2005] Lloyd's Rep I R 251; *Synergy Health (UK) Ltd v CGU Insurance plc* [2011] Lloyd's Rep IR 500.

95 *Schoolman v Hall* [1951] 1 Lloyd's Rep 139.

96 Supra n. 26.

97 The liabilities may be in the tort of deceit or negligent misstatement, see *HIH Casualty and General Insurance Ins Ltd v Chase Manhattan Bank* [2003] UKHL 6, [2003] Lloyd's Rep IR 230[5] per Lord Bingham.

contract.[98] It is however uncertain to what extent the courts will exercise this discretionary power in relation to insurance contracts.[99]

The duty to make fair presentation of the risk requires, in part, that '*every* material representation as to a matter of *fact* is *substantially* correct, and every material representation as to a matter of expectation or belief is made in good faith'.[100] The concept of 'materiality' in this context bears the same meaning as with the duty of disclosure.[101]

the demands of the law vary with the nature of the representation:

Where the representation is *factual*, it must be 'substantially' correct.[102] It is considered to be so, if a prudent insurer would not regard the difference between what has been represented and what is actually the case as material.[103] In this event the inaccuracy does not prejudice the insurer's assessment of the risk. At the same time it indicates that the qualification is of limited significance.

By contrast, where the representation relates to an *expectation or belief*, the accuracy of which can never be judged with certainty, the required standard is good faith.[104] The assured must have honestly believed in the truth of the expectation or belief that has been expressed.[105] Beyond this the reasonableness of the belief does not come into issue.

In addition, a representation may be withdrawn or corrected at any time before the contract of insurance is entered into.[106] This provides the assured with the opportunity to recover the position.

Although there is a clear theoretical distinction between the duty to disclose and the duty not to misrepresent, in practice they may be closely intertwined.[107] The possibilities are many. Where an insurer embroiled in litigation raises a defence based on breach of the duty to make fair presentation reliance may be placed on material omissions and misrepresentations. It is equally possible that there may be a close interplay between the two. If an assured utters a falsehood in the placement process, in concealing the truth material information may also not have been disclosed. If an assured discloses only some material facts, beyond failing to make disclosure of the remaining material facts, there may also be an implied misrepresentation that there are no further material facts to disclose.[108]

Furthermore, the Act does not address the question that may arise in particular with regard to corporate and unincorporated assureds, namely the representations that may be attributed to the assured. The key issue in this regard is the concept of authority. The assured bears responsibility for the misrepresentations of any person who has the authority to speak on behalf of the assured.[109] The fact that an intermediary with authority has

---

98 Misrepresentation Act 1967 s 2(2) which provides that in the case of a misrepresentation that is not fraudulent the court may award damages in lieu of the remedy of avoidance.

99 *Highlands Insurance Co v Continental Insurance Co* [1987] 1 Lloyd's Rep 109.

100 IA, s. 3(3)(c).

101 Supra under the title 'Material Circumstances'.

102 IA, s. 3(3)(c).

103 IA, s. 7(5).

104 IA, s. 3(3)(c).

105 *Economides v Commercial Union Assurance Co Ltd* [1997] 3 All E R 636.

106 IA, s. 7(6).

107 *Pan Atlantic Insurance Co Ltd v Pine Top Insurance Co Ltd* [1995] 1 AC 501(HL), per Lord Mustill

108 Ibid p 549, where Lord Mustill observes 'in practice the line between misrepresentation and non-disclosure is often imperceptible'.

109 *International Lottery Management v Dumas* [2002] Lloyd's Rep IR 237; *Arbory Group Ltd v West Craven Insurance Services* [2007] Lloyd's Rep IR 491.

made a misrepresentation will not take the representation outside the scope of the authority conferred.

III. Remedies for Breach of Duty under the Insurance Act 2015[110]

The Act in this regard makes major changes to the position under preceding law. The remedy for breach is no longer restricted to avoidance of an insurance contract in all circumstances. It may vary according to the nature of the breach and the impact of the breach on the insurer. But, as under the preceding law, the availability of a remedy is dependent on the breach being causative. In the absence of a causative connection there is no remedy.

A. Causation a Pre-Condition[111]

Before 2015, a causal requirement was not expressly written into the law but was nonetheless implied with regard to the disclosure obligation under section 18 and misrepresentations under section 20 of the MIA 1906.[112] At this time the language of the common law referred to the requirement that the insurer prove inducement.[113]

However, under the 2015 Act, it is *expressly* provided that the insurer has a remedy for breach of the duty to make fair presentation of the risk *only if* the breach was causative. The burden of proof is on the insurer.[114] It must establish on a balance of probabilities that, 'but for' the breach, it (a) would not have entered into the contract at all, or (b) would have done so on different terms.[115] This is traditionally described as the 'but for' test. Where causation is established, the breach is characterised as a 'qualifying breach', thereby indicating that a remedy is available.[116] Nevertheless, the 'but for' test of causation is problematic and how generally it is to be applied is the source of continuing debate.[117] In the present situation where there is a single cause and effect, it probably works acceptably well.[118] Expressed in non-technical terms the insurer has to prove that had all material information been disclosed and/or statements made had been honest and accurate the risk would not have been underwritten or would have been underwritten on different and less favourable terms. On the other hand, if the insurer would have accepted the risk on the same terms even if the assured had fully discharged the duty to make fair presentation of the risk, a causal link is not established.

The question of causation raises predominantly issues of fact to be determined in the context of individual cases and on the balance of probabilities.[119] The test relates to how the underwriter in question would have responded to the proposal in the circumstances

---

110 The remedies are set out in Schedule 1 to the 2015 Act.

111 Causation was also an element in the preceding law, see *Pan Atlantic Insurance Co v Pine Top Insurance Co Ltd* [1995] 1 AC 501, where the requirement was implied into section 18(1) of the MIA 1906 (now repealed).

112 *Pan Atlantic Insurance Co Ltd v Pine Top Insurance Co Ltd* [1995] 1 A.C 501.

113 Ibid.

114 IA, s. 8(1).

115 IA, s. 8(1).

116 IA, s. 8(3).

117 For a recent judicial analysis of the "but for" causal test, see *The Financial Conduct Authority v Arch Insurance (UK) Ltd* [2021] UKSC 1; [2021] Lloyd's Rep I R 63, paras 160–185.

118 Cf. *Zurich Insurance Plc v Niramax Group Ltd* [2021]EWCA Civ 590; [2022] Lloyd's Rep IR 56, where the causal tests of 'efficient cause' and 'but for' are analysed.

119 *Fage UK Ltd v Chobani Ltd* [2014] FSR 29.

then prevailing.[120] It may be presumed that evidence of causation will be given primarily by the underwriter directly concerned, when this is possible, supported by evidence of the underwriter's previous practice and that of the wider market. The test would appear to be primarily subjective but with objective criteria capable of being introduced. As for the evidence of the underwriter it will necessarily be cautiously assessed and tested. The process is highly hypothetical in nature, with it easy for the underwriter to be convinced that had the assured acted in accordance with the duty to make fair representation, the risk would have been responded to differently.[121]

There is no necessary link between causation and materiality, the former being predominantly subjective and the latter objective.[122] Simply because an omission or misrepresentation is material, it does not follow that the test of causation is also satisfied. Nonetheless, such an association is some and may even be strong evidence in support of a causal connection: as is the case when the breach of duty is intentional or reckless.[123] In these kinds of cases there may exist, in the language of the pre-Act law, a 'presumption of inducement', in the sense that inducement may be inferred. But even if this is a correct analysis, it is important to appreciate that the presumption is not one of law but of fact. It amounts to an acceptance that on the facts of individual cases it may be justifiable to recognise an inference of fact that the insurer was induced, but the inference is no more than prima facie and may be rebutted by counter evidence.[124]

B. Qualifying Breaches and Remedies

Once a breach of duty is established as a qualifying breach, it may be further characterised as 'deliberate or reckless' or 'otherwise'.[125] This distinction is critical to determining the remedies available for breach.[126]

A breach is deliberate or reckless where the assured knew it was in breach of duty or did not care whether or not it was in breach of duty.[127] A deliberate breach of the duty to disclose is often described as 'concealment'. Examples would be an assured who conceals a material document in the body of a large pile of disclosed documents, a practice described as a 'data dumping', or intentionally lies.

A breach which is neither deliberate nor reckless falls into the residual class 'other breaches'.

---

120 *Marc Rich v Portman* [1996] 1 Lloyd's Rep 430

121 *North Sea Shipping Ltd v Sphere Drake Insurance plc (The North Star)* [2005] 2 Lloyd's Rep 76.

122 Cf. *St Paul Fire & Marine Insurance Co (UK) Ltd v McConnell Dowell Construction Ltd* [1995] 2 Lloyd's Rep 116.

123 *Simner v New India Assurance Co Ltd* [1995] LRLR 240(QBD); *Hayward v Zurich Insurance Co Ltd [2016] 4 All E R 628; AXA Versicherung AG v Arab Insurance Group* [2016] Lloyd's Rep IT 1, affd [2017] EWCA Civ 96(CA). Also Bennett [1999] LMCLQ 165.

124 *St Paul Fire & Marine Insurance (UK) Ltd v McConnell Dowell Contractors Ltd* [1995] 2 Lloyd's Rep 116 (CA), [1996] 1 All E R 96; *Assicurazioni Generali SpA v Arab Insurance Group (BSC)* [2003] Lloyd's Rep I R 131(CA); *Axa Versicherung AG v Arab Insurance Group (BSC)* [2015] EWHC 1939 (Comm), [2016] Lloyd's Rep IR 1.

125 IA, s. 8(4).

126 IA, s. 8(2) and Schedule 1.

127 IA, s. 8(5).

The burden of proof is borne by the insurer to show that a qualifying breach was deliberate or reckless.[128]

In analysing the remedies available for breach of duty it is further necessary to draw a distinction between the 'original contract of insurance' and any 'subsequent agreement to vary the original contract':

Original Contract of Insurance

DELIBERATE OR RECKLESS BREACHES

Where the breach is deliberate or reckless, the insurer *may* avoid the contract and refuse all claims, and is not required to return any of the premiums paid.[129] The effect of avoidance is retrospective. The contract is erased; it is as if the contract never existed. It is sometimes said the contract is cancelled.

However, avoidance is not an automatic remedy: to effect an avoidance the insurer must communicate a notice of intention to avoid the contract to the insured. It is also not a mandatory remedy, as emphasised by the use of the word 'may' in the legislation.[130] It is always open to the insurer to waive the remedy and affirm the contract. The insurer, by reference to its conduct, may also be estopped from exercising the right to avoid the contract.[131] Beyond avoidance, there is a further penal element. The insurer is not required to return any premiums paid, but clearly cannot claim premium payments that fall due post-avoidance.

OTHER BREACHES

Where the breach is neither intentional nor reckless, the remedies available are various and governed by the way the insurer would have reacted in the absence of a qualifying breach by the assured.[132] In other words, had the duty to make fair presentation of the risk been properly performed, how would the insurer have responded:

> If the insurer would not have entered into the insurance contract on any terms, the insurer may avoid the contract and refuse all claims, but is obliged to return premiums paid.[133]
>
> If the insurer would have entered into the contract but on different terms, other than a term relating to premium, the contract is to be treated as if it had been entered into on those different terms if the insurer so requires.[134]
>
> If the insurer would have entered into the contract, whether on the original or different terms[135] (other than a term relating to premium), but would have charged a higher premium, the insurer may reduce proportionately the amount payable on claims.[136] The percentage payable is measured by reference to the proportion that the premium actually charged bears to the higher premium that would have been charged.[137]

---

128 IA, s. 8(6).
129 IA, Schedule 1, para 2.
130 Ibid.
131 Bennett, *The Law of Marine Insurance*, 2nd edn, 4. 162 et seq (OUP, 2006).
132 IA, Schedule 1 para 3.
133 IA, Schedule 1 para 4.
134 IA, Schedule 1 para 5.
135 This takes into account the possibility that terms may have been changed under preceding paragraph.
136 IA, Schedule 1 para 6(1).
137 IA, Schedule 1 para 6(2).

Contract Varying the Original Contract of Insurance

As previously observed, the 2015 Act applies equally to contracts which vary the original contract of insurance.[138] When this is the case, references in the 2015 Act to risk relate to changes to the risk proposed in the variation; and references to the contract of insurance are to be understood as relating to the variation.[139]

A variation creates a different contractual structure. There are two components, the original contract of insurance and the contract to vary that contract. The duty to make fair representation of the risk applies to the preliminary negotiations to each contract. But, in the event of a breach of duty with regard to the contact to vary there arises a particular issue. Are the remedies confined to the contract to vary or may they extend to also affect the original contract of insurance? The 2015 Act provides a varied response to this question.[140]

The distinction between 'deliberate or reckless breaches' and 'other breaches' is again relevant, as discussed below:

DELIBERATE OR RECKLESS BREACHES

The insured may by notice to the assured treat the original contract of insurance as having been terminated with effect from the time the variation was made, and is not obliged to return any of the premiums paid. Beyond the agreement to vary the insurer may give notice to terminate the original contract of insurance, taking effect from the time the variation was agreed. The remedy is unlike avoidance, because the original contract of insurance remains in existence until terminated. In addition, there is the added penal element that the insurer is not obliged to return any premiums paid.

OTHER BREACHES

With regard to 'other breaches', the remedies vary according to the impact, if any, the agreed variation has had on the assessment of the premium payable. Again, the remedies are framed on the response of the insurer, had there not been a breach. There are two possibilities:

(a) Total premium increased or not changed as a result of the variation.

If the insurer would not have agreed the variation on any terms, the insurer may treat the contract as if the variation was never made, but must return any extra premium paid.[141]

If the insurer would have agreed to the variation but on different terms (other than a term relating to the premium), the variation is to be treated as if made on those terms if the insurer so requires.[142]

If the insurer would also have increased the premium by more than it did or simply increased the premium, the amount paid on claims may be reduced proportionately[143]. The

---

138 supra n. 14.
139 IA, s. 2(2).
140 The remedies are set out in Schedule 1, Part 2 of the 2015 Act.
141 IA, Schedule 1, Part 2, para 9(2).
142 IA, Schedule 1, Part 2, para 9(3)(a).
143 IA, Schedule 1, Part 2, para 9(3)(b).

percentage payable to be based on the proportion that the total premium actually charged bears to the premium the insurer would have charged.[144]

(b) Total premium reduced as a result of the variation[145]

If the insurer would not have agreed to the variation on any terms, the insurer may treat the variation as if it were never made,[146] and may reduce the amount paid on claims in the proportion that the total premium actually charged (reduced premium) bears to the original premium.[147]

If the insurer would have agreed the variation on different terms (not relating to premium), the variation is to be treated as if it had been entered into on those terms if the insurer so requires.[148]

If the insurer would have (a) increased the premium, or (b) not reduced the premium, or (c) reduced it by less than it did, payment made on claims may be reduced proportionately. The proportion being that which the total premium actually charged bears to (i) the original premium if the insurer would not have changed it, or (ii) the increased or reduced total premium the insurer would have charged.

C. A Reflection on the New Code of Remedies

The 2015 Act makes significant reforms by introducing new flexible and proportionate remedies for breach of the duty to make fair presentation of the risk. There is in this new approach an emphasis on the *subjective* state of mind of insurers. It is for the insurer to prove how it would have responded, had there not been a breach of duty on the part of the assured. This replicates the corresponding position which exists with regard to causation.[149] There reposes in this approach the same potential difficulty. How is the state of mind of the insurers in question to be determined? It may be readily anticipated that the evidence of the particular underwriter will be supporting the precise remedy sought. But the declaration of the particular underwriter cannot of itself be conclusive. To characterise the process as subjective does not reduce itself to this kind of approach.

It is, ultimately, for the court or arbitrator to decide how a particular underwriter would have responded but for the breach of duty on the part of the assured. The insurer in question will naturally give evidence supporting his assessment of how he would have responded, had the assured's duty been properly performed. But both he and the court/tribunal may look to other supporting evidence. The underwriter may rely on previous risk assessment decisions by him in the same area of risk, or more widely by other underwriters in the same area of risk, or to market practice, or any other external evidence that may be available and relevant generally. The court will be aware of the vulnerabilities associated with the underwriters' position and this will no doubt result in a rigorous examination of the evidence.[150]

---

144 IA, Schedule 1, Part 2, para 9(3)(b) and para 11(3)(a).
145 IA, Schedule 1, Part 2, para 10(1).
146 IA, Schedule 1, Part 2, para 10(2).
147 IA, Schedule 1, Part 2, para 10(2) and para 11(2) and (3)(b).
148 IA, Schedule 1, Part 2, para 10(3)(a).
149 See supra n. 113.
150 *North Star Shipping Ltd v Sphere Drake Insurance plc (The North Star)* [2005] 2 Lloyd's Rep 76, [254], per Colman J.

IV. Contracting Out

It is important to recall that the 2015 Act sets out default rules, which apply when the parties have not agreed anything to the contrary. One of the premises underpinning the Act is that parties are free to contract out of its provisions.[151] This applies equally to substantive and remedial provisions. There are two exceptions to this principle neither of which is relevant to the current discussion.[152]

The duty to make fair presentation of the risk imposes obligations on the assured and gives protection to the insurer, ensuring that the risk is accurately and fairly presented, with accompanying remedies for breach. Nonetheless, the statutory framework may be varied by the agreement of the parties. The precise obligations of the assured may be varied, reduced or extended. And the rights and remedies of the insurer may be similarly varied and even increased.

There is however a degree of protection for insureds in the form of transparency requirements. A term which is disadvantageous to the assured, in so far as it places an assured who is in breach of the duty to make fair presentation in a worse position than would have occupied under the Act,[153] is valid only if certain conditions are satisfied.[154] The term must be:

(i)   clear and unambiguous as to its effect

(ii)   the insurer must have taken sufficient steps to draw the disadvantageous term to the assured's attention before the contract as entered into or the variation agreed (unless the assured or its agent had actual knowledge of the disadvantageous term at the time the contract was entered into or the variation agreed).

(iii)   In determining whether (i) and (ii) have been met the characteristics of the class of assureds to which the assured belongs, and the circumstances of the transaction are to be taken into account.[155]

These conditions temper the freedom of contract stance which the Act otherwise adopts. They preclude the risk of hasty and ill-considered exclusions, and the unfair treatment of assureds.

It may be readily anticipated that issues will arise about the clarity of a condition, and whether it has been brought sufficiently to the attention of the assured pre-contract. These represent well-trodden tracks in the law of contract. The English based P&I Clubs which are members of the International Group have excluded the application of the 2015 Act to the full extent permitted. This has been achieved by appropriately drafted provisions in their Rules which clearly satisfy the stipulated preconditions.

The somewhat surprising consequence of right to contract out is that the parties may agree that their legal and contractual relationship be governed by the law prevailing prior to the coming into force of the 2015 Act.

---

151 IA, s. 16.
152 The exceptions relate to s. 9 (basis agreements); s.13A relating to the implied term of payment within a reasonable time.
153 IA, s. 17(1).
154 IA, s. 16(2).
155 IA, ss. 17(2)–(5).

V. Conclusion

It has previously been observed that the Insurance Act 2015 is the most significant legal development relating to the contract of insurance since the codification of the law in the Marine Insurance Act 1906. It emerged after a decade long period of research and consultation which also generated a library of valuable documentary materials. In this process the views of the market and practitioners were fully taken into account, as also were the views of other interested parties, There is, however, nothing novel in the resulting call for reform. The recognition of the problems associated with the pre-contract duty of disclosure and proposals for reform pre-date this most recent review and the emergence of the 2015 Act by a veritable distance. The imbalance in the relation between assureds and insurers, the unjustified favourable position occupied by insurers, and the stultifying effect of avoidance as the sole remedy for breach have long been identified as significant issues worthy of reconsideration, not least by the judiciary. This historical legacy doubtlessly assisted in giving momentum to the proposal which launched the new Act. But it is also unlikely that the new provisions satisfy the reforming zeal of all interested parties.

The new Act moves the law away from its common law roots towards the pattern adopted in European codes wherein proportional remedies for breach are incorporated. In the abstract this approach appears attractive but questions arise about precisely how the scheme is to work in practice. It is easy to foresee disputes arising and not being readily resolved. There is an inbuilt uncertainty associated with the procedure of proportional remedies with the potential to cause unnecessary delay and even injustice. Parties wishing to avoid the risk of adverse difficulties may decide to contract out of the provisions of the Act. This will enable them to define for themselves contractually the pre-contract duty of the assured and the consequences of breach. There are standard clauses in circulation to facilitate this strategy.

CHAPTER 6

Marine Insurance Law Reform in China

Experiences from the UK

Rui Zheng

I. Introduction

The Chinese Maritime Code ("CMC 1993") came into force as of 1 July 1993. Chapter 12 (Articles 216–256) of the CMC 1993 is those regulating legal issues arising out of and in relation to marine insurance contracts. They are divided into six parts, namely "General Provisions", "Formation, Termination and Assignment of Marine Insurance Contract", "Duties of the Assured", "Obligations of the Insurer", "Loss of the Subject-Matter of Assured and Abandonment", and "Payment of Insurance Compensation". After these articles have been implemented for more than 25 years, it may be safe and confident to say that China has formed a relatively straightforward and comprehensive legal system of marine insurance, which provides the basic and necessary legal framework for the operation of marine insurance business in China.

When drafting Chapter 12 of the CMC 1993, the legislators seriously considered the international marine insurance legislation and practices, particularly the UK Marine Insurance Act 1906 ("MIA 1906") and the standard clauses of the London marine insurance market. Therefore, the basic principles of marine insurance well established in English law, such as indemnity and utmost good faith, also exist in Chapter 12 of the CMC 1993, although the wordings are slightly different.[1]

As it is well-known by the marine insurance academia and practitioners in both China and UK, the marine and commercial insurance law in the UK has undergone significant reform in the past few years. The UK Insurance Act 2015 ("IA 2015"), which came into force in August 2016, transfuses some fresh blood into the UK's archaic and trite marine insurance law.[2] The major topics covered by the IA 2015 are the pre-contractual duty of disclosure for all non-consumer assureds, which introduces the new duty to make a fair presentation of the risk on the part of the assureds, and the new remedies for breach of warranty.

Since the CMC came into force in 1993, the marine insurance practice in China has experienced a significant change. The total amount of marine insurance transactions in

---

1 L. Li, "The Maritime Code of the People's Republic of China" [1993] LMCLQ, pp. 204, 215.

2 A general comment as to the background of the Insurance Act 2015, see David Hertzell, "The Insurance Act 2015: Background and Philosophy", in Malcolm Clarke and Baris Soyer (eds), *The Insurance Act 2015: A New Regime for Commercial and Marine Insurance Law* (Informa Law, 2017).

DOI: 10.4324/9781003160298-7

China has grown hugely;[3] the international and national legal environments have changed rapidly; the Chinese maritime courts have to deal with a great number of marine insurance cases every year.[4] During this period, the legal problems encountered in the structural adjustment and transformation of the marine insurance market are revealed gradually, and various new situations emerge. In this process, the institutional framework constructed by marine insurance law needs to provide a good legal environment for the development of the marine insurance market, promote the creativity of the marine insurance market, and escort the healthy growth of the marine insurance market. In order to achieve these goals, Chapter 12 of the CMC 1993 must march step-by-step with the progress of the market and make necessary amendments. Furthermore, the amendments should be forward-looking to solve new problems and reconcile various conflicts of interest that may arise.

On 5 November 2018, the Ministry of Transport of the People's Republic of China has published "the Chinese Maritime Code (Revised Draft)" on its website for public consultations and comments. Till 7 December 2018, 827 valid replies were received. On this basis and through further research, on 10 January 2020, the Ministry of Transport issued the Notes on the Revision of the CMC 1993 ("2020 Notes"), which identifies several critical points of the revision, accompanied by a detailed reform proposal to amend the CMC 1993 article by article ("2020 Proposal").[5] Both of the documents have been submitted to the Ministry of Justice for further deliberation and consultation in accordance with the legislative procedure in China.

The 2020 Notes point out five key points which the revision of CMC Chapter 12 should achieve as follows:

> (1) to improve the assured's duty to disclose, reflecting the reciprocal nature of the principle of good faith; (2) to adjust the marine warranty regime, reflecting the fairness to the assured; (3) to improve the marine open cover regime, providing specific norms to suit practice; (4) in line with the commercial practice of marine insurance, to stipulate specifically the insurer's obligation to explain the exemption clauses in the marine insurance contract; (5) to stipulate that the provisions of this Chapter shall govern the indemnity obligation of the P&I Club to its members.

The aforementioned two major reforms in English marine insurance law have undoubtfully provided indispensable comparative law references to the revision of CMC Chapter 12, for those two fields are exactly the ones that serious amendments are considered by the revision committee of the CMC 1993. Therefore, by focusing on the above five key revision

---

3 In accordance with the statistics published by the International Union of Marine Insurers (IUMI), since 2015, the premium income of marine cargo insurance and hull insurance in China has occupied the first and second place respectively in the world. See https://iumi.com/statistics/public-statistics. As regards P&I Insurance, the China Shipowners Mutual Assurance Association (also known as China P&I Club, CPI) has become an internationalised P&I Club with 188 members and over 65 million GT P&I Entered Tonnage, which ranks 10th among its global peers in terms of total entered tonnage (GT). See <www.cpiweb.org/>. All internet resources in this chapter were last accessed on 1 January 2022.

4 The statistics published on the website of the relevant maritime courts show: the Shanghai Maritime Court had taken up 263 marine insurance cases from 2012 to 2019 <www.shhsfy.gov.cn>; the Ningbo Maritime Court had taken up 687 marine insurance cases from 2014 to 2018 <www.nbhsfy.cn>; the Xiamen Maritime Court had taken up 55 marine insurance cases from 2016 to 2018 <www.xmhsfy.gov.cn>; the Qingdao Maritime Court had taken up 342 marine insurance cases from 2016 to 2019 <www.qdhsfy.sdcourt.gov.cn>. Up to March 2022, there is no updated data.

5 It is to be noted that both 2020 Notes and 2020 Proposals were internal documents which were only circulated within the interested parties; they were not available for public consultation. So, the author embedded relevant provisions in text of this chapter.

points, this chapter intends to articulate the current laws in China, their flaws, the revisions proposed and analyse the experiences that could be learned from the perspective of English law.

II. Reform of the Assured's Pre-Contractual Duty to Disclose

A. The Current Law

The assured's pre-contractual duty to disclose is a statutory duty. Article 16 of the Chinese Insurance Law 2009 ("IL 2009") provides that where the insurer inquiries about the subject-matter assured or about the assured when entering into an insurance contract, the assured shall tell the truth. Accordingly, the assured shall truthfully answer the insurer's inquiry about the subject-matter assured. As for the matters which are not inquired by the insurer, the assured has no duty to make disclosure. The insurer's inquiry is usually in writing and the assured is required to truthfully fill out the application form.

However, Article 222 of the CMC 1993 provides that:

> Before the contract is concluded, the assured shall truthfully disclose to the insurer of the material circumstances which the assured had knowledge of or ought to have knowledge of in his ordinary course of business and which may have a bearing on the insurer in deciding the premium or whether he agrees to insure or not. The assured need not disclose to the insurer of the facts which the insurer has known of or the insurer ought to have knowledge of in his ordinary course of business if about which the insurer made no enquiry.

As seen from both Articles mentioned above, it is clear that the disclosure modes under the non-marine insurance contract and marine insurance contract differs from each other. Article 184 of the IL 2009 states that the CMC 1993 shall apply to marine insurance, and then the IL 2009 is appliable only if a matter is not specified by the CMC 1993. Therefore, a preliminary issue may exist as to the assured's pre-contractual duty to disclose under the CMC 1993: whether the insurance contract in question is a marine insurance contract. Article 222 of the CMC 1993 can only be applied if the contract in question is found to be a marine insurance contract.[6]

The matters that the assured is obliged to disclose should be limited to material circumstances rather than every detail. There are two criteria for judging the materiality: firstly, the material circumstances have an influence on the insurer in deciding upon the premium or whether to agree to insure or not; secondly, the assured has knowledge of or ought to have knowledge of in his ordinary course of business before the conclusion of the contract. The matter known after the conclusion of the contract will not constitute a breach of the duty of disclosure even if it was not disclosed.

---

6 There are some examples showing that insurance contracts involving the elements of sea or vessel are not necessarily marine insurance contract in Chinese law: Article 2 of the Regulations of the Supreme People's Court on Several Issues about the Trial of Cases Concerning Marine Insurance Disputes 2006 (Fa Shi [2020] No 18) provides that the IL 2009 and other Laws shall apply to the trial of disputes over insurance contracts involving port facilities or wharves as the subject-matter of insurance provided that the loss of damage to as the subject-matter of insurance is not caused by marine accidents. In addition, the Supreme People's Court once held that the IL 2009 shall apply to the disputes as to the disclosure dispute over a shipbuilding insurance contract, as the subject-matter of insurance namely the vessel under construction and with no navigation capability in that case cannot be properly called a "vessel" for the purpose of the CMC 1993, see *PICC Marine Insurance Operation Centre v Taizhou Sanfu Shp Engineering Co Ltd.* (2017) Supreme People's Court's Retrial Judgement No. 242.

The insurer may waive the right to assert that the assured has breached the duty to disclose in certain circumstances. In marine insurance, Article 5 of the Regulations of the Supreme People's Court on Several Issues about the Trial of Cases Concerning Marine Insurance Disputes 2006 ("RMI 2006") provides that if the insurer knows that the assured has failed to truthfully disclose the material circumstance in accordance with Article 222 (1) of the CMC 1993, nevertheless he collects the premium or pays insurance compensations and then alleges to terminate the contract on the basis that the assured has failed to perform the duty to disclose, the court will not support the allegation.

B. The Reform Proposal

The 2020 Note has identified that the key point to revise is the standard of disclosure. Article 279 of the 2020 Proposal provides that:

> Before the contract is concluded, the assured shall truthfully disclose to the insurer of the material circumstances which the assured had knowledge of or ought to have knowledge of in his ordinary course of business and which may have a bearing on the insurer in deciding the premium or whether he agrees to insure or not.

In the absence of enquiry, the assured is not required to disclose if

1) the disclosure already made has given the insurer sufficient information to put him on notice that he needs to make further enquiries;
2) the insurer knows or ought to know the relevant circumstances in the ordinary course of the business.

The only change on the current law made by the above revision is that the assured does not need to voluntarily and fully disclose the material circumstances in all situations. The insurer may have to make further enquiries if he has already received sufficient information as to the risks.

C. English Law Perspective

1. The Current Position of English Law
In English law, even before the IA 2015 came into force, judicial authorities had firmly established that the assured did not need to disclose everything. A classical observation was made by Christopher Clarke J in *Garnat Trading & Shipping (Singapore) Pte Ltd v Baominh Insurance Corporation*:[7]

> A minute disclosure of every material circumstance is not required. The assured complies with the duty if he discloses sufficient to call the attention of the underwriter to the relevant facts and matters in such a way that, if the latter desires further information, he can ask for it. A fair and accurate presentation of a summary of the material facts is sufficient if it would enable a prudent insurer to form a proper judgment, either on the presentation alone, or by asking questions if he was sufficiently put upon enquiry and wanted to know further details, whether to accept the proposal, and, if so, on what terms.

---

7 [2011] 1 Lloyd's Rep. 589, p. [135].

Blair J confirmed the legal basis for this is that the information may be waived by the insurer. His Lordship exquisitely commented that:[8]

> If the facts and matters disclosed give a fair presentation of the risk, the underwriter must ask if he wishes to have more information; further, even if the initial presentation was unfair, waiver might arise if the information disclosed was such as to prompt a reasonably careful insurer to make further inquiries. In short, if the insurers receive information, which taken on its own, or in conjunction with other information known to them or presumed to be known to them, would naturally prompt a reasonably careful insurer to make further inquiries, then, if they omit to do so, they waive disclosure of the material facts and matters which such an inquiry would have revealed.

The IA 2015 reiterated that the assured has a pre-contractual duty to make a fair presentation of the risk to the insurer. Section 3 (4) of IA 2015 provides the assured's disclosure qualifies as a fair presentation in the following two situations: (1) disclosure of every material circumstance which the assured knows or ought to know; (2) failing that, disclosure which gives the insurer sufficient information to put a prudent insurer on notice that it needs to make further enquiries for the purpose of revealing those material circumstances.

The IA 2015 does not fundamentally change the assured's pre-contractual duty of utmost good faith as it applied under the MIA 1906. The duty of fair presentation is just a re-packed and blended duty under Section 18 (1) and the exception of waiver under Section (3) (c) of the MIA 1906.[9]

2. Comments on the Chinese 2020 Proposal from English Law Perspective

Through comparison, it is evident that Article 279 of the 2020 Proposal resembles essentially Section 3 (4) of the IA 2015.

The IA 2015 has designed a dialogue mechanism between the assured and the insurer, so that the insurer should actively participate in the underwriting process instead of playing a passive role in receiving information. As a matter of fact, the insurer's active involvement in the underwriting stage has been recognised by the insurance market as the best practice. The IA 2015 has confirmed this practice by stipulating it in the legislation, undoubtedly encouraging more insurers to follow. The same consideration applies equally and with no difficulty in the context of Chinese marine insurance law and practice. In this regard, it is submitted that the revision committee has made the right move.

However, the IA 2015 has made some fundamental changes, which are not referred to in the Chinese 2020 Proposal at all. One of those changes is the manner of the assured's disclosure. Pursuant to Section 3 (3) (b), a fair presentation of the risk is one which makes that disclosure in a manner that would be reasonably clear and accessible to a prudent insurer. "Explanatory Notes to the Insurance Bill" explains the purpose of this Section as follows:[10]

> It is intended to target, at one end of the scale, "data dumps", where the insurer is presented with an overwhelming amount of undigested information. At the other end, it is not expected that this requirement would be satisfied by an overly brief or cryptic presentation.

---

8 Sea Glory Maritime Co and Swedish Management Co SA v Al SAGR National Insurance Co [2013] EWHC 2116 (Comm), p. [56].

9 Peter MacDonald Eggers QC, "The fair presentation of commercial risks under the Insurance Act 2015", in Malcolm Clarke and Baris Soyer (eds), *The Insurance Act 2015: A New Regime for Commercial and Marine Insurance Law* (Informa Law, 2017), p. 28.

10 UK Parliament, https://publications.parliament.uk/pa/bills/cbill/2014-2015/0155/en/15155en.htm, p. [46].

It is submitted that the same "data dumps" problem may have occurred or will occur with no doubt in the Chinese insurance market. Therefore, this "small but important change"[11] deserves proper consideration by the revision committee of the CMC 1993 as to whether to introduce it into Chinese law in the future.

III. Reform of Marine Warranty Regime

A. The Current Law

Article 235 of the CMC 1993 is the only provision regarding marine warranty, far less than the English counterparts in the MIA 1906 (Sections 33–41). It provides that:

> The assured shall notify the insurer in writing immediately where the assured has not complied with the warranty in the contract. The insurer may, upon receipt of the notice, terminate the contract or demand an amendment to the terms and conditions of the insurance coverage or an increase in the premium.

There are two major issues in Article 235: first, unlike Section 33 (1) of the MIA 1906, it does not provide the legal definition of marine warranty; second, it does not clearly provide the legal consequences of the breach of marine warranty, for instance, it does not clarify what would happen if the assured fails to notify the insurer upon the non-compliance of warranty.

Articles 6 to 8 of the RMI 2006 patched up the aforesaid second issue. First, If the assured has not complied with the warranty and does not notify the insurer, the insurer is entitled to terminate the contract as from the date of the breach. Second, if the assured has been indemnified by the insurer after the occurrence of loss, the insurer will be barred from asserting the assured's breach of warranty and requiring the restitution of insurance payment. In essence, by making the insurance payment, the insurer has waived his right to terminate the contract by reason of the breach of warranty. Third, after receiving the notification, if the insurer cannot reach an agreement with the assured as to the amendment to the terms and conditions of the insurance coverage or an increase in the premium, the insurer is entitled to terminate the marine insurance contract as from the date of the breach.

However, the RMI 2006 still does not define marine warranty for the purpose of Article 235 of the CMC 1993. The explanation given by the Supreme People's Court was that it is improper for a judicial interpretation to define a key concept in the legislation.[12]

---

11 Peter MacDonald Eggers QC, "The fair presentation of commercial risks under the Insurance Act 2015", in Malcolm Clarke and Baris Soyer (eds), *The Insurance Act 2015: A New Regime for Commercial and Marine Insurance Law* (Informa Law, 2017), p. 30.

12 Judicial interpretation is the official interpretation made by the Supreme People's Court on the application of certain laws, and, therefore, has legal binding force. "Regulation" is a kind of judicial interpretation, which interprets norms and opinions about how to promote adjudication work pursuant to the legislative purpose. See Guodong Du, "Knowing Judicial Interpretation in China-China Legal Research Guide" (*China Justice Observer*, 19 March 2020) <www.chinajusticeobserver.com/a/knowing-judicial-interpretation-in-china>, accessed 19 December 2021.

B. The Reform Proposal

The 2020 Note has identified that the marine warranty regime in CMC Chapter 12 shall be revised by referring to the English insurance law and the insurance practice in China; in particular, the ambiguity of the regime need to be clarified.

Article 293 of the 2020 Proposal is a detailed revision of Article 235 of the CMC 1993, which provides as follows that:

> Where the assured has not complied with the warranty in the contract, the insurer is entitled to terminate the contract, or demand an amendment to the terms and conditions of the insurance coverage or an increase in the premium.
>
> Provided that the insurer elects to terminate the contract, he shall notify the assured in writing; the contract will be terminated upon the arrival of the notice to the assured.
>
> The insurer shall be liable for the loss caused by the assured event before the assured's breach of the warranty; the insurer shall not be liable for the loss caused by the assured event occurring from the time when the assured breaches the warranty to the arrival of the termination notice, unless the assured can prove that:
>
> (1) The assured's breach of the warranty has no effect on the occurrence of the assured event;
> (2) The assured event occurs after the assured has remedied the breach of warranty.
>
> The term "warranty" as mentioned in this article refers to a clause in a marine insurance contract stipulating that the assured undertakes that some particular things shall or shall not be done, or the assured ensures the existence or non-existence of some particular states of facts; however, the agreement that does not affect the underwriting risk is not a warranty.

Three observations may be made as to the above article. First, this new article resembles English law. For instance, Section 33 (1) of the MIA 1906 is transplanted to China as the definition of "warranty"; the stipulation that the assured can remedy the breach of warranty and the insurer is still liable for the assured loss caused by the assured event occurring after the remedy clearly finds its origins from Sections 10 (2) and 10 (4) (b) of the IA 2015. Second, the contract can only be terminated as from the arrival of the written notice given by the insurer. In other words, the contract cannot be terminated from the breach date retrospectively. Third, there must be a causal link between the breach of warranty and the occurrence of the assured event for the insurer to escape from the liability.

C. English Law Perspective

1. The Current Position of English Law

In accordance with Section 33 of the MIA 1906 and the authorities, the marine warranty has three characteristics: first, the warranty must be strictly complied with;[13] second, the assured cannot remedy the breach of warranty;[14] third, no causal link is required between the breach of warranty and the loss of the subject-matter of insurance.[15] Unless otherwise provided in the policy, the breach of warranty results in the automatic discharge of the insurer's liability as from the date of the breach.[16]

---

13 *De Hahn v Hartley* [1786] 1 TR 343.
14 Ibid.
15 *Hibbert v Pigou* (1783) 3 Doug KB 213; *Vesta v Butcher* [1989] AC 852.
16 *The Good Luck* [1992] 2 Lloyd's Rep. 191.

However, the English and Scottish Law Commissions had realised that the warranty regime in the MIA 1906 was in great need of reform, identifying that "the greatest and most obvious problem with the law on warranties is that it permits the insurer to escape liability for technical breaches that have nothing to do with the loss in question" and saying they do not think "the present rules on warranties meet the needs and expectations of an international market".[17] The achievements of reform is Sections 9 to 11 of the IA 2015.

The reforms made by the IA 2015 on the warranty regime could be summarised as follows. First, Section 10 (1) provides that "any rule of law that breach of a warranty (express or implied) in a contract of insurance results in the discharge of the insurer's liability under the contract is abolished". Second, Section 10 (2) provides that

> an insurer has no liability under a contract of insurance in respect of any loss occurring, or attributable to something happening, after a warranty (express or implied) in the contract has be breached but before the breach has been remedied.

Third, in accordance with Section 11 "Terms not relevant to the actual loss", if compliance with a warranty or a term of a contract of insurance would tend to reduce the risk of loss of a particular kind or of loss at a particular location or of loss at a particular time, the insurer may not rely on the non-compliance to exclude, limit or discharge its liability under the contract for the loss if the assured can show that non-compliance with the term could not have increased the risk of the loss which occurred in the circumstances in which it occurred. For instance, where the assured breaches the warranty to install the anti-theft facilities, but the loss of the house was caused by the flood, the insurer is still liable for the loss. Fourth, Sections 10 and 11 are not compulsory provisions and therefore can be excluded by the insurer if he can satisfy the transparency requirement of Section 17 of the IA 2015.

In essence, the IA 2015 does not abolish the warranty regime; it only alleviates or mitigates the legal consequences of the breach of warranty. The reform is not a novel solution or a castle in the air but is established on the grounds of persuasive academic researches, best practices of the insurance market and solid judicial authorities over the past 20 years.[18]

2. Comments on the Chinese 2020 Proposal from English Law Perspective

It may be observed that the 2020 Proposal only partly refers to the current English law position; therefore, there are deficiencies in several aspects.

First, in addition to the core provision of the IA 2015, namely Section 10 (2), there are two important accompanying regimes: (1) the situation in which the warranty is inapplicable; (2) the test of determining when the breach can be seen as remedied.

In accordance with Section 10 (3) of the IA 2015, the warranty does not apply in the following three situations: (1) because of a change of circumstances, the warranty ceases to be applicable to the circumstances of the contract; (2) compliance with the warranty is rendered unlawful by any subsequent law; (3) the insurer waives the breach of warranty.

---

17 The Law Commission Consultation Paper No 182 and The Scottish Law Commission Discussion Paper No 134, "Insurance Contract Law: Misrepresentation, Non-Disclosure and Breach of Warranty by the Insured", pp. [8.21], [8.114].

18 An academic authority representing the highest quality of research in this topic, see Baris Soyer, *Warranties in Marine Insurance* (3rd edn, Routledge 2017).

There is no similar Article in the 2020 Proposal aforesaid. The first two situations may find their counterparts in Chinese contract law, but the third situation, namely waiver, may find it difficult to locate its equivalently functional provision in Chinese law. The main reason is that the wavier regime, especially waiver by estoppel, stems from the equity in English law and has its unique growth soil and complex operational foundation. The waiver issue has generated numerous helpful academic and judicial comments in English law,[19] but it is not clear whether and how those opinions can provide a valuable reference to the Chinese judges facing similar issues.

In accordance with Sections 10 (5) and (6) of the IA 2015, a breach of warranty is to be taken as remedied: (1) if the assured ceases to be in breach of the warranty; (2) in the case where the warranty in question requires that by an ascertainable time something is to be done or not done, or a condition is to be fulfilled or something is or is not to be the case, and that requirement is not complied with, if the risk to which the warranty relates later becomes essentially the same as that originally contemplated by the parties. The 2020 Proposal explicitly borrows the expression "remedy the breach", but does not define the meaning of "remedy" as English does. In addition, Section 10 (4) (b) of the IA 2015 acknowledges that some breaches cannot be remedied ("if the breach can be remedied") but there is no similar provision in the 2020 Proposal.

In conclusion, it is unclear what is the intention of the revision committee: to leave the definition of "remedy" to the future judicial interpretation issued by the Supreme People's Court of China (SPC), or to leave it to the judges by reference to English law?

There are two more discrepancies between the IA 2015 and the 2020 Proposal, which may also expose the problems contained in the proposals.

The first discrepancy is regarding the statutory legal consequences for the breach of warranty, neither the MIA 1906 nor the IA 2015 provides that the insurer is entitled to terminate the contract by written notice. Under the IA 2015, the effect of breach of a warranty will be equated with breach of suspensory provisions.[20] Providing the right to terminate to the insurer under the 2020 Proposal may cause at least two problems.

In the first place, according to the definition of warranty given by the 2020 Proposal, a warranty may be a clause in which the assured ensures the existence or non-existence of some particular states of facts. The insurer may require those state of fact to exist before underwriting the risk to rating the scope of the proposed assured risk. For instance, the policy may contain a warranty to the effect that the assured yacht has been surveyed within the last six months and all of its recommendations have been complied with. In English law, if this warranty is breached, the risk never attaches and the premium is refundable due to total failure of consideration.[21] However, in Chinese law, it is submitted that this warranty shall be interpreted as the condition precedent to the effectiveness of the insurance contract. If the yacht has not been surveyed within the last six months, the insurance contract is ineffective. There exist significant controversies within the Chinese contract lawyers as to whether the ineffective contract can be terminated, and no consensus has been reached so far.[22]

---

19 A useful summary, see ibid., Chapter 6.
20 Ibid., p. [2.38].
21 Ibid., pp. [1.7], [1.16].
22 See Han Shiyuan, *The Law of Contract* (4th edn, Law Press, 2018) pp. 653–656 (in Chinese).

In the second place, in the literal interpretation of the 2020 Proposal, it is arguable that even if the assured event occurs after the breach of warranty has been remedied, assuming that the subject matter of insurance only suffers a partial loss, the insurer can still terminate the contract after paying the indemnity. Whether this is fair to the assured is open to question. In comparison, it should be noted the breach of warranty only suspends the cover under the IA 2015; unless otherwise agreed, the insurer is not entitled to terminate the contract.

The second discrepancy is regarding the causation requirement between the breach of warranty and the subject matter of the assured's loss. Under Section 10 of the IA 2015, no causal link is required, despite that Section 11 may introduce causation test by the back door.[23] In contrast, under the 2020 Proposal, provided that the assured's breach of the warranty has no effect on the occurrence of the assured event, the insurer is still liable for the loss. "No effect" test introduces a certain degree of causation into the warranty regime, but it is difficult to explain what kind of "effect" is required for the insurer to undertake the liability.

3. Observations as to the Future Reform of the Marine
    Warranty Regime in Chinese Law

From the perspective of risks, the warranty has two essential functions: (1) protecting the insurer against the alteration of the risk by the assured during the currency of the policy(2) assisting the insurer in assessing the scope of the risk he is undertaking.[24] Only by fully understanding these two essential functions can the existing laws be better revised.

The long-term judicial practices and recent legislative reform have proved that the two basic functions of warranty in English law can be effectively performed. It is submitted that if the Chinese revision committee insists on learning from the warranty regime in English law, it should be learned in an all-around way. The core reference is to define the consequences of the breach of warranty as suspension of the insurer's liability rather than termination of the insurance contract.

It is submitted that there is no obstacle to introducing the core regime in IA 2015 into Chinese law. On the macro level, the purpose of revising Article 235 of the CMC 1993 is to make the regime fairer to the assured, which Section 10 of the IA 2015 shares the same value. On the micro level, the suspension of cover is not an unfamiliar concept to the Chinese insurance law and insurance market. For example, Articles 36 and 37 of the IL 2009 provide that if the contract provides for the payment in installments of the premium, and the assured, after payment of the initial installment of the insurance premium, fails to pay an installment within 30 days after the date of a reminder from the insurer or within 60 days after the specified time limit, the validity of the contract shall be suspended. If the effect of a contract is suspended its validity shall be restored after the insurer and the assured agree through consultations and the assured pays the outstanding insurance premium. Although those two Articles are in the Chapter of Life Insurance of the IL 2009, there is no reason that the expression of "suspension of cover" cannot exist in the property and marine insurance contract. For instance, in some fishing vessel insurance contracts in the Chinese market, it is easy to find a contractual clause stating that if the assured leases

---

23 Ibid., p. [5.60].
24 Ibid., p. [1.7].

the vessel, the insurer's liability is suspended. It is confident to say that the Chinese courts have no difficulty in determining whether the cover is suspended or not.

Of course, if the core provisions of the IA 2015 were introduced, further research would be needed to determine the proper wording of the revised Article 235 of the CMC 1993.

IV. Reform of the Marine Open Cover Regime

A. The Current Law

Articles 231–233 of the CMC 1993 regulate the marine open cover regime. Article 231 provides that:

> The assured may conclude an open cover with the insurer for the goods to be shipped or received in batches within a given period. The open cover shall be evidenced by an open policy to be issued by the insurer.

Article 232 states that:

> The insurer shall, at the request of the assured, issue insurance certificates separately for the cargo shipping in batches according to the open cover.
>
> Where the content of the insurance certificates issued by the insurer separately differs from those of the open policy, the insurance certificates issued separately shall prevail.

Article 233 provides that:

> The assured shall notify the insurer immediately on learning that the cargo assured under the open cover has been shipped or has arrived. The items to be notified shall include the name of the carrying ship, the voyage, the value of the cargo and the assured amount.

Those Articles do not define the marine open cover in a precise manner. The SPC is of the opinion that, unless otherwise agreed, the marine open cover is obligatory on both sides, namely the insurer shall not refuse the assured to take out insurance within a given period, and the assured shall take out insurance for all the goods shipped within a given period with the insurer. However, the open cover does not have all the contents of the marine insurance contract stipulated in Article 217 of the CMC 1993; it cannot directly produce the rights and duties of the marine insurance contract, and the assured cannot claim the insurance indemnity in accordance with the open cover only.[25]

In addition to the agreed duties, the assured also bears the statutory duty to notify or declare as stipulated by Article 233 cited above. However, the flaw of this Article is that it does not specify the legal consequences of the assured's failure to notify or declare.

B. The Reform Proposal

Article 289 of the 2020 Proposal has revised Article 231 of the CMC 1993 and defined the marine open cover as "an insurance agreement in which the insurer undertakes to indemnify the assured for the goods transported in batches in a given period in the future, and the assured pays the premium". It further requires that an open cover shall be concluded in writing.

---

25 See (2011) the Supreme People's Court's Civil Adjudication Tribunal No. 4's Reply No. 25.

Article 291 of the 2020 Proposal has clarified the assured's duty to notify or declare and provided in detail the legal consequences for the assured's breach. It states that:

> Pursuant to the marine open cover, the name and quantity of the goods to be transported in batches, the name of the carrying ship, the route, the assured value and the assured amount shall be correctly declared to by the assured to the insurer before each carriage; moreover, the assured shall declare all the goods in conformity with the terms of the open cover.
>
> If the assured fails to declare or mistakenly declare a certain batch of the transported goods due to intentional breach of the preceding paragraph, the insurer shall not be liable for the loss caused by the assured event during the transportation, but shall have the right to collect the premium; for the losses caused by the assured event in the subsequent batch of transported goods, the insurer shall still be liable for indemnity as agreed in the contract, unless the declaration is made after the occurrence of the loss.
>
> If the assured fails to declare or mistakenly declare a certain batch of the transported goods due to non-intentional breach of the preceding paragraph, he is entitled to supplement or rectify; even if the assured event occurs after the supplementation or rectification, the assured's right to require the indemnity will not be prejudiced; however, the assured shall have the right to determine the measure of indemnity pursuant to Article 275 (2) of this Code [the measure of indemnity for unvalued policy].
>
> This Article only applies when there is no agreement or different agreement in the marine open cover.

Although it is seemingly complicated, the revision essentially makes clear two points. First, the parties to the marine open cover are free to agree the legal consequences for the breach; the Article only provides for a default position. Second, depending upon the assured's subjective mind, the legal consequences for breach differ; the assured's non-intentional breach is without prejudice to the validity of the cover for the transported goods in question.

Against the background of the expansion of import and export business in China, it is quite understandable for the revision committee to adopt the legal position as stated above. Many enterprises need to ship the goods every day, so it is inevitable that they may unintendedly fail to declare or have trouble to communicate with the insurer in certain circumstances. The law should give them a certain degree of tolerance for the purpose of supporting their business. In addition, this legal position is in accordance with the practice established by the MIA 1906 which will be stated below.

C. English Law Perspective

The MIA 1906 does not provide provisions for the open cover; instead, Section 29 stipulates the floating policy as follows:

(1) A floating policy is a policy which describes the insurance in general terms, and leaves the name of the ship or ships and other particulars to be defined by subsequent declaration.

(2) The subsequent declaration or declarations may be made by indorsement on the policy, or in other customary manner.

(3) Unless the policy otherwise provides, the declarations must be made in the order of dispatch or shipment. They must, in the case of goods, comprise all consignments within the terms of the policy, and the value of the goods or other property must be honestly stated, but an omission or erroneous declaration

may be rectified even after loss or arrival, provided the omission or declaration was made in good faith.

(4) Unless the policy otherwise provides, where a declaration of value is not made until after notice of loss or arrival, the policy must be treated as an unvalued policy as regards the subject-matter of that declaration.

To be precise, the terms in open cover and floating policy cannot be used interchangeably. Open cover is not a term of art and usually has three forms: facultative open cover, facultative/obligatory open cover and obligatory open cover. An open cover arrangement that is obligatory on both sides is very similar to a floating policy, save for the absence of the aggregate limit.[26]

Although the wordings are slightly different, it is quite obvious that Section 29 of the MIA 1906 is the typical foreign legislative reference for the revision of Article 231 of the CMC 1993 in three aspects: first, the parties are free to agree the legal consequences for breach of the duty to declare;[27] second, an unintentional or good faith failure to declare can be rectified even after loss or arrival without prejudice to the validity of the cover; third, the effect of rectification shall render the policy as being unvalued for the purpose of the measure of indemnity as regards the subject-matter of that declaration.

It is submitted that the floating policy regime under the MIA 1906 has been functioned smoothly in practice for quite a long time, and the revision committee of the CMC 1993 has made a good choice to follow the essential provisions of the MIA 1906 in this regard.

V. Reform of the Insurer's Duty to Explain the Exemption Clauses

A. The Current Law

Under Chinese law, if the insurer of marine insurance contract intends to rely on the exemption clause, he must perform the duty to explain pursuant to Article 17 (2) of the IL 2009:

> An insurer shall give a note, which is enough to call attention to the assured on the application form, the policy or other insurance certificate, for the clause regarding the exemption of liability of the insurer as provided in the insurance contract, and shall make clear explanations in respect thereof to the assured in written or oral form, otherwise such clause shall not be valid.

The duty is regarded as an invention of Chinese insurance law and also the most important duty on the part of the insurer. The legal basis of the duty lies upon two aspects: first, it reflects the reciprocal nature of the pre-contractual of utmost good faith—the assured has the duty to disclose and the insurer has the duty to explain; second, it is the requirement of regulating the exemption clause and realising the freedom of contract on the assured's

---

26 Peter MacDonald Eggers QC, "Cargo Insurance and Open Cover", Chapter 14 of *International Trade and Carriage of Goods*, Baris Soyer and Andrew Tettenborn (eds), (Informa, 2016), pp. 226–228; Jonathan Gilman QC and others, *Arnould Law of Marine Insurance and Average*, (19th edn, Sweet & Maxwell, 2018), pp. 318–320.

27 For instance, in *Union Insurance Society of Canton v Wills* [1916] 1 AC 281, the Privy Council held that the parties have agreed the duty to declare as the promissory warranty in the sense of Section 33 of the MIA 1906; in *The Beursgracht* [2001] EWCA Civ 2051, the Court of Appeal held that the parties can agree that the duty to declare as being a condition to the attachment of the cover.

part, for the exemption clause is highly professional and technical, repeatedly studied and formulated by the insurer and put into the contract in advance, which should only be valid if the assured is fully informed and understand its meanings.

B. The Reform Proposal

It should be noted that although the insurer's duty to explain applies to the marine insurance contract, this duty is not provided by the CMC 1993 but the IL 2009. Moreover, the true purpose of this duty is to protect the vulnerable assured in consumer insurance, especially in some kinds of life insurance; it is doubtful that whether or not marine insurance with two parties having equal bargaining power and the assured being advised by the professional insurance brokers and lawyers need the full extent of this duty.

Therefore, Article 281 of the 2020 Proposal slightly revised the application of Article 17 (2) of the IL 2009 concerning the marine insurance contract. It stipulates that:

> An insurer shall give a note, which is enough to call attention to the assured on the application form, the policy or other insurance certificate, for the clause regarding the exemption of liability of the insurer as provided in the marine insurance contract before its conclusion, and shall make clear explanations in respect thereof in accordance with the requirements of the assured.
>
> If the insurer fails to perform the obligation of calling attention to or explanation in accordance with the provisions of the preceding paragraph, the clause shall not be valid.

Pursuant to the revision, the insurer only needs to perform the duty to explain in accordance with the requirements of the assured. In other words, unless the assured so requires, the insurer has no positive duty to explain the meaning of the exemption clause to the assured.

C. English Law Perspective

Both Article 17 (2) of the IL 2009 and Article 281 of the 2020 Proposal find no equivalence in under English law. The closest English legislation in this regard may be Sections 16 and 17 of the IA 2015, which essentially provides that unless transparency requirements are satisfied, contract term (including exemption clause) that put the asinsured in a worse position than he would be under the IA 2015 (disadvantageous term) would be rendered ineffective. Those requirements are: (1) the insurer must take sufficient steps to draw the disadvantageous term to the attention of the assured before the contract is concluded unless the assured or his agent has the actual knowledge of the term; (2) the term must be clear and unambiguous as to its effects. The characteristics of assured persons of the kind in question, and the circumstances of the transaction are to be taken into account in determining whether the above requirements have been satisfied.[28]

It could be observed from the above legislations that the insurer only bears the duty to call the disadvantageous terms to the assured's attention but does not need to explain the meaning of the term to the assured. One possible reason for this is the involvement of the broker during the negotiations of the contract. It is in the course of business of the marine insurance contract concluded in Lloyd's of London that requires the broker to prepare

---

28 Sections 17 (2) to (5) of the IA 2015. See also Robert Merkin, *Colinvaux's Law of Insurance* (11th edn, Sweet & Maxwell, 2016), pp. [8–125].

working of the policy and to exercise reasonable care in responding to any questions by the assured as to the meaning of the clauses or to explain to the assured the terms of the proposed insurance.[29]

It should also be stressed that an otherwise valid clause in a commercial contract will not be easily struck down by English court as it may be regarded as an interference with freedom of contract and undermine the certainty which parties are entitled to expect of the law.[30]

All in all, the English experience says that the exemption clause in a marine insurance contract shall not be rendered ineffective lightly and the broker's role in this regard shall be taken more seriously by the Chinese marine insurance practice.

VI. Reform of the Applicable Law to the P&I Club's Obligation to Indemnify Its Members

A. The Current Law

The CMC 1993 does not specify whether it applies to P&I insurance contract with the nature of mutual insurance. However, the SPC is of the opinion that the insurance contract concluded between the China P&I Club and the members is not commercial insurance contract, hence the IL 2009 does not apply.[31]

The Rule 8 (R) of the China P&I Club's Rules (2020/2021) emphasised the Supreme People's Court's point by stipulating that:

> These Rules and all contracts of insurance made by the Association shall be governed by and construed in accordance with law of the People's Republic of China, except "the Insurance Law".

It is understandable that the IL 2009 does not apply to P&I insurance contract, because this law governs both commercial and consumer insurance; therefore, some Articles are not suitable in the context of P&I Insurance which has nothing to do with the consumers.

B. The Reform Proposal

Article 277 of the 2020 Proposal provides that:

> Where the owner, operator, manager or charterer of a vessel forms a mutual insurance organisation as a member to collect membership fees and bear protection and indemnity liability for the losses, liabilities or expenses incurred by the members in the operation of the vessel, the Articles of this Chapter shall apply *mutatis mutandis* in the absence of any agreement between the mutual insurance organisation and the members.

Under this Article, it is clear that regarding P&I insurance, the Rules of the P&I club will be given priority. Certainly, the condition precedent is that the Rules of the P & I club do not violate any laws. Where the Rules are silent, the relevant Articles of the CMC

---

29 See Robert Merkin, *Colinvaux's Law of Insurance* (11th edn, Sweet & Maxwell, 2016), pp. [16–051], [16–052]; Jonathan Gilman QC and others, *Arnould Law of Marine Insurance and Average*, (19th edn, Sweet & Maxwell, 2018), pp. 214–215.

30 See the Supreme Court's opinion in the context of the penalty rule, *Cavendish Square Holding BV v Talal El Makdessi; ParkingEye v Beavis* [2015] UKSC 67, p. [33].

31 See (2017) the Supreme People's Court's Civil Rulings No. 3702.

1993 shall apply. As the China P&I Club's Rules exclude the application of the IL 2009, the Part III "Contract" of the Civil Code 2020 will apply where the CMC 1993 is silent.[32]

C. English Law Perspective

Section 85 (4) of the MIA 1906 states that: "Subject to the exceptions mentioned in this section, the provisions of this Act apply to mutual insurance".

Mutual insurance is defined by Section 85 (1) as "where two or more persons mutually agree to insure each other against marine losses there is said to be a mutual insurance".

Although Section 85 does not reflect the current P&I Club practice,[33] it is without doubt that the MIA 1906 applies to the P&I insurance contract unless the Club's rules and regulations state otherwise.

It is submitted that, from the perspective of English law, by providing that the CMC 1993 applies to the P&I insurance is beneficial for clarifying the law applicable to the P&I insurance and the integrity and coherence of the marine insurance law.

VII. Conclusion

The marine insurance market is undoubtedly one of the most international commercial markets globally, from which the Chinese market cannot be isolated. It is the clear goal of the Chinese marine insurance law to support the development of the market. In this regard, the international influence of the English marine insurance law, represented by the MIA 1906, the IA 2015 and the correspondent case law must be considered when revising Chinese law.

It is obvious from the above analysis that in respect of the assured's duty to disclose, marine warranty, marine open cover, insurer's duty to explain the exemption clause and the law applicable to the P&I insurance, English law has exerted its remarkable impact on the revision of the CMC 1993. On the one hand, this is helpful to the internationalisation of China's marine insurance law; on the other hand, the Chinese revision committee should realise that the legal transplant is not simply moving the direct related Sections of the MIA 1906 or the IA 2015 into Chinese law; those Sections must be read in the context of the whole legislation and the relevant judicial authorities.

To sum up, further academic and practical research must be conducted in order to localise the English experience in China. The revision of Chapter 12 of the CMC 1993 is an opportunity not to be missed to support the marine insurance sector in China and bring it in line with the global lead; it must be carried forward properly and carefully.

---

32 The Civil Code of the People's Republic of China, adopted at the Third Session of the 13th National People's Congress of the People's Republic of China on 28 May 2020, and came into force as of 1 January 2021.

33 Steven J. Hazelwood, David Semark, *P&I Clubs: Law and Practice* (4th edn, Lloyd's List 2010), p. [2.5].

PART II

LAW IN ACTION

Litigation and Alternative Dispute Resolution

CHAPTER 7

China in the International Commercial Dispute Resolution Arena

The Establishment of the China International Commercial Court

Fa Chen*, **

I. Introduction

Globalisation has led to the boom of cross-border trade, which has, in turn, resulted in an enormous increase in international commercial disputes.[1] For a long time, international arbitration has served as the primary approach to settling international commercial disputes due largely to its merits in neutrality and flexibility.[2] However, the other side of the coin is that international arbitration has considerable weaknesses, such as high costs and the lack of effective sanctions during the arbitral process.[3] Against this backdrop, international commercial courts have mushroomed throughout the world over recent years, aiming to combine the advantages of litigation and arbitration to provide "tailor-made procedures" for cross-border commercial dispute resolution.[4]

In Europe, inspired largely by the success of the UK Commercial Court (now renamed to the Business and Property Courts of England & Wales), France, Holland and Germany have established international commercial courts/chambers, while a similar initiative is

---

* Fa Chen, (MPhil., LLM and LLB) Teaching Associate in Law at the University of Cambridge, and formerly, served as a judge in a Beijing court in China for several years.

** Acknowledgement: This work is a revised and expanded version of a paper titled 'The Establishment of the China International Commercial Court' presented at the London-Dubai International Dispute Resolution seminar, held by Middlesex University Dubai, 28 March 2021. The author would like to thank Professor Eilis Ferran, Professor Rob Merkin, and Professor Howell Jackson and the anonymous reviewers, for their insightful comments. Any remaining errors are my own responsibility. This work was supported by the Erasmus+ Mobility grant (2018), and the UK Higher Education Innovation Fund (2019–2020).

1 Wei Cai and Andrew Godwin, 'Challenges and Opportunities for the China International Commercial Court' (2019), p. 68; International and Comparative Law Quarterly, pp. 869, 869.

2 Dalma R Demeter and Kayleigh M Smith, 'The Implications of International Commercial Courts on Arbitration' (2016), p. 33; Journal of International Arbitration, pp. 441, 441.

3 QMUL and White & Case, '2018 International Arbitration Survey: The Evolution of International Arbitration', p. 10; <www.whitecase.com/sites/whitecase/files/files/download/publications/qmul-international-arbitration-survey-2018-19.pdf>. Unless otherwise stated, all URLs in this work were last accessed on 1 March 2022.

4 Xandra Kramer and John Sorabji, 'International Business Courts in Europe and Beyond: A Global Competition for Justice?' (2019), p. 12; Erasmus law review, pp. 1, 1.

underway in Belgium in the context of Brexit.[5] Also, the creation of a commercial court at the pan-European level has been proposed.[6]

In the Middle East, such courts have been created in Qatar (the Qatar International Financial Center Courts) and UAE (Dubai International Financial Center Courts and Abu Dhabi Global Market Courts) to serve their respective economic objectives.[7] Likewise, in Asia, Singapore established the Singapore International Commercial Court (SICC) in 2015 to consolidate its leading position as a hub of commercial dispute resolution.[8] Inspired by the Singaporean practice, China joined the race for adjudication business through the creation of the China International Commercial Court (CICC) in 2018.[9]

Notwithstanding the domino effect of establishing international commercial courts, these courts differ significantly in many aspects, such as jurisdiction and functioning. Underpinning the distinctions are the different political and judicial appeals of involved countries.

Based mainly on doctrinal and comparative legal studies, this chapter conducts a close examination of the legal framework and operational mechanism of the CICC. It also looks into the challenges surrounding this Chinese legal innovation and explores the way forward.

Following this introduction, Section II broaches the legal framework of the CICC, including its jurisdiction, judge appointment, proceeding language and one-stop dispute resolution platform. Section III figures out the challenges faced by the CICC and endeavours to map the way forward. Section IV concludes.

II. The Legal Framework of the China International Commercial Court

A. Overview

Officially launched in 2013, China's Belt and Road Initiative (BRI) serves as a significant state economic strategy that aims ultimately to reshape global economic governance.[10] However, the BRI relies heavily on non-legally binding norms and agreements such as memorandum of understanding (MOUs) rather than stringent cross-border legal frameworks with rigid rules.[11] This is the background against which moves by the Chinese central authority to promulgate the *Opinion Concerning the Establishment of the Belt*

---

5 Giesela Rühl, 'Building Competence in Commercial Law in the Member States' (2018); European Parliament Study of the Policy Department for Citizens' Rights and Constitutional Affairs, pp. 38–42 <www .europarl.europa.eu/RegData/etudes/STUD/2018/604980/IPOL_STU(2018)604980_EN.pdf>.

6 Ibid., pp. 58–62.

7 For an introduction of the establishment of international commercial courts in the Middle East, see Sheng Zhang, 'China's International Commercial Court: Background, Obstacles and the Road Ahead' (2020), p. 11; Journal of International Dispute Settlement, pp. 150, 152.

8 SICC, 'Report of the Singapore International Commercial Court Committee' <www.sicc.gov.sg/docs/ default-source/about-sicc/annex-a-sicc-committee-report.pdf>.

9 Lance Ang, 'International Commercial Courts and the Interplay between Realism and Institutionalism: A Look at China and Singapore' Harvard International Law Journal online essay, <https://harvardilj.org/2020 /03/international-commercial-courts-and-the-interplay-between-realism-and-institutionalism-a-look-at-china -and-singapore/>.

10 Michael M Du, 'China's "One Belt, One Road" Initiative: Context, Focus, Institutions, and Implications' (2016), p. 2; The Chinese Journal of Global Governance, pp. 30, 30.

11 Heng Wang, 'China's Approach to the Belt and Road Initiative: Scope, Character and Sustainability' (2019), p. 22; Journal of International Economic Law, p. 29.

and Road International Commercial Dispute Resolution Mechanism and Institutions (*BRI Opinion*) to promote international cooperation under the BRI umbrella and resolve associated cross-border commercial disputes are to be considered.[12] The *BRI Opinion* proposes that the Supreme People's Court of China (SPC) should establish the CICC to support the resolution of international commercial disputes arising from the BRI development context in a professional, effective and fair manner via a one-stop mechanism connecting litigation, mediation and arbitration.[13]

To respond to the *BRI Opinion*, in mid-2018, the SPC established the first CICC in Shenzhen, Guangdong Province, and the second CICC in Xi'an, Shaanxi Province, to adjudicate international commercial cases.[14] The pair of locations are purposefully chosen with strategic significance because they are China's southern financial centre and the starting point of the original Silk Road, which are expected to take on commercial disputes arising from the "21st-Century Maritime Silk Road" and land-based "Silk Road Economic Belt", respectively.

The empowering instrument of the CICC is the *CICC Provisions*, a judicial interpretation issued by the SPC in mid-2018, which stipulates the fundamentals of the CICC, such as its jurisdiction, personnel, and the establishment of the International Commercial Expert Committee (ICEC).[15] Apart from the *CICC Provisions*, the SPC has promulgated several other legal instruments to smooth the functioning of the CICC, inclusive of the *CICC Procedural Rules*[16] and *ICEC Working Rules*.[17] The *CICC Procedure Rules* stipulates the detailed rules of CICC-related procedures for filing, serving documents, pre-trial mediation, trial and execution and elaborates on the procedural rules related to the integration of alternative dispute resolution (ADR) mechanisms into the CICC litigation process. In parallel, the *ICEC Working Rules* lays down detailed stipulations on the appointment and entitlement of ICEC experts.

Structurally, the CICC is a divisional arm of the SPC.[18] This echoes the practices of some European countries, such as France and Germany, in which the international commercial court forms a part of their respective domestic judiciary.[19] On these grounds, the establishment of the CICC signifies China's ambition to achieve greater discourse in the realm of *lex mercatoria*.

---

12 Opinion Concerning the Establishment of the Belt and Road International Commercial Dispute Resolution Mechanism and Institutions (BRI Opinion), <http://cicc.court.gov.cn/html/1/219/208/210/819.html>.

13 ibid.

14 CICC, 'A Brief Introduction of China International Commercial Court' <http://cicc.court.gov.cn/html/1/219/193/195/index.html>.

15 Provisions of the Supreme People's Court on Several Issues Regarding the Establishment of the International Commercial Court (CICC Provisions), <http://cicc.court.gov.cn/html/1/219/208/210/817.html>.

16 Procedural Rules for the China International Commercial Court of the Supreme People's Court (For Trial Implementation) (CICC Procedural Rules), <http://cicc.court.gov.cn/html/1/219/208/210/1183.html>.

17 Working Rules of the International Commercial Expert Committee of the Supreme People's Court (For Trial Implementation) (ICEC Working Rules), <http://cicc.court.gov.cn/html/1/219/208/210/1146.html>.

18 CICC Provisions (n 15), Art 1.

19 Pamela K Bookman, 'The Adjudication Business' (2020), p. 45; Yale Journal of International Law, p. 227. European examples of international commercial courts/chambers that are within the domestic judiciary, see the Chamber for International Commercial Disputes of the Frankfurt Regional Court in Germany and the International and European Commercial Chamber of the Paris Court in France.

B. Jurisdiction

As for jurisdiction, cases to be brought before the CICC should be large and complex with potential impacts on the relationship between China and other countries.[20] Yet, cases involving state–state trade or investor–state investment disputes fall outside the jurisdiction of the CICC.[21] In detail, the SPC stipulates five categories of lawsuits, as follows:

1) First instance international commercial cases in which the parties have chosen the jurisdiction of the SPC according to Article 34 of the *Civil Procedure Law of China* (*CPL*) with an amount in dispute of at least 300 million RMB (equivalent to approximately 46 million USD);

2) First instance international commercial cases which are subject to the jurisdiction of the higher courts who nonetheless consider that the cases should be tried by the SPC for which permission has been obtained (referral from high courts);

3) First instance international commercial cases that have a nationwide significant impact;

4) Cases involving applications for preservation measures in arbitration, for setting aside or enforcing international commercial arbitration awards according to Article 14 of these Provisions;

5) Other international commercial cases that the SPC considers appropriate to be tried by the CICC (referral from the SPC).[22]

It should be noted that as for the first category of cases, apart from satisfying the financial threshold of dispute amount of 300 million RMB, involved disputes are bound to the requirements of Article 34 of the *CPL*. According to Article 34 of the *CPL*, the parties to a contractual or other property dispute can choose the jurisdiction of Chinese courts at the place in which "the defendant is domiciled, the contract is performed, the contract is signed, the plaintiff is domiciled, or the subject matter is located".[23] That is to say, cases to be heard in the CICC must have a substantial connection to China. This extra tier of requirement differs from the practice of many international commercial courts, such as the SICC which only requires lawsuits to have an international and commercial nature (see details in the Table below).[24] Besides, the *CICC Provisions* stipulates two routes for cases to be referred to the CICC, i.e. referrals from Chinese high courts and the SPC. This referral mechanism mirrors the practice of Singapore, in which the Singapore High Court can refer cases to the SICC when it is more appropriate for the cases to be heard by the SICC.[25] Implications regarding the differences between the CICC and its global counterparts in jurisdiction will be considered later in Section III.

---

20 Cao Yin, 'International Commercial Courts Eye Expanded Role' (China Daily, 30 January 2019) <www.chinadaily.com.cn/a/201901/30/WS5c50dce6a3106c65c34e72f1.html>.

21 CICC, 'The State Council Information Office Held a Press Conference on the "Opinion on the Establishment of 'The Belt and Road' International Commercial Dispute Settlement Mechanism and Institutions"', <http://cicc.court.gov.cn/html/1/219/208/210/769.html>.

22 CICC Provisions (n 15), Art. 2.

23 Civil Procedural Law of China, Art. 34 <http://english.court.gov.cn/2015-09/11/content_21845452.htm>.

24 SICC, 'Rules of Court' <www.supremecourt.gov.sg/rules/court-processes/rules-of-court>.

25 See Man Yip, 'The Resolution of Disputes before the Singapore International Commercial Court' (2016), p. 65; International and Comparative Law Quarterly, pp. 439, 461.

C. Personnel

Some countries allow their international commercial courts to appoint foreign judges as a means of promoting internationalisation. For example, Singapore has amended its Constitution to permit foreign legal experts to sit on the bench of the SICC.[26] However, it is not the case in China.

Judges of the CICC are selected by the SPC from senior judges who have extensive judicial experience and are familiar with international treaties, international practices and international trade and investment practice with the capacity of using both Chinese and English as working languages.[27] To date, there are 14 judges on the CICC bench, all of whom have worked in the SPC for many years.[28] Moreover, eight of the CICC judges have studied or visiting experience in an overseas jurisdiction.[29] This ensures the professionalism in handling international commercial disputes. However, according to the *Judge Law of China*, Chinese nationality is a prerequisite for getting appointed as a Chinese judge.[30] It means that foreign legal experts cannot sit on the bench of the CICC, which is not helpful to the internationalisation of the CICC. Against this legal obstacle, the CICC mechanism introduces international expertise through its innovative product, the ICEC as discussed above.

The *ICEC Working Rules* serves as the principal legal instrument establishing the ICEC other than the *CICC Provisions*, which stipulates the major powers and duties entitled to the ICEC members. According to the *ICEC Working Rules*, the ICEC is composed of both Chinese and foreign legal experts who are appointed by the SPC.[31] To date, there are 53 experts in the ICEC; of these, 20 are Chinese experts, while the rest 33 are from overseas jurisdictions.[32] It is noteworthy that the experts are selected due mainly to their judicial, academic and arbitral experience in international commercial law, whereas mediators are rare.[33] As for geographical coverage, in the latest round of appointment at the end of 2020, the SPC appointed three Singaporean and four African experts to the ICEC.[34] These experts represent a good source of legal expertise and are entitled to provide advisory opinions on international treaties, international commercial rules, ascertainment and application of foreign laws and other specialised legal issues involved in the trial of cases by the CICC and other courts at all levels.[35] On these grounds, it is expected that the appointment of the Chinese and foreign experts can assist the CICC with the settlement of BRI-related international commercial disputes.

---

26 Constitution of the Republic of Singapore, Art. 95(4)(c) <https://sso.agc.gov.sg/Act/CONS1963>.

27 CICC Provisions (n 15), Art. 4.

28 Data as of 1 September 2021, see CICC, 'Judges', <http://cicc.court.gov.cn/html/1/219/193/196/index.html>.

29 ibid.

30 Judge Law of China, Art. 12(1) <www.npc.gov.cn/englishnpc/c23934/202012/9c82d5dbefbc4ffa98f3dd815af62dfb.shtml>.

31 ICEC Working Rules (n 17), Art. 2.

32 CICC, 'Expert Directory', <http://cicc.court.gov.cn/html/1//219/235/237/index.html>.

33 Weixia Gu, 'China's Law and Development: A Case Study of the China International Commercial Court' (2021), p. 62; Harvard International Law Journal, pp. 67, 77.

34 CICC, 'The Decision on the Appointment of the Second Group of Members for the International Commercial Expert Committee of the Supreme People's Court', <http://cicc.court.gov.cn/html/1/219/208/210/1876.html>.

35 ICEC Working Rules (n 17), Art. 3(2).

D. Litigation Process and Proceeding Language

As a branch of the SPC, the CICC applies the principle of "First Instance Being Final", which means that the CICC establishes a collegial panel consisting of three or more judges to handle the cases, which are first-instance but the judgments are final.[36] However, in light of the *CPL*, where any party considers a judgment to be wrong, (s)he can submit an application to the SPC for a retrial.[37] Such an entitlement is also available to the parties to cases launched before the CICC.

The default law applied to CICC litigation is Chinese law. However, parties can choose a foreign law as the governing law by agreement.[38] As such, the ICEC experts can use their expertise to provide advisory opinions on the ascertainment and application of foreign laws.[39]

In terms of the proceeding language, generally speaking, Chinese courts should use the official language of China, namely Mandarin. In order to cater for the needs of settling international commercial disputes, however, an exception is created to permit a litigant to submit evidence in an English version without providing a Chinese translation, provided the other party has no objection.[40]

From a global perspective, the well-established UK Commercial Court normally uses English as the proceeding language. Given the dominant position of English in international trade and commerce, many international commercial courts/chambers have employed English as their official language to mitigate the competitive demerits compared to the UK Commercial Court (see Table 7.1 above). The difference in proceeding language reflects the potential improvement that the CICC needs to pursue in order to further its internationalisation.

E. One-Stop Dispute Resolution Mechanism

The most remarkable legal innovation of the CICC is perhaps its one-stop dispute resolution mechanism, which integrates litigation, arbitration and mediation to facilitate the settlement of international commercial disputes. For this purpose, the SPC published a *Notice* to introduce the engagement of a pair of Chinese mediation institutions, i.e. the Mediation Centre of China Council for the Promotion of International Trade (CCPIT) and the Shanghai Commercial Mediation Centre (SCMC), in CICC dispute resolution, under which litigants can opt for mediation before or during the litigation process.[41] In detail, if both parties reach a mediation agreement under either CICC-recognised mediation institution, they can ask the CICC to issue either a "conciliation statement" or "judgment based on the mediation agreement".[42] The incorporation of institutional mediation

---

36 CICC, 'A Brief Introduction' (n 14).
37 Civil Procedural Law of China (n 23), Art. 199.
38 CICC Provisions (n 15), Art. 7.
39 ICEC Working Rules (n 17), Art. 3(2).
40 CICC Provisions (n 15), Art. 9(2).
41 Notice of the General Office of the Supreme People's Court of China on Inclusion of the First Group of International Commercial Arbitration and Mediation Institutions in the 'One-Stop' Diversified International Commercial Dispute Resolution Mechanism (SPC Notice), <http://cicc.court.gov.cn/html/1/219/208/210/1144.html>.
42 ibid.

Table 7.1 Comparison between the CICC and International Commercial Courts

	Disputes should have a connection with the place of the courts	Foreign judges can sit on the bench	English as the proceeding language
CICC	Yes	No	No
SICC	No	Yes	Yes
UK Commercial Court	No	No	Yes
Germany International Commercial Court	No	No	Yes
Netherlands International Commercial Court	No	No	Yes
International Chamber of the Paris Court of Appeal	No	No	No

Compiled by the current author.

agreements into court judgments is unprecedented in China's judicial practice, which represents a ground-breaking innovation of the CICC mechanism.[43]

Apart from the participation of the CCPIT and SCMC in mediation, the ICEC members are entitled to mediate international commercial cases brought before the CICC and issue mediation settlement agreements.[44] Thereafter, the CICC can issue judgments based on the mediation settlement agreements.[45] Thus, the engagement of ICEC experts in mediation is an integral part of the CICC's effort to establish the one-stop dispute resolution mechanism that envisages using ADR mechanisms as a top priority for dispute settlement.[46] Moreover, in order to compete with global counterparts in the international commercial dispute resolution market, the CICC needs to show "internationalisation, professionalism and transparency".[47] As such, the participation of foreign legal experts can also mitigate the concerns and doubts about the lack of international elements of the CICC.[48]

From the discussion above, it could be seen that the incorporation of mediation settlement agreements into a CICC judgment can be achieved through two parallel routes:

1) Mediations concluded by either the CCPIT or the SCMC;
2) Mediations provided by ICEC experts.

Notably, the latter route is more striking, given that foreign legal experts are, *de facto*, allowed to get involved in CICC judgment making with an effect of "semi-adjudication".[49] It is noteworthy that China has become a signatory of the *United Nations Convention*

---

43 Gu, 'China's Law and Development' (n 33), p. 74.
44 ICEC Working Rules (n 17), Art. 3(1).
45 ICEC Working Rules (n 17), Art. 13.
46 Weixia Gu, 'Piercing the Veil of Arbitration Reform in China: Promises, Pitfalls, Patterns, Prognoses and Prospects' (2017) 65 The American Journal of Comparative Law, p. 799.
47 Cai and Godwin (n 1), p. 901.
48 Gu, 'China's Law and Development' (n 33), pp. 78–79.
49 Cai and Godwin (n 1), p. 880.

on International Settlement Agreements resulting from Mediation since 2019, which has further facilitated the usage of mediation in the one-stop dispute resolution platform.[50]

Furthermore, the one-stop dispute resolution mechanism connects five accredited Chinese arbitration institutions with the CICC,[51] which can utilise their expertise in international commercial dispute resolution. Also, the CICC provides support for the arbitration institutions to smooth their participation. According to the *SPC Notice*, parties to arbitration at an endorsed arbitration institution can ask the CICC for judicial assistance such as preservation of evidence, assets or acts.[52] Moreover, after the issuance of an arbitral award, either party can ask the CICC to revoke or enforce the award.[53]

It should be mentioned that the "one-stop" dispute resolution mechanism is not a Chinese invention coming out of thin air, which instead echoes the notion "multi-door courthouse" put forward by the Harvard academic Professor Frank Sander in the 1970s. According to Professor Sander, litigants should have the entitlement to choose different routes to dispute resolution on "a menu of options" provided by the courts.[54] Horizontally, the CICC one-stop dispute resolution mechanism mirrors the practice of its Singaporean counterpart which incorporates ADR mechanisms into the litigation process of the SICC to form a multi-tiered litigation-arbitration-mediation trio.[55] Also, ADR mechanisms are used widely in the UK Commercial Court, in which judges can recommend that involved parties reach a consensus through ADR mechanisms at any stage of the litigation process.[56] Theoretically, the integration of private actor-led ADR mechanisms into state-based litigation could take advantage of the synergy and coordination between public and private institutions to generate legal agglomeration effects.[57] In reality, however, the extent to which the supposed synergy would facilitate China to compete in the international commercial dispute resolution arena as an emerging power remains to be seen.[58]

III. The Areas for Improvement and the Feasible Way Forward

The establishment of the CICC with remarkable innovations has marked a significant step in the development of China's judicial system. Nevertheless, there is still room for improvement, compared to its European and Asian competitors. This section broaches the areas for improvement and explores the way forward.

---

50 See Ministry of Commerce of China, 'China Signs the United Nations Convention on International Settlement Agreements Resulting from Mediation', <http://english.mofcom.gov.cn/article/newsrelease/significantnews/201908/20190802891357.shtml>.

51 These include the China International Economic and Trade Arbitration Commission, Shanghai International Economic and Trade Arbitration Commission, Shenzhen Court of International Arbitration, Beijing Arbitration Commission and China Maritime Arbitration Commission.

52 SPC Notice (n 41).

53 ibid.

54 Matthew S Erie, 'The New Legal Hubs: The Emergent Landscape of International Commercial Dispute Resolution' (2020), p. 60; Virginia Journal of International Law, pp. 225, 229.

55 Gu, 'China's Law and Development' (n 33), p. 69 (footnote 7).

56 Business and Property Courts of England & Wales, 'The Commercial Court Guide', pp. 62–63; <https://assets.publishing.service.gov.uk/government/uploads/system/uploads/attachment_data/file/672422/The_Commercial_Court_Guide_new_10th_Edition_07.09.17.pdf>.

57 Michael Hwang, 'Commercial Courts and International Arbitration—Competitors or Partners?' (2015), p. 31; Arbitration International, pp. 193, 197.

58 Gu, 'China's Law and Development' (n 33), p. 86.

A. The Narrowly Defined Jurisdiction Needs to Be Broadened

As discussed above, cases to be settled at the CICC must have a substantial connection to China. In practice, however, the parties to an international commercial dispute may have uneven bargaining power, which does not nevertheless rule out the possibility that they may choose a neutral court in a third country to which the dispute has no connection.[59] As such, the substantial connection requirement stipulated by the *CPL* definitely excludes many international commercial disputes from the jurisdiction of the CICC. This positions the CICC at a competitive disadvantage in the global arena, given that most of its peers do not employ such a substantial connection requirement.

It is noteworthy that the *Special Maritime Procedure Law of China* has removed the substantial connection restriction by permitting parties to a case without any substantial connection to China to confer jurisdiction on Chinese courts through a written agreement.[60] Given this, it is well worth Chinese authorities' consideration about ruling out the substantial connection restriction imposed on the jurisdiction of the CICC so as to enhance its global competitiveness.

Besides this, the CICC does not have jurisdiction over investment disputes. Although the *CICC Provisions* does not define "commercial disputes", the jurisdiction of the CICC clearly excludes investment disputes as mentioned previously. This narrowly defined jurisdiction seems inconsistent with the objective of the establishment of the CICC that aims to promote international cooperation while facilitating BRI-related dispute resolution. Instead, under the present legal framework, the resolution of investor-state disputes relies heavily on the bilateral investment treaties (BITs) that China has entered. However, a close examination of the BITs that China has concluded with BRI-related countries reveals that those BITs are too narrow in the jurisdiction to provide sufficient protection in need, which calls for a well-structured legal framework.[61] Given above considerations, to provide broader coverage of jurisdiction over international commercial disputes will enhance the demand for the service of the CICC.[62]

Nevertheless, due attention should be paid to the legal hurdles that bar the CICC's jurisdiction from covering investment disputes. In its judicial interpretation on implementing the *New York Convention*, the SPC specifies that commercial legal relations refer to economic rights and obligations arising from contract, infringement or related laws and regulations, excluding disputes between foreign investors and the host state.[63] Thus, considering the existing judicial interpretation, it is necessary to make special stipulations regarding the CICC's jurisdiction if it is to be expanded to cover investment disputes in the future. However, given that the SICC defines commercial disputes broadly to contain those arising from investment,[64] it is necessary for the CICC to enlarge its jurisdiction to enhance its global competitiveness.

---

59 Zhang (n 7), p. 162.

60 Special Maritime Procedure Law of China, Art. 8 <http://english.court.gov.cn/2015-09/11/content_21845453.htm>.

61 Zhang (n 7), p. 163.

62 Zhang (n 7), p. 163.

63 Notice of the Supreme People's Court on Implementation of the 'Convention on the Recognition and Enforcement of Foreign Arbitral Awards' Acceded to by China <http://cicc.court.gov.cn/html/1/219/199/201/698.html>.

64 Andrew Godwin, Ian Ramsay and Miranda Webster, 'International Commercial Courts: The Singapore Experience' (2017), p. 18; Melbourne Journal of International Law, pp. 219, 226.

B. The Level of Internationalisation Needs to Be Improved

Internationalisation is a core competence of international commercial courts. For the purpose of further internationalisation of the CICC, improvement in the areas of judge appointment, proceeding language and foreign engagement is imperative, compared to its global peers.

First, the CICC personnel needs to be further internationalised. As discussed above, judges sitting on the bench of the CICC must be Chinese nationals, which prevents foreign legal experts from becoming Chinese judges. Although the SPC has appointed over 30 foreign experts to the ICEC to fill the internationalisation gap, compared to the SICC in which foreign judges can sit on its bench to showcase the neutrality and credibility, it is evident that the internationalisation level of the CICC needs to be enhanced in the area of judge selection.

To solve this insufficient internationalisation problem, it may rely on the people's assessor mechanism. Unlike common law jurisdictions, China does not employ a jury system, which instead allows people's assessors to join a collegiate panel to hear cases. When sitting in a collegiate panel, people's assessors have equal power to judges except serving as the presiding judge.[65] As such, a feasible way forward is to select people's assessors from retired judges of Hong Kong or Macau to join a collegiate panel to hear cases, which can incorporate international expertise on the one hand while without contradicting the *Judge Law of China* on the other.[66] In practice, a Shenzhen local court in China Guangdong Province has served as the first experimental field to do so, which had selected people's assessors from Hong Kong jurors to hear 172 cases by the end of 2018.[67] This marks a roadmap for the CICC to carry out a similar breakthrough.

Another issue related to the insufficient internationalisation of the CICC lies in the lack of participation of foreign lawyers and foreign arbitration institutions. Most countries ban foreign lawyers from practising law in their domestic courts,[68] so does China which disallows foreign lawyers to practise law in Chinese courts, including the CICC. However, the SICC represents a departure from the standard global practice on this issue. Under the legal framework of the SICC, foreign lawyers can conduct either full registration or restricted registration at the SICC. The former circumstance entitles foreign lawyers to represent on behalf of parties in cases (with no substantial connection to Singapore) held by the SICC.[69] This is compared to foreign lawyers under restricted registration, who can only participate in a much narrower range of specific cases to make submissions on specific questions of foreign law.[70] Back to the Chinese legal framework, the *CPL* clearly stipulates that only Chinese lawyers can represent on behalf of litigants as a lawyer in

---

65 Decision of the Standing Committee of the National People's Congress Regarding Perfecting the System of People's Assessors, Art. 1 <www.lawinfochina.com/display.aspx?lib=law&id=3678&CGid=&EncodingName=big5>.

66 Zhang (n 7), p. 168.

67 Legislative Council Panel on Administration of Justice and Legal Services, 'Opportunities for Hong Kong's Legal and Dispute Resolution Services in the Greater Bay Area', p. 7 <www.legco.gov.hk/yr18-19/english/panels/ajls/papers/ajls20190325cb4-665-4-e.pdf>.

68 Hwee Hwee Teh and Justin Yeo, 'The Singapore International Commercial Court in Action: Illustrations from the First Case' (2016), p. 28; Singapore Academy of Law Journal, pp. 692, 708.

69 Legal Profession Act (Chap 161), s 36P(1), <https://sso.agc.gov.sg/Act/LPA1966#pr36P->.

70 Ibid., s 36P(2).

cases held by Chinese courts.[71] Thus, to enhance the global competitiveness of the CICC, it is desirable to admit foreign lawyers to participate in lawsuits.

Moreover, foreign arbitration institutions are yet to be introduced to the one-stop dispute resolution platform. The thing underlying this situation is the legal barrier that prevents foreign arbitration institutions from entering the Chinese arbitration service market. According to the *Arbitration Law of China (ALC)*, a valid arbitration agreement must reach a consensus in the designation of an arbitration commission which should be registered at a competent Chinese authority.[72] Thus, in order to introduce foreign arbitration institutions to the CICC one-stop dispute resolution platform, rules that apply especially to the CICC mechanism need to be formulated to break through the stipulation of the *ALC*.

It should be noted that China employs an increasingly open attitude toward foreign entry into the Chinese legal service market. This can be exemplified by the fact that the Lin-gang Area of the Shanghai Free Trade Zone has served as the first-mover to allow foreign arbitration institutions to establish branches in its territory from 2020 to settle civil and commercial disputes related to international commerce, maritime or investment.[73] This maps the way forward for the CICC to promote further liberalisation by incorporating foreign arbitration and mediation institutions into the one-stop dispute resolution mechanism.[74]

Apart from the aspects discussed above, proceeding language is a potential area calling for change. English is the prevalent language of international trade, and thus, courts that aim to race in the adjudication business market need to attract international commercial disputes by conducting their proceedings in English as a "selling point".[75] Considering the fact that most international commercial courts/chambers use English rather than their respective national language as the official language, it is necessary for the CICC to stay in line with prevalent global practice.

C. The Recognition and Enforcement of Chinese Judgments Need to Be Promoted

International commercial courts settle cross-border commercial disputes. This is associated with the fact that the assets of the parties to a case may not be located in the country of the involved international commercial court, thus generating the issue of the recognition and enforcement of judgments.[76] Unlike international arbitral awards that can be recognised and enforced under the *New York Convention*, court judgments are not ensured recognition and enforcement by an equivalent treaty. Thus, the recognition and enforcement of judgments is crucial to the viability of international commercial courts, a chal

---

71 Civil Procedural Law of China (n 23), Art. 263.

72 Arbitration Law of China, Arts. 10 and 16 <http://english.mofcom.gov.cn/aarticle/policyrelease/internationalpolicy/200705/20070504715852.html>.

73 See Linklaters, 'Overseas Arbitration Institutions able to administer Foreign-Related Arbitrations in Shanghai Lin-Gang Pilot Free Trade Zone from January 2020', <www.linklaters.com/en/insights/publications/asia-news/asia-dispute-resolution/2020/overseas-arbitration-institutions-able-to-administer-foreign-related-arbitrations-in-shanghai>.

74 See Lin Jingchu, 'Improving the "Belt and Road" One-stop Dispute Resolution Mechanism' (People's Court Daily, 28 August 2019), <http://rmfyb.chinacourt.org/paper/html/2019-08/28/content_159456.htm?div=-1>.

75 Kramer and Sorabji (n 4), p. 5.

76 Anselmo Reyes, 'Recognition and Enforcement of Interlocutory and Final Judgments of the Singapore International Commercial Court' (2015), p. 2; Journal of International and Comparative Law, pp. 337, 338.

lenge that is also faced by the CICC.[77] At present, the available routes to the recognition and enforcement of Chinese judgments are bilateral treaties and the reciprocity principle. As of September 2018, China had concluded 20 judicial assistance treaties related to commercial matters; of these, 18 had been effective.[78] The insufficiency of judicial assistance treaties in commercial matters leads inevitably to the reliance of the recognition and enforcement of CICC judgments on the reciprocity principle.

Reciprocity contains *de facto* reciprocity and *de jure* reciprocity. The former requires the existence of a precedent to demonstrate that a Chinese judgment has been recognised and enforced in a foreign jurisdiction or the other way round. In practice, Chinese courts have applied the *de facto* reciprocity principle prudently.[79] This casts doubts on the reliance on reciprocity to support the recognition and enforcement of CICC judgments.

Considering the aforesaid problem, Chinese authorities need to promote the recognition and enforcement of Chinese judgments in overseas jurisdictions so as to pave the way for the further internationalisation of the CICC. In fact, China has been on the track to do so. Over recent years, the SPC has increased communication with its sophisticated overseas counterparts to transplant their experience in international commercial dispute resolution into the Chinese legal soil.[80] Most recently, the SPC concluded a Memorandum of Guidance with the Supreme Court of Singapore in August 2018 to promote the recognition and enforcement of money judgments in commercial cases, which set a template for the achievement of similar judicial cooperation with other courts worldwide.[81]

Moreover, positive changes have emerged in the promotion of judicial reciprocity. In the context of the BRI, in 2015, the SPC indicated its plan to promote the conclusion of bilateral and multilateral judicial assistance agreements so as to promote judicial reciprocity with BRI-related countries.[82] In 2016 and 2017, Chinese courts recognised the judgments made by the Singapore High Court and a US court respectively, thereby using the reciprocity principle to recognise and enforce civil judgments of Singapore and the US for the first time.[83] Moreover, in the second China-Association of Southeast Asian Nations held in 2017, the joint declaration established a broad reciprocal relationship, under which signatory countries without concluding international treaties of recognising and enforcing foreign civil and commercial judgments could be presumed to have a reciprocal relationship between each other, provided there is no precedent for refusing to recognise and enforce

---

77 Zhengxin Huo and Man Yip, 'Comparing the International Commercial Courts of China with the Singapore International Commercial Court' (2019), p. 68; International and Comparative Law Quarterly, pp. 903, 935.

78 Ministry of Foreign Affairs of China, 'List of Judicial Assistance Treaty Concluded by China', <http:// new.fmprc.gov.cn/web/ziliao_674904/tytj_674911/tyfg_674913/t1215630.shtml>.

79 See Qisheng He, 'The Recognition and Enforcement of Foreign Judgments Between the United States and China: A Study of Sanlian v Robinson' (2014), p. 6; Tsinghua China Law Review, pp. 23, 35–37.

80 See Yin (n 20).

81 Memorandum of Guidance Between the Supreme People's Court of China and the Supreme Court of Singapore on Recognition and Enforcement of Money Judgments in Commercial Cases, <www.supremecourt .gov.sg/docs/default-source/default-document-library/spc-mog-english-version---signed.pdf>.

82 Several Opinions of the Supreme People's Court on Providing Judicial Services and Safeguards for the Construction of the Belt and Road <http://www.lawinfochina.com/Display.aspx?lib=law&Cgid=251003>.

83 See Gareth Thomas, Dominic Geiser and Rachel Yu, 'Chinese Court Recognises a US Commercial Judgment for the First Time Based on Principle of Reciprocity' (Herbert Smith Freehills Notes, 22 September 2017), <https://hsfnotes.com/asiadisputes/2017/09/22/chinese-court-recognises-a-us-commercial-judgment -for-the-first-time-based-on-principle-of-reciprocity/>.

civil and commercial judgments on the ground of reciprocity.[84] Also, China joined the *Hague Choice of Court Convention* in 2017, under which signatory countries are bound to recognise judgments made by the chosen courts. Most recently, China became a member state of the *Convention on the Recognition and Enforcement of Foreign Judgments in Civil or Commercial Matters* in 2019. The afore-discussed progress can promote the recognition and enforcement of Chinese judgments in foreign countries and *vice versa*. Considering China's willingness and effort, there is solid ground to expect the development of the recognition and enforcement of CICC judgments in the foreseeable future.

IV. Concluding Remarks

Globalisation has boosted the prosperity of international trade and has, in turn, sharpened the need for cross-border commercial dispute resolution. Even though international arbitration remains the primary resort, international commercial courts have emerged worldwide to provide an alternative resolution. Following the global trend, China established the CICC in 2018 to settle BRI-related international commercial disputes and seek greater discourse in the harmonisation of *lex mercatoria*.

The establishment of the CICC has been associated with a number of remarkable innovations such as the introduction of foreign legal experts to the ICEC, the mediation power granted to the ICEC experts, and the incorporation of ADR mechanisms into the CICC litigation process, thus signifying a remarkable step forward in the development of China's judicial system.

Compared to its global competitors, however, the CICC still has room for improvement for the furtherance of internationalisation. This typically lies in the areas of jurisdiction, judge appointment, proceeding language and the recognition and enforceability of CICC judgments. Notwithstanding the challenges and statutory impediments, Chinese authorities have been on the track to promote the further internationalisation of the CICC, such as through broadening judicial cooperation. Given this, the future of China as an emerging power in the international commercial dispute resolution arena to generate impacts on the BRI *lex mercatoria* is well worth expecting.

---

84 See CICC, 'The Nanning Declaration at the 2nd China-ASEAN Justice Forum', <http://cicc.court.gov .cn/html/1/219/208/209/800.html>.

CHAPTER 8

Cultural and Linguistic Sensitivity in International Arbitration

Simon Croall and James M. Turner[1]

I. Introduction

What follows is said to be the transcript of a recent radio conversation between a US warship and Canadian authorities:

> *Americans: Please divert your course 15 degrees to the North to avoid a collision.*
> *Canadians: Recommend you divert YOUR course 15 degrees to the South to avoid a collision.*
> *Americans: This is the Captain of a US Navy ship. I say again, divert YOUR course.*
> *Canadians: No. I say again, you divert YOUR course.*
> *Americans: This is the aircraft carrier USS Lincoln, the second largest ship in the United States' Atlantic fleet. We are accompanied by three destroyers, three cruisers and numerous support vessels. I demand that YOU change your course 15 degrees north, that's one five degrees north, or countermeasures will be undertaken to ensure the safety of this ship.*
> *Canadians: This is a lighthouse. Your call.*

This conversation is of course untrue. It is a version of a joke that has been around for more than 90 years.[2] A moment's thought is all that is needed to realise that it is obvious (if entertaining) nonsense. Yet when one of the current authors told this joke at a 2019 conference held in a Far East country not known for its love of the United States, a show of hands revealed a majority of those present to believe it.

The following story, by contrast, is both closer to home and true:

> In a London arbitration in the mid-2010s, in a dispute between a Chinese shipyard and a European buyer, a shipyard employee, a young sub-manager in the design department, was being cross-examined by the advocate for the buyer – through an interpreter – about the authorship of an email. The witness's evidence was that he wrote it; the advocate challenged that evidence, suggesting that its English was far too good for him to have done so; the witness bridled and insisted that he was its author.
>
> At this point the chairman of the tribunal, a very senior retired judge, obviously thought that he had the short answer to this debate. He interrupted to ask: *"But how could you have typed an email in English using a Chinese keyboard?"*
>
> The long silence that followed reflected the perfect storm of cultural dissonance stirred up by these exchanges:

1 Quadrant Chambers, London.
2 See a version of this conversation https://en.wikipedia.org/wiki/Lighthouse_and_naval_vessel_urban
_legend#History, accessed 26 March 2022.

DOI: 10.4324/9781003160298-10

1) The witness, as an employee, driven by loyalty to his employer to say what he thought was expected of him.

2) The same witness was reluctant to lose face by accepting that his English was not good enough to have written the email.

3) The all-too-common English assumption that spoken ability in a language inevitably correlates with written ability in that language, and that a non-native speaker giving evidence through an interpreter is either incompetent in English or deliberately hiding behind the interpreter to give themselves more time to think.

4) An assumption, on the part of the arbitrator, that keyboards in China do not have the Western alphabet on them, whereas in fact Chinese is often typed on Western keyboards using the *pinyin* system.

5) The deference accorded to older and more senior individuals in Chinese society, added to the reluctance to cause your interlocutor to lose face. These combined to make the witness reluctant to explain why the arbitrator's question was founded on ignorance.

Those of us who practise as advocates and arbitrators in international commercial arbitration, no doubt pride ourselves on our well-developed sensitivity to cultural and linguistic differences. Yet this example shows that such pride may be misplaced and that there is good reason – and every necessity – for all involved in the process of resolving international disputes to reflect more deeply.

After all, the very perception that one is aware of and tolerant of differences must carry with it recognition that there exist real differences in the way different people from different commercial worlds and cultures may react or respond to the same situation. Indeed, that perception may even carry with it an element of intolerance – or else there is nothing for us to tolerate.

In this chapter, the authors pose the following questions: first, why does or should cultural and linguistic sensitivity matter in the arbitral process? Second, what does it actually mean to be "sensitive" in this sense? In particular, is this "sensitivity" a passive or an active state of mind? Third, what practical consequences does or should it have? Should those practical consequences be left to the lawyers, or should the Tribunal itself be involved?

There is a limit to the extent to which this chapter can explore these questions. The current authors are lawyers, and not social scientists, linguisticians or psychologists. Our evidence base is limited, by and large, to observations made, over several decades, in English-language arbitrations conducted along conventional Anglo-Saxon adversarial lines, often between Far Eastern and European parties.

Neither of those factors undermines the enquiry, however; if anything, they allow it to be seen in sharper focus. Why does linguistic and cultural sensitivity matter?

II. Why Does Linguistic and Cultural Sensitivity Matter?

Every professional participant in the arbitral process would (or should) wish to ensure that the parties, their representatives, witnesses, the Tribunal and everyone else involved in the process are treated courteously and with respect.

That may – and is capable of being – no more than good manners. But that is not to imply that courtesy and respect can or should be confined to the superficial. We should remind ourselves that in most arbitrations – in the Anglo-Saxon tradition at least – one party must win and the other must lose.

This is not necessarily the case in Chinese arbitration, where there is scope for the tribunal to recommend a settlement to the parties, which the parties can then consider whether to accept or reject.

> In a London shipbuilding arbitration in the early 2010s, the owner of the shipyard came to give evidence. His answer to nearly every question – to the bafflement of the English lawyers and arbitrators – was that the fair resolution to the dispute was a particular form of settlement.
>
> It turned out, of course, that he had simply assumed that a London arbitration would be like a Chinese one, and that he was trying to get the tribunal to adopt his settlement idea and propose it to the parties. But such a role on the part of the tribunal is unknown in English arbitration and so of course his pleas fell on deaf, uncomprehending ears.

Human nature being what it is, not every losing party will accept defeat with philosophical equanimity; in other words, many are likely to feel hard done by.

The goal of the linguistic and cultural sensitivity deployed by those in the arbitral process must be to eliminate any legitimate cause for a losing party to feel that it has lost because it has been misunderstood or, which is even worse, discriminated against.

Here lies the core challenge. It is essential to the process that parties and witnesses participating in arbitration are not only heard but understood. Without that understanding, there is a real risk of failing to ensure that the parties are given a fair hearing.

III. The Significance of the Issue

The UNCITRAL Model Law on International Commercial Arbitration 1985 (as amended in 2006) forms the basis for International Commercial Arbitration worldwide. A cornerstone principle is enshrined at Article 18 (*Equal treatment of parties*), stating that

> The parties shall be treated with equality and each party shall be given a full opportunity of presenting his case.

The right to a fair hearing is a core requirement of every international arbitration regime; it is designed to ensure that parties are allowed to put forward their position on the issues and to have their account of events heard and case properly understood. We see this principle in almost all arbitral regimes, e.g., Arbitration Act 1996 (UK) s 33, Hong Kong Arbitration Ordnance s 46, by the application of the model law by the Singapore International Arbitration Act s 3, Federal Arbitration Act 9 U.S.C § 306 and the Rules of the China International Economic and Trade Arbitration Commission (CIETAC), Arts 24 and 35.

The significance of this requirement cannot be overstated – compliance with it is essential if parties are to have confidence in the arbitral process and are able to accept the resulting decision.

However, compliance requires more than simply allowing a party the opportunity to set out its position in writing or orally. It also requires that the process is equipped with adequate tools so that all involved can properly understand what is being said and make a fair assessment, not only of the oral and written evidence but also of the actions and conduct of the parties which may be (or said to be) relevant to the issues.

It is obvious, for example, that it is essential that any written or oral evidence submitted by either party will require translation or interpretation as may be necessary so that the parties (through their representatives), any witnesses and the Tribunal can understand (in their mother tongue) that evidence.

The importance of the role of the translator/interpreter is often underestimated – a subject to which we will return below. However, just as the Tribunal (and the parties) will often need assistance in order to understand the actual words used by those involved in the dispute, they will often require similar assistance in understanding the actions of those involved.

Anyone involved in international arbitration will have encountered disputes between corporations, institutions and even governments from different parts of the world operating in the context of very different commercial cultures. Such differences in commercial cultures might manifest themselves in a variety of ways, for example:

1) Different attitudes to record keeping;
2) Different internal corporate governance;
3) Different responses to issues/disputes: in some commercial cultures outward signs of confrontation/disagreement will be avoided at almost all costs and in others confrontation/disagreement will be actively sought out;
4) Different modes of communication: in some cultures all potentially important communication will be in writing, in others the norm is a telephone call or face to face discussion;
5) Very considerable differences in IT setup and use.

Any experienced arbitral tribunal – in any jurisdiction – is informed in its decision-making process by its own cultural norms and expectations. As a result, invisible and frequently unacknowledged rules and assumptions develop, for example that an argumentative witness, or one who does not answer the question, has something to hide or is being deliberately evasive – a view which then licenses an arbitrator to reject, in whole or in part, other evidence which that witness has given. These unwritten rules can often play a large part in determining whether one account or another is preferred.

> In London arbitration, it is easy to think of cases where a Tribunal is invited (or pre-disposed) to prefer the case advanced by one party rather than another, because the conduct of one of the parties is said to be inconsistent/consistent with the case they now advance, or because the case advanced is not supported by documents which it is said would exist if what they were saying were correct.
>
> In such cases the Tribunal is invited to attach significance (potentially decisive significance) to the actions/practices of one party or another. If it follows such a course, it will be making a judgment as to the meaning and significance of those actions. And yet equality to the parties and their right to a fair hearing demand that such a judgment should only be made in the light of an understanding of the commercial context in which those actions took place.

The result may be that persons from the same culture or commercial background may be more likely to reflect those norms than someone from a quite different background – irrespective of the veracity of their evidence.

Fairness, therefore, demands an appreciation of cultural and commercial differences in order to make an accurate and informed (and thus fair) assessment of a witness and their evidence.

A. A Particular Issue for International Arbitration

When assessing the commercial actions of parties or the demeanour and credibility of a witness, a Tribunal (and indeed those who represent the parties in the process) will not typically have (or seek) assistance from anyone able to explain the relevant commercial culture/context.

This may not be necessary: the parties, their representatives, the witnesses and the arbitrators may all come from the same essential commercial culture. In such circumstances there is no reason to think that the action or conduct of parties will be or may be misunderstood.

However, in international arbitration it is a commonplace for the Tribunal to be composed of members from different backgrounds, or for the Tribunal to be from a different commercial background to one or more of the parties or witnesses. In this event the starting point should be that assistance in understanding the relevant commercial context may be required.

It is tempting to think that experienced arbitrators can make a sound judgment of the significance of a person's conduct or demeanour even if from a different commercial background. This may sometimes be true – but will not invariably be so, as the examples given above show.

Every member of a Tribunal, indeed everyone involved in the arbitration, is bound to be influenced by their own experiences and commercial/legal upbringing. It is inevitable he or she will instinctively see things and interpret actions through that prism. This is not a criticism – it is an inevitable reality.

The problem arises when, in interpreting those actions, the arbitrator subconsciously applies commercial/cultural norms with which they are familiar, but which do not necessarily reflect the commercial context in which the actions were taken. It is easy to say that experienced arbitrators should be trusted to have this in mind and to avoid this pitfall, but that is only possible if: first, arbitrators are aware that they may unwittingly/subconsciously assess conduct against the wrong commercial culture; and second, arbitrators are given the tools/information which would allow them to apply the right yardstick.

IV. Solutions/Recommendations

A. Acknowledge the Issue

The current authors suggest that the first and most important step is for all involved – the Tribunal, the respective legal teams, the parties and witnesses (with the guidance and encouragement of their legal teams) – to recognise the possibility (if not likelihood) that findings of fact can be influenced by commercial and cultural preconceptions.

If all are aware of and recognise the potential for misunderstanding, then there is immediately much less scope for it to occur. Arbitrators will be on guard to ensure that they are aware of – or at least do not make assumptions about – the relevant commercial and cultural context; legal teams will be astute to draw such matters to the attention of the Tribunal; and the parties, where necessary, can explain the relevant context.

- Such awareness should not be assumed. Cultural awareness is easy to achieve in the context of a talk about that very topic. It is much less obvious that it would necessarily be achieved on day 6 or 16 or 60 of the evidence in a hard-fought arbitration involving many substantive and technical issues.
- It is not enough that arbitrators are expected to be vigilant to prevent potential misunderstandings. Those representing parties in arbitrations need to be equally vigilant, to anticipate such issues and to work with the clients and witnesses to

maximise understanding of the process and the role of all within it. In an appropriate case they can then ensure that the Tribunal is provided with assistance as to the appropriate context.

B. The Need for Dialogue

Underpinning that assistance is the need for and power of dialogue. First of all, dialogue between lawyers, their clients and their witnesses is of course essential. Those who flatter themselves with the badge "international lawyer" are duty-bound to put in the hard work that goes with acting not merely as a lawyer, but as a cultural bridge between the client and the tribunal which will decide its dispute. This can involve lengthy discussion with the client well in advance of the hearing. Second, it is also important, of course, that there is dialogue between advocate and tribunal, in which cultural issues are openly addressed; as the keyboard example highlights, one cannot simply assume that all arbitrators are knowledgeable about all cultures, let alone the influence that the witness's culture will have on the evidence they have to give (and how they give it).

In addition, that dialogue, sometimes, may need to be formalised or reinforced.

C. Admit Evidence / Material of Relevant Context

Wherever there is a dispute as to how and in what context actions/conduct should be understood, consideration should be given to admitting evidence/material of the commercial/cultural context.

- Often this will involve no more than eliciting further information from existing witnesses or an interpreter and perhaps receiving short submissions or statements on the point. If necessary and disputed there may be need for material from more than one party or even cross examination.
- In some cases, expert evidence may be necessary.

What procedure is put in place to ensure fairness, minimise expense and limit costs will ultimately be a matter for the Tribunal.

These proposals are not a radical departure from current practice in many contexts. Indeed, it has long been the case in most common law jurisdictions that evidence is admissible of relevant customs and practices where they are said to be of relevance to disputes.

For example, the English commercial court has admitted evidence of different cultural/historical and commercial practices where it was regarded as important to an understanding of actions and conduct of the parties. *Berezovsky v Abramovich*[3] involved a dispute about whether a certain agreement had been made between two individuals in late 1990s Russia. The judge, Gloster J, stated this:

> The dispute between the two men has to be evaluated against the sometimes turbulent political and economic backcloth of Russia in the late 1990s and early 2000s, and in the context of the deterioration of their relationship. Nonetheless, the dispute is in essence a commercial one, which, like any other tried in this court, has to be decided on the factual evidence, both

---

3 *Berezovsky v Abramovich* [2012] EWHC 2463 (Ch), p. [38].

oral and documentary, relating to the specific transactions in issue. And, although this court necessarily views that evidence *"Under Western Eyes"*, it has to be careful about applying what it might regard as conventional Western European business standards to judge the conduct of businessmen operating in the very different, and largely unregulated, commercial and political environment of Russia at the material times. As I remind myself: *" ... this is not a story of the West of Europe".*[4]

There may be built-in limitations. The relevance of any such evidence to the issues may depend upon the applicable governing law. Equally what evidence of this kind and character may be admitted will depend upon the powers of the Tribunal and the applicable curial law.

However, if one party seeks to place emphasis on certain actions and suggest a factual or legal conclusion, such material will frequently be relevant. Under most procedural rules a Tribunal will have the power necessary to admit evidence and place sensible limitations upon that evidence.

D. Arbitrator's Culture?

It might be thought that some of the concerns in this chapter might serve as an encouragement for parties to appoint arbitrators from their own commercial culture. It ought not to do so. On the contrary, so long as the arbitral process (and those engaged in it) are aware of the potential pitfalls to which we have alluded then it ought to be unnecessary for parties to feel that they should appoint an arbitrator who is from their commercial culture. In many cases, doing so may even be counter-productive.

Good arbitrators in whom parties can have confidence and trust must have all different types of skills. No one single factor is sufficient to make a good arbitrator and no single factor (such as the commercial background of the arbitrator) should outweigh all other factors when considering who to appoint.

E. Language Differences

The receipt of evidence (written and oral) in the mother tongue of the party adducing or providing the evidence is common and is almost always interpreted into the language of the arbitration.

For all the same reasons that are applicable when interpreting conduct, it is vital that the process is not only carried out efficiently but also that the result is a translation which reliably reflects the meaning of the language used by the witness or in the document.

It is therefore important that that process is carried out by someone who is striving accurately to reflect the meaning of the words used (rather than simply to translate each word).

This will not depend solely upon the skills or qualifications of the interpreter. It will also depend upon the extent to which the interpreter has been given a proper opportunity to prepare, so as to be familiar with technical terms which are likely to be used, as well as the specific names of the various individuals and companies involved in the dispute.

---

4 Ibid., p. 38 (Gloster J)

It is all too often the case that parties who have spent time and money investing in the careful preparation of their respective cases fail to give adequate consideration to the need for a skilled and experienced interpreter – and to give that person the assistance, time and documentation necessary to prepare to do the job properly.

Parties' lawyers and arbitrators should be encouraged to focus more carefully on this important role. In particular interpreters should be given more opportunity to become familiar with the relevant material in advance of the actual process of interpretation.

Insofar as parties are required to agree a protocol for this exercise they should be encouraged to do so.

V. Conclusion

The issues and ideas canvassed in this chapter are put forward because of the need to ensure that the arbitration process is one in which the parties can reasonably and confidently expect to have their positions and arguments heard and understood.

This chapter has sought to highlight the scope for misunderstanding, for cultural dissonance and for misplaced assumption to disrupt the dispute resolution process. The current authors have suggested that the key to minimising such disruption is for there to be dialogue between the client and their advocate and between the advocate and the tribunal.

Ultimately, of course, it will remain for the Tribunal, once they have understood the material in its proper context, to determine what, if any, significance to attach to any disputed language or conduct. We are not in any way suggesting that parties' conduct should always be excused or regarded as having little effect in law; the authors simply emphasise the need to be sure that such conduct has been properly understood before a judgement is made upon its significance.

> In the arbitration in which the keyboard example occurred, the shipyard's lawyers were able to defuse the situation by getting the witness to explain the pinyin system in re-examination.
> They were also able to make submissions about aspects of Chinese social and business culture in our closing argument. All those submissions were accepted by the Tribunal.

To adapt the words of Lord Goff, a great English judge, in *Spiliada Maritime Corporation v Cansulex Ltd.*[5]: *we are all pilgrims on the road to justice. Justice asks of us all that we take off the spectacles of cultural assumption to see better the fellow human before us.*

---

5 *Spiliada Maritime Corporation v Cansulex Ltd.* [1987] AC 460, 488.

CHAPTER 9

Compulsory Consolidation in Arbitral Proceedings

An Infringement on Party Autonomy?

Lijun Liz Zhao* and Catherine Green**

I. Introduction

International commercial transactions are often complex, involving multiple parties and multiple contracts. Under many circumstances, the parties are domiciled in various countries. Maritime trade transactions are no exception. As such, commercial and maritime disputes can regularly involve a number of parties from different jurisdictions. The 2014 *OW Bunker* bankruptcy[1] and the 2021 *Suez Canal Obstruction* demonstrate the point.[2] This can give rise to parallel proceedings involving inter-related contracts, the same or some of the same parties and related issues in dispute, but with no single arbitration agreement binding all parties to that series of contracts which would otherwise result in a single arbitration proceeding.

The same dispute or several closely related disputes may risk an outcome where there are inconsistent, if not conflicting, decisions and awards, causing problems in practice for

* Dr Lijun Liz Zhao, Senior Lecturer in Corporate and Commercial Law, City, University of London.
** Catherine Green, Arbitrator, Executive Director of the New Zealand International Arbitration Centre (NZIAC). Acknowledgement: Both authors contributed equally to this research. This research was supported by the Higher Education Innovation Fund [HEIF2020LZ] and Major Project of the China National Social Fund [15ZDB178]. We would like to thank reviewers for their thoughtful comments and efforts towards improving this research. All errors remain our own. All internet-based resources were last accessed on 1 March 2022.

1 OW Bunker (OWB), a Danish marine fuel (bunker) company, was the world's largest bunker supplier until its collapse in 2014. It was an intermediary supplier of bunkers to ships: in many cases, it obtained fuel from wholesale suppliers on credit. As such, at the time of bankruptcy of OWB, hundreds of shipowners were impacted. They found themselves subject to double liability for the fuel cost for the supplier as there were a number of parallel proceedings related to fuel cost involving OWB in many jurisdictions, including the UK and the USA.

2 In March 2021, the Suez Canal was blocked for six days after the grounding of a mega container vessel 'Ever Given'. This incident impacted on a number of parties, located in different jurisdictions: firstly, as regards ownership, the ship Ever Given is owned by Shoei Kisen Kaisha (a ship owning and leasing subsidiary of the large Japanese shipbuilding company Imabari Shipbuilding). Secondly, as regards chartering, the ship is time chartered and operated by the container transportation and shipping company Evergreen Marine, headquartered in Taiwan. Thirdly, as regards ship registration and daily management, Ever Given is registered in Panama, its technical management is undertaken by the German ship management company BSM and the Crew include 25 seafarers, all Indian, Lastly, as regards ownership of onboard cargos, about 80% of cargos are from China, to be shipped to Rotterdam, and the vessel itself and its cargo are insured, separately. The UK Club has insured the owner of Ever Given for certain third-party liabilities.

DOI: 10.4324/9781003160298-11

parties and their legal advisers. Much research has discussed the consolidation of parallel proceedings by arbitration agreements in the area of international investment law.[3] However, scant attention has been paid to these problems from the standpoint of commercial and maritime law.[4] This is where this research kicks in.

In order to fill this gap, this chapter endeavours to map out a limited number of circumstances, under which compulsory consolidation is allowed. It also evaluates the issues and difficulties associated with the consolidation. Given that consolidation by the parties' agreement is not controversial[5] on the basis of party autonomy, this aspect of the consolidation will not be analysed here. Instead, this chapter probes into the more controversial aspect, namely of compulsory consolidation. In other words, consolidation in the absence of an agreement to arbitrate.

II. The Need to Mitigate Challenges for the Business Community in Multi-Party Disputes

A. An Overview of Compulsory Consolidation

The case of *Compania Espanola de Petroleos SA v Nereus Shipping SA* (1975)[6] demonstrates how the challenges outlined above might arise for the business community in the transnational commercial and maritime law context. In that case, a three-year charterparty was entered into by Nereus Shipping SA (a Liberian corporation; agent for the owners) ("Nereus") and Hidrocarburos Derivados SA (a Venezuelan corporation engaged in the oil business) ("Hideca") for the transportation of petroleum products. Six months later, an addendum was agreed between these first two parties and a third party, Compania Espanola de Petroleos SA ("CEPSA"), guaranteeing the charterparty. A dispute arose following the alleged default by Hideca in its performance under the agreement during the third year. Nereus initiated two separate arbitration proceedings – one against Hideca, and the other against CEPSA. This scenario then gave rise to procedural disputes as to whether CEPSA was also bound by the agreement to arbitrate in the charterparty (to which it was not a signatory), and whether the two separate arbitrations initiated by Nereus could be consolidated by court order.[7]

The United States Federal Arbitration Act does not clearly provide for compulsory consolidated arbitration, and the US case law is not very clear on the point. It is noted that,

---

3 Bernardo M. Cremades, and Ignacio Madalena, 'Parallel Proceedings in International Arbitration', *Arbitration International*, 24(2008)4, pp. 507–540.

4 T. Evan Schaeffer. 'Compulsory Consolidation of Commercial Arbitration Disputes', Saint Louis University Law Journal 33(1989), p. 495.

5 Philip Allen Lacovara, 'Class Action Arbitrations – the Challenge for the Business Community', *Arbitration International*, 24(2008)4, pp. 541–560.

6 527 F2d 966 (2d Cir 1975).

7 The Court in that case found that the addendum incorporated the charterparty and the accompanying arbitration clause by reference and upheld an order to consolidate two arbitrations which had been initiated under the US Federal Arbitration Act. This case has not been without criticism and subsequent judgments have clarified that Federal Courts do not have authority to order consolidation absent express consent: See for example *Weyerhaeuser Co v Western Seas Shipping Co* 743 F2d 635 (9th Cir 1984).

in the case of *Nereus* (1975), the US Second Circuit Court supported the consolidation of arbitrations where certain factors were present.[8] Those factors included:

1) Whether the proceedings involve common questions of law and fact;
2) Whether the possibility exists of conflicting awards or inconsistent results;
3) Whether a substantial right might be prejudiced if separate arbitral proceedings are conducted;
4) Whether a substantial right might be prejudiced if consolidated proceedings are conducted.[9]

However, the US Supreme Court reversed the aforementioned approach in the *Nereus* case which had been developed by the Second Circuit and denied consolidation of arbitrations in the subsequent *Moses H. Cone Memorial Hosp. v. Mercury Construction Corp* (1983) case.[10] On that basis, current US law does not allow multi-party arbitrations to be compulsorily consolidated by court order.

In the earlier case, it is easy to see how the relevant set of circumstances lent itself to a desire on the part of Nereus to consolidate the two separate arbitrations. A key objective of consolidation is to aid in promoting efficiency of process and to avoid inconsistency in decisions between what would otherwise be entirely independent and disconnected arbitration proceedings relating to the same project or chain of contracts.

However, and putting aside the specific facts in the case of *Nereus*, an express agreement to consolidate after a dispute has arisen cannot be assured. To address this limitation, some possible solutions are employed.

The first type of solution is that a limited number of pioneering legislatures and national courts have been willing to provide for or order the consolidation of arbitral proceedings in the absence of party consent (as in the case of *Nereus*).[11] In addition, the second type of solution is that many arbitration rules provide for a form of compulsory consolidation.[12] The rest of this work evaluates these two solutions.

B. Party Autonomy

A key issue embedded in consolidation is that this approach, whilst perhaps positively encouraging much desired efficiency of process, necessarily infringes on a key pillar of arbitration, namely "party autonomy", and the underlying concept of "consent". Since arbitration is commonly referred to as a "creature of contract", consent to arbitration is an

---

8 *Compania Espanola de Petroleos, S.A. v. Nereus Shipping, S.A.*, 527 F.2d 966 (2d Cir. 1975), cert. denied, 426 U.S. 936 (1976); see also *Elmarina, Inc. v. Comexas, N.V.*, 679 F. Supp. 388 (S.D.N.Y. 1988); *Cable Belt Conveyors, Inc. v. Alumina Partners of Jamaica*, 669 F. Supp. 577 (S.D.N.Y. 1987); *Sociedad Anonima de Navegacion Petrolera v. Cia. de Petroleos de Chile S.A.*, 634 F. Supp. 805 (S.D.N.Y. 1986); *Shoyo Shipping Co. v. Shipmair, B.V.*, 1986 A.M.C. 2374 (S.D.N.Y. 1986). Cf. *Ore & Chem. Corp. v. Stinnes Interoil, Inc.*, 606 F. Supp. 1510, 1512-13 (S.D.N.Y. 1985)

9 ibid. See also T. Evan Schaeffer. 'Compulsory Consolidation of Commercial Arbitration Disputes', Saint Louis University Law Journal 33 (1989), pp. 502–503.

10 460 U.S. 1 (1983).

11 See details in the analysis in following sections.

12 A full review of all instances of consolidation across global arbitration institutions falls outside the scope of this paper. However, it is worth observing that the inclusion of consolidation provisions in institutional arbitration rules, although not introduced by all institutions, is perhaps now the norm rather than the exception.

indispensable feature of arbitration.[13] The importance and centrality of party autonomy is reflected in Article 1(e) of the UNCITRAL Model Law on International Commercial Arbitration:

> [W]here a provision of this Law refers to the fact that the parties have agreed or that they may agree or in any other way refers to an agreement of the parties, such agreement includes any arbitration rules referred to in that agreement.

C. Scope and Aims of this Chapter

This chapter examines whether this infringement, by virtue of compulsory consolidation of arbitration, is justifiable or whether it is a step too far, by reference to two mechanisms for consolidation, namely, court ordered consolidation under the Arbitration Acts of the Netherlands and Hong Kong, and consolidation under the LCIA Arbitration Rules ("LCIA Rules") (consolidation under institutional rules).

The Dutch and Hong Kong legislative positions and the LCIA Rules, whilst not the only examples available, provide clear and well-established examples of court ordered consolidation and consolidation under institutional rules. In that regard, both provide a useful demonstration of how each of these approaches work in practice. Hence, these are chosen here for our analysis.

III. Court Ordered Consolidation

In most jurisdictions, compulsory consolidation of arbitrations involving multiple parties is not permitted unless there is consent from all parties concerned. The US and China are examples of jurisdictions falling within this category.

With respect to the US, as explained above, the form of compulsory arbitration that was endorsed by the US Second Circuit in the *Nereus* case (1975) was subsequently overruled by the US Supreme Court in the *Moses H. Cone Memorial Hosp. v. Mercury Construction Corp* (1983) case.[14]

Turning to China, the Arbitration Law has not provided for compulsory consolidation;[15] rather, the Chinese Supreme Court issued a Judicial Interpretation of the Arbitration Law in 2006, which is legally binding throughout China. Although the 2004 draft version (i.e. green paper) of the Judicial Interpretation,[16] published for public comment, considered the introduction of compulsory consolidation in commercial arbitration in China,[17] the final version of the Judicial Interpretation deleted the draft provision on compulsory

---

13 T. Evan Schaeffer, 'Compulsory Consolidation of Commercial Arbitration Disputes', Saint Louis University Law Journal 33 (1989), p. 496.

14 See the analysis in the former section.

15 National Congress of PR. China, Arbitration Law of the People's Republic of China (enacted in 1994, amended in 2008 and 2017).

16 Supreme People's Court of China, Interpretation of the Supreme People's Court on Several Issues Concerning the Application of the Arbitration Law of the People's Republic of China (Draft for Public Comment) (equivalent to a green paper), 2004, www.chinacourt.org/article/detail/2004/07/id/125211.shtml.

17 Ibid, Article 15.

consolidation.[18] That is to say, Chinese law is still silent regarding consolidated arbitration by court order.

Nevertheless, such a regime remains up for debate in China and potentially will be enacted in the future. As such, it is of great value to investigate the law and practice of the court ordered consolidation elsewhere.

Although not widely favoured,[19] some jurisdictions have enacted legislation that allows for the consolidation of arbitral proceedings absent party consent. However, it should be noted that only a small number of national laws allow compulsory consolidation by court order.

An example of this form of legislation that clearly permits compulsory consolidation is the Dutch Arbitration Act 1986, which empowers the president of the District Court in Amsterdam to order the whole or partial consolidation of two or more connected arbitrations in the Netherlands, unless the parties agree otherwise.[20] Article 1046 of the Dutch Arbitration Act provides "Consolidation of Arbitral Proceedings" as following:

1. If arbitral proceedings have been commenced before an arbitral tribunal in the Netherlands concerning a subject matter which is connected with the subject matter of arbitral proceedings commenced before another arbitral tribunal in the Netherlands, any of the parties may, unless the parties have agreed otherwise, request the President of the District Court in Amsterdam to order a consolidation of the proceedings.

2. The President may wholly or partially grant or refuse the request, after he has given all parties and the arbitrators an opportunity to be heard. His decision shall be communicated in writing to all parties and the arbitral tribunals involved.

3. If the President orders consolidation in full, the parties shall in consultation with each other appoint one arbitrator or an uneven number of arbitrators and determine the procedural rules which shall apply to the consolidated proceedings. If, within the period of time prescribed by the President, the parties have not reached agreement on the above, the President shall, at the request of any of the parties, appoint the arbitrator or arbitrators and, if necessary, determine the procedural rules which shall apply to the consolidated proceedings. The President shall determine the remuneration for the work already carried out by the arbitrators whose mandate is terminated by reason of the full consolidation.

4. If the President orders partial consolidation, he shall decide which disputes shall be consolidated. The President shall, if the parties fail to agree within the period of time prescribed by him, at the request of any of the parties, appoint the arbitrator or arbitrators and determine which rules shall apply to the consolidated proceedings. In this event the arbitral tribunals before which arbitrations have already been commenced shall suspend those arbitrations. The award of the arbitral tribunal appointed for the consolidated arbitration shall be communicated in writing

---

18 Supreme People's Court of China, Interpretation of the Supreme People's Court concerning Some Issues on Application of the Arbitration Law of the People's Republic of China, Interpretation No. 7 [2006] of the Supreme People's Court, August 2008.

19 Chi Manjiao, 'The Fading of Compulsory Consolidation of Arbitration: A Fight between the Principles of Efficiency and Party Autonomy in International Commercial Arbitration', (2008) 4 Fudan Journal of the Humanities and Social Sciences, p. 119.

20 Code of Civil Procedure 1986 (The Netherlands), Article 1046 (1).

to the other arbitral tribunals involved. Upon receipt of this award, these arbitral tribunals shall continue the arbitrations commenced before them and decide in accordance with the award rendered in the consolidated proceedings.

5. The provisions of Article 1027(4) shall apply accordingly in the cases mentioned in paragraphs (3) and (4) above.

6. An award rendered under paragraphs (3) and (4) above shall be subject to appeal to a second arbitral tribunal if and to the extent that all parties involved in the consolidated proceedings have agreed upon such an appeal.[21]

Similar to the Dutch Arbitration Act, it is worth noting that Hong Kong, one of the global international trade hubs and popular seats of arbitration, has also adopted a similar approach. Under Section 2 of Schedule 2 to the Hong Kong Arbitration Ordinance (Cap 609), "Consolidation of arbitrations" is prescribed as follows: [22]

(1) If, in relation to 2 or more arbitral proceedings, it appears to the Court—
 (a) that a common question of law or fact arises in both or all of them;
 (b) that the rights to relief claimed in those arbitral proceedings are in respect of or arise out of the same transaction or series of transactions; or
 (c) that for any other reason it is desirable to make an order under this section, the Court may, on the application of any party to those arbitral proceedings—
 (d) order those arbitral proceedings—
  (i) to be consolidated on such terms as it thinks just; or
  (ii) to be heard at the same time or one immediately after another; or
 (e) order any of those arbitral proceedings to be stayed until after the determination of any other of them.

(2) If the Court orders arbitral proceedings to be consolidated under subsection (1)(d)(i) or to be heard at the same time or one immediately after another under subsection (1)(d)(ii), the Court has the power—
 (a) to make consequential directions as to the payment of costs in those arbitral proceedings; and
 (b) if—
  (i) all parties to those arbitral proceedings are in agreement as to the choice of arbitrator for those arbitral proceedings, to appoint that arbitrator; or
  (ii) the parties cannot agree as to the choice of arbitrator for those arbitral proceedings, to appoint an arbitrator for those arbitral proceedings (and, in the case of arbitral proceedings to be heard at the same time or one immediately after another, to appoint the same arbitrator for those arbitral proceedings).

(3) If the Court makes an appointment of an arbitrator under subsection (2) for the arbitral proceedings to be consolidated or to be heard at the same time or one immediately after another, any appointment of any other arbitrator that has been made for any of those arbitral proceedings ceases to have effect for all purposes on and from the appointment under subsection (2).

---

21 Ibid.

22 See Section 2 of Schedule 2 to the Hong Kong Arbitration Ordinance (Cap 609). www.elegislation.gov.hk/hk/cap609?xpid=ID_1438403522100_002.

(4) The arbitral tribunal hearing the arbitral proceedings that are consolidated under subsection (1)(d)(i) has the power under sections 74 and 75 in relation to the costs of those arbitral proceedings.

(5) If 2 or more arbitral proceedings are heard at the same time or one immediately after another under subsection (1)(d)(ii), the arbitral tribunal—

    (a) has the power under sections 74 and 75 only in relation to the costs of those arbitral proceedings that are heard by it; and

    (b) accordingly, does not have the power to order a party to any of those arbitral proceedings that are heard at the same time or one immediately after another to pay the costs of a party to any other of those proceedings unless the arbitral tribunal is the same tribunal hearing all of those arbitral proceedings.

(6) An order, direction or decision of the Court under this section is not subject to appeal.[23]

The introduction of legislation providing for consolidation in the absence of party consent, however, remains uncommon (the Netherlands and Hong Kong being outliers in this regard)[24] and the willingness of national courts to interfere in party autonomy by ordering consolidation is also rare. To avoid repetition, the analysis below will illustrate the court ordered compulsory consolidation approach by investigating the Dutch approach. Similar analysis applies to the Hong Kong.

Firstly, according to Article 1046 (1) of the Dutch Arbitration Act 1986, the Dutch approach means that, rather than there being no consolidation absent agreement of the parties, the court may order consolidation unless there is agreement to the contrary (where both sets of arbitral proceedings are seated in the Netherlands).

Secondly, amendments approved on 27 May 2014,[25] permit the parties to nominate a third party (this might be for instance an arbitral institution) to determine the party's application to consolidate. That third party's power is broader than the Court's, in that the third party nominated may also determine a consolidation application where one arbitration is seated in the Netherlands and the other is seated elsewhere.[26]

Moreover, under the Dutch statutory regime, not only can the District Court consolidate proceedings but, where there is no agreement between the parties as to how to proceed, the Court can also determine the procedure to be followed.[27] This, on its face, appears to be a radical departure from traditional arbitration which is based entirely on the agreement of the parties.

The result of this approach is to give the Dutch District Court the power to not only enforce arbitration agreements but also to effectively reformulate them.[28] This means of addressing the question of consolidation strikes at the very essence of the arbitral process in that it expressly overrides party autonomy.

---

23 Ibid.

24 Illustrated by the aforementioned case *Compania Espanola de Petroleos SA v Nereus Shipping.*

25 Gerard Meijer and Bo Ra Hoebeke 'The new Dutch Arbitration Act and the new NAI Arbitration Rules' (*Lexology*, 15 January 2015), www.lexology.com/library/detail.aspx?g=32745dfa-99b2-42f3-b691 -c0cecb75328f.

26 Code of Civil Procedure 1986 (The Netherlands), Article 1046 (1).

27 Code of Civil Procedure 1986 (The Netherlands), Article 1046 (4).

28 Juliska M Aponte, 'Compulsory Consolidation of International Arbitral Proceedings: Effects on Pacta Sunt Servanda and the General Arbitral Process', (1994) 2(1) Tulane Journal of International and Comparative Law, pp. 223, 225.

There is a "right to opt out" of the court ordered consolidation provision by means of contractual agreement and, in theory, a party who agrees to arbitration where the expressly chosen seat will bring the arbitral process under the Dutch Arbitration Act, might be said to have consented to the possibility of a court order for consolidation under that chosen law. However, the reality is that it is highly unlikely that a party would necessarily be aware of those legal procedural implications at the time of entering into the agreement; as a result, such parties would not exercise the *theoretical* "right to opt out" of the statutory court ordered consolidation provisions.

A notoriously short period of time is typically allocated to the agreement of a model arbitration clause, particularly where standard form agreements are used as a basis for a contract, with boilerplate dispute resolution clauses being part and parcel of that template agreement. In reality, the likelihood of contracting parties turning their minds to specifically negotiating the clause in a comprehensive way is relatively low. Although the parties might discuss the governing law, seat, or applicable institutional rules, it is certainly not a given that such a discussion would engage in any detail as to specific procedural implications of opting for one seat over another.

On that basis, unless the parties had specific, previous experience in arbitration under the Dutch law which had also raised the question of consolidation, it would be unlikely they could be said to have knowingly consented to such a regime governing and allowing court ordered consolidation.

On the other hand, it should be recognised that arbitration legislation typically does provide for a default procedure to apply absent party agreement (usually based on the UNCITRAL Model Law on International Commercial Arbitration). It is, therefore, arguable that the step taken by the Netherlands to include provision for consolidation and for the procedure to be pursuant to court order in the absence of the parties' consent, is perhaps not as radical as it appears at first blush. After all, absent agreement, any number of other procedural rules will be applied to the proceeding.

Nonetheless, where parties have turned their minds to the arbitration process itself and have consented and agreed to adopt that course vis-à-vis a particular contractual relationship but not another, it is difficult to reconcile "party autonomy" in such a case with the approach adopted by the Dutch legislature or its equivalent.

IV. Consolidation under Institutional Rules

Absent legislation, the starting point is that consolidation cannot be ordered or mandated without the agreement of the parties. Unlike the above stated starting point, there are now many examples of institutional rules which include provisions with respect to consolidation.

For the purposes of this chapter, the authors have scrutinised just one by way of example, namely, the LCIA Arbitration Rules,[29] as the LCIA Arbitration Rules are both relatively well-established and exemplify the approach adopted by many other arbitral institutions. For instance, the China International Economic and Trade Arbitration Commission (CIETAC) provides for a number of circumstances where multi-party arbitrations can

---

29 LCIA, Arbitration Rules, www.lcia.org/Dispute_Resolution_Services/lcia-arbitration-rules-2020.aspx #Article%2022.

be consolidated in accordance with Article 19 of the CIETAC 2015 Arbitration Rules; however, all these circumstances are based on the consent of multiple parties.[30] As such, in this section, the LCIA Arbitration Rules are used to illustrate this type of consolidated arbitration under institutional rules.

Article 22.7(ii) of the LCIA Arbitration Rules 2020 states that the Arbitral Tribunal, with the approval of the LCIA Court, shall have the power to order

> the consolidation of the arbitration with one or more other arbitrations subject to the LCIA Rules and commenced under the same arbitration agreement or any compatible arbitration agreement(s) and either between the same disputing parties or arising out of the same transaction or series of related transactions, provided that no arbitral tribunal has yet been formed by the LCIA Court for such other arbitration(s) or, if already formed, that such arbitral tribunal(s) is(are) composed of the same arbitrators.[31]

In accordance with Article 22.7 of the LCIA Arbitration Rules, the arbitral tribunal, with the approval of the LCIA Court, has a *discretion*[32] to order the consolidation of an arbitration with another upon the application of any party (a) where there is written agreement to consolidate; or (b) where the other arbitration is also subject to the LCIA Arbitration Rules and is commenced under either the same arbitration agreement or a compatible arbitration agreement and is either between the *same* parties or arising out of the *same transaction or series of related transactions*, subject to the proviso that an arbitral tribunal has not yet been appointed for the other arbitration or, if it has, that the arbitral tribunal is composed of the same arbitrators.

In addition, the LCIA Court is similarly empowered to make an order for consolidation pursuant to Article 22.8 of the LCIA Arbitration Rules. This Article provides that

> **22.8** Without prejudice to the generality of Article 22.7, the LCIA Court may:
>
> (i) consolidate an arbitration with one or more other arbitrations into a single arbitration subject to the LCIA Rules where all the parties to the arbitrations to be consolidated so agree in writing; and
> (ii) determine, after giving the parties a reasonable opportunity to state their views, that two or more arbitrations, subject to the LCIA Rules and commenced under the same arbitration agreement or any compatible arbitration agreement(s) and either between the same disputing parties or arising out of the same transaction or series of related transactions, shall be consolidated to form one single arbitration subject to the LCIA Rules, provided that no arbitral tribunal has yet been formed by the LCIA Court for any of the arbitrations to be consolidated.

Article 22.8 is comparable in terms of the criteria for when matters will be consolidated. However, it is noteworthy that the LCIA Court can consolidate arbitrations without the need for a party to make an application.[33]

In both cases, as stated above, any affected party must be given a reasonable opportunity to state their views with respect to the application.

---

30 CIETAC, Arbitration Rules of 2015, Article 19 Consolidated Arbitration, www.cietac.org/index.php?m =Page&a=index&id=65.

31 Article 22.7(ii) of the LCIA 2020 Rules.

32 Emphasis added by the authors.

33 Cf Article 19 of CIETAC Arbitration Rules 2015 (Consolidated arbitrations) must be initiated by one party's application.

The approach adopted by the LCIA, whether under Article 22.7 or Article 22.8, requires the decision to ultimately rest with the institution rather than the arbitral tribunal (even where the arbitral tribunal makes the order, it must do so with the approval of the LCIA Court). There is merit in this approach, as the institution is involved in the administration and procedure of both arbitrations subject to the application to consolidate. Moreover, an arbitral tribunal cannot make a decision which binds another arbitral tribunal (the consolidation order affects both arbitral proceedings). The LCIA Court, however, under the LCIA Arbitration Rules, is able to make such an order effective with respect to both arbitral proceedings.[34]

The increasing incidence of consolidation under the LCIA Arbitration Rules can be seen in the most recent available empirical data and statistics published by the LCIA which record that, in 2019, there were 35 applications for consolidation made in arbitrations administered pursuant to the LCIA Arbitration Rules. Of those, five applications were rejected and six remained undecided as at the end of 2019.

The LCIA also reported that the number of applications for consolidation had increased by over 50% as compared with 2018.[35] Furthermore, in 2020, 50 applications for consolidation were made by parties under the LCIA Arbitration Rules (2014 or 2020), an increase of over 40% compared with 2019; 12 of the 49 applications were made in cases pursuant to the LCIA Arbitration Rules 2020.[36]

From these statistics, it appears that consolidation may be a procedure on the rise with an increasing number of applications for consolidation being reported. One possible reason explaining such an increase is that the LCIA Arbitration Rules which were introduced in October 2020 allow consolidation under broader circumstances.

Taken overall, there is a natural and understandable reticence on the part of institutions to move too far to permit or require consolidation under their arbitration rules, particularly noting such organisations do not have any sovereign regulatory authority.[37] The standard approach seen in those institutional rules which do provide for the consolidation of two or more arbitral proceedings, is to only permit such an application (and subsequent order) where those proceedings are pending under the same institutional rules. The Singapore International Arbitration Centre did release a proposal on cross-institution consolidation in December 2017.[38] However, that proposal does not appear to have gained any real traction.

The present approach to consolidating arbitrations under institutional rules, as illustrated above, is sensible, and in particular, the approach is in line with the principle of party autonomy. The parties agreed to arbitrate under that institution's arbitration rules which include the power to order consolidation (even absent party consent). There can be little objection to this approach – the parties agreed to it.

---

34 Ioannis Giakoumelos, 'The Need for Implementation of a Consolidation Provision in Institutional Arbitration Rules', (2017) 17 Pepperdine Dispute Resolution Law Journal, pp. 23, 61.

35 LCIA, '2019 Annual Casework Report', www.lcia.org/LCIA/reports.aspx, p. 20.

36 LCIA, '2020 Annual Casework Report', www.lcia.org/LCIA/reports.aspx, p. 24.

37 Thomas P Devitt, 'Multiparty Controversies in International Construction Arbitrations', (1983) 17(4) International Lawyer, pp. 669, 675.

38 Singapore International Arbitration Centre, 'Memorandum regarding proposal on cross-institution consolidation protocol' (December 2017) www.siac.org.sg/images/stories/press_release/2017/Memorandum%20on%20Cross-Institutional%20Consolidation%20(with%20%20annexes).pdf.

Consolidation in accordance with an institution's arbitration rules, given the parties have consented to arbitrate under such rules, is, as a starting point, considerably more palatable than consolidation by court order. This mechanism for consolidation under institutional rules relies on the agreement of the parties rather than a power outside of that contractual relationship. That explains, at least partially, why the Dutch and Hong Kong approach to consolidation of arbitrations by court order is not popular on a global scale.[39]

The question remains more broadly as to whether consolidation is, in any event, desirable. As such, the rest of this chapter turns to examine this question. To evaluate this very question, consideration must be given to the advantages and disadvantages which result from consolidation.

V. Evaluation: Advantages and Disadvantages of Consolidation

In theory, the consolidation of arbitral proceedings ought to lead to time and cost efficiencies to the benefit of all parties concerned. However, in practice, there are obvious issues which can arise where the consolidation is ordered absent party consent.

These practical impediments are likely to have the opposite effect, in that they can lead to drawn out and costly procedural arguments where the parties cannot agree the rules of the game or the arbitration becomes much more complicated, extensive and thus costly.

Take for instance the following hypothetical scenario. There are two disputes to be arbitrated which relate to the same project and where there is a common claimant:

> The first arises under a contract which provides for all disputes arising out of or in connection with the contract to be referred to arbitration in accordance with the Arbitration Rules of the Singapore International Arbitration Centre ("SIAC Rules"). The arbitration is seated in Amsterdam; and
> The second arises under a contract which provides for all disputes arising out of or in connection with the contract to be referred to arbitration under the LCIA Rules. The arbitration is seated in London.

As explained in the former sections, there is no power to consolidate the two arbitral proceedings under either the LCIA Rules or the SIAC Rules.[40] However, the first arbitration is seated in the Netherlands and an application to the District Court of Amsterdam for the consolidation of the two proceedings, in the face of the respondent to the second arbitration's objection, is granted. What happens next? Into which arbitration proceeding is the other consolidated?

The adverse implications of mandated consolidation are immediately apparent. Such an order can easily give rise to a complex web of procedural disputes in terms of which arbitration rules apply to the arbitration, the revocation of the appointment of an arbitrator already made, the validity of any order made by that arbitrator before consolidation, and their entitlement to be paid their fees and expenses. While there is considerable

---

39 See analysis in the previous section.

40 Both sets of rules provide for consolidation but only where there is either party consent or where both arbitral proceedings are pending under the same institutional rules. See SIAC Rules 2016, Rule 8, and LCIA Rules, Article 22A.

consistency in approach between different institutions, the SIAC Rules and LCIA Rules are not identical and each of the parties may have very different views as to which rules they wish to apply. After all, they contracted for a specific procedure when entering into the underlying agreement, and it is difficult to see, when the basis of arbitration is agreement, why the parties should be forced into proceeding with arbitration which is not in the form (or jurisdiction) contracted for.

Moreover, the issue may be even more pronounced where a party has opted for arbitration in accordance with an institution's arbitration rules that allow for fixed or capped fees and expedited procedures. The rationale for opting for such rules is clear, and there can be no serious argument that parties to such an agreement should then be forced into full scale arbitration with the attendant costs of such procedures. It cannot be assumed that arbitration would have been agreed to absent such crucial cost controls.

Even where specific institutional rules are not at play, the arbitration agreements may nevertheless have significantly different approaches in terms of, for instance, the formation of the arbitral tribunal, the powers afforded to that tribunal, the language of the arbitration and the seat and governing law of the arbitration (amongst other matters), which can be difficult, if not impossible, to reconcile absent further argument before the courts.

Another consideration is (in)efficiency of process, which arguably is one possible benefit of consolidation. Consolidation does not guarantee efficiency of process. On one hand, this approach, in certain circumstances, may instead lead to unnecessary time and cost for parties in having to engage in a broader dispute than if they were only a party to their individual arbitration.[41] This may be seen in the need to prepare additional evidence and submissions, to engage in otherwise unnecessary procedural argument, or to attend lengthier (or otherwise entirely avoidable) case conferences and hearings. On the other, the arbitral tribunal will also require additional time (for which additional fees will be charged) to consider a wider breadth of dispute and materials. These factors have time and cost implications which a party may wish to avoid.

Aside from the cost and (in)efficiency of process, the other key objective or benefit to consolidation is to ensure consistency in outcomes. Where there are two or more separate arbitrations, there is always the risk of inconsistent awards being rendered. There is significant merit in this argument,[42] particularly in the context of arbitrations involving disputes arising out of contracts consisting of a principal contract and its ancillary contracts, or the same transaction or series of transactions.

Parallel arbitral proceedings may result in inconsistent determinations of fact or of law and give rise to the risk of inconsistent findings on damages, creating the opportunity for a windfall by a party who may obtain double recovery where successful in relation to the same event as against two separate parties in two separate proceedings.[43] Nevertheless, it is a known risk which can be mitigated by the parties before it arises.

In this regard, it is always open to the parties to agree to consolidation or to ensure that related contracts include model arbitration clauses which provide for disputes to be arbitrated under the auspices of the same institution's arbitration rules. This agreement, made

---

41 T Evan Schaeffer, 'Compulsory Consolidation of Commercial Arbitration Disputes', (1989) 33 St Louis University Law Journal, pp. 495, 497.

42 For instance, in *Aiden Shipping Company Ltd v Interbulk Ltd (Vimeira)* [1986] UKHL J0522-1, the arbitral tribunals reached different conclusions as to whether the port is a safe port.

43 See the *Vimeira* case, [1986] UKHL J0522-1.

from the outset and at a time when the parties are not in dispute, would obviate the need to attempt to find a resolution to the issue only after the parties find themselves embroiled in conflict – a point in time which is unlikely to bring with it an agreement on anything.

Multi-party disputes are not uncommon and ought to be readily anticipated in the context of construction and maritime charterparty agreements in particular.[44] Where there are multiple parties to a project, the contracts entered into in respect of that project will commonly ensure other matters are aligned. There is no reason why the dispute resolution mechanism should not be given equal consideration in terms of consistency of approach.

A further tenet of arbitration which is likely to be eroded by multi-party, consolidated arbitrations, is confidentiality. Parties arbitrate because they want to keep their disputes and the often highly commercially sensitive information, which is referenced in the process, confidential, both generally from public view and, more specifically, from competitors or suppliers in their market. This is a key driver for many in the commercial world to engage in arbitration rather than public litigation as was recognised by Justice Leggatt in *Oxford Shipping Co Ltd v Nippon Yusen Kaisha*:[45]

> The concept of private arbitration derives simply from the fact that the parties have agreed to submit to arbitration particular disputes arising between them and only them. It is implicit in this that strangers shall be excluded from the hearing and conduct of the arbitration.

However, consolidation, by widening the dispute and the actors involved, risks undermining confidentiality and is at odds with commercial parties' motivations to engage in arbitration and expectations in terms of how that process will unfold. By whittling away the confidentiality of the process absent consent, this may have serious negative repercussions on users' confidence in engaging in arbitration in the future.

Given the concerns over confidentiality that arise in the context of consolidated arbitration, it has been suggested that such concerns may be alleviated by requiring parties to sign confidentiality agreements or by structuring the proceeding in such a way as it restricts a party's access to information not relevant to its case and to limit the use of such information.[46]

In theory, such suggestions are credible, but in practice, the reality for commercial parties is that the damage resulting from a breach of confidentiality cannot be practically undone or compensated for once committed, with the utility of a confidentiality agreement being relatively limited. Moreover, the added complexity of devising and running an arbitral proceeding which restricts access to some but not all materials and evidence may well easily undo any perceived efficiency benefits of a consolidated process. As such, the procedural arguments alone which might arise as to which specific information or documentation is available to whom, can be protracted and destructive of any efficiency objective. If there were any suggestion that this had been improperly managed by the arbitral tribunal, this may also give rise to judicial review proceedings, which again would counter any efficiency gains.

---

44 Matthew D Schwartz, 'Multiparty Disputes and Consolidated Arbitrations: An Oxymoron or the Solution to a Continuing Dilemma', (1990) 22 Case Western Reserve Journal of International Law, pp. 341, 372.
45 [1984] 2 Lloyd's Rep 373 (QB), p. 379.
46 Ioannis Giakoumelos, 'The Need for Implementation of a Consolidation Provision in Institutional Arbitration Rules', (2017) 17 Pepperdine Dispute Resolution Law Journal, p. 37.

A further, and arguably more serious issue, is the question of enforceability of any award published by an arbitral tribunal which has been appointed with respect to the dispute, other than in accordance with the parties' agreement to arbitrate. Article V(1)(d) of the New York Convention provides that recognition and enforcement of an award may be refused where there is proof that:

> The composition of the arbitral authority or the arbitral procedure was not in accordance with the agreement of the parties, or, failing such agreement, was not in accordance with the law of the country where the arbitration took place.

Accordingly, there is a credible argument that enforcement might be successfully opposed where the arbitral procedure was otherwise than in accordance with the parties' agreement.[47]

Taken overall, the authors claim that there is no overwhelmingly compelling advantage to support compulsory consolidation absent party consent which would outweigh the key principles of arbitration, including party autonomy, consent and confidentiality. In the circumstances, the balance logically lies in promoting party autonomy above the expediency of process which could result from consolidation.

VI. Conclusion

Comparing the two existing mechanisms (first, the court ordered consolidation, and second, consolidation under institutional rules), the institutional rules approach is preferable to that of court ordered consolidation in terms of any mandatory scheme. The arbitral institutions have refrained, to date, from providing for consolidation other than where the parties have already agreed to arbitrate in accordance with that institution's arbitration rules. On that basis, the mandatory nature of the consolidation is fundamentally less intrusive on party autonomy, as compared to consolidation ordered by a court.

It must be recognised that there is a legitimate basis for the proposal that consolidation, in some form, be considered. After all, one of the highly prized benefits of arbitration is that, when conducted appropriately, it can be a much more efficient process for the final resolution of a dispute arising between the parties than commercial litigation. This is particularly so in the international arena where enforcement becomes an issue, with enforcement under the New York Convention being markedly easier than enforcement of a foreign judgment.

Nevertheless, that well-meaning and admirable intention cannot be held above the importance of party autonomy when that shift in balance could result in the agreement of the parties being unreasonably and illegitimately negated.[48]

Moreover, the practical implications of compulsory consolidation are just as likely to result in inefficiencies rather than efficiencies, a contrary end goal to that for which proponents of consolidation are aiming.

Thus, this chapter argues that the balance between the promotion of efficiency in the conduct of arbitral proceedings and party autonomy is best struck by making use of means, other than compulsory consolidation. For instance, utilising institutional arbitration rules

---

47 Matthew D Schwartz, 'Multiparty Disputes and Consolidated Arbitrations: An Oxymoron or the Solution to a Continuing Dilemma', (1990) 22 Case Western Reserve Journal of International Law, pp. 341, 369.
48 See reasons explained in Section V.

which are purposefully designed for the effective delivery of time and cost-effective arbitration processes. This approach underscores and preserves the consensual nature of arbitration and recognises the importance of giving effect to the parties' agreement, whilst promoting sensible and proportionate responses to the parties' dispute.

Overall, compulsory consolidation gives rise to a degree of ambiguity, uncertainty and unpredictability which is undesirable and can jeopardise the entire process, including the enforcement of any award made by the arbitral tribunal. It may be of value to contracting parties, who do not wish to risk being compelled at a later date into a multi-party consolidated arbitration, to proactively include a non-consolidation clause in their arbitration agreement.[49] Regardless, non-consenting parties should not be corralled against their will into an arbitral process which is contrary to their wishes and to their agreement. Such an approach flies in the face of the primary tenets of modern arbitration and is likely to hinder and undermine the credibility and success of arbitration in the future.

On a final note, nothing in this chapter should be taken as advocating against the approach currently adopted by several arbitral institutions, such as the LCIA, where there is a power within their arbitration rules for arbitrations to be consolidated (where they are both subject to those rules). That is quite a different matter. The parties have agreed to those rules and, therefore, the argument that their autonomy has been infringed does not withstand scrutiny. Such features of those institutions' rules have been closely considered and incorporated with a clear vision of promoting efficiency in process and the institutions should continue to review and revise their rules with that purpose in mind.

---

49 T Evan Schaeffer, 'Compulsory Consolidation of Commercial Arbitration Disputes', (1989) 33 St Louis University Law Journal 513 (claiming that although the likelihood of parties turning their minds to such procedural concerns at the time of contracting is low).

CHAPTER 10

The Interim Measures Mechanism in International Arbitration in China

Law and Recent Developments

Jing Wang[1] and Weisheng Wang[2]

I. Introduction

With the gradual implementation of China's "Belt & Road Initiative", more and more Chinese enterprises have expanded their business overseas, which has led to an increase in disputes between domestic and foreign parties. Moreover, more and more international commercial entities, including Chinese enterprises, are choosing arbitration as a means of dispute resolution. Arbitration has always been preferred by commercial entities as a fast and confidential dispute resolution method. It is particularly important in arbitration where preservatory measures as a "preliminary" procedural relief are available to ensure fairness of the case and effective enforcement of the final arbitral award. The preservation regime in Mainland China concerning cross-border arbitration has developed rapidly in recent years, thus helping the development of international arbitration in Mainland China. This chapter will examine the development of the application for interim measures in aid of arbitration in Mainland China and highlight the differences in practice.

II. Interim Measures in Mainland China

Interim measures are important to ensure the smooth enforcement of arbitral awards. Under the arbitration law of many jurisdictions, such as the UK, Singapore and Hong Kong, an arbitral tribunal is empowered to order preservation measures (i.e. interim measures).[3] However, there is no equivalent clear support for interim measures under the Arbitration

---

1 Director of the Maritime Law Committee of All China Lawyers Association, Top Ten Lawyers in Foreign-related Legal Practice in Guangzhou, Member of the Expert Committee on Civil and Administrative Litigation Supervision of the Supreme People's Procuratorate, Arbitrator, Founding Partner of Wang Jing & Co. Law Firm, Chairman of Board of Directors and Managing Partner at Wang Jing & GH Law Firm.

2 Member of Chartered Institute of Arbitrators, Arbitrator, PRC Ministry of Justice: National List of 1,000 Lawyers in Foreign-related Legal Practice (practice areas: Cross-border Investment and M&A, Maritime & Admiralty), All China Lawyers Association: Leading Lawyer in Foreign-Related Legal Service, Guangdong Lawyers Association: Leading Lawyer in Foreign-Related Legal Service, Partner at Wang Jing & GH Law Firm.

3 The Arbitration Ordinance in Hong Kong (Cap. 609), s 35; The Arbitration Act 1996 in UK, s 39; The International Arbitration Act in Singapore (CHAPTER 143A), s 12.

DOI: 10.4324/9781003160298-12

Law of PR China[4] or other relevant Chinese laws and regulations. "The Convention on the Recognition and Enforcement of Foreign Arbitral Awards" ("New York Convention") to which Mainland China has ratified contains no provisions relating to interim measures granted by an arbitral tribunal, or the power of an arbitral tribunal to order such measures. Likewise, none of the judicial assistance treaties concluded by Mainland China so far has provisions for interim measures in international arbitration. As such, there is no clear authority regarding interim measures concerning arbitral proceedings. Therefore, in judicial practice in Mainland China, interim measures applications, such as property preservation, evidence preservation or injunctions relating to arbitral proceedings, are not always supported and enforced by Chinese courts. The courts' review standards and results are somehow inconsistent.

Mainland Chinese courts have exclusive jurisdiction to decide a request for preservation measures or review a decision regarding preservation measures and this process is a matter not arbitrable.[5] Therefore, any party who wishes to obtain a preservation order in Mainland China in aid of arbitral proceedings should apply to the competent Chinese court per the applicable preservation rules.

The aforesaid preservation rules which Chinese courts shall follow when handling such an application for preservation are mainly contained in the Civil Procedure Law of PR China,[6] the Arbitration Law of PR China, the Maritime Procedure Law of PR China[7] and the Interpretation of the Supreme People's Court on the Application of the Special Maritime Procedure Law of the People's Republic of China (the "Interpretation on Maritime Procedure Law of PR China").[8]

A. Preservation Measures under Civil Procedure Law of PR China

Chapter 9 'Preservation and Advance Enforcement' of the Civil Procedure Law of PR China,[9] provides in its Article 100 "property preservation and conduct preservation[10] measures during litigation or arbitration" and Article 101 "property preservation and conduct preservation measures before litigation or arbitration".

Chapter 9 of the Civil Procedure Law of PR China stipulates general provisions relating to preservation measures which serve as a legal basis for property or conduct preservation

---

4 The Arbitration Law of P.R. China (Order No. 76 of the President) came into effect on 1 September 1995 and the latest amendment to it was introduced in 2017 (hereinafter referred to as the "Arbitration Law of P.R. China").

5 *Hemofarn DD v. Jinan Yongning Pharm. Co.* [2008] Min Si Ta Zi No. 11 (a reconsideration for refusal to recognize and enforce foreign arbitration award) (Supreme People's Court, reconsideration and binding order).

6 The Civil Procedure Law of P.R. China (Order No. 71 of the President of P.R. China)was first issued in 1991 and the latest amendment to it was introduced in 2017.

7 The Special Maritime Procedure Law of P.R. China (Order No. 28 of the President of P.R. China)came into effect on 1 July 2000 and it was issued by the Standing Committee of the National People's Congress (hereinafter referred to as the "Maritime Procedure Law of P.R. China").

8 The Interpretation of the Supreme People's Court on the Application of the Special Maritime Procedure Law of the People's Republic of China came into effect on 1 February 2003 and the latest amendment to it was introduced in 2008. It was issued by Supreme People's Court. It hereinafter will be referred to the "Interpretation on Maritime Procedure Law of P.R. China".

9 The Civil Procedure Law of P.R. China, Arts. 100–101.

10 It should be noted that the term "behaviour preservation" in Chinese legal practice is also very often used. Both behaviour preservation and conduct preservation are interchangeable. This Chapter simply employs the term "conduct preservation".

(i.e., injunction). Article 81 of the Civil Procedure Law of PR China contains general provisions relevant to evidence preservation which serve as a legal basis for evidence preservation. In practice, many preservation applications in arbitral proceedings have been granted and enforced by Chinese courts. Such arbitral proceedings include both domestic arbitration[11] and arbitration involving foreign elements but are administered by arbitration institutions in Mainland China.[12] The provisions of the Civil Procedure Law of PR China as cited above do not prohibit an application for preservation measures in aid of non-Mainland China seated arbitration. Given that the aforesaid preservation rules apply to both Chinese domestic arbitration and arbitration involving foreign interests elements but administered by arbitration institutions in Mainland China, the possible inference is that they shall be similarly applicable in foreign-seated arbitrations. Article 101 of the Civil Procedure Law of PR China reads, inter alia, "the interested party may, before instituting an action or applying for arbitration, apply to the people's court ... for taking preservative measures". While conferring the right of application on the interested parties to arbitration, Article 101 does not distinguish foreign arbitration from the domestic one or arbitration involving foreign elements. A possible interpretation of this rule is that the Civil Procedure Law of PR China does not exclude preservation measures in aid of overseas arbitration. However, in judicial practice, except for some special circumstances, there is no precedent that an application for preservation in aid of non-Mainland China seated arbitration is granted.[13]

Article 272 of the Civil Procedure Law of PR China deals with preservation measures for arbitration involving foreign interests elements, which reads,

> [w]here a party applies for a preservation measure, the arbitral institution of the People's Republic of China handling cases involving foreign interests elements shall transfer the party's application for a decision to the intermediate people's court at the place of domicile of the respondent or at the place where the respondent's property is located.

Since this Article expressly targets those arbitration cases administered by arbitration institutions in Mainland China handling cases involving foreign interests elements, this Article is not applicable in arbitrations administered by arbitration institutions or tribunals outside Mainland China.

In a case decided in 2014,[14] related courts in Shanghai dismissed the applicant's preservation application for lacking legal basis. In this case, the parties concerned have submitted disputes between them to the Korean Commercial Arbitration Board for determination; the applicant doubted the respondent's solvency due to the latter's repeated delay in effecting payment, and thus applied for property preservation before the Shanghai No. 1 Intermediate People's Court ("SIPC").[15] However, the court held that because the arbitral proceedings are not conducted within the territory of Mainland China, the property preservation application does not accord with the stipulations of Article 272 of the

---

11 *Hubei Dongsheng Rubber Seal Co. Ltd. v. Wuhan Xiandai Precision Machinery Co., Ltd.* (a property reservation order) [2020] E 01 Cai Bao No. 80 (Wuhan Intermediate People's Court, property reservation order).

12 *Maguro Investment Limited v. Dalian Global International Shipbuilding Co., Ltd.* [2020] Liao 02 Cai Bao No. 21 (Dalian Intermediate People's Court, property reservation order).

13 The Interpretation on Maritime Procedure Law of P.R. China, Art 21.

14 *DONGWONF&B v. Shanghai Lehan Commercial Co., Ltd.* [2014] Hu Yi Zhong Shou Chu Zi No. 2 (Shanghai No. 1 Intermediate People's Court, property preservation order).

15 Ibid.

Civil Procedure Law; thus, the court rejected the application for lacking legal basis. On appeal, the court of appeal, Shanghai High People's Court upheld the decision of SIPC.[16]

As discussed in the previous paragraphs, the Civil Procedure Law of PR China does not address the question as to whether parties in an arbitration seated outside Mainland China can apply before a Mainland Chinese court for preservation measures in aid of arbitration but provides rules for court-ordered interim measures, not distinguishing domestic arbitrations, arbitrations with foreign elements but administered by arbitration institutions in Mainland China and arbitrations administered by foreign arbitration institutions. One explanation of this is that court-ordered interim measures shall be allowed as the rule does not exclude arbitrations administered by foreign arbitration institutions expressively. While the counterargument is that court-ordered interim measures shall not be allowed as the rule does not explicitly allow court-ordered interim measures in arbitrations administered by foreign arbitration institutions. The result of such ambiguity is that, in practice, Chinese courts seldom allow interim measures applications in arbitrations administered by foreign arbitration institutions, except in some special practice areas.[17]

B. Interim Measures under Arbitration Law of PR China

Similar to the position under the Civil Procedure Law of PR China, the Arbitration Law of PR China only provides preservation relating to domestic arbitration and arbitration involving foreign elements. Article 28 of the Arbitration Law of PR China deals with property preservation during arbitral proceedings administered by Arbitration Commissions, and Article 46 deals with evidence preservation during arbitral proceedings administered by Arbitration Commissions. Furthermore, Article 68 of this Law provides that if a party to a foreign-related arbitration applies for evidence preservation, the foreign-related Arbitration Commissions shall pass the application to the intermediate people's court of the place where the evidence is located.

The Arbitration Law of PR China does not define the concepts of "Arbitration Commissions" or "foreign-related Arbitration Commissions", but it provides in Article 10 that

> [a]rbitration commissions may be established in municipalities directly under the Central Government and in cities which are the seats of the people's governments of provinces or autonomous regions ... People's governments of the cities referred to in the preceding paragraph shall arrange the relevant departments and chambers of commerce to organise arbitration commissions in a unified manner ... [t]he establishment of an arbitration commission shall be registered with the administrative department of justice of the relevant province, autonomous region or municipality directly under the Central Government.

A foreign arbitration institution is not organised or registered as per the paragraph above and, therefore, is not likely to be recognised as an "Arbitration Commission" under the Arbitration Law of PR China. As such, the Arbitration Law of PR China merely provides for preservation measures in domestic arbitration or foreign-related arbitration

---

16 *DONGWONF&B v. Shanghai Lehan Commercial Co., Ltd.* [2014] Hu Gao Shou Zhong Zi No. 21 (Shanghai High People's Court, reconsideration and binding order).

17 In accordance with Maritime Procedure Law of P.R. China, maritime courts in China allow interim measures applications in support of arbitrations conducted in foreign countries or Hong Kong SAR.

administered by foreign-related Arbitration Commissions but does not cover preservation measures relating to arbitration administered by foreign arbitration institutions.

On 30 July 2021, the Ministry of Justice of the People's Republic of China published a consultation draft of the revised Arbitration Law of the PRC (the "Consultation Draft"). This Consultation Draft provides an interim measures mechanism, according to which both the arbitral tribunals and the courts can decide on an interim measure application and after an arbitral tribunal makes a decision permitting interim measure application, such a decision can be sent to the courts for compulsory enforcement. It is unclear in the Consultation Draft whether an interim measure order made in a foreign arbitration proceeding can be enforced in the same way.

C. Enforceability of Interim Measures under New York Convention or Other International Treaties

In accordance with Article V(1)(e) of the New York Convention, to which China is a contracting state, recognition, and enforcement of an arbitral award may be refused, if the award has not yet become binding on the parties. It is controversial whether or not interim measures ordered by arbitral tribunals could be enforced under the New York Convention.[18] On the one hand, tribunal-ordered interim measures lack finality, and can be revised or withdrawn at any time by the tribunals. From this perspective, it is not certain whether tribunal-ordered interim measures can be "arbitral awards" defined under the New York Convention. On the other hand, New York Convention does not require an arbitral award to be final, it uses the word "binding" and it provides for the refusal of recognition and enforcement of awards when the awards "have been set aside or the enforcement of which have been suspended". Interim measures ordered by an arbitral tribunal is binding on the parties, and as long as it is not set aside or suspended, such an award remains binding. From this perspective, New York Convention does not preclude its application on the enforcement of interim measures.

In judicial practice, courts of different jurisdictions also diverged on this issue. In *Resort Condominiums International Inc. v. Ray Bolwell and Resort Condominiums (Australasia) Pty Ltd.*,[19] the dispute was submitted to arbitration in the US, and an injunction was issued during the arbitration proceedings. However, when the injunction was sought to be recognised and enforced in Australia, it was dismissed by the Australian court. In its reasoning, the court held that interim measures may be changed during the arbitration proceedings, thus if it is enforced, it could make the dispute resolution process even more complicated.

While in *Sperry Int'l Trade, Inc. v. Government of Israel*,[20] the United States Court of Appeals, Second Circuit affirmed that although the tribunal had not definitively resolved the issues, a decision requiring that funds be placed in escrow was severable and thus, it is a final award on a severable issue and shall be enforced.

The Chinese courts take a comparatively conservative stance. In Hemofarn DD v. Jinan Yongning Pharm. Co., the Supreme People's Court of China considered the arbitral award as in violation of public policy under the New York Convention and rejected

---

18 *Société Sardisud v. Société Technip* [1994] Rev Arb 391 (the Supreme Court of Queensland).

19 *Resort Condominiums International Inc. v. Ray Bolwell & Resort Condominiums (Australasia) Pty. Ltd.*, [1993] 118 ALR (Supreme Court of Queensland), pp. 655–657.

20 *Sperry Int'l Trade, Inc. v. Government of Israel*, 689 F.2d 301(2nd Cir. 1982).

the enforcement application.[21] Therefore, it is commonly believed that the foreign tribunal's decision on interim measures is unenforceable under the New York Convention in Mainland China.

Besides the question of enforceability under the New York Convention, another question is whether tribunal-ordered interim measures can be enforced under bilateral treaties concerning civil judicial assistance between China and various countries. As of now, Mainland China has concluded 37 bilateral treaties concerning civil judicial assistance.[22] Generally, these mutual assistance treaties cover matters including the service of legal documents, evidence collection, recognition and enforcement of foreign judgments, etc. Furthermore, in some cases, the recognition and enforcement of arbitral awards are also included. Nevertheless, none of them mentions the enforcement of foreign interim measures, issued by arbitral tribunals. Therefore, tribunal-ordered interim measures are not directly enforceable under these bilateral treaties concerning civil judicial assistance.

One unclarified question is that whether tribunal-ordered interim measures, after being entered as judgments, can be enforced through mutual judicial assistance treaties or other similar arrangements. There is a mutual judicial assistance treaty between Mainland China and Singapore, which, however, does not provide for recognition and enforcement of court judgments. While since 2016, courts of each of the two countries have started to recognise and enforce civil judgments made by the courts of the other country. The recognition and enforcement are arranged under Reciprocity Principle. As such, a judgment made by the Singapore court can now be enforced in Mainland China. In the meantime, Article 46 of the Singapore Arbitration Act provides that:

> (1) [a]n award made by the arbitral tribunal according to an arbitration agreement may, with leave of the court, be enforced in the same manner as a judgment or order of the court to the same effect. (2) [w]here leave of the court is so granted, judgment may be entered in the terms of the award.

If an interim measure is issued by a tribunal in Singapore and such interim measure is converted as a judgment by the Singapore court, the question is whether such a judgment by the Singapore court can be enforced in mainland China under the same Reciprocity Principle. So far, there is no official interpretation or clarification on this issue.

D. Interim Conclusion

In general, in the commercial arbitrations seated in Mainland China (including domestic ones and those involving foreign elements), the parties concerned can apply for property preservation and evidence preservation before the arbitration institutions, who will pass on the applications to the competent mainland courts for decision and enforcement. Regarding general commercial arbitrations seated outside Mainland China, in practice, an application by a party to such arbitration for the property, evidence, conduct preservation, or a request for recognising and enforcing interim measures ordered by tribunals will

---

21 *Hemofarn DD v. Jinan Yongning Pharm. Co.* (a reconsideration for refusal to recognize and enforce foreign arbitration award) [2008] Min Si Ta Zi No. 11 (Supreme People's Court, reconsideration and binding order).

22 Ministry of Justice of the People's Republic of China, 'Civil and Commercial Judicial Assistance Treaties' <www.moj.gov.cn/Department/node_358.html> accessed 15 February 2022.

normally not be supported because there is no clear authority under Chinese law, the New York Convention or judicial assistance treaties concluded by Mainland China.

III. Special Rules on Preservation Measures in Maritime Arbitration in Mainland China

Maritime arbitration is a special type of commercial arbitration in Mainland China to which special procedures apply. Compared to preservation measures applicable to general commercial disputes, the maritime preservation mechanism provides essential protection to successfully enforce court judgments or arbitral awards in maritime disputes.

A. Background to Maritime Preservation Measures

Due to the involvement of many parties from multiple jurisdictions and because ships, goods, and other pertinent subject matters are usually mobile globally, maritime disputes are inherently international. China's maritime arbitration preservation mechanism refers to international conventions such as the International Convention on Arrest of Ships and other international practices (hereinafter referred to as "The International Convention on Arrest of Ships").

Previously it was controversial at the international level whether or not a court should take preservation measures for international arbitration. For instance, in *McCreary Tire & Rubber Co. v. Ceat S.p.A.*, the 3rd Circuit Court held that the parties' application to a court for preservation measures aimed at "evading" the arbitration agreement, which is contrary to the objectives of the New York Convention.[23] In the subsequent cases, US courts considered that an application to a court for ship arrest belongs to a conventional maritime relief, which should be distinguished from the scenario of *McCreary Tire & Rubber Co. v. Ceat S.p. A.* The International Convention on Arrest of Ships also includes provisions supporting international arbitration.[24] Consequently, the practice of court granting preservation measures in aid of maritime arbitration by relevant nations eventually contributed to the amendment to the relevant international convention.

Under the International Convention on Arrest of Ships, a ship arrest applicant can commence arbitration in a jurisdiction other than the place of ship arrest, and the grant of the ship arrest application is not conditional on the urgency of relevant circumstances.[25]

B. Interim Measures under Maritime Procedure law of PR China

The preservation mechanism in Mainland China's maritime litigation referred to the International Convention on Arrest of Ships. The scope of maritime claims protected under it is consistent with the international practice, covering both property preservation, conduct preservation, and evidence preservation, and the attachable property including ships, cargoes, bunkers and provisions.

---

23 *McCreary Tire & Rubber Co. v. Ceat S.p.A. v. Mellon Bank* 501F.2d 1032 (3rd Cir 1974).
24 The International Convention on Arrest of Ships, Arts. 2, 7.
25 Ibid., Art. 2.

Article 21 of the Maritime Procedure law of PR China lists 22 maritime claims based on which an application for ship arrest may be filed. Except for some minor differences, the aforesaid 22 maritime claims are the same as those provided for under Article 1 of the International Convention on Arrest of Ships.[26] But the scope of property attachable in aid of Chinese domestic maritime arbitration is not limited to ships. Maritime claim preservation to which the Maritime Procedure law of PR China applies can be against such properties as ships, goods carried by ships, ship's bunkers and provisions.[27] As for other properties, preservation of maritime claims may still be possible by relying on the preservation rules under the Civil Procedure Law of PR China.[28] Under the Maritime Procedure law of PR China, apart from property preservation under Chapter III, other preservation measures available include conduct preservation in the form of the maritime injunction and evidence preservation stipulated in Chapter V.

Article 21 of the Interpretation on Maritime Procedure law of PR China stipulates that an application for preservation of maritime claims before litigation or arbitration shall be dealt with per Article 14 of the Maritime Procedure law of PR China; where the maritime case has been accepted by a foreign court or the relevant disputes have been submitted for arbitration, if the property involved therein is located within the territory of Mainland China, and if the parties apply for preservation of maritime claims to the maritime court of the place of location of such property, the said maritime court shall accept such application for review and decision. Article 41 and Article 47 of this Interpretation contain similar provisions relating to the maritime injunction and maritime evidence preservation. Therefore, the Supreme People's Court of China confirms expressly by judicial interpretation that property preservation, conduct preservation in the form of the maritime injunction, and evidence preservation are feasible for overseas maritime arbitration. However, the maritime preservation mechanism in Mainland China does not clarify whether interim measures ordered by overseas arbitral tribunals can be recognised and enforced by Chinese maritime courts. In judicial practice in Mainland China, maritime courts follow the inference relating to interim measures granted in general commercial arbitration adopted by other mainland courts, i.e. recognising and enforcing such interim measures lacks legal basis under either the New York Convention or bilateral judicial assistance treaties concluded by Mainland China. In short, in Mainland China, a party is not able to file for recognising and enforcing the interim measures granted by foreign arbitral tribunals even for maritime arbitration, but the party can apply for preservation of maritime claims as per the aforesaid provisions relating to maritime preservation (i.e., a court-ordered interim measure relief).

In *Dampskibsselskabet NORDEN A/S v. CAI International, Inc.*,[29] the charterer's delay in redelivery of the ship fundamentally breached the Charterparty, causing a loss of USD 5,436,443.5 and the dispute was submitted to an arbitration seated in London. As the charterer went bankrupt subsequently, the shipowner applied for property preservation in Mainland China. Though the arbitration was held outside Mainland China, Tianjin Maritime Court decided to accept the owner's application in accordance with the

---

26 Ibid., Art. 1.

27 The Interpretation on Maritime Procedure Law of P.R. China, Art. 18.

28 Ibid.

29 *Dampskibsselskabet NORDEN A/S v. CAI International, Inc.* (a preservation order of maritime claims) [2014] Jin Hai Fa Bao Zi No. 7–1 (Tianjin Maritime Court, preservation order of maritime claims)

Interpretation on Maritime Procedure law. As for the legal basis, the court cited Article 12 of the Maritime Procedure law, which defines preservation as a "compulsory measure against property". Accordingly, the equivalent value of the bank deposit in the charterer's account was frozen.

The aforementioned legal rationale was followed in many maritime cases.[30] As the stipulation in the Interpretation on Maritime Procedure law is unequivocal, property and evidence preservations have been frequently adopted in aid of foreign maritime arbitrations. However, in practice, we see few successful maritime injunction applications relating to maritime arbitrations incurred outside of Mainland China.

C. Interim Conclusion

In commercial arbitrations conducted in Mainland China (including domestic arbitrations and those involving foreign elements), parties can apply for property preservation and evidence preservation before the arbitration institutions, who will then submit the applications to the competent mainland courts for decision and enforcement. As for general commercial arbitrations conducted outside Mainland China, in practice, an application by a party to such arbitration for the property, evidence, conduct preservation, or a request for recognising and enforcing interim measures ordered by tribunals normally will not be supported as mainland courts consider such application or request lacks legal basis under the prevailing law of PR China or the New York Convention, or judicial assistance treaties concluded by Mainland China.

Regarding overseas maritime arbitrations, in judicial practice in Mainland China, property and evidence preservation applications in aid of overseas maritime arbitrations are often granted as there is a legal basis under the applicable Chinese laws and regulations. However, interim measures issued by foreign arbitral tribunals even in a maritime arbitration will not be supported as China's maritime courts take the view that it lacks legal basis under the New York Convention or judicial assistance treaties concluded by Mainland China.

Due to the significant differences between the legal systems of Hong Kong and Macau and that of Mainland China, the same rules apply to foreign arbitrations to those conducted in Hong Kong or Macau. In other words, similarly, mainland courts would not approve an application by a party to Hong Kong or Macau seated arbitration for the property, evidence, conduct preservation or a request for recognising and enforcing interim measures ordered by tribunals.

Therefore, It follows that for interim measures granted by a foreign-seated arbitral tribunal (including Hong Kong and Macau), due to the lack of applicable laws and regulations, the parties concerned may neither apply for the issuance of interim measures from Mainland Chinese courts, nor apply for enforcement of one issued by a foreign arbitral tribunal in Mainland China, except in maritime cases. Consequently, the rights and interests of the parties may not be adequately protected, and the enforcement of the final award may

---

30 *China Resource Chartering Limited v. Fuqing Tianyi Building Material Co., Ltd.* [2020] Min 71 Cai Bao No. 17 (Xiamen Maritime Court, property preservation order); *CAI International, Inc. v. Daxinhua Logistics Holding (Group) Co., Ltd.* [2013] Jin Hai fa Bao Zi No. 68–1 (Tianjin Maritime Court, preservation order of maritime claims) 1; *Zhoushan Shipping Co., Ltd. v. Han* [2010] Yong Hai Fa Zhong Bao Zi No. 1 (Ningbo Maritime Court, preservation order of maritime claims).

face difficulties. To address and solve this problem, as a pioneering move, Mainland China and Hong Kong have signed a series of judicial arrangements to facilitate the enforcement of interim measures and arbitral awards involving the two sides.

IV. Recent Developments – the New Arrangement Regarding Arbitration in Hong Kong

A. Arrangement

On 2 April 2019, the Supreme People's Court of China and the Department of Justice of the Hong Kong Special Administrative Region signed the Arrangement Concerning Mutual Assistance in Court-ordered Interim Measures in Aid of Arbitral Proceedings by the Courts of the Mainland and the Hong Kong Special Administrative Region (the "Arrangement"). The Arrangement came into force on 1 October 2019. The Arrangement entitles a party to arbitral proceedings in Hong Kong to make an application for interim measures before a competent mainland court for the future enforcement of the final arbitral awards. The Arrangement also regulates a party involved in arbitral proceedings in Mainland China seeking interim relief before a Hong Kong court. The Arrangement is about court-ordered interim measures and does not relate to tribunal-ordered interim measures. Notably, for a party in Hong Kong arbitration seeking interim relief in Mainland China, the entities for receiving its application and transfer of the same to a competent court in Mainland China, are several recognised arbitral institutions, not the arbitral tribunal.

Before the Arrangement going into effect, in a Hong Kong arbitration for general commercial disputes, a party was not able to apply for interim relief before a court in Mainland China. While in a Hong Kong arbitration for maritime disputes, a party can apply for interim relief before a competent maritime court in Mainland China. Under this Arrangement, in those Hong Kong arbitrations administered by the recognised arbitral institutions, the parties can now seek court-ordered interim relief.

On the other hand, since the principles of the UNCITRAL Model Law on International Commercial Arbitration ("UNCITRAL Model Law") is adopted in Hong Kong, a Hong Kong court can grant interim reliefs on the application of a party to arbitration proceedings that have been or are to be commenced in or outside Hong Kong.[31] And the enforceability of interim reliefs granted by an arbitral tribunal outside Hong Kong is also accepted.[32] Therefore, it is normally permissible to enforce interim reliefs in Hong Kong.

The Arrangement mainly fills the gap of the enforcement of interim measures in Mainland China for arbitrations seated in Hong Kong.

B. Main Contents of the Arrangement

The Arrangement, for the first time, addresses brief answers to such issues as (1) who can apply for interim measures to Chinese courts in aid of arbitral proceedings in Hong Kong; (2) when contracting parties can apply for such interim measures; (3) types of interim measures; (4) procedures and documents required, etc.

---

31 The Arbitration Ordinance.
32 Ibid., s 61.

C. *Arbitral Proceedings in Hong Kong*

Article 2 of the Arrangement sets out qualifications of arbitral proceedings in Hong Kong to apply for such interim measures before Chinese courts. First, the seat of arbitration shall be Hong Kong; second, only arbitration proceedings administered by specified institutions or permanent offices of relevant organisations in Hong Kong satisfy the requirements of the Arrangement. Therefore, *ad hoc* arbitrations are excluded under the Arrangement.

Six Hong Kong arbitral institutions and permanent offices have been approved since the promulgation of the Arrangement. They include Hong Kong International Arbitration Centre ("HKIAC"), China International Economic and Trade Arbitration Commission ("CIETAC"), International Court of Arbitration of the International Chamber of Commerce-Asia office, Hong Kong Maritime Arbitration Group, South China International Arbitration Center (HK), and eBRAM International Online Dispute Resolution Centre.

D. *Timing of Applying for Interim Measures*

A party to arbitration seated in Hong Kong may apply for interim measures before the competent Chinese court before or after the arbitration institution or permanent office accepts the arbitration case. If a party makes an application for interim measures before the acceptance of the arbitration case, a letter from the institution or permanent office certifying its acceptance of the arbitration case is required to be sent to the relevant court in Mainland China within 30 days from the date of the enforcement of the interim measures. Otherwise, the court will lift the interim measures. In light of the formalities of accepting arbitration cases, issuing and sending out the certifying letters to courts in Mainland China, 30 days might be inadequate.

Some qualified institutions and permanent offices have issued guidelines for such applications. For instance, HKIAC suggests that a party to HKIAC arbitral proceedings should follow the steps below:

1) The party to apply interim measures under the Arrangement;
2) After the court in Mainland China grants the application, the party to commence arbitration proceedings in HKIAC;
3) The party to request a Letter of Acceptance from HKIAC;
4) If HKIAC decides to issue the Letter of Acceptance, it may send the Letter of Acceptance to the requesting party or the related mainland court on the court's request.[33]

E. *Competent Courts*

The competent courts in Mainland China for accepting such interim measures applications are intermediate people's courts. For the recognition or enforcement of the final arbitral awards issued in Hong Kong's arbitral proceedings, it is necessary to make the court grating interim measures in aid of arbitral proceedings consistent with the court

---

33 'Hong Kong-Mainland China Arrangement on Interim Measures' (*HKIAC*, 2019) <www.hkiac.org/arbitration/arrangement-interim-measures> accessed 20 February 2022.

recognising or enforcing the final arbitral awards. Therefore, both the courts recognising or enforcing the final arbitral awards and the courts accepting interim measures applications are intermediate people's courts of the place of residence of the respondents or the place where the respondent's property is located.

The competent court in Hong Kong for accepting such interim measures applications is the High Court of the Hong Kong Special Administrative Region.

F. Types of Interim Measures

In accordance with the Arrangement, interim measures in Mainland China include property preservation, evidence preservation, and conduct preservation. Specifically, the preservation measures can be freezing of balance in bank accounts, attachment of real property or chattels, attachment of stocks, bonds or other securities or shareholding in private companies or interests in private entities, balance in WeChat Pay accounts or Alipay accounts, seizure of evidence, court injunctions preventing a party from acting or requesting a party to act in a certain way, etc.

While in the case of Hong Kong, interim measures include: (1) injunction and other interim measures to maintain or restore the status quo pending the determination of the dispute; (2) taking action that would prevent, or refraining from taking action that is likely to cause, current or imminent harm or prejudice to the arbitral proceedings; (3) preserving assets; (4) or preserving evidence that may be relevant and material to the resolution of the dispute.

G. Security Requirement

As per the Arrangement, a people's court of the Mainland may require the applicant to provide security, etc., while a Hong Kong court may require the applicant to give an undertaking or provide security for costs, etc.

H. Exclusion of Ad Hoc Arbitration

Contracting parties can choose to have disputes between them resolved through institutional arbitration or *ad hoc* arbitration. *Ad hoc* arbitration is not completely recognised in Mainland China. In accordance with the Arbitration Law of PR China,[34] in Mainland China, an application for arbitration may only be submitted to an Arbitration Committee, and if in an arbitration clause, no Arbitration Committee is nominated expressly or implicitly, such an arbitration clause cannot be enforced under the Arbitration Law of PR China. As discussed above, the Arbitration Committee under the Arbitration Law of PR China is an institution, properly organised and registered, and therefore cannot conduct *ad hoc* arbitration. Over time, such restriction under the Arbitration Law of PR China becomes more and more incompatible with the development of the economy. Recently, *ad hoc* arbitrations in Mainland China under certain specific circumstances are allowed.[35]

---

34 The Arbitration Law of P.R. China, Art. 16.

35 Opinions of the Supreme People's Court on Providing Judicial Guarantee for the Building of Pilot Free Trade Zones came into effect on 30 December 2016 and was issued by the Supreme People's Court. <http://en.pkulaw.cn/display.aspx?cgid=441e185f12e602a2bdfb&lib=law> accessed 19 February 2022 (hereinafter

Nevertheless, the Arrangement does not include *ad hoc* arbitrations, and therefore parties in *ad hoc* arbitrations cannot rely on the Arrangement for applying for interim measures. As a result, for those Hong Kong *ad hoc* arbitrations for general commercial matters, parties cannot apply for or enforce interim measures in Mainland China. For those Hong Kong *ad hoc* arbitrations for maritime matters, parties can apply for interim measures before maritime courts in Mainland China relying not on the Arrangement, but the Maritime Procedure Law of PR China, and related judicial interpretations.

1. Whether a Party Can Apply for Compulsory Measures after the Arbitration
    Award Is Issued and before the Arbitration Award Is Recognised and Enforced

As discussed in this chapter earlier, the Arrangement entitles a party to Hong Kong seated arbitral proceedings to apply to the mainland court for interim measures before or after the request for arbitration is accepted by the relevant arbitration institution. Therefore, before a Hong Kong arbitration starts or during a Hong Kong arbitration, a party can rely on the Arrangement to apply for a court-ordered interim measure in Mainland China. However, the Arrangement is silent on whether any compulsory measures can be taken after the final arbitration award is issued, but before the arbitration award is recognised and enforced by mainland courts. There is usually a several-month time gap between the time a final arbitration award is issued and the time the arbitration award is recognised and enforced by mainland courts. It is possible that during this time gap a respondent's assets evaporate, and court-ordered compulsory measures in this period are needed if an applicant has not yet applied for interim measures before or during the arbitration proceedings. Parties are not able to rely on the Arrangement as the Arrangement applies to the period before and during the arbitration, but after the arbitration award is rendered, the arbitration proceedings have ended, and the tribunal is *functus officio*. After the promulgation of the Arrangement, other arrangements were promulgated to address this issue. A more detailed discussion will be given below.

I. Timeframe for Granting Interim Measure in Mainland China

Article 8 of the Arrangement provides that a court shall examine a party's application for interim measures expeditiously. As to courts in Mainland China, there are no specific rules regarding the timeframe for reviewing and granting an application for interim measures under the Arrangement. Since there is no detailed requirement under the Arrangement, mainland courts may follow the provisions under the Civil Procedure Law of P.R. China and the Provisions of the Supreme People's Court on Several Issues Concerning the Handling of Property Preservation Cases by People's Courts. This means mainland courts may issue a ruling within 48 hours after accepting the application if the circumstance is urgent, or they may issue a ruling within 5 days after the applicant provides security or

---

referred to as "Opinions of the Supreme People's Court on Providing Judicial Guarantee for the Building of Pilot Free Trade Zones"); Ad Hoc Arbitration Rules in Hengqin Free Trade Zone came into effect on 15 April 2017 and was issued by Zhuhai Court of International Arbitration. <www.zhac.org.cn> accessed 19 February 2022 (hereinafter referred to as "Ad Hoc Arbitration Rules in Hengqin Free Trade Zone"); SCIA Arbitration Rules came into effect in 2019 and was amended in 2020. It was issued by Shenzhen Court of International Arbitration<www.scia.com.cn/home/index/rulelist.html> accessed 19 February 2022 (hereinafter referred to as "SCIA Arbitration Rules")

after the application is made.[36] While in practice, the review period is not likely to be within 48 hours or 5 days. Quite often, the courts request supplementary documents, explanation or additional security to support a party's application, and the period for providing these are not included in the calculation of the 48 hours or 5 days. Therefore, very commonly the actual review period exceeds 48 hours or 5 days.

J. The Supplementary Arrangement Filling the Gap

1. Obtaining Interim Measures in Mainland China Before or after an
   Application for Enforcement of a Hong Kong Arbitral Award

The Supplementary Arrangement Concerning Mutual Enforcement of Arbitral Awards between Mainland China and the Hong Kong Special Administrative Region (the "Supplementary Arrangement") was promulgated by the Supreme People's Court on 26 November 2020.

One of the positive developments under the Supplementary Arrangement is that preservation or compulsory measures can be taken by courts in Mainland China if a party makes such an application for preservation or compulsory measures before or after the courts accept an application for enforcement.[37] This provision fills the gap discussed above.

As discussed above, as per the Arrangement, a party to Hong Kong arbitration can apply for interim measures before Mainland China courts prior to the commencement of or during the Hong Kong arbitration. But after the arbitration award is rendered, a party cannot rely on the Arrangement to apply for compulsory measures before courts of Mainland China. The Arrangements of the Supreme People's Court on the Mutual Enforcement of Arbitral Awards between the Mainland and the Hong Kong Special Administrative Region[38] does not address this issue either. Such enforcement mechanism between the Mainland and Hong Kong is different from those in the Arrangement between the Mainland and the Macau SAR on Reciprocal Recognition and Enforcement of Arbitration Awards[39] and the Provisions of the Supreme People's Court on Recognition and Enforcement of Arbitral Awards of Taiwan Region.[40]

Before the promulgation of the Supplementary Arrangement, there are still some judicial precedents where mainland courts ruled to grant applications for compulsory measures against respondents before the recognition of a Hong Kong arbitral award.

---

36 The Civil Procedure Law of P.R. China, Arts. 100–101; The Provisions of the Supreme People's Court on Several Issues Concerning the Handling of Property Preservation Cases by People's Courts (Fashi [2020] No. 21), which came into effect on 1 January 2021 (hereinafter referred to as the "Provisions Concerning the Handling of Property Preservation Cases"), Art. 4.

37 The Supplementary Arrangement, Art. IV.

38 The Arrangements of the Supreme People's Court on the Mutual Enforcement of Arbitral Awards between the Mainland and the Hong Kong Special Administrative Region (Fashi [2020] No. 3) came into effect on 1 February, 2000.

39 The Arrangement between the Mainland and the Macau SAR on Reciprocal Recognition and Enforcement of Arbitration Awards (Fashi [2007] No. 17) came into effect on 1 January 2008 and was issued by the Supreme People's Court, Art. 11.

40 The Provisions of the Supreme People's Court on Recognition and Enforcement of Arbitral Awards of Taiwan Region (Fashi [2015] No. 14)came into effect on 1 July 2015 and was issued by the Supreme People's Court, Art. 10.

In *Guangdong Yuehua International Trade Group Co., Ltd. v. Sinotide Holdings Limited and Junxiang Ke*,[41] Guangzhou Intermediate People's Court, Guangdong Province, ruled to approve the applicant's application for freezing bank accounts or other compulsory measures before the recognition and enforcement of the Hong Kong final award.

The court in *Farenco Shipping Pte. Ltd. v. Eastern Ocean Transportation Co., Ltd.*[42] also approved such applications. The court in *Farenco Shipping Pte. Ltd. v. Eastern Ocean Transportation Co., Ltd.* held that:

Firstly, since the Arrangement between the Mainland and the Macau SAR on Reciprocal Recognition and Enforcement of Arbitration Awards and the Provisions of the Supreme People's Court on Recognition and Enforcement of Arbitral Awards of Taiwan Region provide expressly that a party involved in Macao or Taiwan arbitration proceedings could apply for compulsory measures to Mainland China courts before the recognition and enforcement of the final award, the court could deal with the current matter involving Hong Kong arbitration on the same principle. In this circumstance, the applicant was entitled to apply to take property preservation measures against the counterparty, and the court should review the application per relevant laws and regulations of Mainland China.[43]

Besides this, the Supreme People's Court's Reply Letter to Hubei Provincial Higher People's Court concerning Issues involved in the Application for Property Preservation in the Case of Application for Recognition and Enforcement of the Arbitral Award of the Hong Kong Special Administrative Region by Automotive Gate FZCO (reference No.: the Supreme People's Court Minta No. 129(2017)) states that

> even though there is no specific law or regulation (before the issuance of the Supplementary Arrangement), referring to Article 100 of the Civil Procedure Law of PR China, a court may support an application for interim measures after accepting the application for recognition and enforcement of the Hong Kong arbitral award provided that the applicant can provide adequate security.

Therefore, it is reasonable for the court, in this case, to grant the application for property preservation before the filing of the application for recognition and enforcement of the Hong Kong arbitral award since the applicant had provided a letter of guarantee for its application.[44]

The *Farenco* case was selected as the Ten Exemplary Cases in 2019 by Guangzhou Maritime Court. In 2020, during the press conference held by the PRC Supreme Court for announcing the promulgation of the Supplementary Arrangement, the PRC Supreme Court's speaker also mentioned the *Farenco* case and stated that before the Supplementary Arrangement, no law addresses this issue, but in practice, in the *Farenco* case, the Guangzhou Maritime Court permitted such applications and supported the smooth enforcement of the Hong Kong arbitration awards, and Article Four of the Supplementary Arrangement was based on such beneficial practical experience.

---

41 *Guangdong Yuehua International Trade Group Co., Ltd. v. Sinotide Holdings Limited and Junxiang Ke* (recognition and enforcement of arbitration award)[2014] Sui Zhong Fa Ming Si Chu Zi No. 42 (Intermediate People's Court of Guangzhou City, Guangdong Province, first instance).

42 *Farenco Shipping Pte. Ltd. v. Eastern Ocean Transportation Co., Ltd.* (property preservation) [2018] Yue 72 Cai Bao No. 78 (Guangzhou Maritime Court, property preservation and biding order).

43 Ibid.

44 Ibid.

The Supplementary Arrangement is an improvement in the regime of assistance between Hong Kong and Mainland China in respect of the application for interim measures or compulsory measures in aid of arbitration. The Supplementary Arrangement reduces the risk that a losing party in the arbitration seeks to transfer its assets quickly before Hong Kong arbitral awards are recognised and enforced in Mainland China, and thus the interests of the winning parties can be better protected.

V. Different Criteria for Granting Interim Measures in Hong Kong and Mainland China

As discussed, it is now open to a party in Hong Kong arbitration to seek interim measures in Mainland China or a party to Mainland-seated arbitration to seek interim measures in Hong Kong. However, under both the Arrangement and the Supplementary Arrangement, the factors that courts should consider for granting interim measures are not clearly expressed. Article 8 of the Arrangement merely provides that the court of the requested place shall decide for interim measures under the laws or regulations of the requested place. In this regard, related laws and rules in Hong Kong and the Mainland provide the necessary criteria.

A. Criteria for Granting Interim Measures in Hong Kong

In Hong Kong, arbitral tribunals and courts can grant interim measures concerning arbitration proceedings.[45]

1. Test Adopted by Arbitral Tribunals

Hong Kong adopts the principles of the UNCITRAL Model Law as the basis for its arbitration laws or regulations. The Arbitration Ordinance of Hong Kong stipulates the conditions for granting an interim measure based on Article 17 of the UNCITRAL Model Law. This article provides three conditions, namely: (1) whether harm not adequately reparable by an award of damages is likely to result if the measure is not ordered; (2) the arbitral tribunal or court needs to consider the balance of interests of the parties concerned; they have to consider whether such harm substantially outweighs the harm that is likely to result to the party against whom the measure is directed if the measure is granted;[46] and (3) whether there is a reasonable possibility that the requesting party will succeed on the merits of the claim.[47]

These are just the preliminary conditions necessary to be met. In practice, the test under Article 17(A) of the UNCITRAL Model Law is similar to the American Cyanamid test, which include the following questions: (1) whether the requesting party has a good arguable case; (2) whether there is "balance of convenience" in support of granting interim measures.[48]

There are still other conditions necessary to be considered and it depends on the types of interim measures the parties seek. The practice on the grant of Mareva injunctions or

---

45 The Arbitration Ordinance s 36, 45; the High Court Ordinance s 21M.

46 The Arbitration Ordinance, s 36(1).

47 The Arbitration Ordinance, s 36(2).

48 *American Cyanamid Co. Appellants v. Ethicon Ltd.* [1975] AC 396 (HL).

the reference to the Chartered Institution of Arbitrators (CIArb) Guideline on Applications for Interim Measures (2016) may also be accepted by tribunals in Hong Kong arbitration proceedings.

2. Test Adopted by Courts

Generally, there is a two-stage test by Hong Kong courts for granting or refusing a request for interim measures in aid of foreign-seated arbitral proceedings. The two-stage test is: (1) whether the facts of the case warrant the grant of interim relief if substantive proceedings were brought in Hong Kong, and (2) under s21M (4) of the High Court Ordinance, whether it is unjust or inconvenient for the court to grant the interim relief.[49]

In the first-stage test, the relevant common law principles concerning granting interim measures in Hong Kong will apply.[50] For example, the American Cyanamid test may be applied. Courts will see whether the claimant has good arguable reasons to seek interim measures. And courts will also consider whether there are adequate damages for each party and whether there is a balance of convenience in granting interim measures.[51] Courts should grant or refuse a request for interim measures based on the principle of minimising damages to the parties concerned.[52] There are different requirements for Hong Kong courts to satisfy before granting interim reliefs in aid of arbitration proceedings. For instance, for granting a freezing order,[53] the court needs to consider whether the assets of the respondent will be liquidated or dissipated in Hong Kong[54] before the final award is issued.

Article 21M(4) of the High Court Ordinance provides that:

> The Court of First Instance may refuse an application for appointment of a receiver or interim relief under subsection (1) if, in the opinion of the Court, the fact that the Court has no jurisdiction apart from this section concerning the subject matter of the proceedings concerned makes it unjust or inconvenient for the Court to grant the application.

According to Article 21M(4) of the High Court Ordinance, the court will consider whether it is unjust or inconvenient to grant interim injunctions. And the factors in the Motorola Credit Corporation v Uzan (No 2) [2004] 1 WLR 113 are for consideration when granting interim measures during the second-stage test.

B. Criteria for Granting Interim Measures in Mainland China

Interim measures in Mainland China include property preservation, evidence preservation, court injunctions preventing a party from acting or requesting a party to act in a certain way.

---

49 *Top Gains Minerals Macao Commercial Offshore Ltd v. TL Resources Pte Ltd HCMP* 1622/2015 [23]; *Compagnia Sud Americana De Vapores SA v. Hin-Pro International Logistics Ltd* [2015] 2 HKLRD 458; *Pacific King Shipping Holdings Pte Ltd v. Huang Ziqiang* [2015] 1 HKLRD 830 [27].

50 *Chen Hongqing v. Mi Jingtian* HCMP 962/2017 [27], [29].

51 *American Cyanamid Co. Appellants v. Ethicon Ltd.* [1975] AC 396 (HL).

52 *National Commercial Bank Jamaica Ltd v. Olint Corp Ltd* [2009] 1 WLR 1405.

53 *Mareva Compania Naviera SA v. International Bulk Carriers S4 (The MAREVA)* [1980] 1 All ER 213, [1975] 2 Lloyd's Rep 509 (CA).

54 *Intercontinental Housing Development Ltd v. Quek Teck Huat* [1986] HKLR 1153 (CA).

Regarding property preservation and injunctive relief, the test is whether it is possible that due to the respondent's acts or other reasons, it becomes difficult to enforce the final award or a party's interest would be damaged.[55] It is not a very difficult test. In practice, many property preservations or injunctive relief applications have been permitted and enforced by courts.

As for the preservation of evidence, the test is whether the relevant evidence may be lost or difficult to obtain at a later stage.[56] It is also not a very difficult test and in practice, many evidence preservation applications have been permitted and enforced by courts.

Overall, the Arrangement and the Supplementary Arrangement allow parties in Hong Kong arbitration to apply for interim measures in Mainland China, and parties in Mainland China's arbitration proceedings to apply for interim measures in Hong Kong. The criteria adopted by courts, although not expressed in the Arrangement, or the Supplementary Arrangement, are similar to those applied in court proceedings relating to arbitration in Hong Kong or Mainland China. Such a mechanism benefits the arbitrations in both the Mainland and Hong Kong and increases the chance of successful enforcement of arbitral awards.

VI. Power to Order Interim Measures: Courts or Tribunals

A. The Practice in Hong Kong

Hong Kong arbitration law adopted most of the principles under the UNCITRAL Model Law. Interim measures are available from an arbitral tribunal,[57] a court[58] and even an emergency arbitrator[59] in Hong Kong. An order on granting interim measures by an arbitral tribunal is enforceable by the Hong Kong court. The practice is summarised as follows:

1. Arbitral Tribunal

Under s31 of the Arbitration Ordinance, which is based on the principles of the UNCITRAL Model Law, an arbitral tribunal can grant interim measures at the request of a party. The arbitral tribunal can request a party to maintain or restore the status quo, to take action to prevent harm or prejudice, to give a method of preservation of assets out of which a subsequent award may be satisfied, and to preserve relevant evidence which is important to the dispute resolution.

Also, the order concerning interim measures issued by the arbitral tribunal, no matter in or outside Hong Kong, with the leave of the court, is enforceable in the same manner as an order of the court. It is worth noting that, if the order is made outside Hong Kong, the leave of the court can only be granted if the order belongs to the type of order that may be made in arbitration proceedings.[60]

---

55 The Arbitration Law of P.R. China, Art 28.
56 Ibid., Art. 46.
57 The Arbitration Ordinance, s 35.
58 The High Court Ordinance, s 21; the Arbitration Ordinance, s 45.
59 The Arbitration Ordinance, part 3A.
60 The High Court Ordinance, s 61.

2. Emergency Arbitrators

A party can appoint an emergency arbitrator and apply for emergency relief before the tribunal is constituted. An order on emergency relief granted by the emergency arbitrator, no matter in or outside Hong Kong, can be enforced in the same manner as the order or direction of a court in Hong Kong.[61]

Since Hong Kong is an international arbitration hub, most arbitration institutions in Hong Kong include the emergency arbitrator mechanism in their current rules. For instance, HKIAC has rules for emergency arbitrators.

3. Courts

Hong Kong courts can grant interim measures in aid of arbitral proceedings, and they will follow the two-stage test in the Top Gains Minerals Macao Commercial Offshore Ltd v TL Resources Pte. Ltd. when deciding whether to grant interim measures.[62]

Compared to jurisdictions where the power of granting interim measures is limited to only national courts, there is the question of allocating such power to arbitral tribunals and domestic courts in Hong Kong. The Arbitration Ordinance of Hong Kong provides that an interim measure can be declined if the court considers that it is more suitable to be handled by an arbitral tribunal. The court in the Leviathan Shipping Co v. Sky Sailing Overseas Co. followed such provision.[63]

B. The Practice in Mainland China

Unlike most common law jurisdictions such as Hong Kong and Singapore, in Mainland China the power of granting interim measures is only vested in courts. If a party to arbitral proceedings wishes to apply for property preservation, the arbitration commission would pass on the application to the competent court under the Civil Procedure Law of PR China.[64] If a party to arbitral proceedings makes an application for the preservation of evidence, the arbitration commission shall pass the application to the court of the place where the evidence is located.[65] In short, the arbitration commission will pass on the application for interim measures to the competent court if such application is submitted by any party to arbitral proceedings after receiving the same from the applicant. The court will decide to grant or refuse such an application. And the decision will be served on the arbitral parties and the arbitration commission.[66] However, there are various limitations to court-ordered interim measures. Firstly, some of the aims of choosing arbitration for dispute resolution may be impaired, e.g. confidentiality and expertise, since the parties concerned normally prefer their cases to be handled confidentially by a neutral tribunal of experts in related fields. And in some cases, court procedures for interim measures may be inefficient. Arbitrators are more familiar with the cases in most circumstances and thus the tribunals can be in a better position to consider and decide whether to grant the interim measures.

---

61 The Arbitration Ordinance, part 3A.
62 *Top Gains Minerals Macao Commercial Offshore Ltd v. TL Resources Pte Ltd* HCMP 1622/2015 [23].
63 *Leviathan Shipping Co v. Sky Sailing Overseas Co* [1998] HKCFI 549.
64 The Arbitration Law of P.R. China, Art. 28.
65 Ibid., Art. 46.
66 The Provisions Concerning the Handling of Property Preservation Cases, Art. 3.

Nevertheless, in practice, some leading arbitration institutions in Mainland China follow the international trend to grant tribunals and even emergency arbitrators the power to decide on interim measures. For example, the CIETAC rules[67] currently in effect provide that "[a]t the request of a party, the arbitral tribunal may decide to order or award any interim measure it deems necessary or proper under the applicable law or the agreement of the parties and may require the requesting party to provide appropriate security in connection with the measure."[68] It follows that if some pre-conditions are met, a CIETAC arbitral tribunal is entitled to decide to order or award any interim measure it deems necessary. Also, CIETAC explores the emergency arbitrator mechanism. CIETAC grants an emergency arbitrator the power to decide on emergency relief and the emergency arbitrator shall make a reasonable effort to ensure the validity of the decision on emergency relief.[69]

Even though there are some developments in some of China's arbitration institutions concerning tribunal-ordered interim measures, it still lacks a proper mechanism regarding the enforcement of the tribunal's order on interim measures in Mainland China. The effect of such grants of interim reliefs by tribunals or emergency arbitrators is still limited. The rules of some of China's arbitration institutions have made advancement while the interim measure mechanism in the arbitration law system, as a whole, lags. Legislators are suggested to consider apportioning more rationally the power concerning interim measures between national courts and arbitral tribunals to further enhance the feasibility of cross-border dispute resolution in Mainland China.[70]

VII. Conclusion

Under the laws of Mainland China, the power of granting interim measures is vested in national courts. In commercial arbitrations, those arbitration commissions registered in Mainland China and their tribunals can accept and pass on the application of interim measures to the competent national court. Although those arbitration commissions outside of Mainland China and their tribunals can decide on the application of interim measures, their awards are not likely to be enforceable in Mainland China. A special mechanism exists in maritime arbitrations that allows court-ordered interim measures before and during the arbitration proceedings. Following the global trends and development of international arbitration, the Arrangement and the Supplementary Arrangement were promulgated, to facilitate court-ordered interim measures in Mainland China relating to arbitrations administered by certain arbitration institutions in Hong Kong.

Moreover, some leading arbitration institutions in Mainland China, such as CIETAC, have changed rules to empower emergency arbitrators to grant interim measures and permit tribunal-ordered interim measures. However, it still lacks proper mechanisms regarding the enforcement of tribunal-ordered interim measures in Mainland China. Without

---

67 The China International Economic and Trade Arbitration Commission (CIETAC) Arbitration Rules came into effect on 1 January 2015 (hereinafter referred to as the "CIETAC Rules") <www.cietac.org/index.php?m=Page&a=index&id=106&l=en >accessed 19 February 2022.

68 The CIETAC Rules, Art. 23.

69 The CIETAC Rules, appx III.

70 The Consultation Draft suggests amendment allowing both the arbitral tribunal and the courts to decide interim measure application and provides an enforcement mechanism for arbitral tribunal's decision of interim measure. Yet it is unclear how this enforcement mechanism can be applied in cross-border arbitration scenarios.

such a proper mechanism, the international dispute resolution process might be hampered because parties do not have the certainty of quick and smooth enforcement of arbitration awards. With the development of the economy, China has become the centre of many important economic activities. A well-functioning dispute resolution process is indispensable to an environment boosting economic activities. Therefore, laws in Mainland China should be revised, supplemented or further clarified to ensure and facilitate the parties' rights in both domestic and international arbitrations.

CHAPTER 11

Chinese Experiences of Commercial Litigation and Mediation in Italy

Francesco Munari

I. The Importance of the Trade between China and Italy and the International Agreements Fostering Bilateral Cooperation

For many years China's importance and leadership in global business has become a fact. It will grow further in connection with the enhanced role of Chinese (economic) power and with ambitious projects that are being implemented, such as the Belt & Road Initiative (BRI, also known as One Belt – One Road), which is expected to bring many Chinese interests also in European countries, including Italy.[1]

On this basis, together with the establishment of diplomatic relations between China and Italy in 1970, bilateral relations have developed rapidly, bearing important and successful results in various fields. Today, as one of the largest economies in the European Union (EU), Italy is also an important partner of China in Europe, and the two countries have deepened pragmatic cooperation since establishing a comprehensive strategic partnership in 2004.

Indeed, China and Italy complement each other in terms of resources, and therefore, trade cooperation can be considered the cornerstone of their relationship. In this context, Belt & Road projects have already helped the expansion of shipping trade in the Mediterranean, creating an unprecedented development of opportunities for Italy's major ports.

This process has been strengthened since March 2019 with the execution between the Italian and Chinese governments of the Memorandum of Understanding between Italy and China "*on Cooperation within the Framework of the Silk Road Economic Belt and the 21st Century Maritime Silk Road Initiative*".[2] Under this MoU, the two parties shall be in the position of establishing better connectivity and promote globalisation and free trade between the two Countries. The signing of the MoU has been met with some criticism within the EU, mainly because of the independent move of one Member State in a strategic matter which might be of interest for the whole EU foreign and security policy. However, such a criticism does not seem persuasive, for different reasons: firstly, because even without an MoU, many other EU Member States have developed over the last years important strategic and commercial relationships with China; secondly, and as a matter

---

1 See World Bank, *Belt and Road Economics. Opportunities and Risks of Transport Corridors* (29 March 2018, updated in 2019) www.worldbank.org/en/topic/regional-integration/brief/belt-and-road-initiative. All website resources in this chapter were last accessed 1 March 2022.

2 The text of the MOU is available also on the Italian Government official website: http://www.governo.it/sites/governo.it/files/Memorandum_Italia-Cina_EN.pdf.

DOI: 10.4324/9781003160298-13

of fact, because a true EU foreign and security policy is still to be truly implemented, Member States tend to pursue their own interests in the foreign policy arena without caring too much of any EU actual or potential common interest.

In this vein, as long as this MoU – as it appears from its text – is not constraining in any way EU actions within China, nor is exclusive of other Member States' interests, there seems to be no room for any legal nor political concern: the formalisation of a bilateral cooperation framework between China and Italy such as the one arising out of the MoU and China will foster the achievement of the common goals stemming from the BRI, i.e. a long-term ambitious project that can encourage connectivity and economic development. And any fears of Italy not being able to control the outcome of Chinese investments in strategic infrastructures appear to be ungrounded, as long as Italy retains its golden power on foreign investments in infrastructural assets and facilities under the provisions of the *decreto legge* No. 21 of 2012, as specifically implemented by the *decreto del Presidente della Repubblica* No. 85 of 2014.[3]

In terms of figures, China has become one of the largest cooperative partners of Italy in terms of imports and exports. In November 2018, the bilateral trade volume has reached $48.25 billion, more than the total for the whole of 2017, making Italy China's ninth-largest export destination and third-largest source of imports. Moreover, concerning technology and made in Italy brands, in recent years Italy has become one of the main destinations for Chinese firms' overseas investments, and their amount is steadily increasing.

II. Business and Dispute Settlement: Courts and Other ADR Mechanisms

The development of trade between the two countries will necessarily bring about the risk of commercial disputes between Italian and Chinese entities. In the international business community, such disputes are governed by well-established rules and principles. Italian or Chinese companies will be able to protect their rights in the national jurisdiction of their respective states, in international arbitration, or in other ADR mechanisms.

From an Italian perspective, it seems opportune to develop a few considerations concerning possibility for Chinese companies, on the one hand, to start proceedings before Italian courts and, on the other hand, to be sued before Italian courts. In this perspective, the Italian legal system and relevant jurisdictional rules are very clear in establishing a full parity of the arms between Italian and non-Italian parties before national courts, especially in matters of business and international trade.

Indeed, Italian rules on transnational litigation apply to all non-EU parties the same regime which is established at EU level within the European space of freedom, security and justice, in respect of litigation on civil and commercial matters. This creates a very friendly environment for non-European firms appearing before Italian jurisdiction: e.g. in a litigation involving a Chinese party before an Italian court:

1) the Chinese plaintiff is not subject to any requirement (including taxation or security to be deposited before the court to ensure payment of expenses) other than those applied to Italian plaintiffs;

---

3 See respectively OJ of the Italian Republic of 15 March 2012, No. 63 (as amended by *legge* No. 56 of 2012) and of 6 June 2014, p. 129 ff. In essence, these provisions establish that investments or acquisitions by foreign entities in strategic sectors must be notified to the Italian Government which can veto them or subject them to specific undertakings by investors.

2) if defendants are abroad, terms for appearing before the Court are extended (e.g. in ordinary cases 150 days instead of 90), thus giving a foreign defendant more time to prepare its statements of defence;

3) interim measures can be adopted by an Italian court only if they need to be enforced in the Italian territory or if the Italian court is competent on the merits;

4) *Lispendens* principles apply also in case the previously seized court is located in a non-EU Member State.

Finally, a foreign judgment is recognised automatically in Italy and can be therefore enforced there, once very basic principles have been complied with by the foreign court: e.g. this court has jurisdiction on the matter under parameters analogous to those existing in Italy, the writ of summons has been properly served and notified to the defendant, the judgment is final and is not inconsistent with *ordre public*.

Again, Italy applies rules acknowledging a sort of relativism of jurisdiction, implying in essence that all courts throughout the world can and will adjudicate in international civil and commercial matters involving Italian parties, without any interference by the Italian legal system to "protect" Italian interests abroad, as long as basic jurisdictional standards are applied by the foreign court.

III. Specialised Courts for Dealing with (Many) Transnational Litigations

Quite often, transnational litigations arise from different interpretations of complex relationships that are governed by sophisticated contracts. Like other countries, also the Italian legislator has paid attention to this specific feature of transnational commercial litigations, and has thus established judicial bodies specialised in the field of commercial and business matters.[4] In particular, under the applicable Italian law on civil procedure, only selected courts sitting in a few towns are competent to hear disputes relating to:

1) Intellectual and property law;

2) Italian and European competition law;

3) Corporate law, and particular all corporate matters, transfer of shareholdings, shareholders' agreements and any litigation concerning companies' directors or shareholders;

4) Public procurement contracts.

The underlying rationale of this legislative choice is to convey this kind of litigation to specialised judges having a specific expertise, with a view to achieving a competent cohort of professionals capable of dealing efficiently and more rapidly in respect of business disputes. This further enhances attractiveness both of Italy as a place where foreign investments can be carried out, and of Italian firms when operating abroad.[5]

When business litigation is transnational, the Italian legal system further provides that non-Italian defendants can be sued only before nine (plus two) selected (commercial)

---

4 A. Graziosi, 'Dall'arbitrato societario al tribunale delle imprese: a dieci anni dalla riforma del diritto societario' (2014) 1 Rivista Trimestrale di Diritto e Procedura Civile, p. 77.

5 M.A. Iuorio, 'Il tribunale delle imprese' (Judicium, 25 September 2013) <www.judicium.it/wp-content /uploads/saggi/501/M.%20Iuorio.pdf> accessed 10 December 2020; L. Tenaglia, 'L'istituzione del tribunale delle imprese' (2012) 5 Corriere Giuridico, pp. 75, 79.

tribunals sitting in Bari, Cagliari, Catania, Genoa, Milan, Naples, Rome, Turin and Venice (plus Trento and Bolzano), of Italy.

The outcome of this choice is manifold: (i) Italian commercial court judges develop specific skills in these areas of law; (ii) their approach is closer to international business and trade; (iii) proceedings enjoy a fast track compared to other areas of litigation.

In addition, when it comes to private antitrust enforcement, the *decreto legislativo* No. 3 of 2017 implementing Directive No. 2014/104/EU,[6] introduces a specific set of rules aimed at regulating actions for compensation for damage resulting from violation of Italian and European competition law, which also include important innovations for discovery and burden of proof of damages to the benefit of the parties that have suffered damages because of the infringement of competition rules.[7]

Moreover, in order to push further forward efficiency and specialisation of Italian judges, for this kind of disputes only three tribunals are competent in Italy, i.e. Milan, Rome and Naples, respectively, for Northern, Central and Southern Italy.

IV. Arbitration in Italy Involving Chinese Parties: The Circulation and Recognition of Arbitral Awards

Transnational commercial parties often choose international commercial arbitration as the solution to settle their disputes, for this mechanism of dispute resolution is perceived as more neutral by businessman and their legal counsel when negotiating and executing contracts with foreign counterparts. And as a matter of fact, arbitration has become the first best solution for companies to resolve international disputes with their foreign counterparts,[8] also because parties can appoint either the sole arbitrator or the arbitration panel competent to decide the matter among highly specialised professionals.

The *favor* offered by the Italian justice system to foreign plaintiffs or defendants is not, therefore, exclusive of other features of the Italian legal system fostering Italian openness to trade with foreign countries and firms.

And indeed, Italian law is adamant in progressively enhancing ADR mechanisms and arbitration in particular. The Italian code of civil procedure dedicates a special book to the arbitration, i.e. Title VIII of Book IV, from section 806 to section 840. Under these rules, all civil and commercial disputes can be adjudicated by arbitrators and special provisions apply to arbitration concerning company law disputes (*decreto legislativo* of 17 January 2003 No. 5).[9]

Under Italian law, and along the same rationale of opening the Italian legal system to foreign entities, an arbitration subject to the above statutory provisions can anyway be conducted in any language, and thus not only in Italian.

Moreover, and due consideration being taken to the growing importance of arbitration institutions to promote (transnational) ADR, the Italian statutes expressly recognise these institutions and entrust them with an important role as a partner to develop ADR mechanisms.

---

6 OJ of the Italian Republic of 2 August 2017, No. 179 (*Supplemento ordinario*).

7 P. Manzini, Il risarcimento del danno nel diritto della concorrenza – Commento al D.lgs. n. 3/2017, (Giappichelli, 2017).

8 R.D. Fischer and R.S. Haydock, 'International Commercial Disputes Drafting an Enforceable Arbitration Agreement', (1996) 21 William Mitchell Law Review, p. 942 (also available in open access at <https://open.mitchellhamline.edu/cgi/viewcontent.cgi?article=2191&context=wmlr>).

9 OJ of the Italian Republic of 22 January 2003, No. 8 (*Supplemento ordinario*).

In Italy the main player is certainly the Chamber of national and international arbitration of Milan (CAM), an established institution which is very active in promoting arbitration and other ADR mechanisms at national and transnational level. Arbitration institutes normally push arbitrators to reduce as much as possible the time to solve a dispute and provide certainty as to the costs of the arbitration.

In addition, the possibility to tailor the arbitration procedure through an efficient case management allows claimants and respondents to optimise their needs even in the unfortunate case of a litigation.

This option is clearly available also within Italian–Chinese commercial relationships. As a matter of fact, both China and Italy favour arbitration. In the first place, both China and Italy are parties of the most important convention on International Commercial Arbitration, i.e. the 1958 New York Convention on the recognition of the foreign arbitral awards. Thus, arbitral awards pronounced in Italy can be enforced in China and *vice versa*.

Secondly, most international disputes introduced by Chinese companies are settled by international commercial arbitration in the China International Economic and Trade Arbitration Commission (CIETAC), an institution availing itself of a roster composed by more than 400 arbitrators. Chinese law on arbitration is grounded on Chinese general Civil Procedure Law (CPL) and China Arbitration Law (CAL), and is significantly modelled on the (UNCITRAL) Model Law on International Commercial Arbitration, adopted by the United Nations Commission on International Trade Law.

The Chamber of national and international arbitration of Milan grounds its procedural rules on the (UNCITRAL) Model Law too, as well as on the basis of the principles of international commercial arbitration as elaborated by the business arbitration community.

In this perspective, no wonder that Chinese companies have already carried out arbitrations before CAM, and other proceedings are pending as of the time in which this chapter is written. And apparently, this practice will grow in importance and frequency, together with the improvement of the bilateral commercial relationships between the two states.

Trade relations between Italy and China have also been implemented in international maritime trade and, as a result, also the number of disputes between operators in this sector has increased.

Maritime arbitration is another well established procedural instrument in order to settle disputes between shipping operators worldwide. Maritime law is international by definition, and the same applies to relevant disputes among maritime players. The maritime arbitration falls under the broader genus of international commercial arbitration, and even if this area of law is highly specialised, from the procedural viewpoint its footprints are those of international commercial arbitration.[10]

This explains also why the Genoa maritime arbitration chamber has been incorporated by the CAM through an agreement executed in 2017. The purpose and the auspice of this advancement is that of deviating part of the maritime arbitration traditionally captured by the UK legal system towards civil-law legal systems that share analogous models of law and are more connected with the matter under dispute. In a prospective Chinese-Italian bilateral commercial relationship stretching also in the maritime field, the incorporation

---

10 S.M. Carbone, A. La Mattina, 'Prospettive dell'arbitrato marittimo in Italia' (2016) 1 Giurisprudenza Arbitrale 102.

of "legal places" where disputes can be settled according to tailor made solutions which are nevertheless coherent with best practices and international standards seems to be clearly instrumental to an overall improvement of the bilateral commercial relationships.

Finally, as far as it concerns the treatment in Italy of foreign arbitral awards, sections 839 and 840 of the Italian code of civil procedure set out the rules for their recognition and enforcement. Pursuant to these provisions, the party wishing to enforce a foreign arbitral award in Italy must file an application to the Court of Appeal of the place where the other party is domiciled. If the other party is domiciled abroad, the Rome Court of Appeal is competent. In this case, the President of the competent Court of Appeal verifies the formal regularity of the application and of the attached documents; once this easy survey is done, the Court issues an order making the award enforceable in Italy: the only exceptions to the enforceability of a foreign award are the inconsistency of the award with *ordre public* and the ascertainment by the Court that the award concerns matters that, under Italian law, cannot be resolved by arbitration: for the sake of this comment, suffice it to mention that this is not the case for civil, commercial and maritime matters.

V. Peculiarities of Disputes Involving Chinese Parties

A. Cultural Diversity and Methodologies to Turn a Problem into an Opportunity: The Italy-China Business Mediation Centre ("ICBMC")

The above having been said, a general *caveat* should be highlighted: litigation and arbitration are widely accepted in Western culture as a tool to solve a dispute. Such an approach, however, is not shared worldwide. In order to bridge the cultural diversities concerning Italian-Chinese trade and business relationships that may encounter problems, other ADR mechanisms have been envisaged, focused on mediation.

Indeed, mediation has been part of China's cultural fabric for thousands of years and the process of a respected neutral assisting parties in the resolution of a dispute has existed since ancient times.

In preparing the growing potentialities of conflicts whose increase is proportional to that of trade relations between Italy and China, a necessity was felt to find solutions capable of being mutually satisfactory for both Chinese and Italian partners.

In this regard, it is worth noting the agreement signed on 7 December 2004 among CAM, the Special Agency of the Milan Chamber of Commerce, the Italian-Chinese Chamber of Commerce and the Mediation Centre of the China Council for the Promotion of International Trade-Mediation Centre (CCPIT, now CCOIC). Such an agreement defines the rules and procedures for the operation of the Mediation Centre between Italy and China (Italy-China Business Mediation-Centre - ICBMC), and is meant exactly to amicably settling potential frictions and conflicts arising out of the intensification of the bilateral commercial relations between players respectively coming from China and Italy.[11]

Mediation is meant to cope with the concern that the business community – especially when trying to boost increasing commercial relationships – is unwilling to sustain time-consuming, expensive and serious economic disputes whose outcome is uncertain almost by definition. Uncertainties related to judicial proceedings and arbitrations are the main

---

11 See <www.china-italy.it/it/icbmc>.

causes persuading many business Italian and Chinese operators that it is in their inter-est to explore an alternative dispute resolution tool in order to keep fluidity of trading relationships and promote their development. The ICBMC is meant to provide a quick, economical and confidential means to solve disputes that may arise between Italian and Chinese entrepreneurs.

More specifically, through this institution they have the possibility to deal in a collabo-rative and informal way with extremely complex problems, with a view to achieving more easily a mutually satisfactory solution of any critical issue arising out in their relationship.

The ICBMC also offers the parties the expertise of mediators who have special train-ing in the resolution of Italian-Chinese trade disputes, and of qualified and experienced personnel able to assist the parties at every stage of the proceedings.

The most important advantages of the ICBMC can be summarised as follows:

1) the requests for mediation are managed both in Italy and China, depending on the place where the request for mediation is filed;
2) ICBMC, as a double-nationality entity, enhances trust in the mediation procedure, works to overcome cultural and linguistic differences and achieves promising results;
3) a mediator is appointed for cases above 100,000 EUR. Fees are quite reasonable (2% of the disputed amount, with a cap of 25,000 EUR);
4) if mediation is successful the mediation agreement is signed as a contract between the parties.

The ICBMC has proved so far to be a quick and successful ADR mechanism, in which hundreds of cases have been so far dealt with, and a percentage of solved disputes shortly below 50% so far. Such a percentage is remarkable, for it implies also that, in the same number of cases, litigation has been avoided, and with it the inevitable negative commer-cial implications, as well as costs and difficulties in enforcing arbitral awards or judgments.

VI. Conclusion

The business relationships between Italy and China are inevitably going to grow, and the two parties, their enterprises and workers shall benefit thereof. The legal environ-ment hosting these relationships is prepared to accompany this evolution, and the Italian legal environment is particularly friendly for a partner like China. Even though legisla-tion is different, and sometimes cultural gaps are still to be bridged, lawyers must make all efforts to sharpen all existing tools capable of fostering the development of a recently established relationship, which is nevertheless probably among the most promising ways to enhance mutual benefits for all parties concerned.

In this vein, the fact that Italy is a founding member of the EU does not seem capable of hampering in any way the bilateral relationships between Italy and China; indeed, the contrary seem true: the EU as such has been always advocating multilateralism and free trade, for a smooth and peaceful development of international relationship, and has always maintained with China friendly and respectful attitude in all political and commercial for a in which China's presence is becoming more and more important. Within the EU rules and principles Italy shall certainly move towards achieving the goal of establishing a high-level commercial friendship with a global player like China. Lawyers shall have to contribute to this goal.

CHAPTER 12

Recent Chinese Experience in London Maritime Arbitration and Litigation

Ian Gaunt[1,2]

I. Introduction

It is estimated that as many as 90% of international shipbuilding contracts are governed by English law and that of these at least 80% are subject to London arbitration, many of them on the Terms of the London Maritime Arbitrators Association (LMAA).[3]

Since 2009 the shipbuilding industry has suffered a prolonged depression, with occasional but generally short-lived recoveries. Many arbitrations have resulted, with owners trying to get out of shipbuilding contracts or renegotiate terms, in particular to delay deliveries or reduce prices, or to cancel contracts altogether. There has been a general perception in China that Chinese parties have lost a disproportionately large number of these cases. This chapter will show that the above perception is based on a rather partial view. In detail:

It is true that Chinese (and other) shipyards have lost cases where the yard could not meet the long stop cancelling date and the buyers chose to cancel in a depressed freight market. However, in cases where the quality of the ship as tendered has been in issue, and in cases involving post-delivery warranty claims, Chinese (and other) shipyards have been much more successful in London arbitration.

Also, outside the shipbuilding field, in traditional maritime claims, Chinese parties have been successful in many cases in London arbitration. One, in *Jiangsu Shagang Group Co. Ltd. v Loki Owning Company Ltd.*,[4] has also had a notable recent success in defending a claim under a corporate guarantee of charterparty liabilities in which the English court was ready to recognise particular Chinese corporate practice. Chinese parties have been successful in securing the enforcement of Chinese arbitration awards in the English courts under the New York Convention and the recognition by the English courts of Chinese court judgements under the Senior Courts Act without there being in

1 Barrister, MA (Cantab), FCIArb, DiplCArb, The author is Immediate Past President of the London Maritime Arbitrators Association and co-author of Curtis, Gaunt and Cecil, The Law of Shipbuilding Contract 5th edition. The views expressed are personal.

2 This article is based on a paper delivered at the International Commercial and Maritime Law conference held in London by CECCA on 7 December 2018. The author acknowledges the invaluable assistance given by Ms Jing Ren LLM, PhD (cand) (Soton).

3 See more via LMAA, Procedural Rules and Guidance, https://lmaa.london/the-lmaa-terms/. All internet resources in this chapter last access on 1 March 2022.

4 [2018] EWHC 330 (Comm).

DOI: 10.4324/9781003160298-14

place any bilateral treaty in respect of the enforcement of court judgments between the two countries.

This chapter will further highlight some cases involving bills of lading and the potential clash of jurisdiction between the Chinese maritime courts and English arbitration tribunals and the use of English anti-suit injunctions in these cases and in shipbuilding cases in London arbitration.

A. Types of Cases

The typical types of cases which come to London arbitration in the maritime sphere and which involve Chinese parties mostly fall into one of the following categories:

1) Shipbuilding contracts and contracts for construction of units for use in the offshore oil and gas industry.
2) Charterparties of various forms.
3) Contracts of affreightment for carriage of specific quantities of commodities over a given period.
4) Contracts for carriage of goods evidenced by bills of lading.
5) Guarantees for payments under shipbuilding contracts in the form of (1) guarantees of instalments payable by a buyer (2) refund guarantees give for possible repayment obligations of a shipyard in the event of a legitimate cancellation of a building contract; and guarantees of obligations under charterparties.
6) Claims for enforcement of Chinese arbitration awards in England.
7) Claims for enforcement in England of Chinese court judgments.

II. Shipbuilding Contracts

London arbitrators are very often involved in deciding on shipbuilding contract disputes. China is now the world's largest shipbuilder. It has overtaken Korea in most types of shipbuilding and will probably continue in that position, probably to build up an even bigger lead in years to come.[5] Shipbuilding is a major priority of the Chinese Government in promoting economic development, so it can be expected we will see more and more ships built in China, probably involving more Chinese-made equipment components, as well as more sophisticated types of ships.[6]

Nearly all international shipbuilding contracts have traditionally been governed by English law; nearly all of them have arbitration agreements in them; and nearly all the arbitrations have been conducted in London on an *ad hoc* basis. A standard ship may cost anything from USD 10–USD 30 million to build. A cruise ship or an oil rig or other sophisticated ship may cost anything between USD 200 million and USD 1 billion million to build. So these are very high value assets and high value disputes, of a type which in other sectors are more likely to be dealt with in an ICC arbitration or an arbitration under the rules of the London Court of International Arbitration

---

5 C Steidl, L Daniel and C Yildiran, 'Shipbuilding Market Developments Q2 2018' (*oecd.org*, 15 May 2018) <www.oecd.org/sti/ind/shipbuilding-market-developments-Q2-2018.pdf>.

6 Maritime equipment and hi-tech shipping features as a major focus for the PRC Government's 2025 strategy ("中国制造[Zhongguo Zhizao] 2025") announced in 2015.

(LCIA). But usually, in the shipbuilding field, whether there is provision for ICC arbitration or LCIA arbitration or an *ad hoc* arbitration, the parties will provide not merely for English law as the substantive law of the contract but also for arbitration in London. This is partly a matter of tradition and partly because they like what they think is the certainty which is given to them by English law and, I think, thirdly, because London has a good reputation for impartiality.

Almost all of the shipbuilding cases in arbitration in London fall into one of two categories. One is where the ship has simply not been delivered by the "long stop" cancellation date. This is usually a period of either 210 days or 270 days after the scheduled delivery date. If the shipyard has simply not been able to tender the delivery of the ship within that period, the buyer is given a right to cancel the contract (unless the delay is attributable to a small number of delays of the buyer performing obligations imposed on it by the contract, such as payment of instalments or delivery of Owner Furnished Equipment). If the market has fallen, the buyer may not want to take the ship and may try to find any reason for not taking the ship. If the buyer has the opportunity to cancel the contract because the ship has not been tendered for delivery before the long stop delivery date, there is no further permissible delay provision that the shipyard can rely on. There is a permissible delay provision in the traditional shipbuilding contract but the 210-270 day cancellation date is a "drop dead" date or a "longstop" date, so that the buyer can cancel at that point, irrespective of any "force majeure" which has happened.

In a number of cases Chinese shipyards have tried to rely on the so-called "prevention principle" or the general principle of law that a party is not entitled to rely on its own wrong if it has cause the other party to miss crucial deadlines, including a cancellation date. This line of argument has hardly ever been successful because of one of the following objections:

(1) the contract contains a complete code for dealing with the consequences of delay, which is said to exclude the "prevention principle"[7] or
(2) because the contract entitles the shipyard to override the objections of the buyer's site supervisors[8] or
(3) the shipbuilder is unable to show a causal connection between the "prevention" complained of and the delays alleged to have resulted.[9]

In a very recent and rather unusual case,[10] a shipyard was again unsuccessful in seeking to rely on the prevention principle where the buyer's arguably wrongful failure to take delivery of two ships in a series (all ordered by the same buyer) had allegedly caused delay in the delivery of two later ships in the same series due to be delivered from the same shipyard. In this case the court held that the shipbuilding contract for the two earlier ships in the series contained a complete code dealing with delay and that the shipyard could not rely on the "force majeure" delay provisions (among other things) because it had not

---

7 *Multiplex Constructions (UK) Ltd v Honeywell Control Systems Ltd (No 2)* [2007] EWHC 447.
8 *Zhoushan Jinhaiwan Shipyard Co. Ltd. v Golden Exquisite Inc* [2014] EWHC 4050 (Comm).
9 *Adyard Abu Dhabi v S.D. Marine Services* [2011] EWHC 848 (Comm).
10 *Jiangsu Guoxin Corporation Ltd v Precious Shipping Public Co. Ltd.* [2020] EWHC 1030 (Comm). It was unusual in that most shipbuilding contracts are placed in the name of single purpose companies. In this case all the ships in the series were initially ordered in the name of Precious, so that its actions in relation to the earlier ships could theoretically be invoked as actions preventing performance of the later contracts.

given notice of the event giving rise to the delay even though the alleged preventive act (the rejection of the earlier ships) was within the knowledge of the buyer and allegedly caused by the buyer.

Despite this decision, there may still be some, very narrow, scope for the operation of the "prevention principle" where there is a specific entitlement under the shipbuilding contract for the shipyard not to proceed further with construction if the buyer, when explicitly required by the shipbuilding contract to do so, has failed to take part in a particular inspection or other procedure. However, in view of the fact that the shipyard is usually given the right to proceed with construction notwithstanding the buyer's failure to give approvals, this line of argument will probably not be helpful to the shipyard in the absence of carefully and individually crafted express provisions in the shipbuilding contract.

A very large number of the cases which have been heard in London are in the delay category because as it turned out shipyards took on, at a certain point in the market cycle, far too much work and when it came for delivery of the ships and they were not able to deliver, the market had fallen very severely. The buyers didn't want the ships in a depressed market and exercised their rights to cancel. It was very difficult for the shipyards to defend those types of cases successfully.

The other types of cases have been those where the shipyard has been able to offer the ship for delivery, but the quality of the ship, or its compliance with the specification, is the issue in the dispute. In those sorts of cases, although they are fewer in number, the Chinese shipyards have been much more successful. But the reputation of London maritime arbitration in Chinese shipbuilding cases seems to have developed very much on the basis of the first type of case. That is the cases which are difficult to defend because the ship has not been delivered within the long stop cancelling date. In these cases there have quite often been parallel proceedings in the Chinese maritime courts where the shipyard usually, or its trading house partner, has alleged fraud of some kind and tried to assert jurisdiction challenging the arbitration agreement and trying to stop an arbitration award which would result in a payment out of the refund guarantee.

SHIPYARD SUCCESSES

The following is a selection of Chinese shipyards which are recorded in publicly reported cases as having been successful in London arbitration or on appeal. These cases do not include successes by Chinese shipyards in cases which they have won in private and confidential arbitrations which have not been reported. There are however known to be a significant number of such cases:

- *Shanghai Waigaoqiao Shipbuilding Co. Ltd.*
- *Jiangsu Eastern Heavy Industry Co. Ltd.*
- *Wuhan Ocean Economic & Technical Cooperation Co. Ltd.*
- *Wuhan Guoyu Logistics Group Co. Ltd.*
- *Zhoushan Jinhaiwan Shipyard Co. Ltd.*
- *Foreign Economic & Technical Cooperation Co. of China.*

I have mentioned the two main categories of shipbuilding contract cases, cancellation for delay and rejection on grounds of quality, and it is no secret that Chinese parties have lost a large number of the first type of shipbuilding contract cases in London. Some people would tell you that Chinese shipyards have lost *all* their cases in London, but this is not at all true. The cases that have been lost are nearly all cancellation-for-delay-type cases. There are two possible approaches to this experience on the part of Chinese shipyards. One is that they can say that London arbitrators are biased against them and redirect their cases somewhere else – to Singapore or Hong Kong. The other is that they can analyse why the shipyards have not been able to deliver the ships within the allotted time and before the cancellation date or in future contracts look to try to modify them to be more advantageous, or less disadvantageous, to the shipyard in delay situations.

I have referred to some of the criticisms that have been raised of London maritime arbitration. At the Marintec conference which was held in Shanghai two years ago it was alleged that the Chinese shipyards "were not being fairly and impartially treated in London arbitration" and that "the Chinese shipyards' current management standards operation mode and idea about dispute resolution did not accord with the practice of London arbitration". One of these quotations comes from the China Maritime Arbitration Commission; the other one from a very prominent maritime lawyer in China who also suggested that because the shipbuilding industry in England was not flourishing ("不兴旺" BuXingWang in Chinese) parties should be more inclined to look to Chinese law and arbitration to resolve disputes under international shipbuilding contracts. This, it is respectfully suggested, is not really a relevant consideration in choosing a system of law and or a dispute resolution venue in an international shipbuilding contract. What parties seek above all is neutrality and predictability, both of which are regarded by most international parties in the shipping industry as particular hallmarks of London arbitration. If anything, the absence of English or British shipowners and shipyards from the international marketplace tends to mean that London is even more than in the past a neutral venue for the determination of international shipbuilding disputes. Coupled with this is the availability of a right of appeal from the award of an English-seated arbitration tribunal to the English Commercial Court on a point of law. This is much favoured by those in the shipping industry as a "safety valve" even if few such appeals are ultimately successful, but it is a procedure not available in almost any venue other than England, since almost all other countries have adopted the UNCITRAL Model Arbitration Law which does not allow for such a right of appeal. In the current circumstances, and possibly not for some years to come, it is probably not realistic to expect that foreign parties will be prepared to choose Chinese law and/or arbitration in international shipbuilding contracts, even though the reputation of some arbitral bodies in China, notably CIETAC continues to gain international recognition and traction.

It is suggested that a more reflective approach might be useful in these circumstances, and to look at the things which might be done – some of them a matter of contract management – some of them a matter of litigation management or arbitration management – to avoid losing these types of cases in future. Some of these are matters for the shipyards' internal management processes to avoid disputes coming to the surface at all; others are matters of litigation or arbitration management when a dispute has arisen or is likely to arise.

FOCUS POINTS FOR SHIPYARDS: CONTRACT AND ARBITRATION MANAGEMENT

- Whole process review of contract <u>and</u> specification with involvement and participation of legal personnel;
- Strict compliance with contract;
- Do not be afraid of serving notices of delay to comply with contract;
- Select and appoint lawyers timely and appropriately;
- Selection and appointment of arbitrator;
- Determine an overall strategy at outset and then find out all essential defence points;
- Witness statement preparation.

The selection and appointment of the arbitrator is obviously extremely important. Preparation of witness statements is also very important as is a serious approach to the process of document disclosure. Recently, the LMAA held a seminar to try to make London arbitrators aware of the differences between Chinese practice in arbitration and litigation and that in London. One of the big differences we found is that we rely heavily on witness evidence in London arbitration. In commercial proceedings in China, there is little cross-examination of witnesses or indeed witness evidence at all. In London, cross-examination of witnesses is likely to be the main part of a hearing and witnesses are subject to really quite testing cross-examination. They may not like it. The witnesses may be quite senior officers in some of these companies and they may not like being asked really very direct questions by counsel in London arbitration. So, it is quite important to prepare them for what is going to happen to them in the arbitration hearing; otherwise they will go to the arbitration and they will immediately be put in the headlights. In practice, we do not have oral "evidence in chief". In other words the witness is not invited to tell his or her story. The witness will have given a written statement. The arbitrators will have read the witness statement and they will know exactly what the witness wants to say in the witness statement. So, when the witness gives evidence he or she will immediately be subjected to cross-examination and that can be a very unsettling experience. I have given evidence in an American case some time ago and it can be quite unnerving. So it is a good idea to make sure that the witness in a London arbitration is going to be well prepared. There are limits, of course, to the extent to which you should be "preparing" a witness and telling them what to say but nevertheless they should be given a flavour of what they are likely to be asked and the process in the arbitration room.

This is one example of the way in which shipyards can improve their litigation or arbitration case management. The last ten years since the financial crisis have been a very bitter experience in many cases, but it seems now that Chinese shipyards have learned important lessons, not only in terms of their internal management procedures, but also in terms of the way in which they manage and present their cases in London arbitration.

Most of the maritime cases publicly reported in England are appeals from arbitration awards. Of course, arbitration awards are private, as is the case in China. The proceedings are confidential, and is not permissible to report them unless both the parties agree to it. Sometimes the parties' agreement is obtained but very often the losing party doesn't want the result of the arbitration publicised, so it doesn't become public. But if the losing party appeals the arbitration award, then that will come into the public arena because the appeal will go to the Commercial Court and those proceedings are public and may be published in the Law Reports.

Finally on the subject of shipbuilding contracts, I would mention anti-suit injunctions (a subject which will be expanded on in the next section in connection with cases concerning bills of lading and contracts for the carriage of goods by sea). In spite of the express agreement for London arbitration in most international shipbuilding contracts, there have been several cases in recent years, where the shipyard has deliberately taken steps to instigate competing proceedings in local courts in order to serve its interests, including two important reported English cases. In these cases a fraud allegation was made before a Chinese maritime court, as a result of which it is argued that the shipbuilding contract and the associated refund guarantee issued by the shipyard's bank were tainted by illegality and thus unenforceable. The aim is to relieve the bank refund guarantor from its payment obligations under the guarantee (and thus to relieve the shipyard of the need to reimburse the guarantor under its counter-indemnity).

This was the situation in the English Commercial Court case of *Spliethoff's Bevrachtingskantoor BV v Bank of China Ltd*.[11] There, the newbuildings, the subject matter of two shipbuilding contracts between the buyer, Spliethoff's Bevrachtingskantoor BV, one of the largest Dutch ship operating companies, and a Chinese shipyard (Rongsheng Shipyard, usually known in China as "Xi Xia Kou"), had not been delivered on time. Both contracts contained the usual provisions entitling the buyer to terminate the contracts if the ships were not delivered within the "long stop date". This had passed and the buyer duly claimed to terminate the contracts. Both contracts provided for dispute resolution by way of arbitration in London. Having terminated the contracts, the buyer asked for a refund of the advance instalments which was rejected by the shipyard. The buyer then commenced arbitration proceedings in London pursuant to the arbitration clause contained in the contracts and obtained an award in its favour. In parallel, the shipyard instituted proceedings against the buyer and the manufacturer of the ships' main engines (Wärtsilä) in the Qingdao Maritime Court in China, claiming that the buyer had committed fraudulent conspiracy by agreeing with the engine manufacturers that second hand engines would be supplied to the yard for installation in the ships. *Ex parte* interim orders were made by the Chinese court thereafter, preventing any payment out under the refund guarantees provided by the Bank of China for what was apparently a limited period. It was clear that at that stage the Chinese litigation was almost certainly in contradiction to the arbitration clause agreed in the contracts. The buyer therefore successfully applied to the English High Court for anti-suit injunctions in support of London arbitration, restraining the yard from continuing its proceedings in China.[12] This case excited great controversy in China and the "fraud" proceedings went all the way to the Supreme People's Court before being dismissed.

---

11 [2015] EWHC 999 (Comm). For a further discussion on the issue of recognition and enforcement of Chinese court judgments in England see below.

12 The scope of the orders made by the Chinese maritime court as a matter of Chinese law was disputed in the English proceedings; the Chinese legal experts who gave evidence differed as to whether the orders were time limited and had expired and as to whether Bank of China might incur penalties in China if it did not comply with them.

Another prime example is *Crescendo Maritime Co. & Anor v Bank of Communications Company Limited & Ors*,[13] a case concerning the false backdating of a shipbuilding contract (a practice which became quite common in an attempt to avoid the need to comply with new regulatory requirements relating to tank coatings or, more recently, Tier III low emission engines.)The contract in this case was terminated following the breakdown of the parties' relationship and the buyer claimed to be entitled to terminate the contract, again for delay beyond the contractual "long stop date". London arbitration was commenced in accordance with the terms of the shipbuilding contract. The refund guarantor, a Chinese bank, refused to pay out under the guarantee, on the ground that it was unaware of the backdating issue, which had amounted to fraud. The tribunal had in fact joined the bank as a party to the arbitration proceedings.[14] The bank however did not participate in the arbitration and commenced proceedings in China, seeking declarations of non-liability under the refund guarantees. The bank managed to obtain a ruling to that effect. On learning of the parallel Chinese litigation, the buyer of the ship sought an interim anti-suit injunction from the English Commercial Court in favour of the London arbitration. On the other side, the arbitration proceeded to awards, where the bank was found to be conscious of the backdating and the allegations of fraud were therefore dismissed. Finally, a permanent anti-suit injunction was granted to stop the bank from proceeding against the buyer in China.

The above decisions have demonstrated the English courts' pro-arbitration approach and their willingness to grant anti-suit injunctions to uphold the sanctity of arbitration agreements, even in cases where fraud-based claims are asserted in parallel proceedings in China. In a case where the refund guarantor's assets are likely to be available to be attached outside China to enforce the payment obligation under a refund guarantee, the parallel Chinese proceedings are likely ultimately to prove ineffective to prevent the refund guarantor from having to pay out under the guarantee, as both Bank of China and Bank of Communications found in the above cases.

III. Charterparties

The second type of contract which is very often involved in maritime business is the charterparty. In simple terms charterparties are contracts for the hire of ships, and they fall into three principal categories. One is the bareboat charter where the owner gives up the whole of the management of the ship to the charterer and probably only retains a financial interest in the ship. That is of interest at the moment in China because there are many leasing companies, for example subsidiaries of banks like ICBC, who are involved in ship leasing activities. In fact, Chinese leasing companies have now become one of the most important sources of finance in the shipping industry. It may well be that in a ship financing transaction a single purpose subsidiary of, say, ICBC will buy a ship, a new ship from a shipyard or a second hand ship from its previous owner, and will charter it out or lease it out on a bareboat charter. In accounting terms this is the same, effectively, as a finance lease where the owner recovers substantially the whole of the investment cost of the ship

---

13 [2015] EWHC 3364 (Comm).
14 There was a London arbitration agreement in the refund guarantee as well as in the shipbuilding contract.

over the period of the charter. The charterer will insure and provide crew for the ship and often let it out to another charterer to use in its business of carrying cargo.

Another type of charterparty is a time charter which is a contract for the leasing of a ship for a finite period and may be anything from one trip, for example, from Shanghai to Indonesia and back or it might be for a period of time, like five or ten years. But in this case the owner, or effective or "disponent owner" will have some responsibility for the appointment of the Master and crew and operation and management of the ship and will not contract this out to the charterer as in the case of a bareboat charter, although the charterer will be responsible for the supply of fuel oil or "bunkers" to the ship.

A third type of charterparty is a voyage charter where someone who owns or charters the ship will let it out just for one voyage. For example, from Shanghai to Brazil.

Internationally, like shipbuilding contracts, most charterparties are governed by English law which is expressly chosen by the parties and a very high proportion of them are subject to London arbitration on the Terms and Procedures of the LMAA.[15] They are very rarely the subject of court proceedings in the first instance. However, appeals from arbitration awards to the Commercial Court and beyond are generally published in the official Law Reports and therefore form part of the body of the English common law.

There are many hundreds of English court decisions on particular aspects of the obligations arising under standard form of charterparties and the relative certainty which derives from being able to refer to this body of decisions is an important factor in the selection of English law and frequently English arbitration in relation to such charter contracts.

Many of the established Chinese shipowners and operators, like COSCO, SINOCHART, SINOTRANS and SINOPEC are thoroughly familiar with conducting arbitrations in London to enforce charter obligations and it is fair to say that they have a good success rate in winning such cases.

IV. Contracts for the Carriage of Goods: Bills of Lading and Anti-Suit Injunctions

Bill of lading disputes are also, unfortunately, a common source of friction between the Chinese courts and London arbitration. The following is an example of the sort of case. A cargo is delivered from Africa to a Chinese port by a ship which is on a time charterparty. The time charterer issues bills of lading for the carriage of the goods. The bills of lading are the title for the goods, they are a receipt that the goods have been loaded on board the ship and they also are evidence of the contract of carriage of goods by sea between the shipowner and the holder of the bill of lading. Ultimately the bill of lading will have to be presented to the Master by the consignee of the cargo to have the goods released at the delivery port. There are often major disputes as to whether arbitration agreements which are contained in the time charterparty (or sometimes a voyage charterparty) have been effectively incorporated into the bill of lading so as to bind the consignee in China. So, for example the goods, a cargo of iron ore, are delivered at Qingdao and the consignee in China, the person to whom the goods are to be delivered, says "you have not delivered enough of it". There is a short delivery or "the goods are not in the condition in which I expected to receive them". The first thing that will happen is that the consignee will go to

---

15 The London Maritime Arbitrators Association.

the maritime court in Qingdao and have the ship arrested as security for the cargo claim. The shipowner, and the charterer, will say "but there is an arbitration agreement" in the bill of lading because there was one in the charterparty and it is referred to and effectively incorporated in the bill of lading. The problem then is that the English rules about incorporation of arbitration agreements and bills of lading and the Chinese rules about incorporation of arbitration agreements of charterparties and bills of lading are different, so that the Chinese courts will assert jurisdiction and the shipowner will say "No, the English arbitration tribunal has jurisdiction" on the basis that the underlying charterparty and the bill of lading are both expressly governed by English law and subject to English arbitration . A very major conflict will develop.

A consequence of this may be an application to the English court (or in one controversial case the Chinese court) for an anti-suit injunction. This is a frequent source of friction. In the situation described above, where there is a short delivery or a complaint about the condition of the cargo being delivered in China, the consignee will go to the Chinese court and the owner will say "no, I want arbitration in London" and he or she will try to get an anti-suit injunction from the London court to stop the proceedings in China. It is important to understand that an anti-suit injunction is not directed at the Chinese court; it is not a derogation of Chinese sovereignty. It is directed at the parties to the proceedings. It doesn't attempt to bind the Chinese court. The Chinese court can do whatever it does but there are consequences if one of the parties disobeys the anti-suit injunction. For example, if they come within the personal jurisdiction of the English court then they could be, for example, arrested for contempt of court if they come to England, even just transiting through London airport.[16] Also a party may be liable in damages for breach of the arbitration agreement by trying to litigate in the Chinese court.

In these types of cases, the receiver frequently seeks to sue the shipowner in the local Chinese court where the goods are delivered, while the shipowner on the other hand, wants to have the dispute resolved by English arbitration pursuant to the relevant bill of lading which purports to incorporate the arbitration clause of an underlying charterparty. The English and Chinese law principles governing the incorporation of charterparty terms into bills of lading are significantly different. The Chinese courts have adopted a rigid approach and tend to reject the validity of the arbitration clause incorporated in the bill of lading, whereas the English courts will frequently give effect to it. In such circumstances the use of an English anti-suit injunction is an important technical device in the armoury of the shipowner to protect its contractual right to arbitrate in England.

A real case in point is *Starlight Shipping Co. v Tai Ping Insurance Co. Ltd.*[17] The owner had chartered its vessel, Alexandros T, subject to an arbitration agreement which was incorporated into a bill of lading. The vessel was lost together with her cargo on a voyage from Brazil to China. The insurers of the cargo, having paid out on the loss of the cargo, brought court proceedings in China against the owner, the manager and the head charterer, maintaining that the arbitration clause in the bill of lading was ineffective as a matter of Chinese law. The cargo owners and insurers also began arbitration in London under a

---

16 For an recent example of the consequences of disobeying the order of the English court in relation to a freezing order see the report of *Lakatamia Shipping Co. Ltd. v Morimoto* [2019] EWCA Civ 2203: https://7kbw .co.uk/court-of-appeal-restores-e27m-worldwide-freezing-order/.

17 [2007] EWHC 1893 (Comm). For a similar application of the principle see also *Niagara Maritime SA v. Tianjin Iron & Steel Group Company Limited* [2011] EWHC 3035 (Comm).

reservation as to jurisdiction of the arbitral tribunal. The shipowner then applied for an anti-suit injunction to restrain the defendants from taking any further steps in respect of the Chinese proceedings. In granting an interim anti-suit injunction, the English High Court held that, as a matter of English law, the insurers were, as was the case with the cargo receiver, bound by the arbitration clause in the bill of lading, and that Chinese law was irrelevant to the question since "the cargo claim is one which gives rise to a dispute 'arising under the contract' and is therefore arbitrable".[18] The English Court therefore granted the anti-suit injunction even though it was clear that Chinese jurisprudence would not regard the cargo insurers as being bound by the arbitration clause in the bill of lading.

Chinese interests may also be caught in the trap of an English anti-suit injunction even if they are not party to an arbitration agreement. A case in point is *Qingdao Huiquan Shipping Co. v Shanghai Dong He Xin Industry Group Co. Ltd.*[19] The case is particularly interesting in the cargo claim context. In this case it was the Chinese shipowner who sought an anti-suit injunction from the English court to restrain the court action in China. The dispute arose from a settlement agreement between the Chinese shipowner and a cargo receiver, under which the latter agreed to pay a sum of money through the receiver's agent in respect of the time charterers' default in payment of hire in return for the lifting of the lien and the release of the cargo. In the settlement agreement there was an arbitration clause providing for all disputes "arising under, out of or in connection with" the agreement to be resolved by arbitration in London. Note that the receiver's agent was not, in any event, a party to that agreement. Three years later the receiver's agent brought proceedings before a Chinese court, claiming a refund of the sum paid to the owner under the charterparty and alleging that there had been a separate oral agreement between it and the owner not containing an arbitration clause. The Chinese shipowner then applied to the Commercial Court for an anti-suit injunction against the receiver's agent to restrain the Chinese proceedings.

Giving judgment on the owner's application, Bryan J referred to the existing case law which has established that, it was possible to obtain an anti-suit injunction against a non-contracting party when that party asserted its claim on rights arising out of a contract which was subject to arbitration of disputes. In doing so the claimant was bound by the subject contract and in particular, the forum clause contained in it. The question then to be determined was whether the agent's claim was substantively based on the settlement agreement or whether it was independent. The judge found that the agent was effectively seeking to rely upon the terms of and rights arising under the settlement agreement, notwithstanding the fact that its claim in the court proceedings in China was formally based on the alleged oral agreement. As a consequence the agent was also obliged to take the burden of the arbitration clause contained in it. Accordingly, it was held that, where the foreign claimant is indeed bringing a contractual claim inconsistently with a jurisdiction clause in that contract, an injunction will be granted even in cases where privity of contract is not present. This case can be seen as a paradigm of Chinese parties' confidence and maturity in utilising foreign procedural rules to safeguard their interests.

Lastly, I would mention that, while the English court has the power to issue an anti-suit injunction, an unnecessary delay in seeking the injunction where the foreign proceedings

---

18 *Starlight Shipping Co. v Tai Ping Insurance Co. Ltd.* [2007] EWHC 1893 (Comm) at para. 14.
19 [2018] EWHC 3009 (Comm).

were already far advanced may result in an otherwise strong application being rejected by the English court. In such cases Chinese parties have been successful in resisting the potential threat from the English courts. For example In *The Kishore*,[20] the applicant for an anti-suit injunction had waited for more than nine months after the commencement of proceedings in China before it sought an anti-suit injunction in England. The English High court therefore refused the application on the basis that the relief was not sought promptly.

From a carrier shipowner's perspective these problems often arise because of the basic differences between the English and Chinese law approaches to incorporation of charterparty arbitration clauses. The English law on this subject has developed through a significant number of reported cases over the last century and is widely followed by other common law countries.[21] A certain body of caselaw has recently developed in China[22] but it is respectfully suggested that the Chinese decisions at the level of individual maritime courts are not wholly consistent or predictable and in some cases unreasonably favour Chinese consignees or their insurers. For example the Chinese courts have generally refused to recognise that a cargo insurer claiming in right of a bill of lading holder should be bound by the same obligations as the holder of the bill, including the arbitration agreement. No doubt this battle of jurisdictions in cargo cases will continue for some years to come.

The author is aware that there is a view in China that these anti-suit injunctions are a matter of interference with Chinese sovereignty, that they are easily obtained by owners and that they are a frequent bar to proceedings in the Chinese maritime court. In fact, it is quite difficult, and is, as I see it, becoming in fact increasingly difficult for a shipowner to obtain an anti-suit injunction in order to stop the proceedings in China. As in the *Qingdao Huiquan*[23] case cited above however, Chinese shipowners delivering cargo to Chinese ports may find the English approach more appealing even if consignees in China and their insurers will inevitably favour litigation in the Chinese courts.

V. Guarantees

In recent years there have been a number of important decisions involving Chinese parties concerning guarantees issued by banks and other parties for obligations of shipyards and buyers under shipbuilding contracts, as well as guarantees given for obligations of Chinese charterers under long term time charterparties. Some of these have been decided on the basis of the legal distinction to be drawn between an on demand bond on the one hand and, on the other, a guarantee in the sense of a so-called "see to it" guarantee. This distinction is often important in determining whether the party claiming under the guarantee has to

---

20 *Essar Shipping Ltd. v Bank of China Ltd (The "Kishore")* [2015] EWHC 3266 (Comm). See also *Pan Ocean Co. Ltd. v China-Base Group Co. Ltd. (1) & Beihai Xinan Petrochemical Co. Ltd.* [2019] EWHC 982 (Comm), where the judge found that the relevant contract did not contain an exclusive jurisdiction clause in favour of the English courts, and went on to conclude that even if there had been a binding exclusive jurisdiction clause, he would have declined to grant an anti-suit injunction on the basis of delay.

21 *Since Thomas v Portsea Steamship Company Limited* [1912] AC 1.

22 See Liang Zhao and Lianjun Li: The Incorporation of Arbitration Clauses into Bills of Lading under the PRC Law and its practical implications Arbitration International, *Arbitration International*, Volume 33, Issue 4, December 2017, pp. 647–661, and Zhao and Li: Maritime Law and Practice in China, 2017, paragraphs 6.23 through 6.28.

23 [2018] EWHC 3009 (Comm).

prove that the underlying contractual obligation guaranteed has not been performed. In the case of an on demand bond, such proof should not be necessary and the bond can be successfully called on unless it can be shown that the demand is fraudulent or in bad faith. A presumption based on the four so-called "Paget" tests is often invoked to determine what form a bond or guarantee takes. In broad terms, where the bond or guarantee has been issued by a bank as in *Wuhan Guoyu Logistics Company Limited v Emporiki Bank of Greece S.A.*[24] the instrument is more likely to be construed as an on demand bond than where it has been issued by a non-bank, commercial company, as in *Shanghai Shipyard Co. Ltd. v Reignwood International Investment (Group) Company Ltd.*[25]

A different issue of corporate authority concerning a guarantee obligation undertaken by a Chinese company arose in *Jiangsu Shagang Group Co. Ltd. v Loki Owning Company Ltd.*[26] The case involved a guarantee of charterhire payable by a subsidiary and provides an illustration of the extent to which an English court has been prepared to take into account practices in China in sanctioning important transactions entered into by a major company, which were quite different from those which might have been expected in England or many other jurisdictions.

A subsidiary of Jiangsu Shangang Group Limited had entered into a charterparty for a ship to carry iron ore for its steel mill in China. The charterer defaulted in payment of charterhire and the charter was terminated. About USD 70 million was involved in this case. The parent company in the Shagang Group had given guarantees for the obligations of the chartering subsidiary under the long term charter entered into by it. The shipowner who let the ship to the Chinese subsidiary sued the Shagang parent company under its guarantee. There was an arbitration agreement in the guarantee and the arbitration tribunal found in favour of the foreign shipowner and against the Chinese party. The Chinese party which had given the guarantee appealed to the English Commercial Court and won. This is significant because it shows that the English court is prepared to accept that there are different ways of doing business in China to the way which a public company, for example in England or America or Europe, might do business. This was a company which was very much controlled by one shareholder and that shareholder was accustomed to approve or not to approve things which were done by the company with very little corporate documentation.

The judge stated this:

> The absence of any record or formal documentary reaction (either within JSG or Shagang) to the discovery of the Guarantee in late 2010 is surprising, at least to an English lawyer's eyes. However, allowances must be made for differences in working practices. It is clear that much of JSG's dealings (such as the giving of authority by SWM for guarantees) went undocumented. Additionally, it is apparent that JSG's record keeping systems were very far from perfect.

Nevertheless the judge accepted that the guarantee which was the subject of the case had not been properly authorised and the claimant shipowner went away empty handed.

---

24 [2012] Civ EWCA 1629.
25 [2020] EWHC 803 (Comm).
26 [2018] EWHC 330 (Comm).

From cases such as this it would be hard to say that the English court was in some way prejudiced against the position of the Chinese party. The non-Chinese party in this case certainly had a different view.

VI. Enforcement of Chinese Arbitral Awards

Turning to the enforcement of a Chinese arbitration award, *Sinocore v RBRG (UK) Ltd.*[27] is a relatively recent case where an award of a CIETAC arbitral tribunal with a Chinese "seat" was approved for enforcement in England under the New York Convention. This was despite the fact that there was an allegation of fraud and illegality affecting the bills of lading which were involved in the case. Under the New York Convention, public policy can be a defence to an application to enforce a foreign arbitration award. The court drew a distinction between domestic public policy (that is English domestic public policy in this case) and international public policy and decided that as a matter of international public policy the award should be upheld despite the alleged illegality which might have been a bar to enforcement in the case of a domestic English arbitration award. It thus appears that a Chinese party can be confident that awards which are properly rendered by Chinese arbitration tribunals will be enforced under the New York Convention in England.

Conversely, we know from our experience in the LMAA that awards made by "*ad hoc*" LMAA tribunals are regularly approved for enforcement, where necessary by the Chinese Supreme People's Court, and that very few have actually been refused enforcement.

VII. Recognition and Enforcement of Chinese Court Judgements

Finally, on the recognition of Chinese court judgments, there is no multi-lateral treaty governing the enforcement of court judgements as there is governing the enforcement of arbitration awards. There is no equivalent of the New York Convention regarding the mutual recognition of court judgments. However, the question whether the English court would enforce the judgement of a Chinese court came for decision in the case of *Spliethoffs Bevrachtingskantoor BV v Bank of China Ltd.* (mentioned above in the context of parallel proceedings in China in a shipbuilding contract dispute).

This case aroused considerable controversy in China. The shipowner claimed in arbitration for the refund of instalment payments under its contract with the shipyard[28] on the basis that it had properly cancelled the contracts for delay. The shipyard brought parallel proceedings in the Qingdao maritime court in China claiming against the shipowner and the supplier of the main engines, Wärtsilä and alleging that they had conspired to supply engines which were not the new engines as required by the shipbuilding contracts. These Chinese proceedings eventually went to the Supreme People's Court which dismissed the claim by the shipyard. The reported English case concerned a refund guarantee given by Bank of China. Bank of China tried to challenge the arbitration award and avoid payment under the refund guarantee because the bank claimed that it was restrained from paying out by an order of the Qingdao Maritime Court. There was some controversy

---

27 [2018] EWCA Civ 838.
28 The shipyard in question is known in China under its name Xi Xia Kou ("XXK") (in English the shipyard is usually known as "Rongsheng").

about whether the Chinese court judgement was in fact binding on the Bank of China and whether it did in fact prevent it from making the payment. But the English court did quite clearly recognise that the Chinese court's judgement was enforceable as such as a matter of principle under the English Senior Courts Act and so could be enforced. The judge (the same judge as in *the Shagang* case mentioned above) said this:

> In my judgment, it is clear as a matter of English law that, in choosing to fully defend the claims against it in the [Chinese] proceedings after the final dismissal of its jurisdictional challenges in the Supreme Court, [Spliethoffs] is to be treated as having "otherwise submitt[ed]" to the jurisdiction of the Chinese courts, subject to s.33(1)(c) of the CJJA" ... "Here, having unsuccessfully challenged jurisdiction, [Spliethoffs] appeared at trial and made substantive submissions on the facts and the law. When it lost in the [Qingdao Maritime court], it appealed to the Shandong High Court and then applied to the Supreme Court for a retrial. Under English law principles of private international law, that was submission" ... [Spliethoffs] seeks to rely on s.33(1)(c) of the [English Civil Jurisdiction and Judgments Act] on the basis that it should not be regarded as having submitted because it appeared in China to protect or obtain the release of property seized or threatened with seizure in the proceedings. The difficulty for [Spliethoffs] is that, whilst it did submit for the purpose of seeking to lift the [Chinese court] orders, it was unsuccessful in doing so and then went on to defend the claims fully on the merits ... I therefore conclude that [Spliethoffs] is to be treated as having submitted to the jurisdiction of the Chinese courts.

This decision is also likely to be important in considering the question of reciprocity. In proceedings in future to enforce an English court judgement in China, the Chinese courts, if asked to enforce an English court judgement, will inevitably ask the question "will the English courts enforce a Chinese court judgement?" and the answer is in principle yes, at least if the foreign party has defended the Chinese proceedings and effectively submitted to the jurisdiction of the Chinese court.[29]

VIII. Conclusion

This chapter summarises and may give some insight into shipbuilding cases and other maritime arbitration proceedings in London and related litigation involving Chinese parties.

Based on the analysis above, it may help to dispel the suggestion that the English courts and English maritime arbitration tribunals are in some way biased against Chinese parties. This chapter demonstrated that it is clear from these recent decisions that they will decide the cases which come before them strictly in accordance with the contractual agreements entered into by the parties, the law and the evidence presented to them.

---

29 See: Recognition and enforcement of foreign court judgment in China – from the perspective of recognizing an English court judgment: Yang, Luo and Xiao; The Ninth International Conference of Maritime Law, Shanghai October 2018.

PART III

LIABILITY REGIMES

CHAPTER 13

Deficiency and Remedy of a Cargo Lien Clause under Multiple Charterparties

From the Perspective of Chinese Law

Shengnan Jia[1]

I. Introduction

In the chartering industry, the nature of a shipowner's cargo lien appears to be unquestionable, given that it is generally accepted to be a legal possessory security in China. Unlike contractual security, the creation of a cargo lien does not depend on mutual agreement between a shipowner and a charterer to a charterparty. If only the condition precedent is satisfied, including possession of the cargo and the debt is due, the law will give the shipowner a security interest on the cargo in accordance with the Chinese Maritime Code 1992 (hereinafter referred to "CMC 1992").[2]

In this context, as far as the shipowner's cargo security is concerned, the interrelation between the legal and the contractual solution might be described as a combined product of primary and secondary security mechanisms. The legal cargo security plays a primary role in protecting the shipowner, while contractual cargo security plays a secondary role in strengthening the protection of the shipowner.

From the perspective of the origin of the shipowner's cargo security, this interrelation is inevitable, because traditionally the shipowner must possess the charterer's cargo during the performance of the charterparty. In response to the charterer's default, trade usage and the law grant the shipowner the legal security on the cargo. However, in the modern chartering industry, a single charterparty model has been replaced by a string of charterparties, namely multiple charterparties. A vessel may involve multiple charterparties, including bareboat, time and voyage charterparties.[3] In this connection, the different parties to multiple charterparties inevitably interlink with the cargo on the same vessel.

A question arises as to whether the legal cargo security may contribute all creditors, including a shipowner, a disponent shipowner and sub-disponent shipowners under

---

1 Dr Shengnan Jia is an Associate Professor, Navigation College, Jimei University, Xiamen, China; Co-Founding Director, China–Europe Commercial Collaboration Association (CECCA) (London) and Chair of the Board, Stichting CECCA (Netherlands).

2 Maritime Code of the People's Republic of China 1992 (hereinafter referred to as "CMC 1992") was adopted on 7 November 1992 at the Twenty-Eighth Session of the Seventh National People's Congress of People's Republic of China and came into effect on 1 July 1993. See Article 87 of The Maritime Code 1992.

3 Lars Gorton and others, *Shipbroking and Chartering Practice* (7th edn, Informa 2009), p. 126.

DOI: 10.4324/9781003160298-16

multiple charterparties to claiming against the debtor. After all, the condition precedent of the legal cargo security for the creditor is to possess the cargo physically. However, it is evident that not all creditors may possess the cargo physically and the condition of the legal possessory security cannot be satisfied. For this reason, the legal cargo security is untenable unless the legislation persists in granting a shipowner a legal right.

In the Chinese legal framework, although Chinese maritime law has adopted several international conventions and some common law concepts into its legal regime, the essential principles and philosophy regarding civil and commercial law are from German law. Furthermore, like German law, the theory of secured transactions law has been incorporated into the CMC 1992. Even so, in comparison with German law, because of the absence of the developed secured transactions law, some theories, like indirect possession,[4] are only present in academic literature making it difficult to discern and determine the value orientation of the legislator. In this context, in a chain of charterparties, the theory of indirect possession cannot play a role in determining that the disponent shipowner or sub-charterer may enjoy the indirect possession on the cargo while the actual shipowner may perform the lien on the cargo. Furthermore, in Chinese law, the absence of some provisions results in that the legislator's real purpose not being readily discernible. Therefore, it is anticipated that the controversy in terms of the legal nature and effect of shipowner's cargo security is evident in practical and academic circles. This chapter will explore the deficiency and remedy of a cargo lien clause under multiple charterparties through Chinese legislation, scholarly opinions and judicial decisions.

II. Brief Account of the Chinese Maritime Code

In the structure of a contract for carriage of goods and charterparties under Chinese law, a voyage charterparty and a bill of lading have been codified into a Chapter entitled "contract of carriage of goods" under the CMC 1992 where all provisions for a voyage charterparty are not mandatory, while time and bareboat charterparties have been incorporated into a Chapter captioned as "charterparties" where the provisions are regarded as being elective and only binding when parties have not provided for them in the relevant agreement.

Based on this, under the CMC Chapter "contract of carriage of goods", a voyage shipowner, as a carrier, enjoys a (contractual) security (lien) provided by legislation which states that:

> If freight, contribution in general average, demurrage to be paid to the carrier and other necessary charges paid by the carrier on behalf of the owner of the goods as well as other charges to be paid to the carrier have not been paid in full, nor has appropriate security been given, the carrier may have a lien, to a reasonable extent, on the goods.[5]

Similarly, under the chapter entitled "charterparties", a time shipowner is entitled to invoke a security on the cargo belonging to the time charterer. Article 141 provides "in case the charterer fails to pay the hire or other sums of money as agreed upon in the

---

4 It is noted that the foundation of indirect possession has been explicitly provided under Section 868 of the German Civil Code, but due to the limited space, no further discussion on the indirect of possession.

5 CMC 1992, Art. 87.

charter, the shipowner shall have a lien on the charterer's goods, other property on board and earnings from the sub-charter".[6]

In essence, Article 87 provides for a carrier's statutory security on the cargo. As discussed earlier, in Chinese law, a voyage charterparty is deemed to be a contract of carriage of goods and a voyage shipowner's rights and obligations provided by legislation are compatible with those of a carrier.[7] In this connection, although the legislation does not expressly point out that a voyage shipowner acts on a carrier, after this kind of a charterparty is deemed to be a contract of carriage of goods, the corresponding shipowner's role is deemed to be that of a carrier. Subsequently, considering the notion of "carrier" in Chinese law, it is recognised that the carrier may invoke a statutory lien.[8] Furthermore, from the entire legal system in China, a statutory lien is provided not only by property law which is to concentrate on the protection of an owner's security over his property, but also by the law of contract, which is to stress the protection of the obligatory right to enhance the dynamic transaction.[9] Therefore, in the context of a voyage charterparty, the voyage shipowner as a carrier actually enjoys a statutory lien and the purpose of the carrier's lien is to remedy an obligatory right.[10]

In addition, in accordance with the CMC 1992, the carrier has been divided into "carrier" and "actual carrier". The former indicates that "the person by whom or in whose name a contract of carriage of goods by sea has been concluded with a shipper",[11] while the latter refers to "the person to whom the performance of carriage of goods, or of part of the carriage, has been entrusted by the carrier, and includes any other person to whom such performance has been entrusted under a sub-contract".[12] In this connection, a voyage shipowner may be a contractual or actual carrier.

In terms of a time charterparty, the foundation is different. The legislation does not precisely provide for a time charterer being a carrier. Furthermore, because the majority

---

6 Ibid.

7 It should be noted that the CMC 1992 is undergoing revision by the lawmaking bodies in China. The revision of the CMC 1992 has been listed in the current National Legislation Plan of the Thirteenth National People's Congress for the period from 2018 to 2023, as one of the 47 draft statutes in the second tier of the hierarchy to be submitted for review when the draft becomes mature. In November 2018, the Ministry of Transport of P.R.C. issued the Revision of the CMC 1992 (Draft for Comments). Based on this Revision, the SPC submitted that the majority opinion in the SPC proposed to divide a carriage of goods by sea contract and a voyage charterparty into the different chapters on the ground that both the carriage contract arising from a bill of lading and the voyage charterparty are fundamental different, while the minority opinion contended that the voyage charterparty belonged to the carriage of goods by sea contract; see, Beiping Chu, "Internal Harmonization and International Transplant of the Revision of the CMC 1992" (Impact of the Civil Code on Shipping Legislation and Judicial Practice, Yangtze River Maritime Law Association, 26 November 2020); However, the Ministry of Transport of P.R.C on 7 January 2020 actually submitted the Revision of the CMC 1992 (Draft for Approval) to the State Council of P.R.C. In this Draft, the voyage charterparty still stands in the Chapter of "Contract of Carriage of Goods". See "Application of the Ministry of Transport of P.R.C. for the Review of the Revision of the CMC 1992 (Draft for Approval)" (Jiao Fa Fa [2020] No. 10).

8 Art 836 of The Civil Code of P.R.C. 2020 (hereinafter referred to "Civil Code 2020") provides that "[W] here the consignor or consignee fails to pay the freight, storage fees and other expenses, the carrier is entitled to lien on the relevant carried cargoes, except as otherwise agreed upon by the parties". The Civil Code was enacted on 28 May 2020 and came into force as of 1 January 2021. It abolished the General Principles of Civil Law of 1986, the Contract Law of 1999, the Tort Law of 2010 and the Property Law of 2007.

9 Ziming Weng and Xiaohan Yu, "Carrier's Lien—Study on Article 315, Contract Law of P.R.C." (2001) 1 People's Court Daily.

10 Ibid; But this point always gives rise to the controversial proposition.

11 CMC 1992, Art. 42 (1).

12 Ibid. at Art. 42 (1).

proposition in China is that the time charterparty reflects the nature of a "lease" contract, some Chinese scholars directly assert that only the time charterer may act as the carrier, because he "has leased the ship from the shipowner".[13] Certainly, this rationale is untenable. Whether a disponent shipowner under a time charterparty may count as a carrier depends on whether he issues the bill of lading.

III. Deficiency of Substantive Law Protection

Following the above brief account, this section will be divided into two aspects to explain the deficiency of the Chinese substantive law. One aspect is to look at the general deficiency regarding shipowners, disponent shipowners and carriers; another is to look at the impact of the deficiency on the disponent shipowner.

A. Deficiency under a Single Charterparty

The current legislation cannot provide sufficient legislative protection to all shipowners when they resort to exercising their right to cargo security. Because the purpose of this chapter is to demonstrate that the contractual solution should be used to protect the shipowner's cargo security, the object here is to illustrate how the deficiency of the substantive law impacts on the protection of the shipowner.

As noted above, the CMC 1992 is a special law to deal with maritime disputes; whereby, the shipowner's cargo security is firstly subject to the CMC 1992. With regard to the scope of the secured cargo, both Articles 87 regarding the voyage shipowner's cargo security and 141 regarding the time shipowner's cargo security of the Maritime Code, do not extend the scope of the secured cargo to the third party's property.[14] More specifically, the provision of the scope under the CMC 1992 follows that of the BALTIME Form which is that the shipowner shall have a lien on all cargos belonging to the time-charterer.[15]

In addition, it should be noted that in comparison with Article 141 expressly providing for "a lien on the charterer's goods",[16] Article 87 of the CMC 1992 provides:

> if the freight, contribution in general average, demurrage to be paid to the carrier and other necessary charges paid by the carrier on behalf of the owner of the goods as well as other charges to be paid to the carrier have not been paid in full, nor has appropriate security been given, the carrier may have a lien, to a reasonable extent, on the goods.[17]

Although this article in the official English translation does not limit the scope of the secured cargo belonging to the charterer, in the Chinese version, prior to the term "goods", the word "its" has been inserted. The meaning of "its" in terms of Chinese practice and

13 Meirong Zhou, Yi Yang and Wei Tan, "An Analysis of the Legal Issues in Lien Clause in the Time Charter Party" (2009) 1 China Ocean Law Review, pp. 365, 365.

14 CMC 1992, Art. 87; in the draft of revision of the CMC 1992, the scope of the cargo has been extended to the third parties' cargo. But this revision has not been issued officially so far.

15 The BALTIME 2001 form, Art. 16 provides that "the Owners shall have a lien upon all cargoes and sub-freights belonging to the Time-Charterers and any Bill of Lading freight for all claims under this Charter, and the Charterers shall have a lien on the Vessel for all moneys paid in advance and not earned".

16 CMC 1992, Art. 141 provides that "in case the charterer fails to pay the hire or other sums of money as agreed upon in the charter, the (time) shipowner shall have a lien on the charterer's goods, other property on board".

17 Ibid. at Art. 87.

in academic circles has been hotly debated. Chinese Maritime Courts for Presidents 2001 and Judgment of the Supreme People's Court involving Foreign-related Commercial and Maritime Legal Issues 2008 have provided a definitive response by stating that in the internal water transport, regardless of whether or not the cargo belongs to the charterer, the shipowner is entitled to exercise his legal cargo security on any cargos on board; but in accordance with the CMC 1992, in the international water transport, the secured cargo should be confined to the debtor's cargo.[18] The debtor signifies the charterer. Therefore, from the point of view of the legislation, apart from the charterer's property, the shipowner is not entitled to detain the third party's cargo.

Notably, the legislation is contrary to the Chinese general law. In Part III "Contract" of the Civil Code 2020, the carrier is entitled to detain the cargo regardless of whether this cargo belongs to the consignee or the consignor, while under the CMC 1992 the specific provision stresses that the secured cargo must belong to the charterer.[19] However, as previously mentioned, the general law is only applied when the special law is inadequate in relevant provisions. It should be noted that in the draft of revision of the CMC 1992, the scope of the cargo has been extended to the third parties' cargo. However, this revision has not been issued officially so far.[20]

Nevertheless, Articles 94 regarding the voyage charterparty and 127 regarding the time charterparty in the CMC provide the alternative approach to addressing the issue of the scope of the secured cargo.[21] In accordance with the above two Articles, Articles 87 and 141 are not mandatory; they are only to be applied when in the charterparties used by the parties, the relevant clauses are absent. In addition, when there are no different clauses in the chosen charterparties by parties, Articles 87 and 141 can be applied. From the viewpoint of literal interpretation, Articles 94 and 127 imply two meanings. First, the parties to voyage and time charterparties are entitled to negotiate the contractual rights and obligations; secondly, the parties are entitled to draft a clause which may not be compatible with Articles 87 and 141. In other words, if the parties draft a lien clause over cargo in their voyage or time charterparties; or they choose to use the NYPE Form which does not limit the scope of the secured cargo, regardless of which option will be compliance with the legislation. Articles 87, 141 and other Articles are only regarded as backup contractual clauses. In light of this rationale, the legislation in essence grants party autonomy to par-

---

18 Chinese Maritime Courts Seminar for Presidents (全国海事法院院长座谈会纪要), July 2001, Art. 4; Judgment for Foreign-related Commercial and Maritime Legal Issues (涉外海事商事审判实务问题解答) 2008, Art. 138; It should be noted that decisions laid down by "Chinese Maritime Courts Seminar for Presidents" and "Judgment for Foreign-related Commercial and Maritime Legal Issues" can be regarded as judicial interpretations which should be applied by all Chinese courts, Xuyu Hu, "Research on International Carrier's Cargo Lien by Sea" (2013) 175 (8) Jinan Journal (Philosophy and Social Sciences), p. 62.

19 The Civil Code 2020, Art. 836 provides that "[W]here the consignor or consignee fails to pay the freight, storage fees and other expenses, the carrier is entitled to lien on the relevant carried cargoes, except as otherwise agreed upon by the parties".

20 The Ministry of Transport of P.R.C on 7 January 2020 actually submitted the Revision of the CMC 1992 (Draft for Approval) to the State Council of P.R.C. See "Application of the Ministry of Transport of P.R.C. for the Review of the Revision of the CMC 1992 (Draft for Approval)" (Jiao Fa Fa [2020] No. 10).

21 CMC 1992, Art. 94 provides that "the other provisions in this Chapter (a contract of carriage of goods) regarding the rights and obligations of the parties to the contract shall apply to the shipowner and the charterer under voyage charter only in the absence of relevant provisions or no different provisions in the voyage charter". And Art. 127 stipulates that "[T]he provisions concerning the rights and obligations of the shipowner and the charterer in this Chapter (charterparties) shall apply only when there are no stipulations or no different stipulations in this regard in the carter party".

ties when they draft the cargo security clause. Nevertheless, this conclusion gives rise to strong debate.

The prevailing view is that the principle of *numerus clausus* is unshakable in Chinese legal system, although the understanding and application of this principle in recent years is gradually loose. Accordingly, even if Articles 87 and 141 are not mandatory provisions, the cargo security, in accordance with the Civil Code 2020, is a legal security right. The scope of the secured cargo, the requirement of exercise this clause and other conditions must be subject to Part II "Property Rights" of the Civil Code 2020. Party autonomy is excluded. Whereas the scope of the secured cargo in Part II "Property Rights" of the Civil Code 2020 simply refers to the debtor's movable property,[22] the shipowner's cargo security cannot apply to the third party's property. From the carrier's perspective, the bill of lading holder is the carrier's debtor; therefore, it is possible to detain the consignor's property. But from the shipowner point of view in a charterparty, there is no possibility for the shipowner to detain the consignor's property.

Against the above discussion, there are two main conflicts. First, the conflict between the general law and the special law. While the general law, Part III "Contract" of the Civil Code 2020 grants the carrier the secured right on all relevant carried cargoes,[23] the special law, the CMC 1992 simply allows the carrier to lien on the debtor's cargo. In the context of charterparties, the debtor's cargo refers to the charterer's cargo. In light of the principle of *lex specialis derogate legi generali*, the CMC 1992 takes priority.

The second conflict arises from the law of contract and property law. While from the perspective of contract law, the provisions regarding a voyage and time charterparty in the CMC 1992 are not mandatory, the property law in the Civil Code 2020 provides the concept and application of the lien over the debtor's movable property.

It is observed that the scope of the secured cargo in charterparties is simply confined to the charterer's cargo in the current legal framework, although the narrow scope has given rise to strong criticism of the legislation. Furthermore, Chinese judicial practice normally takes a conservative and cautious approach to exercising of the shipowner's cargo security. More specifically, traditionally the cargo lien (security) is a legal security interest which must be subject to the legislation. It does not matter whether the legislation is reasonable or not.

In the typical Chinese cases reported officially, all relevant courts are not in favour of shipowners claiming cargo security against consignees. Furthermore, all shipowners have to be liable for damages because they detain the consignees' cargo. The foundation of the courts is completely uniform which is that the scope of the secured cargo in the CMC 1992 is simply to identify the charterer's cargo, not including the cargo of others, and pointing out that the broad scope provided by Part III "Contract" of the Civil Code 2020 cannot be applied. Most importantly, although there is no judgment made by the SPC in an application for a shipowner's retrial, the SPC rejected the shipowner's application. In other words, the SPC is in favour of applying a narrow scope to the secured cargo.[24]

---

22 The Civil Code 2020, Art. 447 provides that "in case an obligor (debtor) fails to pay debt due, the obligee (creditor) may take the lien on the obligor's movable property which he lawfully possesses and be entitled to seek preferred payments from these movable property".

23 The Civil Code 2020, Art. 836.

24 *Xiamen Liangxiang Shipping Company v Jiangsu Weitai Logistics Company* [2016] MMZ No. 1393; *Jiangsu Weitai Logistics Company v Guangxi Xinminhang Shipping Industry* [2016] M72 M C No. 227;

It can be seen that a legislative remedy for any shipowners is limited. The legal cargo security is not useful in China from the viewpoint of the scope of the secured cargo because in practice the possibility for the charterer's cargo being on board is nearly zero.

B. Deficiency under Multiple Charterparties

The purpose of the above section was to look at the deficiency of a shipowner's cargo security in a single charterparty. This section will examine what is the dilemma of the disponent shipowner under multiple charterparties.

With regard to the voyage charterparty chain, as discussed in section III.A, although the legislation does not expressly point out that a voyage shipowner acts as a carrier, after a voyage charterparty is deemed to be a contract of carriage of goods and a voyage shipowner's rights and obligations provided by legislation are compatible with those of a carrier, his role is deemed to be that of a carrier. Furthermore, under the voyage charterparty chain, both a head shipowner and a disponent shipowner are carriers. Just the head shipowner is the actual carrier, and the disponent shipowner and sub-disponent shipowner are contractual carriers. In accordance with Article 87 of the CMC 1992, these carriers enjoy the statutory cargo security. The limitation of this statutory cargo security is discussed above in section III.A.

With regard to the time charterparty chain, regardless of the shipowner's cargo security or the disponent shipowner's cargo security, both are difficult to achieve the remedy. To start with, the foundation is different. The legislation does not provide a precise answer for a time charterer being a carrier. Furthermore, because the majority proposition in China is that the time charterparty reflects the nature of a 'lease' contract, a deep-rooted idea is that this time charterparty cannot have any connections with a carriage of goods by sea contract. Even if in practice there is no doubt that under a time charterparty, either a shipowner or a time charterer may issue the bill of lading, but after examining Chinese cases, it is found that Chinese parties often worry about the time shipowner' or the disponent shipowner's legal status. Therefore, when time shipowners claim the cargo security, they tend to persuade the judge to consider that their time charterparties are in fact voyage charterparties rather than time charterparties. In other words, if the disputed charterparties can be deemed to be voyage charterparties, the shipowners, as the carriers are entitled to detain the consignee's cargo, not just to detain the charterer's cargo.

For example, in *Xiamen Yichengda Shipping Company v Qinzhou Xiangli Logistic Company*,[25] Yichengda time chartered his vessel to Xinminhang Company. After Xinminghang Company stopped all business and could not pay for the hire, Yichengda detained Xiangli Logistic' cargo. However, during the litigation proceedings, Yichengda simply contended that he voyage-chartered his vessel to Xinminghang Company. Although Yichengda did not express his intention for this contention, the court pointed out that Yichengda ventured to demonstrate this contract was the voyage charterparty so that he was a qualified actual carrier. In the end, at the first instance and the second (final) instance, both Xiamen Maritime Court and Fujian Higher Court held that Yichengda and

---

QinZhou Xiangli Logistics Company v Xiamen Yichengda Shipping Operator Company [2016] M72 MC No. 960; *Xiamen Liangxiang Shipping Company v Jiangsu Weitai Logistics Company* [2017] ZGRMS No. 1698.
    25 [2017] MMZ No. 419.

Xinminghang Company entered into the voyage charterparty rather than the time charterparty. Therefore, Yichengda was simply entitled to claim the hire against the charterer, Xinminghang, rather than the consignee, Xiangli Logistic.[26]

It can be seen that in theory, Yichengda is the actual carrier who is entitled to claim the freight against Xiangli Logistic. However, because of the clear line between the time charterparty and the carriage of goods by sea contract, if Yichengda was a voyage charterparty shipowner, he was entitled to claim the freight against the consignee; by contrast, if he was a time charterparty shipowner, he forfeited his right against the consignee.

Apart from the time head shipowner, the time disponent shipowner encounters more difficult. This is because although the head shipowner cannot lawfully detain the consignee's cargo, in practice, he takes possession of the cargo and often forces the consignee to sign a contract with him before unloading the cargo. Otherwise, he refuses to proceed to port. By contrast, the disponent shipowner has no right to control the cargo physically.

In the author's opinion, in the current legal framework, as far as a time disponent shipowner is concerned, the crucial issue is whether, like German law, indirect possession or constructive possession can be applied under Chinese law. Because the disponent shipowner does not possess the cargo physically, he has to claim constructive possession in order to exercise his lien. However, the Property Law does not provide the theory of indirect possession even though this theory is generally accepted in practical and academic circles.[27] In practice, there is no decided case applying the theory of indirect possession to support the time shipowner's lien. However, in a recent dispute between a freight forwarder and a principal, the Shanghai Maritime Court applied the provision of Property Law regarding "possession" to recognise the application of indirect possession on the cargo in legal practice.[28] However, this case was heard the Shanghai Maritime Court. It is an underlying viewpoint in China that academics, the judiciary and practitioners in the southern coastal provinces are inclined to hold a broad view. In this context, the local court very often renders a decision compatible with commercial reality even if the legislation does not provide a clear answer. In contrast, courts in the northern and western provinces, tend to maintain a conservative attitude towards the recognition and creation of a new legal rule, even if this new rule can find support in legal theory.

In short, from the viewpoint of substantive law, the protection of both shipowners and disponent shipowners is limited. Although the legislation seems to stipulate specific provisions for the exercising of the shipowner and the voyage disponent shipowner's cargo security, and only protection of the time disponent shipowner's cargo security, it is arguable that the legal requirement of the secured charterer's cargo gives rise to the legal barrier to exercising the cargo security. A positive factor is that the legislator has noted this

---

26 *QinZhou Xiangli Logistics Company v Xiamen Yichengda Shipping Operator Company* [2016] M 72 MC No. 960; *Xiamen Yichengda Shipping Operator Company v QinZhou Xiangli Logistics Company* [2017] MMZ No. 419.

27 Guang Sun, "Research on Legal System of Possessory Lien on Goods Carried by Sea" (PhD Dissertation, Dalian Maritime University 2014), pp. 27–28.

28 *Shanghai TOPFOR Logistics International Co., Ltd v Shanghai Xuntonggroup* [2016] No. 331, Hu No. 72 Civil Division I, (dispute over Shipping Agency Contract); Chan Yang, "A Freight Forwarder's Lien on Movable Property Based on Indirect Possession" (2017) 5 Navigation 17, pp. 17–22; it should be noted that in 2016 the Property Law referred to the Property Law of P.R.C. 2007. After the Civil Code 2020 came into effect on 1 January 2021, the majority provisions of the Property Law 2007 have been codified into the Civil Code 2020 and the Property Law 2007 was abolished.

legal barrier and accepted the proposal provided by Chinese scholars. In the Revision of the CMC 1992 (Draft for Approval 2020) proposed by the Ministry of Transport of PRC on 7 January 2020, the secured cargo is not confined to the charterer's property.[29] It is anticipated that the revision of the CMC 1992 may contribute to the application of cargo security. However, the revision will only improve matters partially. There is no disponent shipowner's provision appearing in the revision of the CMC 1992.

IV. Remedy in Procedure Law: Arrest of Cargo

In the context of deficiency of substantive law, the procedure law quite commonly plays an important role in protecting the parties. Although the protection of the procedure law normally is temporary and relies on the decision of the competent court, as opposed to the self-help remedy, it is to some extent an effective approach to protect the parties.

With regard to the protection of the disponent shipowner, Article 44 of Special Maritime Procedure Law provides that "a maritime claimant may apply to arrest the goods on board for ensuring the fulfilment of his maritime claim".[30] This special provision grants the parties a right to apply for property preservation which is similar with the concept of interim measure in common law.[31] In terms of the scope of a maritime claimant, the legislation does not stipulate any limitation. Therefore, in theory, all parties, before or during the litigation or arbitration proceedings, are entitled to apply for the arrest of cargos. In practice, after the litigation or arbitration proceedings, whether the application is proper and lawful is subject to the substantive law. In addition, whether the applicant possesses the cargo physically will not impact on the creation of the application for the arrest of cargo.

However, the scope of the arrested cargo on board, in accordance with Article 44, is confined to the counterpart. There is no judicial interpretation to clarify the meaning of "counterpart". Whether the "counterpart" simply refers to parties to a contract, alternatively it may refer to parties in any underlying legal relationship is an issue. To this present author's observations, the "counterpart" in the procedure law can be construed in a broad sense in legal practice. Therefore, a maritime claimant may choose its counterpart. Even if in accordance with the charterparty, in most situations the disponent shipowner's charterer is chosen to be the counterpart, Article 44 provides an opportunity to choose the bill of lading holder/cargo owner to be the co-counterpart. Furthermore, the application of the arrest of cargo by itself may drive the charterer to pay for debt.

In this context, the nature of the disponent shipowner's cargo security is immaterial under procedural law. This procedural protection indeed makes up for the deficiency of the substantive law. However, the deficiency of procedural law is evident.

First, the remedy by way of the arrest of cargo is not a self-help remedy. It is a judicial remedy. Whether a competent court will approve this application and issue an order cannot

---

29 The Ministry of Transport of P.R.C on 7 January 2020 submitted the Revision of the CMC 1992 (Draft for Approval 2020) to the State Council of P.R.C. The Article 87 of the CMC 1992 has been replaced by Article 99 of the Revision of the CMC 1992 (Draft for Approval 2020) providing that the carrier is entitled to lien on the relevant cargos on board; See "Application of the Ministry of Transport of P.R.C. for the Review of the Revision of the CMC 1992 (Draft for Approval)" (Jiao Fa Fa [2020] No. 10).

30 Chinese Special Maritime Procedure Law, Art. 44.

31 There is no specific definition of interim measure under Chinese law. However, the property preservation and the evidence preservation provided by Chinese law exert the similar function, like interim measure in common law.

be controlled by the applicant. Furthermore, in accordance with Article 16 of the Special Maritime Procedure Law providing that "a maritime court may, in accepting a maritime preservation application, order the claimant to provide a deposit. Where the claimant fails to provide the deposit, his application shall be rejected",[32] the applicant, the shipowner, disponent shipowners or others, all may be required to pay for the deposit. Although this is not a mandatory provision, in practice, the court in most situations will require the applicants to do so to avoid risk. In addition, the court will require the applicants to submit the relevant evidence regarding the application, in order to decide whether the application is proper. After the counterpart applies for a maritime injunction and provides the deposit, it is possible for the court to reject the claimant's application.[33] In short, the feasibility of this legal remedy to a great extent depends on the court's discretion.

Secondly, in comparison with the legal cargo security in the substantive law, the crucial shortcoming in the procedural law is that this protection cannot provide the privileged right. Under Chinese law, with regard to whether the cargo security can be regarded as the property-based lien is in question in academic circles.[34] However, the majority viewpoint is that cargo security is treated as an independent security right which is derived from the real property rights that retain the dominance of *in rem*, even though the creation of the cargo security might rely on the clause of an agreed contract.[35] For this reason, the creditors relying on the cargo security can claim against the debtors and the true owner of the secured property. Even if the cargo is destroyed, the creditor has the privileges right to obtain the cargo damages. The most important thing is that the privileged right due to the cargo security takes priority over other security interests, including the mortgage, pledge and others. The reason is that the cargo security counts as the legal right while other security interests are contractual rights.[36]

However, the procedure law cannot provide this kind of privilege before the disponent shipowner's cargo security is recognised. The cargo owner's other debtors are also entitled to apply for an order to arrest the cargo. In other words, if the disponent shipowner's cargo security cannot be provided by legislation, this disponent shipowner simply counts as the general creditor.

In light of the above discussion, it can be found that the procedural approach for protecting the disponent shipowner may make up for the deficiency of the substantive law. However, its application is dependent on the judicial remedy, as opposed to the self-remedy. Furthermore, the feature of the shipowner or the disponent shipowner's cargo

---

32 Chinese Special Maritime Procedure Law, Art. 16.

33 In accordance with the Chapter IV, Maritime Injunction of Special Maritime Procedure Law of P.R.C, the maritime claimant may apply for an injunction. In practice, when the shipowner detains the cargo, the cargo owner often applies for a maritime injunction. Although in theory the shipowner or the disponent shipowner, as the maritime claimant applies for an order to arrest the cargo, it cannot exclude the counterpart to apply an injunction.

34 Huixing Liang and Huabin Chen, *Real law* (2nd edn, Law Press China 2003)351; Yulin Fu, "Comparative Research on The Function of the Cargo Lien by Sea" in Huixing Liang (ed) *Civil and Commercial Law Review* Vol. 16, (Law Press China, 2000); According to the theory of the source of the right, "liens" are divided into property-based liens and claim-based liens. More specifically, some jurisdictions, such as China, Switzerland, Japan and Taiwan Province contend that liens, as the property-based security, are derived from the real property rights that retain the dominance *in rem* while some countries, such as Germany and France, think that liens stem from the claim against the debtors' default; therefore, they are called the claim-based liens.

35 Huixing Liang and Huabin Chen, *Real law* (2nd edn, Law Press China 2003), p. 351.

36 Yinbo Xu, "Application and Rethinking of Liens under Property Law" (2017) 2 Science of Law 88.

security is to provide the privileged right to the shipowner or the disponent shipowner through the secured cargo. However, when the cargo security cannot be recognised by legislation, the procedural law merely provides a general protection to the shipowner or the disponent shipowner, like other debtors.

V. Observations

The Chinese legal framework regarding the protection of the shipowner by way of the security over cargo is not comprehensive. Even the head shipowner who physically possesses the cargo cannot be protected well because the CMC 1992 merely provides for the secured cargo belonging to the charterer, not the cargo owner. Furthermore, there is no provision regarding the disponent shipowner's cargo security. Apart from the substantive law, the remedy of the procedural law is the alternative. For the disponent shipowner, this remedy is very useful because lack of possession is no longer a legal barrier. However, the disadvantage is also obvious.

In practice, owing to the deficiency of the legislative remedy to the shipowner's cargo security, both the shipowner and the disponent shipowner quite often refuse to seek access to the port before the charterer, the consignee or other relevant party promises to pay the freight or hire. An Agreement on Payment between the shipowner/disponent shipowner and consignee is a general form to ensure the performance of the promise. However, after unloading the cargo, it is quite common that the consignee may bring arbitration or litigation proceedings against the shipowner/disponent shipowner. The convincing argument is that the Agreement is signed under duress. In most situations, this consignee's argument can be accepted by Chinese courts because the scope of the secured cargo is derived from the *numerus clausus*. The Agreement on Payment itself violates the principle of *numerus clausus*.

In short, the legislative solution to the shipowner and the disponent shipowner's cargo security is not sufficient and the contractual solution is feasible only in theory, but fails to achieve it in China.

VI. Conclusion

It is observed that the purpose of this chapter has explored the deficiency and remedy of a cargo lien clause under multiple charterparties through Chinese legislation, scholarly opinions and judicial decisions. It is safe to say that the legislation in the context of both a single charterparty and multiple charterparties is deficient. Because of the application of *numerus clausus* in secured transactions law, parties have no room to provide contractual cargo security. Although combining the substantive with procedural law generates to a great extent the legal effect of the shipowner and the disponent shipowner's cargo security, the procedural law cannot secure the shipowner and the disponent shipowner for them to exercise their privileged rights. To some extent, the advantage of security interests disappears. For this reason, this author argues that if Chinese law sticks to the principle of *numerus clausus* in a strict sense, the possession requirement in secured transactions law should be construed in a broad sense. Like German law, possession should contain direct possession and indirect possession. In this case, it is possible for the disponent shipowner to exercise the cargo security. Alternatively, the legislation provides the disponent shipowner's cargo security as a statutory right.

CHAPTER 14

Multimodal Transport in German Case Law

The Beginning and the End of the Sea Carriage

Tobias Eckardt

I. Introduction

The German Commercial Code (Handelsgesetzbuch (HGB), hereafter referred to as "GCC"), which contains the central provisions of the transport law, was enacted over 100 years ago. As the world of transport evolved, pressure built upon the legal system to accommodate the new factual situation. In particular, the rise of containerised transport vastly increased the instances in which transports were carried out by more than one means of transport.[1] Courts, also in Germany, were more frequently faced with cases relating to a multimodal carriage of goods. Over the years, German courts created a certain amount of case law, thereby outlining principles applying to the multimodal carriage.[2]

The solution developed by the German Federal Supreme Court (BGH) followed the "network system" approach.[3] That is to say that the transport carried out is broken down into various components, for example cross-border road haulage, followed by an inland waterway shipment, followed by a sea transport leg and concluded by domestic road carriage. The courts' approach was to determine which of the applicable legal regimes provided for the strictest liability and to then apply that liability to loss or damage to the cargo.[4] If the carrier should want to rely on a less strict regime of liability, the carrier would have to prove that the loss of or damage to the cargo did occur during that relevant part of transport.

The approach, while consistent with the statutory legal situation at that time, created a number of difficulties. One was the need to ascertain all potentially applicable legal regimes and determine the liability thereunder. Another difficulty arose in determining the "strictest" liability regime. For example: one regime provides for liability of five special drawing rights (SDR) per kilogram and a time bar of six months, and the other provides for liability of four SDR/kg but a time bar of two years – which is stricter?

In the 1990s, steps were taken to reform German transport law. The reform was split into two parts, the first relating to the rules applicable to the carriage of goods by any

---

1 Herber in Münchener Kommentar zum Handelsgesetzbuch: HGB, Band 7: §§ 407–619 Transportrecht, 3rd ed., Munich 2014 (hereafter MüKo/Herber) § 452, para 7.

2 Cf. MüKo/Herber, Vor § 452 para 15.

3 Cf. BGH, decision dated 24 June 1987, I ZR 127/85, TranspR 1987, 447.

4 MüKo/Herber § 452, para 2, 10.

 DOI: 10.4324/9781003160298-17

means save for sea transport and the second part was focused on the sea transport. The new rules were enacted in 1998 and 2013, respectively.[5]

II. The Context of the Rules of Multimodal Carriage

The reform of 1998 introduced sections 452–452d GCC as a distinct subchapter of the GCC. Currently the (abbreviated) Structure of the German Commercial Code is as follows:

Book One – Commercial Entities (ss. 1–104a)
Book Two – Trading Companies (ss. 105–237)
Book Three – Account Books (ss. 238–342e)
Book Four – Commercial Transactions (ss. 343–475h)
    Chapter 1 – General Provisions (ss. 343–372)
    Chapter 2 – Commercial Purchases (ss. 373–382)
    Chapter 3 – Commission Business (ss. 383–406)
    Chapter 4 – Freight Business (ss. 407–475h)
        Subchapter 1 – General Provisions (ss. 407–450)
        Subchapter 2 – Carriage of removal goods (ss. 451–451h)
        Subchapter 3 – Carriage by several modes of transport[6]
            Section 452 – Contract for the carriage of goods by several modes of transport[7]
            Section 452a – Localised place of damage[8]
            Section 452b – Notice of damage; limitation periods[9]

---

5 Cf. for example: Eckardt "The Major Changes of the Recent Reform of German Maritime Law", Tijdschrift Vervoer & Recht (TVR), 2015, p. 58.

6 The following translation was provided by the Deutsche Gesellschaft für Transportrecht eV.; freely available at https://transportrecht.org/wp-content/uploads/HGB4Buch2013DGTRen.pdf.

7 This section reads: "If carriage of goods is performed by several modes of transport under a single contract for the carriage of goods, and if, had separate contracts been concluded between the parties for each part of the carriage involving one mode of transport (transport leg), at least two of these contracts would have been subject to different legal provisions, then the provisions of the Subchapter 1 shall apply to the contract, unless the following special provisions or applicable international conventions provide otherwise. This shall also apply if part of the carriage is performed by sea".

8 This section reads: "If it has been established that the loss, damage or event which caused delay in delivery occurred on a specific transport leg, the liability of the Contractual Carrier shall, in derogation from the provisions of subchapter 1, be determined in accordance with the legal provisions which would apply to a contract for the carriage of goods on this transport leg only. The burden of proving that the loss, damage or event which caused delay in delivery occurred on a particular transport leg is borne by the person alleging this".

9 This section reads:

    "(1) Section 438 shall apply irrespective of whether the place of damage is unknown, is known or becomes known later. For the purposes of compliance with the form and time limit for the notice of damage it shall also suffice if the provisions which would have been applicable to a contract for the carriage of goods on the last transport leg have been observed.

    (2) If the limitation period in respect of claims for loss of, or damage to, the goods or for delay in delivery shall commence on the time the goods were delivered, delivery to the consignee shall be the relevant point of time. Even if the place where the damage occurred is known, the claim shall be time-barred at the earliest in accordance with Section 439".

Section 452c – Removal contract relating to carriage by several modes of transport[10]

Section 452d – Deviating agreements[11]

Chapter 5 – Freight forwarding business (ss. 453–466)

Chapter 6 – Warehousing business (ss. 467–475h)

Book Five – Maritime Trade (ss. 476–619)[12]

The legislator decided to treat the contract for multimodal carriage as a variation of a contract of carriage rather than a contract *sui generis*[13] as can be seen from the systematic position of the rules. Also, the designation as "Carriage by several means of transport" demonstrates that multimodal carriage contracts do not constitute their own type of contract.[14]

Treating the multimodal transport as a variation of unimodal transport allowed the legislator to employ the existing rules without the need to create a new legal regime for cases of multimodal transport.[15]

III. The Contents of the Rules of Multimodal Carriage

A. Sections 452, 452a

1.

The constituent parts of a multimodal contract of carriage, as per sect. 452 GCC, are that it is a single contract of carriage covering the transport by different means of transport and different legal regimes being applicable to the contracts which hypothetically would have

---

10 This section reads: "If the contract for the carriage of goods is for carriage of removal goods by several modes of transport, the provisions of subchapter 2 shall apply to the contract. Section 452a shall only apply insofar as the transport leg on which the damage occurred shall be governed by provisions of an international convention binding on the Federal Republic of Germany".

11 This section reads:

"(1) Any agreements deviating from the provisions in the first sentence of Section 452b (2) may only be made, if they have been individually negotiated, whether agreed for one or several similar contracts between the same parties. Any agreements deviating from the other provisions of the present subchapter may only be made insofar as the provisions referred to therein permit deviating agreements.

(2) In derogation from subsection (1), also standard contract terms may provide that in cases where the place of damage is localized (Section 452a) liability shall be determined in accordance with the legal provisions of subchapter 1
1. irrespective of on which transport leg the damage will occur, or
2. where the damage occurs on a particular transport leg specified in the agreement.

(3) Agreements purporting to exclude the application of mandatory provisions of an international convention applicable to a particular transport leg and binding on the Federal Republic of Germany shall be void".

12 A translation of the Fifth Book provided by the Deutsche Gesellschaft für Transportrecht eV. is freely available at https://transportrecht.org/wp-content/uploads/HGB5.Buchenglischv.21.3.22.pdf.

13 Bundestagsdrucksache (Bundestag printed paper) No. 13/8445, dated 29 August 1997, available at http://dipbt.bundestag.de/doc/btd/13/084/1308445.pdf (hereinafter: Bundestagsdrucksache.13/8445), page 99.

14 MüKo/Herber, Vor § 452 para 1.

15 Bundestagsdrucksache 13/8445, page 100.

had to be concluded if the parties had broken down the transport into individual contracts for each mode of transport.[16]

German law requires that the parties to the multimodal contract of carriage have contracted for a transport by more than one mode of transport. If the parties have only agreed to carry the goods by one mode of transport and the goods are then actually carried by more than one mode of transport, this contract is not deemed a contract for the carriage by several modes of transport.[17]

It follows from the description of the multimodal carriage that a transport by an inland waterway vessel followed by a transport leg by a different seagoing vessel constitutes two different legs of transport given that different rules apply to inland waterway and maritime transport.[18] On the other hand, cargo handling between two instances of (for example) sea carriage constitute only one leg of sea carriage so that any cargo handling in between these unimodal forms of transport forms part of that particular leg of carriage.[19]

2.

The approach taken by the German legislator is rather straightforward: Section 452 GCC states the general rules of transport law (Subchapter 1 – General Provisions, ss. 407–450 GCC) apply to multimodal transport regardless of which means of transport are being employed. Only in cases where the loss, damage or event which caused the delay in delivery (herein together the "loss") can be localised to a specific leg of the transport the rules which would have applied to this leg of transport had the parties concluded a separate contract for this specific leg, applies; sect. 452a GCC.

If the place of the loss can be localised, German law will use the liability regime applicable to that leg of transport. In doing so, German law allows for the applicability of international conventions or foreign law.

The distribution of the burden of proof means that in cases where the party seeking to establish a liability regime other than that of subchapter 1 bears the burden of demonstrating that the alternative liability regime applies. Not meeting that burden will mean that a *"non-liquet"* situation arises. In such a situation the rules of subchapter 1 apply.[20]

The statutory provisions also set out that the burden of proof regarding the localisation of loss is upon the party who wished to apply rules other than those which would apply in case of unlocalised loss. In cases of multimodal carriage involving a sea leg, it is likely to be the carrier who wishes to apply the rules of maritime transport law due to the fact that liability is hereunder limited to 2 SDR/kg or 666.67 SDR/pcs (whichever is higher) vs. 8.33 SDR/kg under the general rules. Also, certain other provisions may prove beneficial to the carrier such as a more restrictive approach to liability for servant's acts and omissions.[21]

---

16 Bundestagsdrucksache 13/8445, page 99.
17 MüKo/Herber § 452, para 12.
18 MüKo/Herber § 452 para 19.
19 BGH, decision dated 18 June 2009, I ZR 140/06, TranspR 2009, 327, para 22.
20 Bundestagsdrucksache 13/8445, p. 101.
21 Cf. MüKo/Herber § 452 paras. 62 et seq. for an overview.

B. Section 452b

Section 452b GCC aims to provide legal certainty to the parties to the contract of carriage. In order to ensure that the need to notify the loss and length of time bar does not suddenly change when during the dispute the applicable legal regime changes due to the place of loss becoming localised or un-localised, sect. 452b GCC provides that regardless of whether the place of loss is known or unknown the notification requirements of sect. 438 GCC[22] apply. Similarly, sect. 452b, second paragraph GCC stipulates that the length of the time bar shall not be shorter than as set out in sect. 439 GCC[23] – that is to say one or three years, depending on the level of negligence/intent.[24]

C. Section 452c

The statute also contains a specific section for multimodal removal contracts. This became necessary as removal contracts are treated in subsection 2 of the fourth book of the GCC.

---

22 Section 438 reads:

"(1) If loss of, or damage to, the goods is apparent and the consignee or the Consignor fails to notify the Contractual Carrier of said loss or damage at the latest on delivery of the goods, then the presumption shall be that the goods were delivered in their entirety and in undamaged condition. The notice must describe the loss or damage in sufficiently clear terms.

(2) The presumption pursuant to subsection (1) above shall also apply if the loss or damage was not apparent and no notice was given within seven days of delivery.

(3) Claims for delay in delivery shall expire if the consignee does not notify the Contractual Carrier of the delay in delivery within twenty-one days of delivery.

(4) Any notice of damage given after delivery must be in text form. Timely dispatch of the notice shall suffice for purposes of compliance with the respective time limit.

(5) Where notice of loss, damage or delay in delivery is given on delivery, it shall suffice for such notice to be given to the party delivering the goods".

23 Section 439 reads

"(1) Claims resulting from carriage to which the provisions of this Subchapter apply shall be-come time-barred after one year. In the event of intent or of fault considered to be equivalent to intent pursuant to Section 435 the limitation period shall be three years.

(2) The limitation period shall commence on expiry of the day the goods were delivered. If the goods were not delivered, the limitation period shall commence on expiry of the day the goods should have been delivered. In derogation from the first and second sentence, the limitation period in respect of recourse claims shall commence on the day on which the judgment against the recourse claimant becomes final and binding or, if there is no final and binding judgment, on the day on which the recourse claimant has satisfied the claim; this shall not apply if the recourse debtor was not informed of the damage within three months after the recourse claimant became aware of the damage and of the recourse debtor's identity.

(3) The running of the limitation period in respect of a claim against the Contractual Carrier shall also be suspended by a declaration whereby the Consignor or the consignee asserts his claims to compensation; the suspension continues until the Contractual Carrier refuses to satisfy the claim. Both the assertion of the claims and the refusal to satisfy the same must be made in text form. Any further declaration concerning the same claim to compensation shall not result in an additional suspension of the running of the limitation period.

(4) The time bar in respect of claims for damages resulting from loss of, or damage to, the goods or from delay in delivery may be shortened or otherwise eased or prolonged or otherwise impeded only by an individually negotiated agreement, whether for one or several similar contracts between the same parties".

24 Bundestagsdrucksache 13/8445, pp. 102, 103.

As the general rule contained in sect. 452a GCC refers back to subsection 1, the rules for removal contracts were not covered by that reference.[25]

D. Section 452d

Section 452d GCC contains rules on in how far the stipulations of this subchapter may be deviated from by general terms and conditions.

E. The Unanswered Question

The question that is not directly answered by statute and on which the focus here will be is: Where does the sea leg of transport start, and where does it end? In other words: into how many parts is a multimodal transport to be broken down? For example,[26] technically, the horizontal and vertical movement of a container being unloaded from a ship is a transport of the container which is not effected by a ship, but by a harbour crane. Is this craning operation then an individual leg of transport? Or is it a part of the sea transport? Or is it a part of the land transport which brings the goods to their destination?

The legislator was aware of the fact that certain ancillary tasks connected to a certain leg of transport were not explicitly ruled by the statute. The legislator expected that such ancillary tasks were either intrinsically linked to a certain leg of transport, thereby leading to the applicability of the rules for that certain leg, or if they possessed such quality that they ought to be treated as a leg of transport themselves, the then relevant rules should apply.[27]

The question that shall be focused on here is what constitutes the beginning and the end of the sea carriage leg in multimodal transports. A number of decisions by the Federal Supreme Court (BGH) have shed some light on this question.

IV. The Case Law

The question that caused dispute between scholars and courts was the question of how to deal with brief transports between two "main" legs of transport.[28] The same applies to periods where the goods are stored waiting for further transport.

---

25 Bundestagsdrucksache 13/8445, page 103.
26 Cf. MüKo/Herber § 452 paras. 17 et seq.
27 Bundestagsdrucksache 13/8445, page 101.
28 For an overview of current legal issues surrounding the cargo handling see: Drews, "Der Umschlag von Waren unter dem neuen Seehandelsrecht", TranspR 2013, 253 et seq.; Freise, "Der Güterumschlag im Eisenbahnverkehr", TranspR 2013, 260 et seq.; Kirchhof, "Umschlag im Luftrecht", TranspR 2013, 265 et seq.; v. Waldstein, "Umschlag in der Binnenschifffahrt", TranspR 2013, 269; Koller, Transportrecht: TranspR, 9th ed., Munich, 2016 (hereinafter Koller), § 452 para 15c et seq.; Koller, "Die Rechtsnatur des Umschlagsvertrages und ihre Bedeutung für die Teilstrecken", TranspR 2008, 333 et seq.; Koller, "Der Umschlag und die Teilstrecke im Licht des multimodalen Transports", VersR 2014, 309 et seq.

A. First Decision to be Considered (BGH, Decision Dated 3 November 2005, I ZR 325/02; BGHZ 164, 394 = TranspR 2006, 35)

This decision came several years after the reform of German transport law introducing the statutory rules for multimodal transport came into force. By then the preceeding decision of the Hamburg court of appeal[29] had sparked ongoing discussion about the question of whether cargo handling in a port constituted a separate leg of transport.[30]

The case to be decided revolved around a transport of a field laboratory installed in a 30' container. The container was shipped by sea from Tunis to Genoa and picked by there for road transport to Garbsen in Germany. The first instance court found that the laboratory was already damaged when the container was loaded on the truck in Genoa. The court of appeal held that the container handling in the port of Genoa formed part of the sea carriage, thereby deciding that the cargo handling did not in itself constitute its own leg of transport.

The Federal Supreme Court upheld the decision finding that the cargo handling at a container terminal did not constitute a separate leg of transport "unless unusual circumstances" apply.

The reasons given by the Federal Supreme Court were that the cargo handling and storage of containers typically form part of the sea transport. Further, the court argued that a detailed checking of the container will only take place upon loading of the container onto the truck for on-transport. It would thus be difficult to pinpoint the time and place of damage prior to such loading. Finally, the court argued that the sea carrier's obligation to carry and care for the cargo is usually not discharged by the mere unloading of the container from the Vessel. It is further noted that the unloading does not place the consignee into the possession of the goods.[31]

The decision by the Federal Supreme Court did not end the discussions in legal literature. In particular, the rather weak backdoor of "unless unusual circumstances apply" led to criticism.[32]

B. Second Decision to be Considered (BGH, Decision Dated 18 October 2007, I ZR 138/04, TranspR 2007, 472)

The Federal Supreme Court was given the further chance to clarify the issue in 2007.[33] In this decision the court had to consider the following facts: Two crates, each containing a printing press, were lashed and stowed on a so-called Mafi trailer. They were carried by

---

29 OLG Hamburg decision dated 19 August 2004, 6 U 178/03, TranspR 2004, 402, referencing to the commentaries by Koller (5th ed.), § 452 HGB para 15 and Fremuth/Thume/Eckardt Kommentar zum Transportrecht, §§ 407–474 h HGB, CMR, WA und ADSp, Heidelberg, 2000, § 452a para 20.

30 Cf. case comment Herber, TranspR 2004, 404; Herber, "Nochmals: Multimodalvertrag, Güterumschlag und anwendbares Recht" TranspR 2005, 59; Drews, "Warenumschlag im Seehafen als Teilstrecke? – Zur Entscheidung des Hanseatischen OLG Hamburg vom 19.8.2004 (TranspR 2004, 402) sowie Replik auf die Anmerkung von Herber hierzu (TranspR 2004, 404)" in TranspR 2004, 450, 451; Bartels, "Der Teilstreckenvertrag beim Multimodal-Vertrag" TranspR 2005, 203.

31 Cf. OLG Hamm decision dated 26. June 2014, 18 U 148/13 = TranspR 2015, 296 and comment thereon by Eckardt, jurisPR-TranspR 2/2015 Anm. 4 on the point of transfer of possession in the harbour of destination.

32 Cf. the references in MüKo/Herber § 452 para 22; § 452a paras. 32 et seq.; Rabe, "Das Mafi-Trailer Urteil des BGH – ein Fazit", TranspR 2008, 186 et seq.

33 BGH, decision dated 18 October 2007, I ZR 138/04, TranspR 2007, 472.

sea from Bremerhaven, Germany, to Durham/North Carolina via Portsmouth/Virginia. Upon arrival in Portsmouth, the Mafi trailer was unloaded from the ship and pulled for a distance of approximately 300 metres to a storage facility. There the chains securing the two crates were removed and the first crate was loaded on a truck for on-transport by road to Durham. After the loading of the first crate, the Mafi trailer was moved in order to facilitate the loading of the second crate. During this movement the second crate, which was at that point in time no longer secured, toppled off the trailer and the contents were damaged.

The question arose whether the printing press was at that time subject to the sea leg of the carriage or subject to the road carriage to its final destination or, as a third alternative, subject to a separate road transport stage within the port area. The Appellate Court of Hamburg held[34] that the trailer was subject to a carriage by road within the harbour. It was moved to this conclusion because it was felt that the distance of 300 metres for which the trailer was towed could not be considered a part of the unloading of the trailer from the ship. Consequently, the defendants were subject to the higher limits of liability of German road transports, rather than the more beneficial rules of maritime liability.

The matter was appealed and thus came before the BGH. The Federal Supreme Court first noted that the hauling of the Mafi trailer for a distance of approximately 300 metres did not constitute "unusual circumstances" so that the rationale of the earlier decision (I ZR 325/02) applied to the transport by the Mafi trailer. Thus, the transport by the Mafi trailer was still considered part of the sea carriage. However, the court noted that the damage did not occur during the 300 metres haulage but during loading operations onto the road transport vehicle. The court clarified that loading operations relating to the next leg of transport, being a different mode of transport, form part of that next leg of transport. The court pointed to the fact that the chains securing the cargo on the trailer had already been removed in order to load the cargo on the road transport vehicle and that this had indeed already taken place regarding the first crate. The risk created by these acts is, according to the court, associated with the loading operations for the road transport and thus the liability had to be determined in accordance with the relevant road transport regime and not by maritime law.

The court further noted that the sea carrier had agreed to carry the goods according to the INCOTERM "FOT Portsmouth" and thus was obliged to load them on the truck. However, the sea carrier bearing the risk of loading the truck did not change the applicability of general transport law. The court pointed out that according to statute the law hypothetically applicable to the leg of transport is decisive. Consequently, an agreement distributing the risk of loss does not affect the question of which liability regime applies.

C. Third Decision to Be Considered (BGH, Decision Dated 11 April 2013, I ZR 61/12, TranspR 2013, 437)

The decision I ZR 138/04 was confirmed in 2013. Here, several machines packed in wooden boxes were stowed on a flat rack container for sea transport from Germany to Savanah, Georgia. When the crates arrived in the United States, US customs did not allow the wooden boxes into the country. It was thus decided to unbox the machines for road

---

34 OLG Hamburg, decision dated 19 August 2004, 6 U 178/03, TranspR 2004, 402.

transport to their destination. The machines were damaged by a forklift either during unboxing or when loading the machines on the truck. Quite in line with the prior decision the court held that the unboxing and loading operations were preparatory steps for the land transport leg and that, consequently, the liability for the loss was not to be determined in accordance with maritime law but road transport rules.

D. Fourth Decision to be Considered (BGH, Decision Dated 1 December 2016, I ZR 128/15, TranspR 2017, 175)

In the very recent decision of the BGH the court had, for the first time, to deal with the question of when the sea leg of a multi modal transport starts. The facts were as follows: Eight wooden crates had to be carried by road within Germany to a sea port to be then shipped to Shanghai. They were picked up from the sender and were transported to Bremen by road, to be packed into the seagoing container there. On short notice it turned out that shipment would not be leaving the port of Bremen, but the port of Hamburg so that a container containing inter alia these boxes was hauled from Bremen to Hamburg. In the harbour of Hamburg, the container was unloaded and the crates were stuffed into a container for shipment to Shanghai. However, mistakenly, two crates were not removed from the container by which they had been transported from Bremen to Hamburg. These two crates ended up in a container destined to Ecuador. By the time this was discovered, the sender had dispatched new goods to Shanghai and consequently claimed losses from the carrier.

The claimants had argued that leaving the two crates in the container was not part of the sea carriage of the cargo and that thus the higher limits of liability under the general rules of transport law applied. The appellate court held that the error occurred during the sea transport leg of the carriage. This finding was upheld by the BGH. The court stated that the test was in the hypothetical scenario that a number of unimodal transport contracts had been concluded (instead of one multimodal transport contract) whether the road haulier or the sea carrier was responsible for the cargo handling or unloading. The Federal Supreme Court followed the appellate court's reasoning that the road carriage had ended upon the unloading of the container from the truck at the container terminal in Hamburg. The subsequent storage of the container on the terminal premises and the combining of the LCL cargos for destination Shanghai was found to be closely linked to the sea carriage. Thus, erroneously leaving boxes in a container was to be seen as part of the sea transport leg.

The Federal Supreme Court approved of this argument and added that as stowing of goods into containers at the terminal was a preparatory step for the sea transport, mismatching crates during the stowing of cargo part also of the sea transport. The court noted that at the time the goods failed to be unloaded from the container the road carrier had no longer custody of them. Rather, the sea carrier, through the terminal operator, had the goods in its care and custody. Consequently, the rules for maritime transport applied.

V. Conclusion

Summarising these cases it is to be concluded that the starting and ending point of the sea carriage leg in multimodal transport is the beginning of the loading operations. It is also to be expected that the differentiation outlined by the Federal Supreme Court will also apply to other means of transport. It is thus probably fair to say that each leg of transport begins with the loading operations for that particular type of carriage and ends when the loading operations for the next leg of carriage begin. Any cargo handling and storage in between these two different modes of transport will be part of that prior mode of transport.

All this is, however, subject to the qualification that "unusual circumstances do not apply", even though there yet has to be a set of facts which the Federal Supreme Court would consider to be unusual in this regard. Sooner or later, however, we can expect a further clarification on this point.

Another question which has as yet been left open explicitly by the Federal Supreme Court is whether the choice of law made by the parties when entering the contract for the multimodal carriage does influence the law applicable to the individual legs of transport.[35]

---

35 See MüKo/Herber § 452 para 31; Koller § 452 para 1a.

CHAPTER 15

Civil Liability for Marine Oil Pollution in China and Europe

Michael Faure and Hui Wang

I. Introduction

Europe has been confronted with spectacular cases of marine oil pollution. The Erika (1999) and Prestige (2002) are well-known incidents that will last in the memory of many Europeans. The European Union has been taking a proactive approach in dealing with major oil catastrophes, through promoting European legislation, thereby equally enhancing the development of international conventions. Moreover, some national courts went even further than the international conventions in order to provide better compensation for oil pollution victims.

Until recently, China had been spared from similar catastrophes, although some major incidents like with *the Tasman Sea* (2002) and *the Sanchi* (2018) also caused substantial damage. China has become the world's largest net crude oil importer in 2017.[1] Most of the oil import is carried out through tanker shipping which increases the risks of oil spilling at sea. Moreover, China has a very long coastline that could potentially be exposed to marine pollution. That raises the question of how China would deal with the compensation of victims and the restoration of the environment after an oil spill.

Thus, this chapter aims to address the question of whether China would be able to compensate potential victims and restore the environment in the event of a marine oil spill. Most European countries have acceded to the international conventions dealing with marine oil pollution compensation, being the Civil Liability Convention of 1992 and the Fund Convention of 1992. China is equally a member of the Civil Liability Convention of 1992. A comparison between the European (hence mainly the international) and the Chinese system will show to what extent damage caused by marine oil pollution can be compensated in those different systems.

This chapter is set up as follows: first, we will briefly review the historical development of the international legal system concerning marine oil pollution compensation, with a focus on the particular role played by major European states collectively through the European Union; (2) then the major features of the international/European legal regime will be analysed; (3) we will focus on the compensation for marine oil pollution in China; (4) we will also compare the applicable rules in both systems; (5) we end with a few concluding observations.

---

1 Ecans, www.ecns.cn/business/2018/02-07/291780.html, last accessed on 9 January 2022.

DOI: 10.4324/9781003160298-18

II. Historical Development of the International Regime and the Role of European States

The international regime specifically dealing with marine oil pollution compensation has been developing since the late 1960s as a reaction to some major oil spill incidents. Initially, in response to the Torrey Canyon spill in 1967, an international convention was introduced to provide compensation for pollution victims, being the International Convention on Civil Liability for Oil Pollution Damage of 1969 (Civil Liability Convention of 1969, or CLC 1969). The CLC 1969 imposes strict liability exclusively on the registered shipowner up to a certain amount.[2] It also requires compulsory insurance or a financial guarantee for pollution liability.[3] However, the strict liability introduced by the CLC 1969 was considered too harsh on the shipping industry, which posed great difficulty for major shipping nations to ratify this convention. Therefore, two years later, another convention was adopted to make the oil cargo interests also contribute to the compensation system in order to strike a balance between the shipping and the oil cargo interests. This was the adoption of the International Convention on the Establishment of an International Fund for Compensation for Oil Pollution Damage of 1971 (Fund Convention of 1971). The Fund Convention of 1971 made the oil cargo owners contribute to the Fund,[4] and it was believed that the harsh burden on the shipping industry could be alleviated to a certain extent.[5] These two conventions came into force in 1975 and 1978. Since then, an international regime on marine oil pollution compensation has been established.

Later catastrophic oil pollution incidents illustrated the insufficiency of the international regime (e.g., the Amoco Cadiz in 1978, the Tanio in 1980, and the Exxon Valdez in 1989). As a result, these two international conventions were revised in 1992,[6] whereby the amount of compensation was substantially increased and the scope of compensation was expanded. Despite the changes, the general principles of liability sharing between the shipping and oil industry, strict liability, limitation of liability, compulsory insurance and channelling of liability remain.

Again, later incidents, Erika in 1999 and Prestige in 2002, triggered further changes to the international conventions. The amount of compensation was increased by approximately 50% in 2000.[7] Later in 2003, a Supplementary Fund Protocol was adopted to

---

2 Articles III and V of the CLC 1969.

3 Article VII of the CLC 1969.

4 Article 10 of the Fund Convention of 1971.

5 See Article 2.1 of the Fund Convention of 1971; see also Hui Wang, Shifts in Governance in the International Regime of Marine Oil Pollution Compensation: A Legal History Perspective, in 21 *Tort and Insurance Law: Shifts in Compensation for Environmental Damage*. pp. 197, 218–19 (Michael Faure & Albert Verheij, eds., 2007).

6 In fact, the international conventions were first revised in 1984. However, the entry into force of the Protocols in 1984 relied on the ratification of the United States. According to Article 13 of the 1984 Protocol, it only enters into force "twelve months following the date on which ten States including six States each with not less than one million units of gross tanker tonnage have deposited instruments of ratification, acceptance, approval or accession with the Secretary-General of the Organization". Since the United States decided to take its own action through the Oil Pollution Act of 1990, it was clear that the United States would never ratify the international conventions. On the other hand, the occurrence of major pollution incidents shows that changes in the Protocol of 1984, such as an increased amount of compensation, were needed. As a result, major changes in the Protocol of 1984 were adopted in the CLC 1992 and the need for U.S. ratification was eliminated. See Wang, supra note 5, pp. 204–205.

7 Wang, supra note 5, p. 209.

establish a so-called Supplementary Fund to provide a third tier of compensation.[8] Membership in the Supplementary Fund is optional, and any state that is a member of the 1992 Fund may join the Supplementary Fund. On January 9, 2020, 32 states have ratified or acceded to the Supplementary Fund Protocol,[9] 140 states have ratified or acceded to the CLC of 1992,[10] and 117 states had ratified or acceded to the Fund Convention of 1992.[11]

It is worth mentioning that the European Union may have played an important role in the introduction of the Supplementary Fund. Already after the occurrence of the Erika incident, the European Commission adopted several legislative proposals tackling the insufficiency of the then available international regime. In the so-called Erika II legislative proposals, the Commission proposed to set up a European fund (the Fund for Compensation for Oil Pollution in European waters, referred to as the COPE Fund) with an updated ceiling of EUR 1 billion (instead of EUR 200 million under the international conventions).[12] The European Council preferred to refer the discussion to the competent international body, namely the International Maritime Organization (the IMO), in order to obtain a similar agreement, but one which can be applied worldwide.[13] A Protocol to the Fund Convention, modelled on this European COPE Fund, was later established and adopted by the IMO in May 2003. Therefore, there was no longer any need for a special European COPE Fund for oil pollution, although the EU Proposal to set up such a fund may have influenced the international decision-making by the IMO. Indeed, the new amount available in the IOPC Fund is probably not by accident almost the amount that was proposed in the European COPE Fund (EUR 1 billion). It was also thanks to the activism of the EU Member States that the Supplementary Fund Convention could become effective quickly in 2005.[14]

The current status of these conventions is as follows: the CLC 1992 replaced the CLC 1969; although the Fund 1971 and the Fund 1992 are coexisting, the Fund Convention of 1971 has been denunciated by most countries, and it ceased to be in force as of May 2002. The Fund of 1971 does not handle new cases and only focuses on the unsettled cases. The European states are mainly parties to the CLC 1992 and the Fund 1992. Therefore, the discussion in this chapter will mainly focus on the Civil Liability Convention of 1992 and the Fund Convention of 1992.

---

8 Protocol of 2003 to the International Convention on the Establishment of an International Fund for Compensation for Oil Pollution Damage, 16 May 2003, (hereinafter Supplementary Fund Protocol). The Supplementary Fund Protocol entered into force on 3 March 2005.

9 Parties to the International Liability Compensation Conventions, IOPC FUNDS, www.iopcfunds.org/about-us/membership, last accessed on 9 January 2022.

10 International Maritime Organization, Status of Treaties – Comprehensive information on the status of multilateral Conventions and instruments in respect of which the International Maritime Organization or its Secretary-General performs depositary or other functions (9 January 2020), available at www.imo.org/en/About/Conventions/StatusOfConventions/Documents/Status%20-%202020.pdf, p. 276, last accessed on 9 January 2022.

11 Ibid., at 306.

12 See in this respect the amended proposal for a regulation of the European Parliament and of the Council on the Establishment of a Fund for the Compensation of Oil Pollution Damage in European Waters and Related Measures, Official Journal C227 E/487 of 24 September 2002.

13 The Transport Council in December 2000 adopted conclusions on the need to achieve improvements to the existing international regime, including "a substantial increase in liability and compensation ceilings".

14 The Member States of the European Union were urged by the Commission in a document in September 2003 to ratify the 2003 Supplementary Fund Protocol as soon as possible. And indeed, among the first countries that ratified the 2003 Protocol, except for Japan, all the other are EU member states (Denmark, Norway, Finland, France, Ireland, Germany and Spain).

III. The Main Features of the International Conventions: European Regime

A. Basis of Liability

The CLC 1992 provides that the registered shipowner shall be held strictly liable for pollution damage caused by the discharge of oil from the ship.[15] Moreover, it further provides that the liability is exclusively imposed on the shipowner, and there is a list of parties whose liability for oil pollution damage compensation is explicitly excluded.[16] This is the so-called "channelling provision" whereby the liability is directed at one particular party – in this case, the shipowner.

Pollution damage is defined in the CLC 1992 as

(a) loss or damage caused outside the ship by contamination resulting from the escape or discharge of oil from the ship, wherever such escape or discharge may occur, provided that compensation for impairment of the environment other than loss of profit from such impairment shall be limited to costs of reasonable measures of reinstatement actually undertaken or to be undertaken;

(b) the costs of preventive measures and further loss or damage caused by preventive measures.[17]

This definition delimits the scope of compensable environmental damage. It provides that environmental damage *per se* is compensable but only so far as it is reasonable and only where reinstatement is actually undertaken or to be undertaken.[18]

B. Amount of Compensation

Under the international regime, the liable party is not required to pay the full amount of compensation, but instead, his liability is capped at a certain amount.[19] The amounts of compensation under the CLC have been increased a few times since its adoption. Table 15.1 summarises the compensation amount under the international regime throughout history.

C. Compensation Instruments

1. Insurance

To guarantee the availability of compensation, the CLC regime requires compulsory financial security. The CLC requires the owner of a ship registered in a contracting state and carrying more than 2,000 tonnes of oil as cargo to maintain insurance or other financial security up to his limits of liability.[20] In addition to insurance, the financial security can also be a bank guarantee or a certificate delivered by an international compensation fund.[21] The most popularly used instrument is insurance, especially protection and indemnity policies.

---

15 Article III(1) of CLC 1992.
16 Article III(4) of CLC 1992.
17 Article I (6) of CLC 1992.
18 David Wilkinson, *Moving the Boundaries of Compensable Environmental Damage Caused by Marine Oil Spills: The Effect of Two New International Protocols*, 5 J. ENVTL. L. 71, pp. 84–85 (1993).
19 Article V of CLC 1992.
20 Article VII (1) of CLC 1992.
21 Article VII(2) of CLC 1992.

Table 15.1 Amount of Compensation by the Shipowner under the International Regime

	CLC 1969 (SDR)	CLC 1992 (SDR)	2000 Protocol (SDR)
Ships ≤ 5,000 tonnes	133 (204.41 USD) per ton	3 million (4.61 million USD)	**4.51** million (6.93 million USD)
Ships > 5,000 tonnes	133 (204.41 USD) per ton	3 million (4.61 million USD) + 420 (645.5 USD)/ additional ton	**4.51** million (6.93 million USD) + 631 (969.8)/ Additional ton
Overall limit	14 million (21.52 million USD)	**59.7** million (91.75 million USD)	**89.77** million (137.97 million USD)

Insurance for ocean-going ships is mainly provided by Protection and Indemnity (P&I) Clubs. Thirteen P&I Clubs form the International Group of P&I Clubs (the Group).[22] The Group arranges reinsurance together for the Clubs.[23] It is reported that the thirteen principal clubs provide liability cover for approximately 90% of the world's ocean-going tonnage and 98% of the world's tanker fleet. [24]

2. Compensation Funds

In addition to the financial security, compensation funds are also established to complement the compensation available from the CLC 1992. The current maximum compensation under the 1992 Fund, after an increase in 2000, is 203 million SDR (311.99 million USD) (including the payment under the CLC 1992), and the compensation under the Supplementary Fund reaches 750 million SDR (1,152.69 million USD) (including the payment under the 1992 Conventions).

The total amount available for compensating oil pollution damage under the international regimes is provided in Table 15.2.

Table 15.2 Compensation for Pollution Damage under the International Regime

	CLC 1969 (SDR)	CLC 1992 (SDR)	2000 Protocol (SDR)
Ships ≤ 5,000 tonnes	133 (204.41 USD) per ton	3 million (4.61 million USD)	**4.51** million (6.93 million USD)
Ships > 5,000 tonnes	133 (204.41 USD) per ton	3 million (4.61 million USD) + 420 (645.5 USD)/ additional ton	**4.51** million (6.93 million USD) + 631 (969.8 USD)/additional ton
Aggregate amount	14 million (21.52 million USD)	**59.7** million (91.75 million USD)	**89.77** million (137.97 million USD)
	IOPC Fund 1971 (SDR)	IOPC Fund 1992 (SDR)	2000 Protocol (SDR)
Overall limit	60 million (92.22 million USD)	135 million (207.48 million USD)	203 million (311.99 million USD)

---

22 www.igpandi.org/about, last visited 16 January 2022.
23 Ibid.
24 Ibid.

IV. The Compensation for Damage Caused by Marine Oil Pollution in China

A. Overview of the Chinese Legal Regime

Similar to the regime in Europe, the civil liability and compensation for marine oil pollution in China also consists of two layers, albeit there are some differences which be analysed in section V.

As the first layer, China is a contracting state to the CLC 92, and most domestic legislation in this respect largely reflect the general principles of the international conventions. These domestic legislations mainly include the China Maritime Code (CMC)[25] and the Marine Environmental Protection Law (MEPL).[26] In addition, there is a Regulation on the Prevention and Control of Vessel-induced Pollution to the Marine Environment.[27] As practical guidance, the Supreme Court of China published important legal documents, inter alia, in 2011 a Notice on Issues concerning Compensation for Oil Pollution Damage from Vessels[28] and in 2018 Provisions on Court Hearings of Cases concerning Marine Natural Resource Loss and Ecological Damages.[29]

As the second layer, the IOPC Fund Convention only applies to Hong Kong Special Administrative Region, whereas the mainland China has established a domestic China Oil Pollution Compensation (COPC) Fund in 2012.

B. Basis of Liability

In China, the Marine Environmental Protection Law is the basic law in the field of marine environmental protection and pollution prevention. Article 66 concerns civil liability and compensation for marine oil pollution damages caused by shipping and related activities. This article reads:

> The state shall make perfect and put into practice a responsibility system of civil liability compensation for oil pollution by vessel, and shall establish an insurance system of oil pollution by vessel, compensation fund system of oil pollution by vessel in accordance with the principles of sharing of owners of the vessel and the cargo of the compensation liabilities for oil pollution by vessel.
>
> The State Council shall adopt implementing measures for ship-source oil pollution insurance and oil pollution compensation fund.

This largely corresponds with the international regime whereby a two layer compensation mechanism is established.

Article 89 stipulates that "Those who cause pollution damage to the marine environment shall eliminate the damage and compensate the losses". Thus, the discharger is required to eliminate the damage and pay compensation, both of which are civil remedies

---

25 Adopted on 7 November 1992, effective as of 12 July 1993. It is currently under revision.

26 Originally adopted on 23 Aug. 1982 and has become effective as of 1 March 1983. Major revisions took place in 1999, 2013 and 2016. The most recent revision was on 4 November 2017, effective as of 5 November 2017.

27 This Regulation was originally adopted in 1983 in order to implement the then Marine Environmental Protection Law of 1982. Following the revisions of the Marine Environmental Protection Law, these Regulations have also been revised in 2009, 2013, 2014, 2016 and 2017. The latest revision took place in 2018.

28 http://rmfyb.chinacourt.org/paper/images/2011-06/15/02/2011061502_pdf.pdf.

29 Effective as of 15 January 2018.

for torts recognised in Chinese law. Therefore, a strict liability on the polluter is recognised under the MEPL for the marine oil pollution damage.

The second paragraph of Article 89 stipulates that "If the State suffers heavy losses from the damages to marine ecosystems, marine aquatic resources and marine nature reserves, the departments invested by this law with the power of marine environment supervision and administration shall, on behalf of the State, put forward compensation demand to those who are responsible for the damages". It provides the legal basis for recovery for natural resources. However, it only applies to "heavy losses" caused to the natural resources, and there is no provision on if and how to compensate the losses that are not considered "heavy". Moreover, it fails to define what are the so-called "heavy losses" or to specify what are the standards for damages to constitute "heavy losses". In addition, this article actually only concerns damages to natural resources suffered by the "State"; as for the damage sustained by individuals or other private parties caused by the oil pollution, there is no explicit provision on the scope of damages recoverable or to what extent they can be compensated.

The concept of pollution damage can, however, be interpreted taking into account the conventions that China has joined and the related judicial explanations. China is a party to the CLC, which means that the definition of pollution damage under the CLC also applies to China. However, in practice, there are still debates on the scope of application of the CLC. The CLC applies to "any seagoing vessel and seaborne craft of any type whatsoever constructed or adapted for the carriage of oil in bulk as cargo".[30] The term "oil" is defined as "any persistent hydrocarbon mineral oil such as crude oil, fuel oil, heavy diesel oil, and lubricating oil".[31] Thus, when the pollution involves other types of vessels or crafts, or the damage is caused by nonpersistent oil, the domestic Chinese law applies. However, even when the CLC ships and oil cause damage, there are still debates on whether the CLC applies only to ships with a foreign-related issue or to all types of seagoing vessels and seaborne crafts.[32]

How to interpret this notion of a "foreign-related issue" is also important in determining the application of the CLC.[33]

C. Amount of Compensation

There is no specific provision in the MEPL on the amount to be compensated in the case of a marine oil pollution incident. In practice, when a claimant brings an action for

---

30 Article I(1) of CLC 1992.

31 Article I(5) of CLC 1992.

32 See James Hu & Yang Bo, *Application of Law in Civil Liability for Oil Pollution Damage Caused by Coastal Vessels in China*, in Prevention and Compensation of Marine Pollution Damage: Recent Developments in Europe, China and the US 193, 193–205 (Michael Faure & James Hu, eds., 2006); Michael Faure & Wang Hui, *Financial Caps for Oil Pollution Damage: China and the International Conventions*, in Prevention and Compensation of Marine Pollution Damage: Recent Developments in Europe, China and the US, pp. 317, 329–330.

33 For example, a foreign element may be that one party involved is a foreigner, the cause of the cases happens abroad, and the subject matter is located abroad. See Hu & Bo, in Prevention and Compensation of Marine Pollution Damage: Recent Developments in Europe, China and the US, pp. 193, 198–199 (Michael Faure & James Hu, eds., 2006).

compensation for oil pollution damage, the party accused of discharge of oil often relies on the China Maritime Code to limit his liability.[34]

It is worth noting that the categories of claims that are subject to the limit under the CMC are much broader than oil pollution under the MEPL. Since China is a member state of the CLC, which established a separate liability limit for oil pollution, the limits set in the CMC do not apply to claims for oil pollution under the CLC.[35] There are debates on the applicable scope of the CLC in both academia and case law.[36] This debate also puzzles the determination of the limit for oil pollution. To clarify this issue, the Regulation of 2018 stipulates the following in Article 52:

> With regard to the limitation of liability for pollution damage caused by vessels, provisions of the Maritime Code of the People's Republic of China in respect of the limitation of liability for maritime claims shall apply. However, with regard to the limitation of liability for pollution damage caused by vessels carrying persistent oils in bulk to sea areas under the jurisdiction of the People's Republic of China, the provisions of the international treaties concluded or acceded to by the People's Republic of China shall apply.

According to this provision, the CLC will apply as long as vessels carrying persistent oil cause the damage. Hence, it seems that the foreign-related issue is no longer necessary for the application of the CLC. If the damage is caused by an accident which does not fall into the scope of the CLC, such as damage caused by nonpersistent fuel oil or fuel oil carried by vessels rather than by oil tankers, the limits under the CMC will apply.

D. Mandatory Financial Security

As noted, China is a member state of the CLC, which introduces an obligation for shipowners to seek insurance coverage for potential liability under the convention. Influenced by the CLC, the MEPL requires vessels to carry oil pollution liability insurance and oil funds, and the MEPL also authorises the State Council to promulgate concrete rules on those issues.[37] Similar provisions can be found in the Regulation, which requires the vessels navigating Chinese seas (with the exception of vessels with carrying capacities of less than one thousand tonnes carrying cargo other than oil) to buy insurance or to seek other financial security coverage.[38] As to the specific amount of financial security, the Regulation states that it shall be no less than the amount required under the CMC and the conventions China acceded to.[39] To implement this provision, another document known as the Implementation Measures was published in 2010 to further clarify the types of vessels that are subject to the compulsory financial security requirement and the amount of the required security (Table 15.3).[40]

---

34 Article 207 of CMC.

35 Article 208(2) of CMC.

36 For a different interpretation of the application scope in case law, see Zhang Liying, *Compensation for the Domestic Oil Pollution in China's Coast: Which Law Shall Apply?*, in Maritime Pollution Liability and Policy: China, Europe and the US, pp. 359, 360–69 (Michael G. Faure et al., eds., 2010).

37 Article 66 of MEPL.

38 Article 53 of the Regulation.

39 Ibid.

40 Measures of the People's Republic of China for the Implementation of Civil Liability Insurance for Vessel-Induced Oil Pollution Damage [Zhonghua Renmin Gongheguo Chuanbo Youwu Sunhai Minshi Zeren

Table 15.3 The Types of Vessels and Required Financial Security [i]

Vessels with persistent oil as cargo		Vessels with nonpersistent oil as cargo and non-oil tankers larger than 1000 tonnes (gross tonnage)	
Types of vessels (gross tonnage)	Amount of financial security	Types of vessels (gross tonnage)	Amount of financial security
(1) Lower than 5,000 tonnes	**4.51** million SDR (6.93 million USD)	(1) 20–21 tonnes (not including 21)	27,500 SDR (42,265.3 USD)
		(2) 21–300 tonnes (not including 300)	(1) + 500 SDR (768.46 USD) per ton
(2) Higher than 5,000 tonnes	(1) + 631 SDR (969.8 USD) per ton; but the total amount is no more than 89.77 million SDR (137.97 USD)	(3) 300–500 tonnes	167,000 SDR (256,665.64 USD)
		(4) 501–30,000 tonnes	(3) + 167 SDR (256.67 USD) per ton
		(5) 30,001–70,000 tonnes	(4) + 125 SDR (192.12 USD) per ton
		(6) Above 70,001 tonnes	(5) + 83 SDR (127.56 USD) per ton

[i] Articles 5 and 6 of the Implementation Measures.

The Implementation Measures require that Chinese vessels either buy insurance from insurers authorised by the Marine Safety Agency or acquire other financial security, such as a letter of guarantee or a letter of credit from insurers or other financial institutions determined by the Marine Safety Agency.[41] The requirements for commercial insurance companies and P&I Clubs to be determined as qualified are also clarified in the Implementation Rules.[42] In 2012, 23 insurance companies and P&I Clubs have been acknowledged by the Marine Safety Agency, including the China Shipowners Mutual Assurance Association (CSMAA) (which is basically the China P&I Club), commercial insurers, and some members of the International Group of Protection & Indemnity Clubs (IG Group).[43]

CSMAA is one of the leading P&I Clubs in the Asia-Pacific region, providing coverage for various kinds of third-party liability, including oil pollution. This is a so-called

Baoxian Shishi Banfa] (promulgated by the Ministry of Transport, 19 Aug 2010, effective 1 October 2010). This document was revised in 2013. Available at the official website of the Ministry of Transport, www.gov.cn /gongbao/content/2013/content_2519696.htm.

41 Article 8 of the Implementation Measures.
42 Articles 9–10 of the Implementation Measures.
43 China Maritime Safety Administration, Guanyu Gongbu 2012 Niandu Zhongguoji Chuanbo Youwu Sunhai Minshi Zeren Baoxian Jigou Mingdande Tongzhi [Notice on the List of Insurance Companies Providing Oil Pollution Damage Liability Insurance for Chinese Vessels of 2012] (19 December 2011).

P&I Club, composed of shipowners that adopt a risk-sharing agreement and, in that way, mutually cover each other's losses.[44] The CSMAA, as a P&I Club, formally functions as a risk-sharing agreement and not as an insurer, in the sense that risks are mutually shared and not shifted to a third party.[45] However, from the victim's perspective the crucial point is that P&I Clubs compensate the losses for which the members (usually shipowners) are covered.[46] It is worth noting that the CSMAA is not a member of the IG Group.[47]

Rule 3, section 12 of the CSMAA clearly provides that pollution risks are covered. According to this clause, the following risks are included:

A. Liability for loss, damage or contamination.
B. Any loss, damage or expense which the Member incurs, or for which he is liable, as a party to any agreement approved by the Directors, including the costs and expenses incurred by the member in performing his obligations under such agreements.
C. The costs of any measures reasonably taken for the purpose of avoiding or minimising pollution or any resulting loss or damage together with any liability for loss of or damage to property caused by measures so taken.
D. The costs of any measures reasonabl[y] taken to prevent an imminent danger of the discharge or escape from the entered ship of oil or any substance which may cause pollution.
E. The costs of liabilities incurred as a result of compliance with any order or direction given by any government or authority, for the purpose of preventing or reducing pollution or the risk of pollution, provided always that:
   a. such compliance is not a requirement for the normal operation or salvage or repair of the entered ship; and
   b. such costs or liabilities are not recoverable under the Hull Policies or the Hull Certificates of the entered ship.[48]

This rule contains no specific title concerning restoration costs. These may, however, be partially covered under the title of cleanup costs. Cleanup costs need to be reasonable and actual.[49] Interim losses are, according to the CSMAA, difficult to evaluate and are usually not compensated.[50]

---

44 See T.G. Coghlin, *Protection and Indemnity Clubs*, 1984 Lloyd's Mar. & Com. L.Q. 403, 403–416.

45 The CSMAA is the Chinese version of P&I Club, which means it has also the same characteristics as the P&I Club – being a risk sharing pool rather than commercial insurance. See Michael G. Faure & Ton Hartlief, Policy Issues in Insurance: Insurance and Expanding Systemic Risks, pp. 211–220 (2003), pp. 167–168 (noting the differences between risk sharing and insurance).

46 One important line of the CSMAA's policies is the liability insurance, which covers damage to cargo, personal injury, pollution damage and so on. So from the perspective of the shipowner, though the ships are insured by the groups of ships themselves but not commercial insurers, his or her damage can still be covered.

47 Arthur Gallagher, Marine P &I Commercial Market Review 2013, p. 46 (2013), available at www.ajginternational.com/assets/Marine-PI-Newsletters/Marine-PI-Commercial-Market-2013-09.09.13.pdf.

48 See *The Rules*, China Shipowners Mutual Assurance Ass'n, rule 3, sec. 12(d)(A)–(E), www.cpiweb.org /en_baoxiantiaokuan/1_1.jsp.

49 Interview with representatives of the CSMAA, in Beijing, China (22 Aug. 2011) (interview transcript on file with the authors).

50 Ibid.

E. Compensation Funds

Although China acceded to the CLC in 1980, it is not a member state of the IOPC Fund. After years of discussion, China established in 2012 its own domestic fund, the China Oil Pollution Compensation (COPC) Fund, and the concrete rules to manage the fund were published Management Regulation of Collection and Use of the Vessel-Induced Pollution Damage Compensation Fund.[51]

The Regulation on the Compensation Fund fixed the contribution at RMB 0.3 (USD 0.048) per ton of persistent oil.[52] The fund can be used to compensate or indemnify when (1) the total amount of compensation exceeds the shipowner's limitation of liability; (2) legal defences are available; (3) the shipowner and its insurer/guarantor cannot provide full compensation; and (4) the liable ship cannot be identified.[53] Three exceptions are stipulated when the Compensation Fund does not apply: when the damage is caused by wars, insurrections, or non-commercial vessels/military ships held by the government; when claimants cannot prove that the oil pollution is caused by ships; or when the damage is fully or partially caused by the victims' fault.[54]

One major difference between the Chinese Compensation Fund and the IOPC Fund is that the former establishes priority lists to provide compensation in case of insufficient capacity of the fund. On the one hand, for the claims caused by different accidents, the Chinese Compensation Fund shall deal with the compensation according to the moment of application to the fund.[55] On the other hand, if the claims are caused by the same accident, the compensation shall be provided according to the following order: emergency response costs, cleanup costs, direct economic losses suffered by fishery and tourism industries, the costs of measures to restore the marine ecosystem and natural fishery resources, monitoring costs incurred by the management committee of the Compensation Funds, and finally other costs approved by the State Council.[56] The upper limit of compensation by the fund for one accident is set as RMB 30 million (4.77 million USD).[57]

V. Comparison between the European (International) and the Chinese Systems

A. Basis of Liability

In both systems, a strict liability system is chosen as the basis for the compensation of pollution damage.

This is justified from an economic perspective: the imposition of liability will provide incentives for the potential parties to take preventive measures,[58] and deter the potential

---

51 Management Regulation of Collection and Use of the Vessel-Induced Pollution Damage Compensation Fund [Caizhengbu Jiaotong Yunshubu Guanyu Yinfa Chuanbo Youwu Sunhai Peichang Jijin Zhengshou Shiyong Guanli Banfade Tongzhi] (promulgated by Ministry of Finance & Ministry of Transport, effective 1 July 2012).

52 Ibid., Art. 6.

53 Ibid., Art. 15.

54 Ibid., Art. 16.

55 Ibid., Art. 17.

56 Ibid.

57 Ibid., Art. 18.

58 See Alberto Monti, *Environmental Risk: A Comparative Law and Economics Approach to Liability and Insurance*, 9 Eur. Rev. Private L. 51 (2001) (discussing the role of liability rules as "engineering instruments").

injurer from doing harm to the potential victims.[59] In the case of a bilateral accident where both parties can influence the accident risk (like the case of a marine oil pollution incident), only strict liability is optimal in the sense that both negligence and strict liability can lead to an efficient care level, but only strict liability leads to an efficient activity level of the injurer as well.[60] Moreover, marine oil pollution is clearly a case where the influence of the injurer (tanker owner) on the accident risk is surely more important than the victim's. The party who transports oil, and hence discharges or poses risks to discharge oil into the sea – for example, a tanker owner – has a greater influence on the accident risk than the potential victims. Therefore, it is more important to control the behaviour of the injurer than the victim, and imposing strict liability on the shipowner is justified.[61] On the other hand, the victims may have an influence on the accident risks as well (although their influence is usually less compared with that of the injurer).[62] They should also be given incentives to take precautions; this is often realised by adding a comparative or contributory negligence defence to the strict liability rule.

The CLC 1992 provides that if the pollution resulted wholly or partially from a negligent or intentional act or omission of the victim, the tanker owner will be exonerated wholly or partially from liability.[63] Hence, a comparative negligence defence is added to the strict liability rule to provide the victim incentives to take care as well. As we indicated above, in China a strict liability rule applies on the basis of MEPL.[64] This excludes liability in case of an intentional act or fault of a third party.

However, strict liability may be optimal only when the injurer is solvent. If the amount of damage exceeds the injurer's wealth, as is often the case for oil pollution damage, the injurer will consider the risk as one where he could at most lose his assets and will set his care level according to the amount of his assets, which is lower than the optimal care level required by the actual damage he could cause. Thus, the insolvency risk may lead to underdeterrence.[65] If the injurer were judgment-proof,[66] a regulatory solution has to take care of the danger of underdeterrence resulting from insolvency.[67] This will be further discussed in the section related to financial security.[68]

---

59 The deterrent effect and victim protection functions of tort law have been widely discussed in law and economics literature. See, e.g., Gary T. Schwartz, *Mixed Theories of Tort Law: Affirming Both Deterrence and Corrective Justice*, 75 Tex. L. Rev. 1801 (1997) (showing that the tort rules may serve both the aims of deterrence and corrective justice).

60 See Steven Shavell, *Strict Liability Versus Negligence*, 9 J. Legal Stud. 1 (1980). For a summary, see Hans-Bernd Schäfer & Andreas Schönenberger, *Strict Liability Versus Negligence*, in 2 Encyclopedia of Law and Economics: Civil Law and Economics 597 (Boudewijn Bouckaert & Gerrit De Geest, eds., 2000).

61 See Steven Shavell, Foundations of Economic Analysis of Law, pp. 188–189 (2004).

62 Victims in oil pollution cases can usually not contribute to the prevention of the accident itself, but they can take measures to mitigate the damage after the accident occurred.

63 Article III (3) of CLC 1992.

64 See Article 89 of MEPL.

65 See William M. Landes & Richard A. Posner, *Tort Law as a Regulatory Regime for Catastrophic Personal Injuries*, 13 J. Legal Stud. 417 (1984) (explaining the underdeterrence effects of strict liability).

66 A party is said to be judgment-proof if he avoids the full degree of liability he should rightly face. See Rohan Pitchford, *Judgment-Proofness*, in 2 The New Palgrave Dictionary of Economics and the Law, pp. 380, 380–383 (Peter Newman ed., 1998).

67 See also Steven Shavell, *The Judgment Proof Problem*, 6 Int'l Rev. L. & Econ. 45 (1986).

68 See the discussion in section 5.4.

B. Channelling

The CLC exclusively channels the liability to the shipowner.[69] China is a contracting country to the CLC. Although there is no specific provision in Chinese law excluding the liability of other parties like in the CLC, in practice, it is always the shipowner that is held liable in the case of marine oil pollution.[70]

Channeling means that the convention or statute indicates which of many possible parties can be held liable for the loss, including the damage to natural resources. The liability of other potentially liable parties is excluded.[71] In the oil pollution case, the liability of the tanker owner (to which liability is channelled) is limited to a certain amount, and the effect of the combination of a financial cap with channelling is that the victim can exclusively sue the tanker owner, where he is confronted with a financial cap.[72] The victim has no additional possibility to bring another lawsuit if, as a result, his damages were not fully compensated.[73] A suit based on tort law against the tanker owner for the amount not covered by the cap is excluded in the convention, and a suit against a third liable party is usually excluded as well because of the channelling.

On the other hand, channelling may have the advantage of transaction-cost reduction. Since the victim does not have to investigate who precisely the liable injurer is, he can only sue the shipowner to whom liability is channelled.[74] However, this seems hardly valid: the additional benefit of channelling for the victim is limited (the costs of finding out the registered tanker owner who may be primarily liable are not that high), whereas the disadvantages for the victim are huge (he or she no longer has the possibility to claim damages from other parties who may have contributed to the loss as well). From a victim's and deterrence perspective, one may well argue that a joint and several liability rule may be preferable; in that case, the victim can simply sue any of the available injurers who are all exposed to liability and claim full compensation.

C. Limited Amount of Compensation

Both the CLC and the CMC adopt a limited liability of the shipowner. This limited liability is calculated on the basis of the tonnage of the vessel. Even with the additional compensation through the compensation funds, the total compensation amounts under both regimes are restricted.

The differences in the amount of compensation can be seen in Table 15.4.

At the international level, the limited liability resulted in undercompensation, which can be shown by referring to the historical evolution of the international regime. Every

---

69 Articles II(1)–(2) of CLC 1992.

70 Wang Hui, Civil Liability for Marine Oil Pollution 249 (2011).

71 For a discussion on the channeling of liability, see Michael Faure & Wang Hui, *Economic Analysis of Compensation for Oil Pollution Damage*, 37 J. Mar. Law & Com., pp. 179, 187–188 (2006).

72 Ibid., pp. 206–207.

73 When there is channeling of liability, the victims cannot claim against other parties for their losses. This is the case in the CLC of 1992, which excludes the possibility for victims to claim against a list of parties. See Article III(4) of CLC 1992.

74 See Tom Vanden Borre, Efficiënte Preventie en Compensatie Van Catastroferisico's: Het Voorbeeld Van Schade Door Kernongevallen [Efficient Prevention and Compensation of Catastrophic Risks: The Example of Nuclear Accident Damage], pp. 698–699 (2001) (Neth.).

Table 15.4 Comparison of Compensation Amounts under the International and the Chinese Regimes (USD)

Amount of compensation	CLC 1992 (after 2000 Resolutions)	CMC
First layer of compensation	Ships ≤ 5,000 GT: 6.93 million; Ships > 5,000 GT: 6.93 million + 969.8/additional tonnes; Overall limit: 137.97 million	20 ≤ Ships < 21GT, 42,265.3; 21 ≤ Ships < 300GT, 42,265.3 + 768.46/GT; 300 ≤ Ships ≤ 500GT, 256,665.64; 501 ≤ Ships ≤ 30,000GT, 256,665.64 + 256.67/GT; 30,001 ≤ Ships ≤ 70,000GT, amount above + 192.12/GT; Ships ≥ 70,001 GT, above amount + 127.56/GT.
Second layer of compensation	IOPC Fund (2,000 Resolutions): 311.99 million	China fund: 4.77 million
Third layer of compensation	Supplementary Fund: 1,152.69 million	

time a new incident with higher damage occurred, the limits were again increased since the then-existing limits apparently did not suffice to provide compensation to accident victims.[75] Whereas in China, limitation of liability is not a known concept in tort law or environmental law, but parties of a marine oil pollution incident can limit their liability under the CLC or the CMC. Additional compensation provided through the Chinese compensation fund is only up to RMB 30 million (4.77 million USD) per accident. These are of a lower level compared to the international system.

D. Financial Security

Both the CLC and Chinese law have requirements on compulsory liability insurance for oil pollution damage or other forms of financial guarantee.

Such a compulsory financial guarantee complies with the economic findings: a strict liability rule could be considered efficient only if the injurer has sufficient assets at stake and there is no insolvency risk. As discussed in Section 5.1, when the injurer is insolvent (being his assets are less than the potential damage he could cause), he will choose a care level only corresponding with his assets which will be lower than the optimal care level required by the damage. Insolvency may thus lead to underdeterrence. In the case of insolvency, compulsory insurance might provide a better outcome:[76] when there is a duty

---

75 See Noah Sachs, *Beyond the Liability Wall: Strengthening Tort Remedies in International Environmental Law*, p. 55 UCLA L. Rev. 837 (2008).

76 Peter J. Jost, *Limited Liability and the Requirement to Purchase Insurance*, 16 Int'l Rev. L. & Econ. 259 (1996). A similar argument has been formulated by Mattias Polborn and Goran Skogh. See Mattias K. Polborn, *Mandatory Insurance and the Judgement-Proof Problem*, 18 Int'l Rev. L. & Econ. 141 (1998); Goran Skogh, *Mandatory Insurance: Transaction Costs Analysis of Insurance*, in 2 Encyclopedia of Law and Economics: Civil Law and Economics, supra note 279, at 521 (pointing out that compulsory insurance may save on transaction cost). See also Howard C. Kunreuther & Paul K. Freeman,

to insure, the insurer will have incentives to control the behaviour of the insured. Through setting appropriate premiums, the insurer can make sure that the injurer will take the necessary care to avoid an accident with the real magnitude of the loss.[77]

This economic argument shows that insolvency may cause potentially responsible parties to externalise harm: they may engage in activities causing harm that can largely exceed their assets. Without financial provisions, these costs would be thrown on society and would be externalised instead of internalised. Internalisation can be reached if the insurer is able to control the behaviour of the insured. The insurer could set appropriate policy conditions and require an adequate (risk-related) premium. This shows that, if the moral hazard problem can be cured adequately, insurance leads to an even higher deterrence than a situation without liability insurance and insolvency.[78]

Therefore, the requirement of compulsory insurance or other financial guarantee complies with the economic theory.

E. Compensation Funds

From the above, it follows that if one fears those on which liability for oil pollution damage is placed (e.g. the tanker owner) might be insolvent in the sense that the amount of the damage he or she may cause could be higher than his or her wealth, a duty to seek financial coverage through insurance or alternative mechanisms should be introduced.[79] However, the amount of oil pollution damage may be so large that even traditional insurance mechanisms or pooling by operators may not provide sufficient coverage. Then there is the need for supplementary funding through a compensation fund.

From the economic view, in order for such a fund to function efficiently, the duty to contribute to the fund should, in principle, only rest upon those who actually contributed to the risk and should be related to the amount of risk to which the specific activity contributes.[80] In this way, the contributors to the fund are given incentives for prevention. Bad risks are punished by paying a greater contribution to the fund, and good risks are rewarded by paying less contribution. Such a fund structure is not only important from an efficiency point of view, by providing optimal incentives for prevention, but it also includes a fairness element.

Examining the financing structure of the IOPC Fund and the Chinese Oil Compensation Fund, the oil recipients pay levies and their contribution is calculated on the amount of oil received in a certain period of time.[81] Consequently, the financing structure merely incentivises

---

Insurability, Environmental Risks and the Law, in The Law and Economics of the Environment 302 (Anthony Heyes ed., 2001).

77 The economic literature argues that compulsory insurance can provide better results than under the judgment-proof problem (insolvency). This was supported by inter alia, Jost and Skogh. See Jost, Ibid., p. 77; Skogh, Ibid., p. 77.

78 There are, however, also a few dangers that should be taken into account when a duty to insure is introduced. One of them is that the moral hazard problem should be cured; another is that there may not be concentration on insurance markets. For these potential dangers of compulsory insurance, see Michael Faure & David Grimeaud, *Financial Assurance Issues of Environmental Liability, in* 5 Tort and Insurance Law: Deterrence, Insurability, and Compensation in Environmental Liability, pp. 185–189.

79 See Michael G. Faure, *Alternative Compensation Mechanisms as Remedies for Uninsurability of Liability,* 29 Geneva Papers on Risk & Ins. 455 (2004).

80 See Michael G. Faure, *Financial Compensation for Victims of Catastrophes: A Law and Economics Perspective,* 29 L. & POL'Y 339 (2007).

81 See Article 10 of the Fund Convention of 1992.

the oil industry to adapt the activity level (e.g., transporting less oil) but not to an efficient level of care. Moreover, both funds, in the normal case, only intervene for the amount that is not covered by the limited liability of the tanker owner,[82] which is a small part of the total costs of an oil-pollution incident. It was decided during the conference that only 5% of largescale oil casualties could not be dealt with under the existing rules.[83] Effectively, this means that the oil interests would only intervene for a relatively small part of oil pollution incidents, albeit the incidents where the IOPC Fund intervenes are usually catastrophic.

VI. Conclusion

This chapter compared the way in which damage caused by marine oil pollution is compensated in China and Europe. As in Europe, the international conventions apply (and partially in China as well), it mostly consisted of a comparison between the international regime and Chinese domestic law. Europe has been confronted with cases of major oil spills causing considerable environmental damage. As a result of those incidents the international regime has experienced many developments and refinements. Conversely, the system in China is still in full development; although, as was shown, the compensation for marine pollution damage is rather elaborate and refined when compared to the compensation for other types of environmental damage in China. The reason may be that China incorporated the CLC, which forced it to adopt a strict liability rule and mandatory financial security to guarantee the tanker owner's liability. China did not, however and for obvious reasons, join the International Fund Convention. China is a net importer of oil and, being the largest importer of crude oil in the world, it would have automatically become the largest contributor to the IOPC Fund. Presently, China has suffered less marine-pollution incidents than other countries that are members to the Fund Convention. If China were to join the International Fund Convention, there is a great likelihood that China would be a net contributor to the IOPC Fund; that is, contributing more through taxes on the oil received in China than it would benefit from compensation via the Fund. Understandably, China instead created its own domestic fund that clearly mimics the International Fund Convention. This shows that, notwithstanding their inherent limits, the international conventions constitute an important example for countries with developing economies, like China, even if those countries do not necessarily join the conventions.

China can undoubtedly learn from the experience in the international regime. Chinese practitioners complain of their legal doctrines lacking assessment standards. This limitation makes the judiciaries' task in assessing natural resource damages difficult. Given the increasing oil imports in China and the fact that most of these imports are seaborne, it must be feared that China may be confronted with oil spills resulting in large environmental damage. With increasing environmental awareness in China, demands for adequate restoration measures will undoubtedly also increase. In that respect there is an opportunity for mutual learning by comparing the situation in China with experiences in Europe under the international conventions. It is to this process of mutual learning that this chapter hopes to contribute.

---

82 Articles X, IV(1)(a)–(c) of Fund Convention of 1992. An exception would be the case where the tanker owner is insolvent. In this case, the Fund would, de facto, act as a guarantor towards the victim.

83 International Maritime Organization, *Official Records of the International Legal Conference on Marine Pollution Damage*, pp. 685–686, IMO Doc. LEG/CONF/C.2/SR12, pp. 685–686 (1969).

CHAPTER 16

The Legal Challenges for Seafarers in Claiming Workplace Injury Compensation in China

Desai Shan* and Pengfei Zhang**

I. Introduction

With 808,183 registered seafarers in 2020, China is one of the largest maritime labour sup-plying states globally.[1] Chinese seafarers play an important role in Chinese coastal trade and the global shipping industry in general. They transport over 50% of Chinese domestic trade and more than 93% of China's international trade.

Due to their significant representation among transport workers, Chinese seafarer rights have increasingly attracted attention from regulators.[2] Since 2011, the Chinese Maritime Safety Administration has held annual Chinese Seafarers' Conferences in Shanghai where seafarers' social and economic contributions are recognised and maritime sector labour rights are promoted.[3] In 2015, China ratified the Maritime Labour Convention, 2006, promising to the world that government would ensure decent working conditions for seafarers. In 2016, the Chinese Ministry of Transport issued the *Development Plan of Seafarers (2016–2020)*, emphasising the importance of seafarer rights protection.[4]

Seafaring is well-recognised as an adventurous and hazardous occupation.[5] According to British merchant fleet (2003–2012) statistics, the relative risk of workplace accidental fatalities (14.5 per 100,000) is 21 times greater than that of the general workforce, 4.7 times that of the construction industry, and 13 times that of the manufacturing industry.[6]

---

* Dr Desai Shan is Assistant Professor at Faculty of Medicine, Memorial University of Newfoundland.
** Dr Pengfei Zhao is Professor, Navigation College, Jimei University, Xiamen, China.

1 Ministry of Transport of People's Republic of China, 'Chinese Seafarer Development Report 2020' (June 2020) <www.msa.gov.cn/public/documents/document/mta1/mdqy/~edisp/20211201105042929.pdf>accessed 17 January 2022.

2 Minghua Zhao, Pengfei Zhang and Gaochao He, 'Port-Based Welfare Services for Seafarers in Chinese Ports: Their Roles, Changes and Challenges' (2021) 130 Marine Policy 104190.

3 Pengfei Zhang and Minghua Zhao, 'Maritime Labour Policy in China: Restructuring under the ILO's Maritime Labour Convention 2006' (2014) 50 Marine Policy 111.

4 Ministry of Tranport, of People's Republic of China, 'The Development Plan of Chinese Seafarers (2016–2020)' (2016) <www.gov.cn/gongbao/content/2017/content_5197028.htm> accessed 15 January 2022.

5 AD Couper, B Stanberry, C Walsh and G Boerne, 'Voyages of abuse: Seafarers, human rights and inter-national shipping' (Pluto Press 1999); M Bloor, 'An essay on health capital' and the Faustian bargains struck by workers in the globalised shipping industry' (2011). Sociology of Health & Illness, p. 33 (7). doi:10.1111/j.1467-9566.2011.01347.x; D Shan, 'Mapping the Maritime Occupational Health and Safety Challenges Faced by Canadian Seafarers' (2020). In Governance of Arctic Shipping (pp. 191–205). Springer, Cham; D Kirkby, 'Life Would Be a Misery!" Mental Health and the Safety of Seafarers (2020). Labour History, (119), pp. 197–208

6 S Roberts, D Nielsen, A Kotłowski and B Jaremin, 'Fatal accidents and injuries among merchant sea-farers worldwide' (2014). Occupational medicine, p. 64 (4), pp. 259–266; D Shan, 'Mapping the Maritime

     DOI: 10.4324/9781003160298-19

In China, seafarer occupational injury and fatality related research is mainly limited to those conducted by state-owned shipping enterprises, while nationwide surveys are not available. A 2012 comparative study of work-related casualty rates from 2005 among Chinese state-owned enterprises in the shipping, logistics and shipbuilding sectors suggested that the shipping sector's occupational casualty rate was about four times higher than that of the shipbuilding sector.[7]

Workplace accidents cause considerable physical, emotional and economic damage and loss to workers and their families.[8] Legislators allow victims to claim damages from liable parties through a compensation system to relieve their grievances.[9] There are usually two legal approaches in the compensation system. One is the workers' compensation system where injured workers/beneficiaries can obtain limited no-fault-based compensation from a public insurance fund or the employers' private insurers. The other is a tort liability system where victims can obtain full compensation from their employers if they can prove the accidents were caused by a lack of due diligence.[10]

Work-related disability/death compensation is a crucial component of the seafarers' rights protection regime. Several trials are being conducted to improve the efficiency of governance on seafarers' occupational health and safety in the global shipping industry. International conventions, smart regulations and international trade unions' collective agreements aim to ensure reasonably good working and living conditions, salary and medical treatment for injured seafarers.[11] However, compensation standards and procedures are still largely subject to the diverse domestic laws of labour supply states. Rather than attenuating consequences, the compensation systems in many countries can contribute to the harmful events endured by victims.[12] 45.92% of Chinese seafarers do not have long-term employment relationships as shipowners and managers are more inclined to offer temporary voyage agreements to seafarers.[13] Within the context of precarious and temporary industrial relations in the maritime sector, it is questionable whether Chinese

Occupational Health and Safety Challenges Faced by Canadian Seafarers' (2020). In Governance of Arctic Shipping (pp. 191–205). Springer, Cham.

7 Zhang, Xiao, Gang Zhang, Yunfang Gui, Chen Ailing, Rongping Li, Baoqi Xu and Hui Xie. Analysis of Industrial Injuries to Chinese Seafarers (2012) Navigation of China, p. 35 (1), pp. 113–118.

8 N Krause, LK Dasinger and F Neuhauser, Modified work and returns to work: A review of the literature. (1998) Journal of Occupational Rehabilitation, p. 8 (2), pp. 113–139. doi:10.1023/a:1023015622987; D Shan, Workplace death at sea: Chinese surviving families' experiences of compensation claims. (2017) Relations Industrielles/Industrial Relations, p. 72 (1), pp. 125–148; D Shan. The anti-therapeutic effects of workers' compensation in China: The case of seafarers (2018). International journal of law and psychiatry, p. 58, pp. 97–104.

9 D Shan, Workplace death at sea: Chinese surviving families' experiences of compensation claims. (2017) Relations Industrielles/Industrial Relations, p. 72 (1), pp. 125–148.

10 P Cane and PS Atiyah, 'Atiyah's accidents, compensation and the law', (2006) Cambridge: Cambridge University Press; Morley Gunderson and Douglas Hyatt, Workers' Compensation: Foundations for Reform (Toronto: University of Toronto Press, 2017). https://doi-org.qe2a-proxy.mun.ca/10.3138/9781442683648.

11 Christodoulou-Varotsi I, Pentsov DA. Maritime work law fundamentals: Responsible shipowners, reliable seafarers. Springer Science & Business Media; 2007 October 18; Michael Bloor and Helen Sampson, 'Regulatory Enforcement of Labour Standards in an Outsourcing Globalized Industry: The Case of the Shipping Industry' (2009) 23 Work, Employment and Society 711 <www-jstor-org.qe2a-proxy.mun.ca/stable /23749285?sid=primo&seq=1#metadata_info_tab_contents> accessed 18 January 2022.

12 Quinland M and Mayhew C (1999) Precarious employment and workers' compensation. International Journal of Law and Psychiatry, p. 22: pp. 491–520; D Shan, The anti-therapeutic effects of workers' compensation in China: The case of seafarers (2018). International Journal of Law and Psychiatry, p. 58, pp. 97–104.

13 G Chen, X Zhu and Y Hao, 'The Application of Maritime Labour Convention (2006) in China and Standard Employment Contractual Remedies. (2014). Wuhan: Wuhan University of Technology, Fujian Maritime Safety Administration.

labour laws can provide Chinese seafarers with appropriate labour rights. The research question raised in this chapter seeks to explore whether Chinese seafarers and shore-based workers are entitled to equal legal protection following workplace injuries.

The following three sections will (1) explore the impact of employment-related mobility on seafarer rights protection; (2) introduce the methods applied in this study; and (3) will present the legal obstacles faced by Chinese seafarers during the compensation process. In the concluding discussion, current legal challenges and barriers faced by Chinese seafarers will be critically discussed, and a policy recommendation will be provided.

II. Employment-Related Mobility and Seafarers' Rights

The high-level international mobility creates challenges for seafarers who claim compensation following workplace injuries/fatalities. Two features of employment-related international mobility that may affect seafarers' compensation claims are: (1) the mobility of the workplace; and (2) the mobility of the workers. In the event of seafarer injuries at sea, the mobility of the workplace can increase the complexity of determining which laws to apply. The mobility of Chinese seafarers may affect the jurisdiction they can access to seek redress.

Ocean-going vessels are mobile workplaces navigating between different ports in the world. Container vessels offer regularly scheduled service between fixed ports, contributing to 13.5% of the total deadweight tonnages of the world fleet. The majority of the world's fleet (72%), bulk carriers and oil tankers, operate between a variety of ports which are determined by the charterers' requests.[14] The mobility of the workplace for seafarers employed on bulk carriers and tankers can also be unpredictable since many experience frequent changes in their navigation lines and ports. The likely result of the unpredictability of workplace mobility is that seafarers can sustain injuries in unforeseen locations where it could be difficult to correctly choose the accessible jurisdiction and applicable law.

In the shipping industry, the mobility of workers has become complicated due to the pervasive adoption of the open registry and global maritime labour supply chains. Traditionally, the shipowner, seafarers and the vessel were of one nationality, and the state would be responsible for regulating worker health and safety, working conditions and labour standards on their registered vessels. However, since the 1960s, through the open registry, maritime employers can register their vessels under a flag of convenience to avoid tax obligations and restrictions on crew nationalities.[15] The absence of crew nationality restrictions permits shipowners to recruit seafarers from middle-low income countries.[16] In addition to the flag state vs. port state challenges created by mobile workplaces, worker mobility has also introduced two new regulators into the governance of maritime labour disputes. These are the labour supply state and the state of the shipowner.[17]

---

14 UNCTAD. Review of Maritime Transport 2019. (Geneva: United Nations, 2019).

15 H Sampson, International Seafarers and Transnationalism in the Twenty-First Century (New Ethnographies). (Manchester: Manchester University Press, 2013).

16 Nathan Lillie, 'Global Collective Bargaining on Flag of Convenience Shipping' (2004), p. 42; British Journal of Industrial Relations, p. 47.

17 G Chen and D Shan, Seafarers' access to jurisdictions over labour matters (2017). Marine Policy, p. 77, pp. 1–8. https://doi.org/10.1016/j.marpol.2016.12.004.

The employment-related international mobility of seafaring jobs increases the unpredictability and complexity of maritime workers' labour disputes. This chapter will focus on the legal challenges seafarers may face in compensation claim processes in China, the labour supply state. Chinese seafarers and their families can claim compensation in another jurisdiction, such as the flag state and the port state. As a major labour supply state, a significant number of maritime employment agreements are reached in China, which means that seafarers can seek justice in China when workplace injuries do occur. Additionally, following injury and repatriation, most Chinese seafarers would choose to pursue their claims in their home country as a convenient legal forum. Thus, Chinese law is frequently applicable law to many maritime labour disputes, and Chinese maritime courts are the main forums for entertaining seafarers' claims.

III. Methods

Two qualitative research methods are applied in this chapter. The first author (1) conducted a legal doctrinal study on Chinese seafarers' rights; and (2) interviewed injured seafarers and surviving families to explore their claim experiences following workplace accidents. Important stakeholders, including ship and crew managers, claim handlers, and maritime judges and lawyers were invited to participate in this research.

Legal doctrinal research is a documentary analysis drawing on legal sources to obtain documentary evidence to support and validate statements.[18] The authors conduct legal research using normative and authoritative legal sources, including statutes, regulations, judicial interpretations, administrative policies, judicial precedents and judges' commentaries. While gathering information for this chapter, we have collected statutes and regulations from the State Council of the People's Republic of China website: www.gov .cn; judicial interpretations were collected from the Chinese Supreme People's Court's website: www.court.gov.cn; maritime judgements and judges' commentaries regarding seafarers claims were obtained directly from maritime courts and from the Chinese Foreign-related Commercial and Maritime Trials website: www.ccmt.org.cn; administrative policies were gathered from the websites of multiple ministries of the State Council of China, particularly the Ministry of Transport and the Ministry of Human Resource and Social Security. Based on these legal sources (legal documents), we have identified and critically analysed all of the instruments available for injured seafarers and surviving families.

The first author conducted 41 interviews with injured seafarers and surviving families and 33 interviews with ship and crew managers, claim handlers, maritime judges and lawyers between 2013 and 2019 (see Tables 16.1 and 16.2). All of the interviews with victims were recorded and interview lengths averaged about 90 minutes, ranging from 50 minutes to 4 hours. The participants were from 18 cities in 12 Chinese provinces.

---

18 Katherine Lippel, 'Workers Describe the Effect of the Workers' Compensation Process on Their Health: A Québec Study' (2007), p. 30; International Journal of Law and Psychiatry, p. 427.

Table 16.1 List of Participants (Victims)

Surviving family members (N = 8)	N = 5 Seafarers were killed/disappeared on ocean-going vessels
	N = 3 seafarers were killed/disappeared on coastal vessels
Injured seafarers (N = 33)	N = 20 ocean-going seafarers
	N = 13 coastal seafarers

Table 16.2 List of Participants (Professionals)

Sector	*Representative*
Shipping companies (n = 4)	Senior managers and Claim managers
Crew agencies/manning companies (n = 10)	Deputy directors, senior managers and junior managers
Shipowners' liabilities insurers (n = 3)	Director, claim handlers
Maritime courts (n = 9)	Maritime judges
Maritime law firms (n = 7)	Maritime lawyers.

IV. Findings

Chinese seafarers usually face legal obstacles from three main sources: (1) an unstable legal environment; (2) inconsistencies of judicial judgements from different courts; and (3) the distinctive vulnerability caused by the low social insurance coverage.

A. The Legal Environment Is Undergoing Frequent Changes

In a transition country like China, the frequently changing legal environment can increase legal risks for compensation claims. After the Open and Reform Policy in 1979, Chinese seafarers began working on foreign vessels through dispatch by Chinese state-owned shipping enterprises.[19] Over the next four decades, laws governing seafarer rights have evolved through four major stages.

The first stage was between 1979 and 1991 where seafarers' rights and entitlements were not regulated by law and regulations. Instead, seafarer compensation claims were handled by the enterprises, which were mainly state-owned employers.

The second stage was between 1992 and 2002 where the major legislative achievement was the promulgation of the *Chinese Maritime Code* in 1992. Article 169 stipulates that in the case of loss of life and injury caused by collision, if the vessels involved both have faults to the collision, they shall take joint and several liabilities to the victims. In addition, the Supreme Court issued the *Specific Provisions on Foreign-related Personal Injuries and Deaths at Sea* which was also promulgated in 1992. This document stipulated the compensation standards for victims of personal injuries and death cases at sea, if a foreign element was involved in the accident. Involvement of a foreign element would include a collision with a foreign vessel, an injury on foreign vessel, and an accident

---

19 P Zhang and M Zhao, Maritime Labour Policy in China: Restructuring under the ILO's Maritime Labour Convention 2006 (2014). Marine Policy, p. 50, pp. 111–116.

outside of the Chinese sea. These judicial provisions adopted tort law liability regimes to address personal injury and death claims from marine casualties, such as capsizing and collisions. In the same year, the Ministry of Labour issued an administrative reply on the issues of addressing injuries, disabilities and fatalities of Chinese workers overseas.[20] In it, the Ministry of Labour stipulated that Chinese crew agencies were not liable to compensate the Chinese worker victims if foreign employers caused the workplace accidents. However, Chinese crew agencies should assist the victims to claim compensation from foreign employers. If the crew agencies had made an advance payment for medical treatment, litigation fee and sick pays to the victims, the crew agencies were entitled to deduct the equivalent amount from the final compensation paid by the foreign employers. If the foreign employers refused to make any payment, the crew agencies might compensate the victims according to its enterprise workers' compensation policies. In this stage, limited regulations had been established and the victims of marine casualties were able to claim some compensation, but their claims were highly restricted. The only liable parties were their foreign employers, namely shipowners overseas, or shipowners liable to marine casualties.

The third stage was between 2003 and 2012 where a nationwide workers' compensation system was launched by promulgating the *Work-related Injury Insurance Regulation* in 2003. As a result, the no-fault compensation principle was established and social insurance funds were founded nationwide. The *Interpretations on Damages of Personal Injuries and Deaths* which provides compensation for workers who are not covered by the *Work-related Injury Insurance Regulation* was enforced in 2004. Subsequently, the *Labour Contract Law (2008)* and the *Social Insurance Law (2010)*, were also enforced, improving Chinese workers' rights and the social security system. Additional regulations were made to clarify seafarers' labour rights, such as *the Regulation of Seamen (2007)* introduced by the State Council, and the *Rules of Dispatching Chinese Seafarers on Foreign Vessels (2011)* introduced by the Ministry of Transport. These two regulations attempted to enforce seafarers' rights to social security. During this stage, China has made significant efforts to unify the workers' compensation standards in order to provide social securities for its citizens. The major conflict that arose at this stage was determining whether seafarers should claim workers' compensation or compensation according to the tort law: *the Interpretations on Damages of Personal Injuries and Deaths* and the *Specific Provisions on Foreign-related Personal Injuries and Deaths at Sea*, or could they claim both types of compensation together?

We are currently still in the fourth stage and the *Specific Provisions on Foreign-related Personal Injuries and Deaths at Sea* have been abolished since 1 January 2013. Its CNY 800,000 (about GBP 80,000) limit for compensation liability, set in 1992, became too low to cover the loss of a victim at the time. In 2015, China became the 68th International Labour Organisation member to ratify the Maritime Labour Convention, 2006. To fulfil its obligations as a member state, China is preparing to roll out the next phase of seafarer rights-related legal reforms.

For seafarers and surviving families, the unstable legal environment has been a significant barrier to exercising their legal rights. An example of this is described by a claimant

---

20 Minister of Labour of People's Republic of China, 'The Replies to the Inquiries on Injuries, Disabilities and Fatalities of Dispatched Workers'. [LXZ (1992) No. 16].

who was affected by the sudden abolishment of the *Specific Provisions on Foreign-related Personal Injuries and Deaths at Sea* in 2013. The following are the words of a seafarer who filled a claim in 2012:

> Suddenly, I was informed by the court that my claim is no longer valid. If I would like to obtain compensation, I have to ask another lawyer to recalculate my claim. This made me feel the whole litigation, courts, and lawyers are not reliable. This is really troublesome for me (Chief Officer A).

B. Inconsistencies of Judicial Judgements from Different Courts

The frequency of change in seafarer rights-related legal frameworks has also created instability in judicial practice and impacted judicial opinions among different Chinese courts.

The above review of the evolution of Chinese laws governing seafarer rights to compensation suggest that a division exists between maritime legislation and labour law. Additionally, maritime jurisdiction and labour jurisdiction are also independent. Maritime jurisdiction entertains all disputes occurring in the maritime transport process, and labour arbitration tribunals entertain general labour disputes. In terms of seafarers' compensation claims, theoretically speaking, these two jurisdictions concur. Workplace injuries at sea occur during maritime transport, and are also a labour dispute. In 2002, the Supreme Court instructed that maritime labour disputes be entertained by maritime courts directly.[21] Accordingly, in Stage 3 and Stage 4, Chinese seafarers' claims were usually entertained by maritime courts.[22] When hearing and judging seafarers' compensation claims, maritime courts have to address the possible conflicts between labour law, tort law and maritime law. A judge from a maritime court commented:

> It was not easy for us to adjudicate labour disputes, considering the expertise of maritime judges are arbitrating maritime commercial and tort disputes. If seafarers' claims could be entertained by Labour Arbitration Tribunals, from my point of view, it might help the disputes be solved more efficiently (Maritime Judge G).

Chinese seafarers are an exceptional group that are subject to special maritime jurisdiction, therefore, maritime judges' judicial interpretation of labour law will have a significant impact on seafarers' rights. Shore-based workers are instead protected by Labour Contract Law and Work-related Injury Insurance Regulations. While conducting this research, it was noted that there is diversity in judicial opinions among the maritime courts. When involved in workers' compensation-related legal disputes, judicial opinions regarding the nature of seafarers' employment agreements and crewing agencies' obligations make seafarers' claims unlikely to be fully supported by the courts.

---

21 Supreme Court of People, 'The reply on the inquiry whether the rule of labour arbitration procedures before litigation is applicable to seafarers' labour disputes' [2002] EMSTZ No. 7.
http://fgcx.bjcourt.gov.cn:4601/law?fn=chl323s536.txt. All internet resources were last accessed 17 January 2022.
22 In this research, we find that some seafarers attempted to file claims to a Labour Arbitration Tribunal. Most of the seafarer interviewees reported that their claims were rejected by the Labour Arbitration Tribunal immediately, but some crew managers reported they had disputes with seafarers arbitrated within the labour jurisdiction. Therefore, there might be exceptions that some Labour Arbitration Tribunals entertaining seafarers' claims, although this conduct is not complied with the Supreme Court's judicial reply.

When Work-Related Injury Insurance contribution and compensation disputes arise between seafarers and manning companies, the status of Chinese seafarers has been controversial under Chinese law due to the variety and flexibility of seafarer recruitment approaches.[23] For example, according to the *Work-related Injury Insurance Regulation (2003)*, enterprises must purchase work-related injury insurance for all employees or hired labourers. The term employee applies to those who have entered into labour contracts or who are in an actual labour relationship with enterprises, companies or other organisations. Seafarers employed by crewing agencies are, however, usually regulated by dual contractual relationships. One is a contractual relationship with manning companies/ crewing agencies, and the other is the voyage contract/agreement with shipowners/bareboat charterers. Under the contractual relationship with shipowners/bareboat charterers, the shipowners/bareboat charterers are not recognised as employers according to Chinese law and, therefore, not technically obligated to contribute to or pay for seafarers' Work-related Injury Insurance. Regarding the contractual relationship with crew agencies/manning companies, the Ministry of Transport has defined this contractual relationship as a labour contract relationship, which imposes obligations on manning companies/crew agencies to arrange social insurance for seafarers.[24] To escape this liability, crew agencies/ manning companies give many seafarers' "recommendations" to serve on vessels rather than entering into labour contracts with them.

There has been extensive debate in judicial practice as to whether the labour contract relationship can be established or recognised between seafarers and crew agencies. For example, in 2011, the Supreme People's Court (SPC) provided a judicial reply to the Tianjin Maritime Court's query on the nature of the contract between a bosun and a Beijing manning company (See Table 16.3). In this case, the bosun was sent to work on a vessel owned

Table 16.3 The Nature of Seafarers' Employment Agreements

Court	Judicial Opinions	Source Citation
The Supreme Court	Neither labour contract nor labour service contract and not subject to the Labour Contract Law (2008)	the People's Supreme Court (2011) MSTZ No.4
Qingdao maritime Court	Labour service contract relationship between the agency and seafarers	Chen Yifang & Fu Benchao (2009)
Ningbo Maritime Court	Seafarers have nominal labour contract relation with the agency and presumed contract relation with shipowners.	Case-acceptance and Admiralty Divisions (2012)

---

23 Bin Wu, Vulnerability of Chinese contract workers abroad: A case of the working conditions and wages of Chinese seafarers (2008). An unpublished paper presented to the ICAS 5 Conference, 3 August 2007 (Kuala Lumpur). Wu, B, & Beaverstock, JV (2013). Globalization, mobility and the working conditions of contract Chinese seafarers. In Bin Wu, S Yao, & J Chen (Eds.), China's development and harmonization: Towards a balance with nature, society and the international community (pp. 41–59). London and New York: Routledge.

24 Ministry of Transport and Communication, 'The Rules of Dispatching Chinese Seafarers to Foreign Vessels' (2011). www.gov.cn/flfg/2011-04/11/content_1841530.htm.

by an Israeli shipping company, and the bosun argued that the Beijing manning company should purchase his social insurance, but the Beijing manning company denied being the responsible employer and refused to pay the bosun's social insurance premium. This dispute was initially filed at the Tianjin Maritime Court, and the Tribunal regarded the relationship between the bosun and the manning company as a factual labour relationship, in which case the manning company would be obliged to arrange social insurance for the bosun. However, the Supreme People's Court later corrected this decision and suggested that the contract be subject to the freedom contract.[25] Accordingly, there was no such clause stipulating the crew agencies' obligations to contribute to the seafarer's social security schemes, so the manning company was not liable to compensate the bosun.

The SPC issued its *Provisions on Case Guidance* in 2010 to set out how the precedents might be taken into consideration when the courts decide cases. However, the *Provisions* only have a limited impact on Chinese legal practices due to a lack of systematic working mechanisms. On 1 June 2020, the SPC issued the *Guiding Opinions on Unifying the Application of Laws and Strengthening Similar Case Retrieval (Trial Implementation) and Related Annotations* ("the Guiding Opinions"). The Guiding Opinions aim to integrate the uniform criteria for legal application into the overall trial process across different levels of the people's courts in China (SPC, 2020).

According to the Guide Opinions, "similar cases" are previous cases whose basic facts, focal points of the dispute or issues regarding the application of law are similar to those in the pending case (Art. 1). The judge in charge of the case is responsible for searching and for the authenticity and accuracy of the search results (Art. 3). Therefore, the judge must search for similar previous cases in the following circumstances:[26]

1) A proposal has been made to submit the case to the specialised (presiding) judges' meeting or the adjudication committee for discussion;
2) Relevant adjudication principles are unclear or a unified adjudication principle has not yet been formed;
3) A court president or division head requires that a search for similar cases be conducted under his or her supervision authority;
4) Other relevant circumstances. (Guiding Opinions Art. 2)

Although the opinions of the SPC are highly influential in Chinese judicial practice, it cannot become a binding legal source. According to facts and evidence from different cases, maritime courts may have different judicial opinions regarding whether seafarers are workers subject to labour contract relationships. For example, Qingdao Maritime Court and Ningbo Maritime Court concluded two different opinions on the nature of agreements between crewing agencies and seafarers (See Table 16.3). According to Qingdao Maritime Court's opinion, if the agency and seafarers only establish labour service contract, then seafarers are not entitled to labour rights under Work-related Injury Insurance. However, based on Ningbo Maritime Court's opinion, if seafarers have nominal labour contract relation with the agency and presumed contract relation with shipowners, then seafarers

---

25 'Yang Haishui v. Beijing Xinyusheng Ship Management Co., Ltd. (Dispute over Seafarer Service Contract)' <www.lawinfochina.com/display.aspx?id=1827&lib=case>.

26 L Zhang, 'China: Supreme People's Court Issues Guidance on Similar-Case Searches' (2020) www.loc.gov/law/foreign-news/article/china-supreme-peoples-court-issues-guidance-on-similar-case-searches/.

are able to claim equal labour rights according to *the Work-Related Injury Insurance Regulation.*

At the administrative regulation level, the Ministry of Transport has made efforts to oblige crew agencies to arrange social insurance for seafarers themselves or through other shipping companies. For example, in the *Rules of Dispatching Chinese Seafarers on Foreign Vessels*, the crew agencies must arrange for seafarers to have valid labour contracts with either the crew agency or a shipowner. However, in the judicial review process, the SPC's reply dismisses the obligation of crew agencies as employers defined in Chinese labour law. Consequently, the judicial opinion or practices may undermine the protection from administrative regulations. Thus, as stipulated by the administrative rules, seafarers' rights may not be fully enforceable in court proceedings.

The questionable legal status of Chinese seafarers is peculiar compared with other Chinese workers. In terms of land-based workers in agency employment, the *Labour Contract Law* stipulates that in cases of work-related injuries, agencies are jointly liable for compensation. If agencies and principal employers fail to sign written labour contracts and arrange social insurance for workers, agencies and companies must take joint liabilities for workers' compensation when workplace injuries occur. The *Interim Provisions strengthen this principle on Labour Dispatch (2014)* promulgated by the Ministry of Human Resources & Social Security. However, the *Interim Provisions on Labour Dispatch (2014)* explicitly exclude the application to seafarers. As a result, seafarers' legal status rights and manning companies' obligations are still obscure, increasing seafarers' claims' legal risk.

C. Seafarers' Vulnerability Caused by Low Social Insurance Coverage

The findings in this research suggest that Chinese seafarers' access to Work-related Injury Insurance is more restricted than it is to other Chinese workers. Over half of Chinese seafarers are not covered by the Work-related Injury Insurance. Furthermore, most of the participants in this study reported that they did not receive any compensation from Work-related Injury Insurance Funds.[27] Resulting from insufficient coverage, seafarers have limited institutional support in their claim process.

No-fault based workers' compensation is widely considered to be a more "therapeutic" tool in addressing the harm caused by industrial accidents than fault-based tort compensation is.[28] No-fault based social insurance compensation can increase the chance of success for injured workers to achieve tort law damages by providing essential maintenance for victims.[29] Correspondingly, without access to no-fault-based workers' compensation, workers are unlikely to receive timely remedies

27 G Chen, X Zhu and Y Hao, 'The Application of Maritime Labour Convention (2006) in China and Standard Employment Contractual Remedies. (2014). Wuhan: Wuhan University of Technology, Fujian Maritime Safety Administration.

28 K Lippel, 'Workers describe the effect of the workers' compensation process on their health: A Quebec study' (2007). International Journal of Law and Psychiatry, p. 30 (4–5), pp. 427–443; A Clayton, Workers compensation-the third way (1997). Safety Science Monitor, p. 1 (1), pp. 1–12.

29 Richard Kurt Lewis, The politics and economics of tort law: Judicially imposed periodical payments of damages (2006). Modern Law Review, p. 69 (3), pp. 418–442. 10.1111/j.1468-2230.2006.00590.x.

following workplace accidents. As shown by this study and previous research,[30] most Chinese seafarers cannot obtain no-fault-based compensation following their incidents since their employers do not contribute to the social insurance scheme. The inequity among workers covered by social security schemes and seafarers exposes the later to increased hardship.

In China, it is common for employers to refuse to insure seafarers' against work-related injuries. However, as this chapter outlines below, the vulnerability of seafarers is a legally constructed discrimination, as confirmed by a Supreme Court Judicial Reply [(2011) MSTZ No. 4]. When an employer refuses to contribute the Work-related Injury Insurance, seafarers are forced to bear the risk by themselves, while other workers are entitled to claim compensation either from their employers or the social insurance fund. This legal conundrum is unique to the Chinese seafarers.

Previous studies show that gender, race and nationality contribute to workers being treated discriminatively by social insurance institutions,[31] while occupation-based discrimination constructed by law is rarely noticed. Under Chinese law, employers can exercise substantial control over seafarers. The Supreme Court Judicial Reply [(2011) MSTZ No. 4] confirmed that when there is no explicit labour contractual provisions between a crew agency and a seafarer and the seafarer is dispatched to a foreign vessel, the seafarer is not entitled to worker's rights under Chinese labour law. The relationship between the seafarer and the manning company is regarded to as a "civil agreement". In this relationship, seafarers are no longer recognised as workers protected by Chinese labour law, but instead, they are considered to be an "equal party" with the shipowner and manning companies, who should not claim entitlement to social security benefits. In contrast, if a land-based worker is in a similar situation, he/she will still have an independent approach to seeking compensation and the social insurance fund will cover the payment first and then claim it back from employers by exercising the right of subrogation (See Table 16.4).

V. Concluding Discussion

No-fault based workers' compensation should cover all workers in civilised societies.[32] However, this chapter has revealed that one particular occupational group, Chinese seafarers, have endured significant legal obstacles when attempting to claim damages for work-related accidents. The lack of legal stability makes it difficult for victims to understand their rights. In some cases, claimants may need to re-draft their statement of claim

---

30 G Chen, X Zhu and Y Hao, 'The Application of Maritime Labour Convention (2006) in China and Standard Employment Contractual Remedies'. (2014). Wuhan: Wuhan University of Technology, Fujian Maritime Safety Administration.

31 K Lippel, 'Workers describe the effect of the workers' compensation process on their health: A Quebec study' (2007). International Journal of Law and Psychiatry, p. 30 (4–5), pp. 427–443; Stéphanie Premji and others, 'Are Immigrants, Ethnic and Linguistic Minorities over-Represented in Jobs with a High Level of Compensated Risk? Results from a Montréal, Canada Study Using Census and Workers' Compensation Data' (2010). American Journal of Industrial Medicine. https://onlinelibrary-wiley-com.qe2a-proxy.mun.ca/doi/full /10.1002/ajim.20845.

32 M Quinlan and C Mayhew, 'Precarious employment and workers' compensation' (1999). International Journal of Law and Psychiatry, p. 22 (5–6), pp. 491–520.

Table 16.4 Work-Related Injury Insurance (WRII) for Seafarers and Land-Based Workers

	The Nature of Employment	Compensation Entitlements of WRII	Liable Parties to WRII Compensation	Dispute Resolution Approaches	Burden of Proof
Seafarers covered by WRII	Labour contract	Apply	WRII Fund	Labour Arbitration Committees and Maritime Courts	The facts of work-related injuries, medical expenses, and disability degrees
Land workers covered by WRII	Labour contract	Apply	WRII Fund	Labour Arbitration Committees and Civil Courts	The facts of work-related injuries, medical expenses, and disability degrees
Seafarers not covered by WRII	Presumed civil contract	Not apply	Not apply	Maritime Courts	The existence of working activities on a specific vessel; the work-relatedness of the injury; the loss (including medical fee and disability degrees); whether the injury is caused by the negligence of shipowners or third parties.
Land workers not covered by WRII	Presumed labour contract	Presumably apply	The employers, manpower agencies, and the Social Insurance Fund	Labour Arbitration Committees and Civil Courts	The existence of labour relationships, the facts of work-related injuries, medical expenses, and disability degrees.

which inevitably prolongs the legal proceedings and may further exacerbate their financial difficulties.

The evolving legal environment makes it difficult to predict maritime judgements. Some judicial opinions, such as the one made by the SPC, denied the labour relationship between crewing agencies and dispatched seafarers overseas. As a result, these sources of law make many seafarers' legal status ambiguous and their rights uncertain. In recent years, the SPC has been adopting reference to judicial precedents in the process of the PRC's judicial reform. The New SPC *Guiding Opinions* will improve the consistency of judgements by assisting judges and arbitration tribunals to refer to case precedents when applying the law.[33] While there is no doubt that this will make case results more predictable, further effort is required to improve judgment certainty and consistency.

Moreover, the low coverage of work-related injury insurance makes seafarers' more vulnerable than shore-based workers. Shore-based workers who are not covered by work-related injury insurance are still entitled to claim Work-related Injury Insurance from employers, agencies or the Work-related Injury Insurance Fund.

The Maritime Labour Convention, 2006, stipulates that the labour supply state should provide equal social insurance treatment, including work-related injury insurance to the seafarers residing in their countries. To fulfil this obligation as a member state, China should clarify seafarer rights and entitlements under the Work-related Injury Insurance system and make them equal to those of shore-based workers. If seafarer employers fail to arrange work-related injury insurance for seafarers, seafarer entitlements to Work-related Injury Insurance should not be denied.

The distinct separation between labour jurisdiction and maritime jurisdiction has negatively restricted seafarers' access to domestic labour protection regimes. If seafarers were entitled to make a choice between maritime jurisdiction and labour jurisdiction based on their convenience, this may improve Chinese seafarers' chances of being compensated in a timely manner after industrial accidents.

---

33 Li, L and Yu, C 'New Guiding Opinion from the Supreme People's Court of the PRC: judicial precedents to play a more important role in the PRC's future legal practices' (Hong Kong Lawyer, 7 August 2020) <www.hk-lawyer.org/content/new-guiding-opinion-supreme-people%E2%80%99s-court-prc-judicial-precedents-play-more-important-role> accessed 19 January 2021.

PART IV

LOOKING FORWARD

New Initiatives in the Digital Age

CHAPTER 17

Forward Planning – Regulation of Artificial Intelligence and Maritime Trade

Jason Chuah[1]

This chapter, in concluding this very timely book, evaluates the continuing regulatory challenges for maritime trade in the light of rapid technological changes. The scope of the subject is indeed so wide that a single, discrete chapter would not be able to do it proper justice. There is already much ink spilt on the various technological developments to commercial shipping – from the 1990s issues of electronic bills of lading and dematerialisation of shipping documents to the early 2000s when electronic financial solutions were introduced to supply chains, trade financing and warehousing, and then onwards to more recent times, when autonomous shipping and blockchains became the flavour of the month. This chapter chooses to focus on the emerging influence of artificial intelligence (AI) in shipping and international commerce. AI solutions are incrementally designed for use in shipping – an obvious application is in autonomous ships, but in truth, there are far more "disruptive" applications being developed to optimise business processes, voyage and cargo planning and vessel maintenance. The continuing impact of AI on maritime trade is undeniable. Parallel to this technological momentum in the maritime business, governments, including those from the US, EU, UK and PRC, have been quick to respond with proposals for policy and/or regulatory intervention.

The emphasis in this chapter is the recently published EU proposal for a Regulation to regulate the use of AI across the European single market, to be called the "EU AI Act". The rationale for this focus is that whilst many other jurisdictions, such as the US, UK and PRC, have published various position papers and policy statements on regulating AI, none has gone far as the EU in proposing a single all-encompassing legislative instrument.[2] The

1 *Professor of Commercial and Maritime Law, City, University of London, UK.*

2 In contrast to the UK, although plans are afoot to amend existing laws, the UK Government takes an incremental, cross sectoral approach to AI regulation (www.gov.uk/government/publications/national-ai -strategy/national-ai-strategy-html-version). (For more on the UK AI strategy, please see below. The UK has also chosen to adopt a more technically focused but piecemeal approach. Thus, it is currently developing and agreeing international technical standards working with the International Organisation for Standardisation and International Electrotechnical Commission (ISO/IEC) and the Industry Specification Group on Securing AI at the European Telecommunications Standards Institute (ETSI). As regards the PRC, for example, the State Council released the country's strategy for developing artificial intelligence (AI), entitled "New Generation Artificial Intelligence Development Plan" (AIDP) in 2017 ("新一代人工智能发展规划" State Council Document [2017] No. 35; there is no official translation of the strategy document at the time of writing. An unofficial translation might be found at https://flia.org/wp-content/uploads/2017/07/A-New-Generation -of-Artificial-Intelligence-Development-Plan-1.pdf For an exposition of the AIDP see Roberts, H., Cowls, J., Morley, J., et al. The Chinese approach to artificial intelligence: an analysis of policy, ethics, and regulation. AI & Soc Vol. 36, pp. 59–77 (2021)). This strategy paper sets out the PRC's aims to become the world leader in AI by 2030. In particular, it sees an opportunity to monetise AI into a trillion-yuan industry. The strategy also sets

proposal is likely to attract much controversy and interest; the consultation and deliberations will be protracted. However, it would be remiss not to consider the potential impact on maritime trade the proposed provisions would produce.

In April 2021, the EU Commission tabled a proposal for an EU wide Regulation to provide for a harmonised scheme of governance for AI.[3] As a matter of background, the EU Commission had published a White Paper on AI back in February 2020 which set out the policy options on how best to achieve the objective of fostering subscription to AI and that of managing the risks attendant in the use of AI.[4] The proposed legislation which was laid as a consequence aims to provide for "a high level of protection of health, safety and fundamental rights" for users and European societies, more broadly.[5] However, as expressed by the White Paper, the proposed Regulation also seeks to extend the principle of free movement to AI goods and services. Member States are explicitly prohibited from imposing unsanctioned restrictions on the development, marketing and use of AI systems.[6]

I. Definitions

An important plank in any regulatory scheme is establishing the definitional parameters. As far as the EU is concerned, a formalised definition is provided for in the draft Regulation. Article 3(1) defines AI as

> software that is developed with one or more of the techniques and approaches listed in Annex I[7] and can, for a given set of human-defined objectives, generate outputs such as content, predictions, recommendations, or decisions influencing the environments they interact with.

It is obvious that this definition largely adopts what might be termed, a functional approach. It focuses on the principal functional characteristics of the "software" – in essence, how the software could be deployed to generate content, predictions, recommendations and decisions without substantial manual handling or processing.[8] Those outputs, such as predictions or decisions, are intended to pursue a given set of human defined objectives. However, the EU Commission, intending to keep the regulation as technology neutral as possible, leaves room in the annex of the legislation[9] to specify the type of AI techniques or approaches which fall to be governed by the law.

This definition, predictably, reflects that recommended by the OECD: "An AI system is a machine-based system that can, for a given set of human-defined objectives, make

---

out in general terms the commitment to establish ethical norms and standards for AI. It is clear too from the national strategy paper that maritime trade is envisaged to be a sector which would benefit from AI adoption. (See section 4.1.2 "智能物流").

3 COM (2021) 206 final; 2021/0106 (COD).

4 COM (2020) 65 final.

5 Recital 1, Preamble of the Draft Regulation.

6 See for example Titles V and VIII.

7 Annex 1 describes AI techniques and approaches as: (a)Machine learning approaches, including supervised, unsupervised and reinforcement learning, using a wide variety of methods including deep learning; (b) Logic- and knowledge-based approaches, including knowledge representation, inductive (logic) programming, knowledge bases, inference and deductive engines, (symbolic) reasoning and expert systems; (c)Statistical approaches, Bayesian estimation, search and optimization methods.

8 Recital 6, Preamble.

9 Supra n.6.

predictions, recommendations, or decisions influencing real or virtual environments. AI systems are designed to operate with varying levels of autonomy".[10]

A contrasting position might be had from the PRC's AI Development Plan (AIDP).[11] The PRC's AIDP, though not a legislative instrument, does flesh out what the PRC government considers to be AI for the purposes of legislative intervention. It tends to concentrate on what "basic theories" AI is founded rather than a purely systemic approach in its attempt to define AI. The AIDP considers that AI is premised on the following theories/notions:

Big data intelligence theory
Cross-media sensing and computing theory
Hybrid and enhanced intelligence theory
Swarm intelligence theory
Autonomous coordination and control, and optimised decision-making theory
High-level machine learning theory
Brain-inspired intelligence computing theory
Quantum intelligent computing theory

The PRC's approach is clearly more narrow, preferring to emphasise the presence of some machine learning methods or processes, or logic based procedures, than the EU's. That breadth is not entirely welcome. For example, Annex 1 of the proposed Regulation refers to "Statistical approaches, Bayesian estimation, search and optimisation methods".[12] This reference to statistical approaches is clearly expansive and potentially would cover almost all existing and future software that does not involve an element of machine learning.[13] Statistical approaches could be fairly mathematical. For example, a software which computes the standard deviation of a set of data might well be deemed an AI system if this type of definition is adopted. Although in practical terms, it is entirely legitimate to take a "sensible" interpretation by positing Annex 1 within the wider frame of the EU AI policy, firms, especially startups, might not be prepared to take the risk.

II. Scope of the Proposed Regulation

The Regulation, being a single market instrument,[14] is limited to the use and movement of AI systems or services in a commercial setting alone. AI-guided military uses and AI systems in law enforcement fall outside the legal competency of the EU.[15] Article 2(1) stresses that the Regulation applies to:

---

10 Art. 1, Recommendation of the Council on Artificial Intelligence (OECD/LEGAL/0449 (22 May 2019)).

11 Supra n.1.

12 Supra n. 6.

13 See generally Ehsani S., Glauner, P., Plugmann, P. and Thieringer, F.M. (eds), "The Future Circle of Healthcare: AI, 3D Printing, Longevity, Ethics, and Uncertainty Mitigation" (Springer, 2022).

14 It is noteworthy that the proposed Regulation has as its legal basis, Art. 114 TFEU which is concerned with enhancing the internal market. This commercial trade dimension of the law is important – not only as a matter of understanding the legislative policy but also when the Regulation comes to be interpreted by the courts, the EU law teleological approach to legislative interpretation will require a direct or indirect interaction with this rationale.

15 Arts. 2(3)(4).

(a) providers placing on the market or putting into service AI systems in the Union, irrespective of whether those providers are established within the Union or in a third country;

(b) users of AI systems located within the Union;

(c) providers and users of AI systems that are located in a third country, where the output produced by the system is used in the Union.

The Regulation thus focuses on the human agents behind the AI systems, not to the AI itself. The latter is clearly perceived too radical for the time being; to do so would be confer legal personality on AI.[16] By and large, those who argue for legal personality the autonomous nature of the AI in making informed decisions, decisions of which carry consequences on others, should lead to the recognition of legal competence. On the other hand, the other side argues that legal competence should be underpinned by a moral consciousness which AI systems do not possess. That debate, interesting as it is, contributes little to the task at hand, which is an evaluation of the proposed law in question.

The proposed Regulation will have an extraterritorial reach, as is common with legislation seeking to protect the internal market and fundamental EU rights. Article 2 makes this plain. Providers placing on the market or putting into service AI systems in the EU would be required to comply with the terms of the Regulation, irrespective of whether they are established in the EU or in a third country. The article goes on to state that the Regulation would apply to users based in the EU; it seems from the tenor of the provision that the user is not only entitled to the rights in the Regulation but also subject to the legal duties, where appropriate. The Regulation also extends to "providers and users of AI systems that are located in a third country, where the output produced by the system is used in the Union".[17]

These provisions are quite far-reaching. Taking an example from commercial maritime trade as a case in point: assuming that a company based in the PRC uses an AI-guided cargo operation system for their ships, registered in Panama. When the vessel calls at the Port of Antwerp, the AI system is deployed via the internet by the stevedoring firm to facilitate unloading of the cargo. The Regulation would be engaged because the user is in Belgium, an EU Member State. It does not matter that the system was stored or accessible in cyberspace.

It should be noted that article 2(1)(a) goes even further – there is no requirement that the AI system or service was even actually used. Article 2(1)(a) is activated as long as the AI system is placed on the EU market. "Placing on the market" is defined in article 3(9) as "the first making available of an AI system on the Union market" but take-up from users is not mentioned.

Naturally there might perceptibly be a concern from commercial undertakings as to the regulatory burden despite very nominal interaction with the EU.

---

16 There is increasing literature on AI and legal personhood. See Chesterman, Simon. "Artificial intelligence and the limits of legal personality". International & Comparative Law Quarterly 69.4 (2020): pp. 819–844; Čerka, P., Grigienė, J., and Sirbikytė, G. "Is it possible to grant legal personality to artificial intelligence software systems?". Computer Law & Security Review 33.5 (2017): pp. 685–699; Abbott, R., and Sarch. A., Punishing Artificial Intelligence: Legal Fiction or Science Fiction. (2019) UC Davis Law Review 53: pp. 323–84.

17 Art. 2(1)(c).

III. Opportunities for Innovation

Maritime trade is continually evolving and improving in making greater and better efficiencies. In this section, the provisions in the proposed Regulation on how best to support innovation shall be assessed. The objective is to enable maritime trade stakeholders to contribute to the ongoing deliberations on policy choices. There are two discussion points here – the introduction of a regulatory sandbox scheme to promote innovation, and the provisions to protect essential rights and interests.

A. AI Regulatory Sandbox

While there are different and varied regulatory sandbox models with different policy and strategic emphasis, broadly speaking, a regulatory sandbox is intended to allow the commercial undertaking to test its products with real customers or users in an environment that is not subject to the full panoply of rules that would otherwise be applicable. That does not mean that the sandbox is entirely bereft of the regulator's involvement. The regulator will typically offer guidance and information so as to foster a collaborative relationship between the two sides. From a regulatory theory perspective, the regulatory sandbox might be considered a form of principles-based[18] regulation as it removes some of the more hardcore regulatory hurdles concentrating instead on allowing some flexibility in meeting the basic parameters of the regulatory objectives and concerns.

Articles 53–55 of the draft Regulation sets out the parameters for the establishment of AI regulatory sandboxes within the territories of the different Member States. Article 53 labels the sandbox, "a controlled environment that facilitates the development, testing and validation of innovative AI systems for a limited time before their placement on the market or putting into service pursuant to a specific plan".[19] There follow in that Title of the draft law detailed provisions on how Member States must retain control over data protection and other public interest concerns (such as health and safety, environmental protection, crimes, etc.). What is perhaps of interest is that the level of cooperation or collaboration between regulator and firm is largely left to individual Member States. Certainly, such an approach coincides with the principles of subsidiarity and proportionality – it would not be prudent for a principles-based sandbox scheme such as that in the AI Regulation to fly in the face of flexibility.

There is an increasing volume of literature on the design, use, criticism and defence of regulatory sandboxes generally.[20] This chapter will however consider more narrowly the question as to how useful the proposal scheme might be for maritime trade.

These provisions place the sandbox squarely within the jurisdiction of individual Member States. For maritime trade, which is highly globalised and networked, it is difficult to see how a sandbox located in and firmly controlled by a single Member State would incentivise AI innovation. On the other hand, as a regulatory sandbox scheme, it might well be impractical for all Member States to adopt the same level of involvement. It thus

---

18 As against a rule-based system
19 Art. 53(1)
20 For a good overview including useful references on writings on the subject (albeit with a strong US focus) see Allen, H. J. "Regulatory sandboxes". Geo. Wash. L. Rev. 87 (2019): p. 579.

raises the question as to whether a regulatory sandbox would actually be beneficial to a highly mobile and globalised sector such as maritime trade.

Another observation is that the rights to be guarded by the AI Regulation are deep-seated ones, the derogation from which is likely to attract public opprobrium. The question thus is to what extent would a regulatory sandbox remove or reduce the so-called hardcore or concrete regulatory requirements. Any reduction or removal might risk controversy, especially where the AI providers are established in third countries. The regulator would be under immense pressure (perhaps rightly so) to provide guidance, erring on the side of caution.

Key to a good regulatory sandbox scheme is the provision of guidance by the regulator. In the UK, for example, the Financial Conduct Authority's approach in their sandbox scheme for the fintech sector will give guidance on how it will interpret the application of regulatory requirements to new technology. Such guidance is helpful given that the UK regulations in question "pre-date smartphones, let alone blockchain or biometric identifiers".[21] For the regulator tasked with making the sandbox scheme work successfully, the challenge with AI solutions is that the guidance is really only as good a proper understanding of the risks. Informational competence is thus key. It follows that how each Member State will develop their regulators' informational competencies will be critical.

It is trite to suggest that an effective regulatory sandbox must therefore be properly resourced. Considering the resources required and given the potential limited reach and usefulness of a regulatory sandbox in the maritime business, a vital question thus is whether so substantial an investment is justifiable and proportionate.

The proposed Regulation states that the AI sandbox approach is intended, *inter alia*, to foster AI innovation and remove barriers to the AI market for small and medium enterprises (SMEs) and startups.[22] It has to be questioned as to whether the promotion of innovation, for innovation's own sake, actually serves the social good. In the maritime trade sector many startups which were conceived to develop AI solutions to disrupt ancient, long-established shipping practice regularly face access to finance.[23] Such startups do increasingly end up being acquired by (much) larger technology companies. As one commentator said in respect of the fintech sector,

> to the extent that the technology developed by these startups is ultimately deployed to entrench the market position of large established financial institutions, without any concomitant reduction in cost or increase in efficiency for customers, it will not address any real market need.[24]

The need for finance could also propel startups away from developing AI solutions which respond to a real market need, to simply designing an AI innovation which would make

---

21 See speech by Mr Christopher Woolard FCA Director for Strategy and Competition (11 April 2016) www.fca.org.uk/news/speeches/innovate-finance-global-summit.

22 Recital.

23 As regards a general startup's access to finance see for example Bollaert, Helen, Florencio Lopez-de-Silanes, and Armin Schwienbacher. "Fintech and access to finance". Journal of corporate finance 68 (2021): 101941; for the maritime sector, see in the context of empirical work carried with reference to Germany see Bass, Hans-Heinrich, and Robert Ernst-Siebert. "SME in Germany's maritime industry: innovation, internationalisation and employment". International Journal of Globalisation and Small Business 2.1 (2007): pp. 19–33; for the maritime sector more generally see Van den Burg, Sander WK, et al. "Mobilizing investors for blue growth". Frontiers in Marine Science 3 (2017): p. 291.

24 Allen, Hilary J. "Regulatory sandboxes". Geo. Wash. L. Rev. 87 (2019): pp. 579, 608.

the startup attractive to venture capitalists out to snare the technology deemed to be the flavour of the month.

Lastly, the Regulation calls for the sharing of the startup's intellectual property consisting of data and AI with the relevant authorities.[25] Given that there is no explicit rationale for this requirement, it seems thus to be disproportionate for most firms, especially SMEs and startups.

B. Controlling Harm

Perhaps it is apposite to start by considering what the Regulation does *not* provide for, where harm is concerned. The noticeable omission in the draft Regulation concerns liability for AI systems. It appears that the EU was content to leave that matter of liability to individual Member States. Any dispute or claim over liability for damage caused by an AI system would be resolved using applicable contract and tort/delict laws.

The Regulation's approach to controlling harm is by (a) banning certain AI systems and (b) regulating the delivery of certain AI systems based on their risk profile.

Title II of the proposed Regulation sets out a list of prohibited AI. The regulation has given up the binary low–high-risk framework initially proposed in the Commission's White Paper on AI[26] and replaced it with a four-tier risk framework. The four tiers relate to uses of AI which carry:

(a) An unacceptable risk;
(b) A high risk;
(c) A limited risk;
(d) A low or minimal risk.[27]

Quite predictably those AI technologies which violate fundamental rights would be banned. The prohibitions in the Regulation would also outspread to practices that have a significant potential to manipulate persons through subliminal techniques beyond their consciousness or exploit vulnerabilities of specific vulnerable groups such as children or persons with disabilities in order to materially distort their behaviour in a manner that is likely to cause them or another person psychological or physical harm.[28] Other manipulative or exploitative practices affecting adults that might be facilitated by AI systems could be covered by the existing data protection, consumer protection and digital service legislation that guarantee that natural persons are properly informed and have free choice not to be subject to profiling or other practices that might affect their behaviour.[29] The proposal also prohibits AI-based social scoring for general purposes done by public authorities.[30] Finally, the use of 'real time' remote biometric identification systems in publicly accessible spaces for the purpose of law enforcement is also prohibited unless certain limited exceptions apply.[31]

---

25 Art. 53.
26 COM (2020) 65 final (19 February 2020).
27 Para 5.2.2 Explanatory Memorandum to the Draft Regulation.
28 Ibid.
29 Ibid.
30 Ibid.
31 Ibid.

During the consultation exercise following the publication of the Commission's White Paper[32] most respondents, whether in support or against the proposal for an AI law, complained about the lack of clarity. The criticisms relate to the lack of clarity on what is meant by high risk and low risk.[33] To my mind, whilst acknowledging that the draft law is not flawless, such a criticism is simply too easy. The subject matter for regulation is risk or harm – a highly subjective and fluid notion. One has to acknowledge that either AI regulation is needed for the public interest or not. Most respondents were in one voice that it is needed.[34] It follows thus that we should be realistic about linguistic niceties in the regulation. Quibbling over the precise boundaries of low, limited and high risk is unhelpful. The maritime trade market participants, in their sector replete with standard form contracts where certainty is so highly prized, know too well that certainty is a pipedream.

In the context of maritime trade innovations, many will not attract a high-risk profile. The risk of harm is associated in the draft law to impact on human beings. In maritime trade, the AI solutions tend to be about the deployment of algorithms to collate, learn and process large data sets. For example, the compilation and interpreting of data relating to particular sea voyages to enable the shipmaster better to navigate the vessel or mitigate against equipment failure and defects whilst the ship is at sea. The human factor in the data set, it would appear, is fairly limited and controlled. It might be useful to draw on another example. An increasingly popular AI-led solution in shipping[35] is the use of AI to combat cybersecurity threats. At a benign or defensive end, the AI solution can inform the users as to whether IT communications traffic appears normal or not. At the other end, the AI solution might react by quarantining external files or impeding data traffic which, if not properly executed, could lead to damaging one of those interests adumbrated in Annex III of the draft Regulation referring to high-risk AI systems.

In the case of high-risk AI systems, the proposed law provides for technical documentation requirements in Art. 11 (Technical documentation), registration requirements in Art. 60 (EU database for stand-alone high-risk AI systems) and reporting requirements in Art. 62 (Reporting of serious incidents and of malfunctioning). Whilst some respondents to the White Paper consultation were sanguine about these requirements, others expressed dismay at how heavy handed and burdensome the requirements are. There is no doubt that these requirements could be onerous and there is no provision or facility for a more nuanced approach whereby cases are evaluated on an individual basis. It is also unclear to what extent the regulatory sandbox schemes could be used to avoid the regulatory burden, at least at conception stage.

Given the fact that in the maritime trade AI systems with a high risk profile are relatively uncommon, there is some force for the maritime sector to argue against a single, unifying AI law but merely writing into individual specific legislations dealing with various rights and interests an AI dimension. For example, where the concern is over biometric

---

32 Supra n.

33 Some arguing that low risk can become high risk through the process of development; see Report prepared by the Montreal AI Ethics Institute for the European Commission's Whitepaper on AI 2020 (https://montrealethics.ai/).

34 The author has some sympathy for a non-unified approach to regulating the impact of AI systems on the human subject. See below.

35 The massive cyber-attack sustained by the likes of Maersk in 2017 could not have escaped the attention of the industry. However, ransomware and other forms of cyber-attacks on less widely reported companies continue to plague the industry (Source: Reuters News update 27 June 2017).

data processed by AI, that could be written into any biometric data specific legislation. A unifying horizontal legislation such as the proposed regulation is probably unlikely to be very useful. Similarly, where the concern is about protection of vulnerable persons being profiled by AI systems, that could be addressed by equal rights and anti-discrimination legislation making a reference to AI, if needed.

The UK indeed prefers a so-called cross-sectoral, piecemeal approach to regulating AI. Instead of a single all-encompassing legislation on AI, the UK has chosen to publish a National AI Strategy, a policy instrument rather than a legislation. This cross sectoral approach to regulating AI seems set to remain for the time being, the UK Government states:

> The UK already regulates many aspects of the development and use of AI through "cross-sector" legislation and different regulators. For example, there is coverage in areas like data protection (Information Commissioner's Office), competition (Competition & Markets Authority), human rights and equality (Equality & Human Rights Commission). As well as through "sector-specific" legislation and regulators, for example financial services (Financial Conduct Authority) and medical products (Medicines and Healthcare products Regulatory Agency).[36]

The UK Government's view is that the cross sectoral approach is right because:

(a) The boundaries of AI risks and harms are grey, because the harms raised by these technologies are often non-AI, or extensions of non-AI, issues, and also because AI is rapidly developing and therefore what counts as the AI part of a system is constantly changing.

(b) Use cases for AI, and their wider impacts, can be highly complex in their own right. There is a big limitation in what can be covered in cross-cutting legislation on AI, and regardless of the overall regulatory approach, the detail will always need to be dealt with at the level of individual harms and use cases.

(c) Individual regulators and industries are already starting to respond to the risks of AI, and to work with innovators in their sectors to guide on interpretation of existing regulations, and on what further regulatory responses are appropriate. Enabling and empowering individual bodies to respond is a much quicker response to individual harms than agreeing to an AI regulatory regime that makes sense across all sectors.

(d) AI is not the only ongoing technology change, and its impacts are often interlinked with other innovations and behaviour changes, including increased connectivity, the move to mobile working, the dominant role of major platforms, etc. It is often hard to unpick the specific impact of AI; focusing regulation on the particular use cases where there is risk allows risks to be addressed holistically, and simplifies things for innovators.[37]

There is much in the UK position which makes good sense. It is better suited to avoid over-regulation and in the maritime trade context, much more flexible and pro-innovation.

---

36 UK Command Paper 525 (September 2021), p. 51.
37 Ibid., p. 52.

IV. Conclusion

This chapter has demonstrated using the proposed EU AI law to show how a single, horizontal AI regulatory framework would apply to the maritime trade and argues that such an approach is problematic. The legislation tries to be all things to all people – preferring a principles-based approach both in trying to incentivise AI innovation and to protect against harm, whilst simultaneously trying to provide a harmonised regulatory framework for AI use in the EU. Other than the obvious criticisms around the lack of clarity over its many provisions, its shortcoming is not properly recognising that many parts of the economy do not have the kind of interface with vulnerable human subjects as the Regulation seeks to protect. The net result being, at best, the *perception* of over-regulation by the industry and at worst, a real risk of over-regulation and gilding the lily by regulators.

INDEX